Cases in
INNOVATIVE NONPROFITS

To the memory of my mother's lost family, the Linde and the Jacobson from Latvia, who perished in the Holocaust.
–R.A.C.

To my mother, Hedy Grünberger Kaplan Malki
and the memory of my father, Fred Sroel Kaplan.
–D.V.-K.

Cases in INNOVATIVE NONPROFITS

ORGANIZATIONS THAT MAKE A DIFFERENCE

EDITORS

RAM A. CNAAN
University of Pennsylvania

DIANE VINOKUR-KAPLAN
University of Michigan

SAGE

Los Angeles | London | New Delhi
Singapore | Washington DC | Boston

SAGE

Los Angeles | London | New Delhi
Singapore | Washington DC | Boston

FOR INFORMATION:

SAGE Publications, Inc.
2455 Teller Road
Thousand Oaks, California 91320
E-mail: order@sagepub.com

SAGE Publications Ltd.
1 Oliver's Yard
55 City Road
London, EC1Y 1SP
United Kingdom

SAGE Publications India Pvt. Ltd.
B 1/I 1 Mohan Cooperative Industrial Area
Mathura Road, New Delhi 110 044
India

SAGE Publications Asia-Pacific Pte. Ltd.
3 Church Street
#10-04 Samsung Hub
Singapore 049483

Acquisitions Editor: Maggie Stanley
Editorial Assistant: Nicole Mangona
Production Editor: Natalie Cannon
Copy Editor: Deanna Noga
Typesetter: Hurix Systems Pvt. Ltd.
Proofreader: Kris Bergstad
Indexer: Naomi Linzer
Cover Designer: Glenn Vogel
Marketing Manager: Liz Thornton

Printed in the United States of America

Cataloging-in-publication data is avialable for this title from the Library of Congress.

ISBN 978-1-4522-7770-7

This book is printed on acid-free paper.

SFI Certified Sourcing
www.sfiprogram.org
SFI-00453

14 15 16 17 18 10 9 8 7 6 5 4 3 2 1

Brief Contents

Detailed Contents

PART 4: INNOVATION WITHIN EXISTING NONPROFIT ORGANIZATIONS

PART 5: LESSONS LEARNED

Preface

There are books that originate from a quick initial insight from the author. When the author explains how the book idea originated, he or she talks about a flash discovery that came out of nowhere and suddenly the light shined and the idea emerged. There are books that originate at the footsteps of previous books. An author may write an academic sequel to a previous book or one reads the literature in a certain field and find an uncovered niche. This book, however, evolved slowly and organically.

For quite a few years, we have been fascinated by social innovations in the nonprofit sector. Throughout the years, we heard our colleagues presenting and discussing social innovations of social entrepreneurs who came up with new ideas and better solutions for endemic problems. We also heard about social innovators who perceived or identified new problems or subgroups of people in need and then developed new methods of intervention. We also read many books and articles about social innovation and realized that there is a lot of ambiguity and disagreement about what a social innovation is and how to define it. It seems that every author conceptualized social innovation somewhat differently.

In attending many conferences devoted to the study of the nonprofit sector, we were impressed with the many innovations therein. We attended presentations that depicted amazing innovations that demonstrated the creativity and adaptability of the nonprofit sector. We realized that the level of creativity and ability to think outside the box in the nonprofit sector is remarkable. We discussed this aspect of the nonprofit sector with our academic peers and found out that in many programs of nonprofit education there are courses that cover the topic of social innovation and social entrepreneurship. Our academic peers also told us that while they have books that cover the topic they do not have a good source that demonstrates nonprofit social innovation. They told us that they used a case study from one source and another case study from another source and so on. That gave us the impetus for creating this book.

Nonprofit social innovations are not an American phenomenon. It also became clear to us that many fascinating social innovations have emerged throughout the world. Attending many conferences, and especially the annual meetings of the Association for Research on Nonprofit Organizations and Voluntary Action (ARNOVA), exposed us to the richness of social innovations from other countries. It was clear to us that when one studies nonprofit social innovation, a focus on American-based innovations alone is too limited. Sometimes, organizations in one culture can adopt and replicate an innovation from another culture, and other times the innovation is applicable only in one culture or locale. Regardless, the process of innovation is universal, and we believe that one can learn from successful innovations regardless of where they take place.

Thus we envisioned a book that consisted of selected cases that together would provide a rich array of successful social innovations in the nonprofit sector, an inspiring book that would illuminate various aspects of the process of social innovation. We contacted colleagues whom we knew were engaged in studying social innovation and placed a call among them for papers in a few academic and professional web-based networks. We received many more suggestions than we could include and we had to select carefully. It was exhilarating to know that there were so many nonprofit innovations and so many people willing to write chapters; it was also painful to reject potential contributors because we realized that some of the suggested chapters would be redundant to those we had already accepted; they were not covering the same innovation but the nature of their proposed case was already covered.

When we negotiated with our potential contributors, we sent them an outline around which to construct their chapter. As sometimes happens when smart professors write up their cases, many did not follow the outline; and while presenting fascinating cases, they produced a chapter that was hard to integrate with the other chapters. We realized that we had to bring the authors to one place and have them present their chapters, hear comments from others, and reconfigure their chapters to be more in concert. We applied for funds for such a meeting and were successful. In March 2013, all authors came to the University of Pennsylvania and spent 3 days presenting their chapters, discussing others' chapters, and realizing how they could improve their own chapters. It also became clear that one or two chapters had to be totally rewritten, and the authors willingly did so.

The 3-day expert meeting also reminded us that we were using concepts that are vague and used differently by different scholars. As a group, we decided that we needed two chapters to explain what we mean by nonprofit social innovation and to clarify the similarities and differences between social innovation and social entrepreneurship. Finally, we set deadlines for when revisions and final papers were due. It was a treat to work with colleagues who met the publisher's deadline and whom we did not have to chase. We had heard horror stories from colleagues who edited books and had to pursue contributors who did not meet deadlines. Our contributors were willing and accommodating!

As a result of the expert meeting and the feedback we received from the participants, we have organized the book in the following manner. We start the book with two conceptual chapters. The first chapter, by the editors, attempts to develop a comprehensive definition of the topic of social innovation and to provide a road map both to classify various social innovations and to create a terminology to distinguish among them. In the second chapter, Björn Schmitz provides an analytic review of social innovation and contrasts it with related concepts such as social entrepreneurship, social enterprise, social business, and democratic enterprise. These two chapters give the reader a conceptual understanding of what a nonprofit social innovation is and tools to analyze various social innovations in this volume and elsewhere.

Following the two opening conceptual chapters, the book presents 18 cases of social innovation that are categorized into one of three sections. In the first section, we present cases in which the innovation involved the formation of a new nonprofit organization. This part of the book presents the cases of a new Welfare Reform Liaison Project (WRLP) (Chapter 3), HopeHELPLive (Chapter 4), Café-au-Play (Chapter 5), The Mind Trust (Chapter 6), GiveIndia (Chapter 7), SZIA--The Social Innovation Foundation of Hungary (Chapter 8), Resto van Harte (Chapter 9), Seacology (Chapter 10), Dialogue in the Dark (Chapter 11), and Krembo Wings (Chapter 12).

The second part is composed of cases emphasizing collaboration. While all innovations require some degree of collaboration, in these innovations collaboration is the essential ingredient. This part of the book presents the cases of The Center for Rural Development in Appalachia (Chapter 13), Living Cities (Chapter 14), and the New York City Collaboration (Chapter 15).

The third part of the book consists of cases in which the innovation occurred within an existing nonprofit organization, also known as *intrapreneurship*. In some cases, this meant that the organization as a whole changed, and in others the change was limited or related to a certain part of the organization. This part of the book presents the cases of the YMCA (Chapter 16), Third Sector New England (Chapter 17), Metro TeenAIDS (Chapter 18), the Jungbo Foundation in South Korea (Chapter 19), and two faith-based social service organizations in Germany (Chapter 20).

The fifth section of this book contains the final and concluding chapter is titled "Lessons Learned: What Do We Now Know of Innovative NPOs and Can They Be Replicated?" In this chapter, the editors provide a summary of the themes that emerged from the cases in this book. These themes are practical in nature, because they try to find commonalities between the cases that come from different countries, regions, and fields. The summary provides an understanding of what it takes to be innovative, from the conception of an idea to its full implementation. We should note that the concluding chapter is not a specific action guide, but it provides an outline of the practical dimensions involved in carrying out nonprofit innovations.

Throughout this writing and compilation, we have had three goals. One is educational—to assist and promote the study of nonprofit social innovation by providing one volume that is both conceptual and case-based. The cases are based on a common outline that allows the reader to easily navigate them and make comparisons. Each chapter concludes with discussion questions, references, and, sometimes, additional materials relevant to the case. Our hope is to get feedback from future users of this volume who will inform us if, and how, the book helped them learn.

We have also aimed to present these cases to highlight and publicize the progress and optimism that can be found in the contemporary nonprofit sector. Too often, headlines and other media focus only on the errors or dysfunctions of nonprofits. By focusing on these innovative cases that we have selected and the concepts and analyses that we present in the two introductory chapters and the concluding chapter, readers can gain an appreciation of such positive steps that have been taken. The cases could galvanize them to recall—or be on the lookout for—other success stories. Such could give them a more balanced picture of the sector.

Finally, perhaps some readers will also be inspired to think creatively and initiate new successful nonprofit innovations themselves. We would be most grateful if they can benefit from the material in this book in their quest for their own nonprofit social innovations.

Ram A. Cnaan
Philadelphia, PA

Diane Vinokur-Kaplan
Ann Arbor, MI

Acknowledgments

Many people helped us in the process of planning, editing, and writing this book. First and foremost we want to thank the contributors who were asked to format their chapters in the fashion we envisioned. They revised their chapters a few times to accommodate our vision, and we thank them for their content, patience, and perseverance.

Rachel Easterbrook of the University of Pennsylvania did a heroic job in editing many of the chapters and giving them a uniform voice. She also offered suggestions to the authors about how to organize their chapters, and she helped write the original proposal and the requests for funding. We are indebted to her for her dedication throughout the process of producing this book.

We were financially supported mostly by two sources within the University of Pennsylvania for the 3-day meeting in which authors presented their chapters and colleagues gave constructive criticism. The Dean of the School of Social Policy & Practice, Richard J. Gelles, provided us with funds to bring all the contributors to the expert meeting held in Philadelphia. Additional financial support was provided by the PISF (Provost Interdisciplinary Seminar Fund) award, titled "Nonprofit and Seminar Series." This support enabled us to fund the local hospitality for this expert meeting. Discretionary research funds from the University of Michigan School of Social Work provided the means for the coeditors to meet and finalize the manuscript.

Finally, we would like to thank all those at SAGE Publications who have helped make this book a reality and who supported us in our efforts. They include: the reviewers of the book, who gave us valuable feedback; Acquisition Editors Patricia Quinlin and Maggie Stanley; Editorial Assistants Katie Guarino and Nicole Mangona; Production Editors Laura Barrett and Natalie Cannon; and especially our Copy Editor Deanna Noga for her helpful editing. We are also grateful to those whom we do not know but who contributed to the production of this volume.

ACKNOWLEDGMENTS OF REVIEWERS

SAGE gratefully acknowledges the contributions of the following reviewers:

Jim Morrison
University of Oklahoma

Hugh Sales, PhD
Belmont Abbey College

Michele D. Kegley, PhD
University of Cincinnati, Blue Ash College

Edmund A. Kellerman, EdD
Dial Center for Written and Oral Communication, University of Florida

Timothy Ewest
Wartburg College

Jacqueline C. Harvey
The University of North Texas

Linda K. Gibson
Pacific Lutheran University

Sylvia Ramirez Benatti, EdD
The University of the District of Columbia

Heather Getha-Taylor
School of Public Affairs and Administration, Univers

Paul L. Ewell
Virginia Wesleyan College

C. Douglas Johnson
Georgia Gwinnett College

Bruce Cline
Folsom Lake College

Dr. Misagh Tasavori
Essex Business School

Roland J. Kushner
Muhlenberg College

CHAPTER 1

Social Innovation

Definitions, Clarifications, and a New Model

Ram A. Cnaan

School of Social Policy and Practice University of Pennsylvania and Graduate Institute for Peace Studies Kyung Hee University

Diane Vinokur-Kaplan

School of Social Work University of Michigan

NONPROFIT ORGANIZATIONS AND SOCIAL INNOVATION

According to the Independent Sector (2012), in 2011, there were more than 1.6 million tax-exempt organizations in the United States—a number that has approximately doubled in the last 30 years—and many more worldwide. They are active in many fields, including education, welfare, arts, culture, health, advocacy, and the environment. Their contribution to our quality of life is immense. In fact, without the contribution of nonprofit organizations (NPOs), life in many communities would be quite bleak. Among the noted reasons for the existence of nonprofit organizations, functioning alongside the state and the for-profit sectors is their potential to be innovative and responsive to meet human needs more quickly and creatively than all other types of organizations. This book provides many examples of charitable nonprofits doing just that, and it is limited to those organizations serving the public good (501(c)(3)-type organizations). (Public and business innovation are beyond this book's purview.)

With the emphasis on innovation in nonprofit activities, it is not surprising that a Johns Hopkins University (2010) survey has revealed widespread innovation among the nation's nonprofits. The study found that a vast majority (82%) of responding NPOs reported implementing an innovative program or service within the past 5 years. These are indeed amazing statistics regarding innovation.

Indeed, this estimate of four fifths of all nonprofit organizations innovating seems rather too optimistic. The sample was relatively small (N = 417) and may have attracted the more innovative NPOs to participate. But this was probably only a small part of the problem. The key problem, in our view, is that while nonprofit innovation is highly celebrated in the sector, *there is no clear understanding of what qualifies as innovation and what does not.* For example, if an NPO decides to follow funding opportunities and start serving a new group of clients, is it an innovation or mere survival adaptation or both? If an NPO adds an auditing department, is it an innovation or a normal sign of growing organizational complexity? What qualifies as a real social innovation is a serious dilemma for which there is currently no clear answer.

In this introductory chapter, written by the book editors, we first discuss the problematic nature of deciding what an innovation is; by citing a few of the most commonly used definitions of innovation, we show that they are limited in their breadth coverage. In the rest of the chapter, we try to develop a model that presents a more comprehensive view of nonprofit innovation, one that can be used to define many initiatives as innovations while still distinguishing the unique characteristics of each innovation. It should be noted that this opening chapter concentrates on definitional issues, while Chapter 2 by Björn Schmitz provides a broader conceptual analysis of social innovation, social entrepreneurship, social enterprise, social business, democratic enterprise, and their interrelationships. We opted to avoid duplication and focus in this chapter on an attempt to provide a new conceptual road map to categorizing nonprofit innovations. We are aware that for some readers this road map will be a useful tool in distinguishing between the nature of various innovations, while other readers will prefer to dive directly into the cases.

The two opening conceptual chapters do not cover the "how to" of innovation. These chapters attempt conceptually to tackle the muddy definitional world of nonprofit social innovation. A more practical understanding of the innovation process is reserved for the concluding chapter in part 5. In this final chapter titled "Lessons Learned: What Do We now Know of Innovative NPOs and Can They be Replicated?" we provide a summary of the themes that emerge from the cases in this book. These themes are more practical in nature, because they try to find commonalities between the cases that come from different countries, regions, and fields. The summary provides an understanding of what it takes to be innovative, from the conception of an idea to its full implementation. We should note that the concluding chapter is not an action guide, but it provides an outline of the practical dimensions of carrying out nonprofit innovation.

In addition to these three conceptual chapters in Parts 1 and 5, the book is divided into three parts. In the first part of social innovation cases, we present cases in which the innovation involved the formation of a new nonprofit organization. This part of the book contains Chapters 3 to 12 and contains the cases of Welfare Reform Liaison Project (WRLP) (Chapter 3), HelpHOPELive (Chapter 4), Café au Play (Chapter 5), The Mind Trust (Chapter 6), GiveIndia (Chapter 7), The Social Innovation Foundation of Hungary (Chapter 8), Resto van Harte (Chapter 9), Seacology (Chapter, 10), Dialogue in the Dark (Chapter 11), and Krembo Wings (Chapter 12).

The second part of the cases is composed of cases emphasizing collaboration. While all innovations require collaboration, in some innovations collaboration is the essential ingredient. This part of the book contains Chapters 13 to 15 and contains the cases of The Center for Rural Development in Appalachia (Chapter 13), Living Cities (Chapter 14), and the New York City Collaboration (Chapter 15).

The third group of cases focuses on innovations that occurred within an existing nonprofit organization. In some cases, this meant that the organizations as a whole changed and in others that the change was partial or related to a certain part of the organization. This part of the book contains Chapters 16 to 20 and contains the cases of the YMCA (Chapter 16), Third Sector New England (Chapter 17), Metro TeenAIDS (Chapter 18), the Jungbo Foundation in South Korea (Chapter 19), and two faith-based social service organization in Germany (Chapter 20).

In the classical sense of social innovation, NPOs promote innovation because they are able to see a problem to which most people are oblivious or to come up with an innovative solution. Clearly, such daring organizations are led by people who are courageous and who possess a creative worldview. We aimed to highlight cases of successful innovations both in the United States and internationally. We do so to show that innovation in nonprofit organizations is not exclusively American. Innovation in nonprofit organizations is a worldwide phenomenon. Sometimes, organizations in one culture can replicate and adopt an innovation from another culture and other times the innovation is applicable only in one culture or locale. Regardless, the process of innovation is universal and we believe that one can learn from successful innovations regardless of where they take place. We hope that those who read this book will think creatively and analytically about them. By focusing on the innovative cases we have selected and the thematic analysis we present in these two introductory chapters and the concluding chapter, readers will gain an appreciation and inclination to think creatively and, hopefully, come up with additional successful nonprofit innovations.

THE QUEST FOR SOCIAL INNOVATION

It seems that just about everyone today is encouraged to be innovative. Almost every nonprofit management job advertisement expects the potential candidate to be able to innovate. Every review of directors or presidents of organizations assesses such individuals' achievements in innovating within their organizations. Creativity and innovation are the current major characteristics required of leaders and successful managers, and those individuals who just do reliable, routine, and high-quality work are often looked upon as lacking something. Professional literature reflects the same quest. For instance, in the for-profit realm, Crossan and Apaydin (2010) conducted a meta-analysis and found that articles on innovation in business and economic journals grew, on average, 14% per year from 1981 to 2008.

The quest for innovation is not unique to any sector, because even the public sector has been called on to be innovative (Borins, 2008; Osborne & Brown, 2011). For example, when President Barack Obama was elected to the White House, he reorganized an existing office to become the *Office of Social Innovation and Civic Participation*. One of the Office's principal activities is handling the *Social Innovation Fund*, which holds a total of $124 million. Indeed, social innovation is the current mantra in most human service organizations.

Why this massive quest for innovation? We live in an era of rapid change that has brought forth rising citizen expectations, emerging new social problems, demand for social services that were previously unattended, limited public fiscal resources, and the perception that we face complex social problems that cannot be remedied by standard solutions even if additional resources become available. Complex reality calls for new solutions by all three sectors, and the way to find these solutions is to be innovative.

Indeed, the future of the nonprofit sector is based on social innovations. The special power of nonprofit organizations is to do what public organizations cannot do because of the lack of political will or the regulations they face; or because they produce goods and services that for-profit organizations will not because it is not profitable for them to do so. The ability to identify new needs, to find means to help people who are not served or are not served well, and the courage to initiate and reorganize service delivery are all innovations that make social nonprofits exciting and hopefully more efficient, effective, just, and sustainable. We set out next to provide to students of nonprofit management and leadership an overview of the typical dimensions arising in defining social innovation in the social innovation literature.

DEFINING SOCIAL INNOVATION

Before providing a set of examples regarding social innovation, we should ask what social innovation actually is. The term is illusive, multidimensional, and still means many different things to different people. There are many concepts and theories that guide the thinking about social innovation. There have been many attempts to understand what social innovation is and what its boundaries are. Yet confusion is often the order of the day. When we entered the concept "social innovation" into Google Scholar, we found over 25,100 academic documents that contain this phrase. And yet there is no clear agreement or understanding of what is, and what is not, social innovation.

Anheier and Leat (2006) defined an *innovation* as ". . . an idea, practice, or object that is perceived as new" (p. 4). While this is a solid inclusive definition, for the purpose of this volume, this definition is too inclusive and unspecified. The Center for Social Innovation at The Stanford University Graduate School of Business (2014) defines *social innovation* as ". . . a novel solution to a social problem that is more effective, efficient, sustainable, or just than present solutions and for which the value created accrues primarily to society as a whole rather than private individuals." Another eloquent definition was offered by Murray, Caulier-Grice, and Mulgan (2010), who defined "social innovations as new ideas (products, services and models) that simultaneously meet social needs and create new social relationships or collaborations" (p. 3). In other words, they are innovations that are both good for society and enhance society's capacity to act. This definition was also adopted almost verbatim by the European Union (2012).

Another example of a well-used definition that is too broad to be of much help is the one proposed by Phillis, Deiglmeier, and Miller (2008). They defined *social innovation* as "a novel solution to a social problem that is more effective, efficient, sustainable, or just than existing solutions and for which the value created accrues primarily to society as a whole rather than private individuals." There are many other definitions of social innovation such as the one by Westley and Antadze (2009), who suggest that "social innovation is a *complex process* of introducing new products, processes or programs that profoundly *change* the basic routines, resource and authority flows, or beliefs of the *social system* in which the innovation occurs. Such successful social innovations have *durability* and *broad impact*" (p. 2). The essence here is not on newness but on changing an existing routine, resources and authority flows, or beliefs in a manner that leaves a long-lasting impact. Again, the definition is too general and misses the many nuances of social innovation.

Damanpour (1991) contended that innovation involves change, but not all kinds of change can be termed innovation. Innovation must involve a break from the existing practices and mindsets and the creation of something new. While this definition excludes *regular change* from *innovative change*, it is still difficult to determine its borders. Damanpour and Schneider (2008) stated that innovation can be either radical or incremental, and it can be based on either the generation of an original invention or the adoption and adaptation of known innovations into new places or new contexts.

We could have cited numerous other definitions, but none were not sufficiently encompassing. When definitions try to tackle a complex field that is composed of many variants and to simplify it into a generic definition, the important nuances of social innovations are lost. Instead of celebrating the many variations of nonprofit and social innovation, the definitions are generic and do not help us classify the variety that exists in social innovations. Our aim is to provide a conceptual framework that will capture most forms and variations of social innovation in an organized manner. But before turning to this discussion, we need to clarify the relationships between social innovation and social entrepreneurship. It is clear that any social innovation starts with a great idea about a problem or an issue that is either ignored or underserved (Amabile, Conti, Coon, Lazenby, & Herron, 1996). But ideas are never enough. They are a prerequisite that is not sufficient. While creativity is related to the production of novel and useful ideas, innovation is related to the successful implementation of creative ideas within an organization, a community, or society (Amabile et al., 1996; Oldham & Cumming, 1996). The innovative idea needs champions who advocate for it and persuade others of its relevance and its utility. Hence, social innovation is the combination of a creative idea and someone (or more than one person) investing numerous hours, resources, and skills to make it real. To go back to the French origins of "entrepreneur," it is someone who undertakes to actualize a novel idea. (Note that the concept and role of social entrepreneurs is elaborated in the next conceptual chapter [Chapter 2] and is discussed in the concluding chapter [Chapter 21].)

In sum, it seems that most academic treatments of social innovation regard it as a unidimensional category devoid of real complexity. At times, some authors went as far as offering a two-by-two model of social innovation (cf. Osborne, 1998, 2002), but the reality is that when we critically analyze social innovations, there are more dimensions that can be used to distinguish between them.

We believe that we should complement the many existing sources with a comprehensive view of social innovation that can serve as a guiding theory for describing the complexity of social innovation and its boundaries (DiMaggio, 1995; Van Maanen, Sørensen, & Mitchell, 2007). In this respect, we follow DiMaggio (1995) who contended that "good theory" is multidimensional and that the best theories are hybrids, resulting from combining different approaches to theory. The technique we use in this chapter to highlight the complexity and multidimensionality of social innovations is known as a *mapping sentence*. We explain it later on in this chapter. For now, our concern is if there is a way to say that one nonprofit activity is definitely not an innovation and another activity is definitely a social innovation.

THE BOUNDARIES OF SOCIAL INNOVATION

It is important to note that in many aspects of life, innovation is not always a priority. On an individual level, the authors of this chapter would not like the pilot who flies the plane to be innovative in the sense of not following protocol and possibly endangering lives. We want said pilot to follow procedures, be reliable, and avoid risk taking, unless an emergency warrants it. The pilot should be applauded and rewarded for being precise and following procedures. Yet, on a systematic level, we also want someone to find innovative ways to make flights safer, cheaper, more comfortable, and to meet unforeseen emergencies.

Furthermore, it is not clear if being innovative is always a good thing. If an organization is serving young people with disabilities by effectively helping them find employment year in and year out, and many people with disabilities are being successfully served, why should innovation be instituted? There are many college-counseling services that effectively and efficiently help students prepare for college, and, as such, they do important work. There are soup kitchens that night after night feed numerous homeless people and are effective and nourishing for years without being innovative. These and many other wonderful services do not need to innovate simply because it is fashionable to innovate. If we fail to financially support these routine services and seek only to support new innovations, the world will suffer. Yet the quest for innovation in general, and for social innovations in particular is stronger today and more valued than at any time in history. It seems that social innovation is in high demand, even though what it is and what it does in particular are not always very clear.

The world is changing, resources are fewer, and social innovation is essential. Yet it is important to note that many quality organizations provide high-level services with minimal innovation. In fact, the majority of nonprofit organizations do not fall into the social innovation definition, and that is no way a sign of disrespect or a stain on their reputation.

What we are looking for in this chapter is a means to conceptually define what is, and what is not, a social innovation, and, offer a model that will distinguish between different types of innovation. Maybe the oldest and seminal definition and classification of social innovation is attributed to the economist Joseph Schumpeter (Dodgson, 2011; Pol & Carroll, 2006). Schumpeter introduced new ways to look at innovation, economic transformation, and the notion of creative destruction (Schumpeter, 1912). Schumpeter does not focus on the traditional supply and demand but on innovation, entrepreneurial activities, and market power. For example, he suggests that technological innovation can create conditions that are ripe for monopolies, which are outside the supply-demand equation. He also observed that nearly all businesses that fail are victims of innovation by their competitors (McCraw, 2010).

Schumpeter's contribution to the understanding of innovation outside the market was even greater. He provided us with the first classification of five types of economic innovation. These five types are (1) introduction of a new good or a new quality of a good, (2) implementation of a new production method, (3) accessing of a new sales market, (4) accessing of a new source of supply of raw materials or intermediate goods, and (5) rearranging of the market position (e.g., a bursting of an existing monopoly or market order). The influence of Schumpeter's classification of innovation is so pervasive that it is still the one most used today. For example, the Organization for Economic Co-operation and Development (OECD & Eurostat, 2005) refers to innovation in the following manner: "An innovation is the implementation of a new or significantly improved product (good or service), or process, a new marketing method, or a new organizational method in business practices, workplace organization or external relations" (p. 46).

As such, Schumpeter provides us with the first differential classification and an understanding that not all innovations are the same. We did not use his classification as such, because it is better suited to the economic sphere of production and business, and we follow the footsteps of scholars who contend that for-profit and nonprofit innovations are not the same. For example, Hull and Lio (2006) compared innovations in these two sectors and concluded that key differences exist in vision, strategic constraints, and financial constraints between the sectors. However, Schumpeter's contribution definitely helped shape our thinking, as can be seen in the following section, and it is further addressed in the next conceptual chapter.

MAPPING SENTENCES AND THEIR APPLICABILITY

When attempting to provide a theory of a concept as wide and complex as *social innovation*, one cannot expect to achieve a grand theory that will be all inclusive, but rather to provide merely a systematic overview that offers a wide but limited set of possibilities. One way of systematically organizing the universe of observations regarding a social phenomenon or a field of investigation is through developing a mapping sentence. This method was developed by Louis Guttman (1959) as a means to systematize a field of study.

Mapping sentences proved helpful in many areas of investigation in which the universe of possibilities seemed endless and when no coherent picture of the field had emerged. They were used in areas such as the study of values (Levy, 1976); intelligence (Guttman, 1965; Guttman & Levy, 1991); achievement motivation (Talsma, Van Den Bercken, Houtmans, & De Bruyn, 1992); interpersonal behavior (Schutz, 1992); volunteering (Cnaan & Amrofell, 1995); children's perception of their family environment (Guttman, Goldschmidt, & Fischbein, 1997); developmental psychology (Bergling, 1999); and self-personality (Levy & Sabbagh, 2008).

Guttman proposed that mapping sentences can be used as a definitional system for analyzing a universe of observations to make explicit in a reliable way which items belong to the content universe and which do not. While a mapping sentence can be tested empirically using "facet analysis," its key contribution is taking the variations or different components of any field of study and presenting them in a series of related facets. Each facet contains a limited set of related and often mutually exclusive options or categories.

For example, in analyzing the concept of social innovation, one facet may be "the innovator." This facet can take many forms based on what is most commonly presented in the literature. The social innovator can be a person suffering from the problem area in which the innovation takes place, a person familiar with someone who suffers from the problem, someone not directly related to the problem, a professional working in the field of the problem, a committee charged to study the problem, an organization active in this field, or any combination thereof.

Once a facet is completed, it is related logically to another facet. In our example, the above facet may be linked to the auspices under which the social innovation took place and so on. Once the full sentence with all its relevant facets and their related options and/or categories is established, each social innovation in general, and specifically each one in this book, can be presented as a unique case of the mapped sentence by selecting one or more categories in each facet.

In sum, the mapping sentence specifies the facets and the relationships between them. It is characterized by (1) its domain, which contains information about the conditions that set the stage for recording observations, and by (2) its range (i.e., response facet), which specifies the relevant set of observational outcomes and their meanings. The mapping sentence's phrases link the facets together, and they make available the semantic structural unity implied by the content universe. A mapping sentence also provides a definitional framework that can be used for generating hypotheses about the relationships among both the facets and their elements.

It should be noted that some categories might overlap between facets, while some categories in one facet may be more often linked with a few but not all categories of another facet. For example, the category of "identifying a new target population" appears both in the facet of "*who benefits*" and in the facet of "*what is being innovated.*" Each of these two facets answers a different question, and not in all cases will the presence of "new target population" be appropriate in both facets. Put differently, members of a new population may be the beneficiaries but what is innovated is a new technology and the discovery of a new population. It is possible, for example, that what is innovated is a new method of intervention but that the primary beneficiaries are people who were previously underserved. As such, for each case in the book, we draw the most relevant social innovation mapping sentences based on the proposed facets and categories.

In this chapter, we attempt to apply the logic of mapping sentences to the domain of social innovation. We first provide a set of four facets and their respective options and/or categories. We do so by focusing on each facet separately and providing examples from the book for as many options and/or categories as possible. We then link all the facets into one logical sentence. The final product is a road map for categorizing and understanding what is included under the concept of social innovation and its many possible variations.

MAPPING THE CONCEPT OF SOCIAL INNOVATION

Based on reading many texts that define and explain social innovation, it seems that we need four key facets to capture the domain of social innovation. The first facet deals with *What is being innovated* and consists of six categories. It is followed by analyzing *Who benefits* (consisting of four categories), which is then followed by identifying *Who is the innovator* (consisting of six categories). It concludes with an assessment of the *Magnitude of innovation* (consisting of four categories). Each case in the book and each case of social innovation can find a specific path through these four facets and identify its unique set of relevant categories. At minimum, there are 576 distinct paths if each analysis of social innovation selects one and only one category from each facet. But because it is possible to choose two or more categories within one facet and at times to decide that no category in a given facet is relevant, the number of possible paths is much larger and reflects the complexity and variety of possible social innovations.

Facet 1: What Is Being Innovated?

Often, when we discuss the concept of social innovation, the first thing that comes to mind is an organization that has revolutionized a certain domain for a social purpose; for example, Habitat for Humanity revolutionized the field of building homes for poor families. But innovations can be undertaken in many shapes and forms and still be innovative. In this facet, we discuss six categories of what can be innovative. We are likely not inclusive enough, and the categories are not mutually exclusive. Often an innovation is large scale and spans over more than one category (see Figure 1.1). The key options and/or categories we use that render positive change and produce social benefits are identifying (1) A new group of clients; that is, moving to serve those who are not recognized as people in need or are seriously underserved; (2) A new subgroup of clients for the organization including people who the organization found out to be effective with (as in the case of providing disaster counseling when needed by an organization with the relevant expertise) or a new group of clients that is served by others maybe faraway but not by this specific organization; (3)An innovative intervention that was not used before; (4) A known intervention used differently than others or differently than the organization applied it before; (5) An intraorganizational innovation that changed the way the organization works and moved it to better effectiveness and efficiency; and (6)An innovation in the relationships with stakeholders in the organization's environment (from funders to ex-clients).

The first thing that comes to mind when discussing "real" social innovation is identifying a new target population. While this may be the Holy Grail for all social innovation scholars, the reality is that such social innovation is rare. Among the chapters in this book, HopeHELPLive (Chapter 4) to some extent identified a new target population (people needing or recovering from organ transplants), but it more so identified an innovative way to address their financial need. In the context of South Korea, Jungbu Foundation (Chapter 19) identified a new target population of professional social workers who suffer from severe cases of burnout. However, given that these types of clients are served in other countries, it may be more a case of the second category; that is, a new group of clients that is served by others but not by their home organization.

HopeHELPLive is an excellent example of the third category. While its clients are also identified as an underserved group of people (the first category in this facet), it also developed a new intervention (community-based fundraisings by friends and relatives of those in medical need). After trying to raise funds from foundations and affluent neighbors, the organization's leaders realized that the best source of help is within the ill person's own social network. HopeHELPLive developed a new method of how to guide friends and relatives to fundraise, and a new intervention emerged. Similarly, Krembo Wings (Chapter 12) for disabled children and Dialogue in the Dark for blind people (Chapter 11) offer innovative interventions to known target populations, but for which organizations were not yet developed.

FIGURE 1.1 Typology Of Social Innovations

Social innovation is focused on…

<u>What is being innovated?</u>

(1) A new group of clients that is moving to serve those who are underserved

(2) A new subgroup of clients including those who the organization found to be effective with or new group that is served by others but not by the organization

(3) An innovative intervention that was not used before

(4) A known intervention used differently than others or differently than the organization applied before

(5) An intraorganization innovation that changed the way the organization works and moves it to better efficiency

(6) An innovation in the relationships with the organizational environment

to the benefit of…

<u>Who benefits?</u>

(1) Individuals or families who were previously not served

(2) Individuals or families who were previously served but for whom a new service and/or treatment was invented

(3) Organizations that serve people who can now do their job in a better or more efficient manner

(4) Communities at large where quality of life is enhanced due to the innovation, even if no particular person is served

performed by…

<u>The Innovator</u>

(1) A person suffering from the problem

(2) A person familiar with someone who suffers from the problem

(3) Someone not directly related to the problem

(4) A professional working in the field of the problem

(5) A committee charged to study the problem or an organization active in this field

(6) Any combination hereof

at the following scope…

<u>Magnitude of Innovation</u>

(1) Totally new

(2) New regarding a specific target population

(3) New in a certain region or country

(4) New within a given organization

The Welfare Reform Liaison Project (WRLP) (www.wrlp.net; Chapter 3) is an excellent case of the fourth category in this facet. The clients are known across the United States (welfare-to-work single parents) as those who need technical skills and support. However, WRLP organized itself differently by newly bridging different institutions within a community and as such was socially innovative and effective. Other organizations that applied modified intervention to a recognized group of clients are Café au Play (for parents and their young children; Chapter 5) and Resto van Harte (for the socially isolated; Chapter 9).

Metro TeenAIDS (Chapter 18) is an excellent example of the fifth category of intraorganizational innovation, namely, changing the way the organization works and moving it to better efficiency. The organization kept serving the same target population in the same geographical area, but shifted focus from direct service to advocacy. The client group, the intervention, and the scope are all familiar from other social service organizations. But the internal change within key mode of service was innovative and made the organization more effective in meetings its goals.

Seacology (Chapter 10) is a good example of the sixth category; change the relationships with key stakeholders. While it deals with environmental protection, its key innovation is regarding the relationships it forges with the local inhabitants of the island ecologies it selects to preserve. By applying patience and support to the locals' priorities, Seacology is more effective than most similar environmental protection organizations.

Facet 2: Who Benefits?

Osborne (1998), Osborne, McLaughlin, and Chew (2008), and Walker (2007) talked about the magnitude of the innovation. However, their proposed typology is binary: new customers versus existing customers. This typology, in our view, is too limited, and we thus proposed a more refined facet. The term *new customers* can mean people that were never served before or people who are new to the organization as is discussed in the first facet above. For us, the facet focuses on the people who benefit from the innovation and the degree to which they were served before. The key options and/or categories we use are (1) Individuals or groups who were previously not served, (2) Individuals or groups who were previously served but for whom a new treatment and/or service was invented, (3) Organizations that served individuals or groups and can now serve them in a better or more efficient manner, and (4) Communities at large whose quality of life is enhanced due to the innovation even if no one particular person is specifically served.

HopeHELPLive is one organization in which its founders identified a group of individuals and families who were previously not served and developed a service for them: those medically eligible for heart transplantation but who could not afford it. The second category, individuals or groups who were previously served but a new treatment and/or service was invented for them, includes such programs as Dialogue in the Dark, Resto Van Harte, Jungbu Foundation, Welfare Reform Liaison Project, and Café au Play. The third category, organizations that found ways to serve individuals or groups in a better or more efficient, effective, just, or sustainable manner, includes such programs as GiveIndia (Chapter 7), YMCA (Chapter 16), and Metro TeenAIDS. The final category, communities at large where quality of life is enhanced due to the innovation, includes such programs as presented in the following cases: The Mind Trust, Living Cities, The Center for Rural Development in Appalachia, Third Sector New England, and Seacology.

Facet 3: The Innovator

This facet can take many forms since the literature presents many characteristics of innovators. We start with a few possible characteristics that we do not use, for instance, the demographics of the innovator such as age, gender, nationality, and so on (for example in the case of Krembo Wings, the innovator was a teenager). We elected not to include demographics because they served more to answer the question of how the innovator looks rather than who the innovators are. It seems to us that the most interesting aspect of the innovator is the person/group/organization's relationship to the problem. When viewing social innovation from this perspective of who is the innovator, the following are the key options: (1) It can be a person suffering from the problem, (2) A person familiar with someone who suffers from the problem, (3) Someone not directly related to the problem, (4) A professional working in the field of the problem, (5) A committee charged to study the problem or an organization active in this field, or (6) Any combination thereof.

It seems that in most of the cases in this book, the innovator was not the person directly suffering from the problem, although they somehow had interest or empathy for it. In the cases of Krembo Wings, the innovator was familiar with people who were affected by the problem. In the cases of HelpHopeLive, Metro TeenAIDS, and Seacology, it was someone familiar with the problem but without a personal relationship to it. In the cases of Welfare Reform Liaison Project, The Mind Trust, Resto Van Harte, GiveIndia, and Dialogue in the Dark, the innovator was a professional working in the field or in a related field. Finally, in the cases of the Jungbu Foundation, Third Sector New England, Living Cities, and the YMCA, the innovation came from the work of a collective or a committee within an organization. Only in the case of Café au Play did the innovations start with a person in need. The person behind the initiative found herself a single mother in Portland with no public spaces to meet people like herself.

Facet 4: Magnitude of Innovation

The final but not least important question to be asked is how new a social innovation must be. This book is filled with amazing stories of social innovations. When the authors met to discuss these cases, we were all in awe of the astounding stories and the great diversity regarding social innovations. Yet in many cases people noted that the innovative aspect of what was presented was locally limited, and the innovator might not be the first to come up with the idea and program. If a solution to a problem is invented in Guatemala, and a few years later it was found that the same solution was already in existence in Nepal, is the Guatemalan social innovation no longer considered an innovation? Is the Guatemalan case, although it produced an invention, merely a diffusion of an innovation? As such, one debate is whether an innovation must be totally new and almost like a patent or whether adopting a solution from one place to another is also an innovation.

There are no agreed upon answers to this question regarding the boundaries of social innovation. Instead of answering the above questions, we turn to what the literature tells us about social innovation. So one key facet when assessing social innovations is the degree to which the innovation is absolutely new, at least to the particular site. It seems that in this facet the key categories are (1) Totally new (never been done anywhere in the world), (2) New regarding a specific target population, (3) New in a certain region or country, and (4) New within a given organization.

It is difficult to state that any of the cases contained in the book is indeed totally innovative and that nothing like it has ever been done before. It seems that this category is more an ideal rather than a practical category. In the context of this book, some social innovations were easy to place within the remaining three categories. For example, when HelpHOPELive was founded, it was geared to a totally new population of people needing heart transplantation, but fundraising to help sick people was done formally and informally in many parts of the world. The Center for Rural Development in Appalachia and the focus of the Jungbu Foundation in Korea on helping social workers cope with burnout are good examples of regional and national innovations. Metro TeenAIDS of Washington, DC, is a good example of an organization that existed and was actively helping in the domain of HIV/AIDS but that later innovated its focus to shift from service provision to advocacy.

The overall mapping sentence that includes all four facets is presented in Figure 1.1.

Limitations

In this introductory chapter, we presented a model to understand and differentiate between varieties of social innovations. The drawback of this model is its inability to determine when a change is no longer an innovation. When one organization finally adopts a practice that is commonly used in its geographical environment by many organizations, it may be an in-house innovation but it is not a social innovation. Such cases that others may include as nonprofit or social innovation are, to us, more cases of institutional isomorphism (where organizations mimic others in their environment) than real innovation. Our model is helpful in categorizing and differentiating social innovations; but it is limited by its inability to determine what is *not* a social innovation. Such a determination can only be made independently and subjectively by each observer and is contextually based. Put differently, the boundaries of what is outside the realm of social innovation are still an open challenge to social innovation scholars.

Finally, we did not discuss the conditions that deter or enhance innovations in existing organizations. Three chapters in this volume, about innovations in the YMCA, Third Sector New England, and in a large German social service organization, relate to innovation within existing organizations. There is a large body of literature on conditions that support or prohibit "intrapreneurship" innovation, and we did not include them in Chapter 2. The reader is advised to look for good reviews of this topic to complement the benefit of this mapping sentence. See, for example, an excellent review of this topic by Van Gurp (2012).

SUMMARY AND CONCLUSIONS

There is no doubt that both social innovation and social entrepreneurship are two concepts in vogue. Directors of public benefit nonprofits are expected to possess the ability to innovate and the relevant style of leadership that is associated with it. While we noted that many organizations should not seek innovation simply for the sake of innovation, but rather in accordance with their mission, we also acknowledge that innovation is hard to define and thus hard to explain or teach. Yet progress is predicated on social innovation, and to be able to assess what is and what is not social innovation and to be able to compare various social innovations, we introduced the logic of mapping sentences.

Mapping sentences are logical tools used to bring a sense of order to a field of study that is complex and hard to understand systematically. We use the mapping sentence here in an experiential manner, and we do not test it empirically. It is our hope that when readers encounter a social innovation, they will form a specific and relevant mapping sentence for that nonprofit organization's social innovation. By applying four key facets, with each consisting of four to six categories, and organizing them as a logical sentence, we prepare future discussions of social innovation to be more precise and introduce the possibility for various social innovations to be compared.

REFERENCES

Amabile, T. M., Conti, R., Coon, H., Lazenby, J., & Herron, M. (1996). Assessing the work environment for creativity. *Academy of Management Journal, 39*(5), 1154–1184.

Anheier, H. K., & Leat, D. (2006). *Creative philanthropy*. London, United Kingdom: Routledge.

Bergling, B. M. (1999). Extending facet design to such complex psychological structures as Piaget's theory. *Quality and Quantity, 33*(10), 13–26.

Borins, S. (Ed.). (2008). *Innovations in government: Research, recognition, and replication*. Washington, DC: Brookings Institution Press.

Center for Social Innovation at The Stanford University Graduate School of Business. (2014). *Social innovation*. Retrieved from http://csi.gsb.stanford.edu/social-innovation

Cnaan, R. A., & Amrofell, L. M. (1995). Mapping volunteer activity. *Nonprofit and Voluntary Sector Quarterly, 23*(4), 335–351.

Crossan, M. M., & Apaydin, M. (2010). A multi-dimensional framework of organizational innovation: A systematic review of the literature. *Journal of Management Studies, 17*(6), 1154–1191.

Damanpour, F. (1991). Organizational innovation: A meta-analysis of effects of determinants and moderators. *Academy of Management Journal, 34*(3), 555–590.

Damanpour, F., & Schneider, M. (2008). Characteristics of innovation and innovation adoption in public organizations: Assessing the role of managers. *Journal of Public Administration Research and Theory, 19*(3), 495–522.

Dimaggio, P. (1995). Comments on "What theory is not?" *Administrative Science Quarterly, 40*(3), 391–397.

Dodgson, M. (2011). Exploring new combinations in innovation and entrepreneurship: Social networks, Schumpeter, and the case of Josiah Wedgwood (1730–1795). *Industrial and Corporate Change, 20*, 1119–1151.

European Union. (2012). *Strengthening social innovation in Europe: Journey to effective assessment and metrics*. Retrieved from http://ec.europa.eu/enterprise/policies/innovation/files/social-innovation/strengthening-social-innovation_en.pdf

Guttman, L. (1959). A structural theory for intergroup beliefs and action. *American Sociological Review, 24*, 318–328.

Guttman, L. (1965). A faceted definition of intelligence. *Scripta Hierosolymitana: Studies in Psychology* (pp. 166–181). Jerusalem, Israel: The Hebrew University.

Guttman, L., & Levy, S. (1991). Two structural laws for intelligence tests. *Intelligence, 15*(1), 79–103.

Guttman, R., Goldschmidt, N., & Fischbein, S. (1997, September 22–24). How school children perceive their family environment: Using DISCO to compare twins with singletons, Jerusalem with kibbutz children. In *Proceedings of the Sixth International Facet Theory Conference* (pp. 85–94). Liverpool, United Kingdom.

Hull, C. E., & Lio, B. H. (2006). Innovation in non-profit and for-profit organizations: Visionary, strategic and financial considerations. *Journal of Change Management, 6*(1), 53–65.

Independent Sector. (2012). Scope of the nonprofit sector. Retrieved from http://www.independentsector.org/scope_of_the_sector#sthash.pVzmnQZf.dpbs

Johns Hopkins University, Center for Civil Society Studies. (2010). *Nonprofits, innovation and performance measurement: Separating fact from fiction*. Baltimore, MD: Author.

Levy, S. (1976). Use of mapping sentence for coordinating theory and research: A cross-cultural example. *Quantity and Quality, 10*, 117–125.

Levy, S., & Sabbagh, C. (2008). The wellbeing of the self's personality: A structural analysis. *Social Indicators Research, 89*, 473–485.

McCraw, T. K. (2010). *Prophet of innovation: Joseph Schumpeter and creative destruction*. Cambridge, MA: Harvard University Press.

Murray, R., Caulier-Grice, J., & Mulgan, G. (2010). *The open book of social innovation*. London, United Kingdom: The Young Foundation.

OECD & Eurostat. (2005). *Oslo manual: Guidelines for collecting and interpreting innovation data* (3rd ed.). Paris, France: OECD. Retrieved from http://www.oecd.org/sti/oslomanual

Oldham, G. R., & Cumming, A. (1996). Employee creativity: Personal and contextual factors at work. *Academy of Management Journal, 39*(3), 607–634.

Osborne, S. (1998). Naming the beast: Defining and classifying service innovations in social policy. *Human Relations, 51*(9), 1133–1154.

Osborne, S. (2002). The voluntary sector in the UK: Key trends and emerging issues. *Nonprofit Review, 2*, 11–21.

Osborne, S. P., & Brown, L. (2011). Innovation, public policy and public services delivery in the UK: The word that would be king? *Public Administration, 89*(4), 1335–1350.

Osborne, S., McLaughlin, K., & Chew, C. (2008). The once and future pioneers? The innovative capacity of voluntary organizations and the provision of public services: A longitudinal approach. *Public Management Review, 10*(1), 51–70.

Phillis, J. A., Jr., Deiglmeier, K., & Miller, D. T. (2008, Fall). Rediscovering social innovation. *Stanford Social Innovation Review, 6*(4), 36.

Pol, E., & Carroll, P. (2006). *An introduction to economics with an emphasis on innovation*. London, United Kingdom: Thomson.

Schumpeter, J. A. (1912). *Theorie der wirtschaftlichen Entwicklung*. Berlin, Germany: Duncker und Humbolt.

Schutz, W. (1992). Beyond FIRO-B—Three new theory-derived measures—Element B: Behavior, element F: Feelings, element S: Self. *Psychological Reports, 70*, 915–937.

Talsma, P. A., Van Den Bercken, J. H., Houtmans, T. J., & De Bruyn, E. J. (1992). Assessment in the domain of achievement motivation: Facet design based item classification. *European Journal of Psychological Assessment, 8*(2), 135–148.

Van Gurp, S. A. (2012). *Innovation in the nonprofit organizational context: Examining the strategic significance of systems trust and individual resistance to change* (Unpublished doctoral dissertation). Iowa City: University of Iowa. Retrieved from http://ir.uiowa.edu/cgi/viewcontent.cgi?article=3150&context=etd

Van Maanen, J., Sørensen, J. B., & Mitchell, T. R. (2007). Introduction to special topic forum: The interplay between theory and method. *Academy of Management Review, 32*(4), 1145–1154.

Walker, R. (2007). An empirical evaluation of innovation types and organizational and environmental characteristics: Towards a configuration approach. *Journal of Public Administration Research and Theory, 18*, 591–615.

Westley, F., & Antadze, N. (2009). Making a difference: Strategies for scaling social innovation for greater impact. *Innovation Journal: The Public Sector Innovation Journal, 15*(2), article 2. Retrieved from http://www.innovation.cc/scholarly-style/westley2antadze2make_difference_final.pdf

CHAPTER 2

Social Entrepreneurship, Social Innovation, and Social Mission Organizations

Toward a Conceptualization

Björn Schmitz

Philiomondo

INTRODUCTION

New buzzwords have entered the nonprofit research arena in the last two decades, including "social enterprise," "social entrepreneurship," and "social business," which represent a melding of business and altruistic behaviors (Bishop, 2006; Bornstein, 2004; Drayton, 2002, 2005; Mair & Martí, 2006; Mair, Robertson, & Hockerts, 2006; Nicholls, 2006). What started as a promising new field of research is still suffering from a relatively weak level of theorizing and empirical research. Furthermore, there is no common definition of the terms; thus, research from different scholars can hardly be compared. As a result, scientific progress is at a low level.

Within the last 5 to 10 years, the term *social innovation* also has been added to these buzzwords, and it has occupied the agendas of practitioners, policy makers, and researchers alike. But social innovation has only contributed to the messy situation because it is also a very ill-defined term. When we are dealing with this kind of terminology—and in this book these terms are highly relevant and prevalent—we need to get a better grip on what these terms mean. While the linkages between the concepts have been stressed in many ways, their relationships have hardly been made clear in an understandable and fruitful way for research.

In this chapter, this author briefly introduces these concepts and reveals the similarities and differences between them. This author also distinguish between social entrepreneurship, social enterprise, social business, and democratic enterprise as forms of social mission organizations, by analyzing these concepts with regard to three main features of the discourse: innovativeness, democratic participation, and earned-income strategies. The innovativeness part is further defined when explicating the social component of social innovation. This distinction is made by demarcating social innovation from both social change and from technical as well as economic innovation.

But social innovation also points to an understanding of an overall process including four phases: claims, invention, implementation, and diffusion. When finally linking social innovation with the above mentioned concepts of social mission organizations, four possible conceptual points of departure are presented. One very promising starting point is to couple the process of understanding social innovation with a functional role model perspective of social mission organizations. Deriving from this model it is claimed that social mission organizations are a required part of social innovations for societies.

SOCIAL ENTREPRENEURSHIP, SOCIAL ENTERPRISE, AND SOCIAL BUSINESS

Since the early 1990s, social entrepreneurship, social enterprise, and social business are concepts that have increasingly occupied the research agendas of nonprofit scholars studying business and those studying organization (Dacin, Dacin, & Tracey, 2011; Hjorth & Bjerke 2006; Short, Moss, & Lumpkin, 2009). These concepts go beyond the traditional nonprofit sector organizations because they also embrace for-profit legal forms that have a social mission. This blend of business and nonprofit features has also been discussed under the term *hybrid organizations* (Billis, 2010; Boyd, Henning, Reyna, Wang, & Welch, 2009; Brandsen, van de Donk, & Putters, 2005; Cooney, 2006; Evers, 2005; Glänzel & Schmitz, 2012; Hasenfeld & Gidron, 2005; Powell, 1987). The concept of hybrid organizations hints at the increased blurring of sector boundaries in the last two decades (Anheier & Then, 2004; Billis, 2010; Dees, 1998; Emerson, 2004; Weisbrod, 1998). In this chapter, this author therefore uses the concept of social mission organizations, which also includes nonprofits, to reflect this line of discourse. This author defines a *social mission organization* as an organization whose primary goal is a social cause (addressing a social problem or a social need) regardless of their legal form. Profit making is secondary to these organizations. What is more, potential profits will be reinvested in the social cause.

When looking at the definitions of the three concepts social entrepreneurship, social enterprise, and social business, two things become apparent. First, the concepts themselves overlap heavily, and often enough they are used synonymously. Second, there is a multitude of attributes that are associated with these concepts. They range from social and environmental responsibility, innovativeness, social change, social transformation, resource mobilization, double bottom line, entrepreneurial means, social needs orientation, social justice, making connections, empowering disadvantaged groups, helping the hardest to help, and sharing the problem and the solution, as well as diffusion and scaling (e.g., Office of the Third Sector, 2009; Schmitz & Scheuerle, 2012). Teasdale (2012) states that "it is unlikely that any single social enterprise possess all of these attributes. The positive attributes associated with each of the different organizational types would appear to have been aggregated to create a mythical beast" (p. 115).

What is more, there are differences in the understanding of the terms in different countries, especially between Europe and the United States. For example, Bacq and Janssen (2011) explained this difference by referencing Albert (1991), who emphasized the two different types of capitalism in Europe and the United States. While the American model is based on individual and financial success, media attention, and short-term financial gain, the Rhineland model puts collective success, consensus, and long-term planning in the foreground. Also, the European discussion is more focused on service providers and democratic governance, whereas the Anglo-Saxon perspective emphasizes the dividing line between charity and social entrepreneurship and embraces for-profit product providers and nonprofit earned-income strategies (e.g., Galera & Borzaga, 2009; Ridley-Duff, 2007).

Several authors have suggested the need to distinguish between different schools of thought. With these attempts the authors provide structure in the field and among the different meanings scholars and practitioners give the three concepts. Table 2.1 gives an overview of the distinguished schools of thought by six authors.

Another important distinction has been introduced by Defourny and Nyssens (2010). They distinguish between two versions of *earned-income schools*: an earlier version that focused on commercial activities of nonprofit organizations and a later version called the *mission-driven business approach*, which is broader and also includes for-profit businesses that trade for social purposes. The distinction here is that the former is an additional

TABLE 2.1 Differentiating Schools of Thought in Social Entrepreneurship Research

		Authors With a Schools-of-Thought Classification					
		Alvord, Brown, & Letts (2004)	Mair & Martí (2006)	Dees & Anderson (2006)	Hill, Kothari, & Shea (2010)	Defourny & Nyssens (2010)	Bacq & Janssen (2011)
Schools of Thought	Earned Income	x	x	x	x	x	x
	Social Innovation	x		x	x	x	x
	Catalyzing Social Transformation	x	x				
	Social Responsibility Activities (cross-sector partnerships)		x				
	Broader Stakeholder Inclusion				x	x	x
	Multiple Bottom Lines				x		

TABLE 2.2 Different Schools of Thought, Their Key Features, and Organizational Forms

School of Thought	Key Feature	Organizational Form
Earned Income I	Commercialization of nonprofits	Social Enterprise
Earned Income II	Trade for social purposes	Social Business
Innovation	Innovation	Social Entrepreneurship
EMES	Democratic governance and stakeholder participation	Democratic Enterprise

source of income for the organizations, whereas the latter also embraces social mission organizations that cover all their activities by earned income (social business) (Yunus, 2006). The second school is the *innovation school*. Here the innovation activities and the social entrepreneur being the change maker are the essential ingredients of discourse (Dees, 2001; Young, 1986). And third, there is a school of thought proposed by the EMES network that stresses the importance of democratic and participatory governance models within the social enterprise discourse. For this school of thought this author would like to introduce the term "democratic enterprise." This differentiation is summarized in Table 2.2 and is the basis for the subsequent discussion.

Instead of focusing on the importance and soundness of different schools of thought or definition criteria, it seems more fruitful to accept the various forms of social mission organizations and discuss the landscape of the various organizational forms and the functional importance of all forms (e.g., Neck, Brush, & Allen, 2009).

Social Entrepreneurship

Social entrepreneurship is commonly linked to innovation emphasizing the centrality of innovation for the concept of entrepreneurship. Peter Drucker (2007) stated, "Innovation is the specific tool of entrepreneurs, the means by which they exploit change as an opportunity for a different business or a different service" (p. 17). The identification of business opportunities and their exploitation is commonly understood as commercial entrepreneurship (Shane & Venkataraman, 2000).

Obviously this emphasis is linked to Schumpeter's ideas of innovation and economic transformation, as well as the notion of creative destruction (Schumpeter, 1912). Innovation and transformation are blended in his approach, setting high criteria for what an innovation exactly is about. Schumpeter (1912) distinguishes five different kinds of innovations: (1) introduction of a new good or a new quality of a good, (2) implementation of a new production method, (3) accessing of a new sales market, (4) accessing of a new source of supply of raw materials or intermediate goods, and (5) rearranging of the market position (e.g., burst of an existing monopoly or market order).[1]

[1] Today, Schumpeter's distinctions are still valid. Take for example OECD's definition (2005), "An innovation is the implementation of a new or significantly improved product (good or service), or progress, a new marketing method, or a new organisational method in business practices, workplace organisation or external relations" (p. 46).

Spear (2006) criticizes that Schumpeter's approach "excludes a large amount of entrepreneurial activity which involves the creation of new organizations but which may not be significantly innovative" (p. 404). However, it remains a question whether the ideas of Schumpeter can be easily transferred to the concept of social entrepreneurship. Schumpeter's (1950) theory is about competitiveness and rivalry between businesspeople. Businesspeople consider innovations important because they expect a high potential to generate higher margins and profits by them. It remains a question whether it is possible to transfer this motivation to the context of social needs or problems that seek solutions.

Commercial entrepreneurship is different from social entrepreneurship in two ways. First, social entrepreneurs pursue a social mission, whereas commercial entrepreneurs are seeking financial profit. Second, possible financial gains of a social entrepreneurship venture will be reinvested for the social mission, while the commercial entrepreneur distributes the profits to the shareholders or reinvests them for the commercial activities (Bacq & Janssen, 2011). Neck et al. (2009) point out that the main difference is not about social outcomes because otherwise every organization could be considered social, at least in the sense that it generates jobs, which leads to economic growth and finally to wealth for society. Thus, the difference between commercial and social entrepreneurship is about the input, be it either the sources of opportunity or the organization's founding mission as starting points.

Thus, social entrepreneurship is not only about innovation, but it is also about *social* innovation, and several authors have directly linked these concepts with each other (e.g., Leadbeater, 2007; Schmitz & Scheuerle, 2012; Westall, 2007). Zahra, Gedajlovic, Neubaum, and Shulman (2009, p. 519) have emphasized that social innovation is the core of social entrepreneurship.[2] From a slightly broader perspective, the main characteristics of social entrepreneurship are innovation, proactiveness, and risk taking for a social cause (Helm & Andersson, 2010).[3] Thus, the main link between social mission organizations and social innovation can be detected in the concept of social entrepreneurship.

Social entrepreneurship definitions are most often not limited to the founding of start-up organizations but also mention innovations in mature nonprofits. However, empirical research has concentrated on social entrepreneurs who have started new ventures and have been subsequently selected and awarded as social entrepreneurs by practitioner groups or fellowship organizations (e.g., Nicholls, 2010). The general assumption is that mature nonprofits are unresponsive and inflexible to changing environments and demands (Dees, 2001). The result of this bias is a lack of research about social entrepreneurs within

---

[2] Obviously social change related to detected unsolved social problems is often the main characteristic that describes the emergence and goal of social entrepreneurs. Regarding social change or—expressed more stronger—social transformation, two main questions arise, because social change is not an aim in itself. First, why do we need social change or social transformation? And second, what is the direction of social change and who determines and defines this direction? As the first question remains to be at minimum partially answered by the drivers mentioned above, the second question is predominantly left aside in the social entrepreneurship discourse. One reason for this might be the assumption that social transformation and social innovation are positive things in themselves because everything else beside the current state is an improvement.

[3] Still, there is the perception that charity and social entrepreneurship are totally different concepts, and social entrepreneurship has been portrayed as extremely positive to play off the advantages of the concept against charity (e.g., Dees, 2012; Trexler, 2008). Until today, social entrepreneurship lacks the proof of its power. There are very few studies qualitatively and especially quantitatively that have shown the full range of impact that social entrepreneurship promises. Andersson (2012) states that the term *social entrepreneurship* serves as a dream catcher.

mature organizations, a phenomenon usually referred to as *social intrapreneurship*. As Seelos and Mair (2012) state, ". . . much social innovation research has explored the entrepreneurial establishment of new social organizations, much less is known about the ability of already established organizations to innovate continuously" (p. 45).

Social Enterprise

Instead, mature nonprofits have been investigated regarding economization processes, commercialization, and the increase of earned-income strategies (e.g., Dees, 1998; Emerson & Twersky, 1996; Weisbrod, 1998). Revenue generation has become a major topic, and studies have shown that an increasing proportion of nonprofits are proactively searching for new potential revenue streams (e.g., Massarsky & Beinhacker, 2002). There are different reasons for this trend such as a probusiness zeitgeist, strive for financial sustainability, favor of commercial approaches, and competition (Dees, 1998). In this area of increased challenges and tensions, nonprofits are searching for new models of financing or the implementation of new solutions. To highlight a few changes among others, marketization can cause a mission-drift, and a shift from serving the poor to serving those who can pay and weeding out difficult customers. It can also result in a higher independence from traditional stakeholders and networks, an increase in short-term thinking and decision making, a decrease in advocacy activities, an overlooking of supporting change in the status quo, discouragement of civic participation, devaluing the work of volunteers, and concentration of power with larger service providers (Eikenberry & Kluver, 2004, p. 135).

"Social enterprises deliberately adopt an uncomfortable position: They are in the market and yet against it at the same time" (Leadbeater, 2007, p. 2). As a result, this leads to rethinking old ways of producing services and goods and forces nonprofits to innovate. As a result, transformations toward being more business-like (Dart, 2004) and the search for earned-income often cannot take place without innovations. Thus, both concepts—social enterprise and social entrepreneurship—have their legitimate overlapping.

Social Business

Revenue generation is the striking feature of social businesses. These organizations recover the full costs they expend by their own generated market or earned income (Huybrechts & Nicholls, 2012). However, the term is academically underdeveloped. The subject being almost totally driven by the discourse around Muhammad Yunus, there are only a few scholars investigating social businesses. Jäger (2010) is an exception, but he does not clearly focus on the core concept of social business. Instead there is an overlapping with the other concepts presented above. In Yunus's 2006 definition, the purpose of social businesses is to change the world, and the negative perception regarding charities is heavily presented in his writings. A social business reinvests its profits for the social cause and does not distribute them to investors or shareholders. With this being said, social businesses can be seen as part of the nonprofit sector because of such a nonlegally defined nondistribution constraint. Thus, social business as a concept is mainly responsible for using the term *social mission organizations* instead of nonprofits because social businesses usually do not have a nonprofit legal form.

Yunus (2010) defined *social businesses* by the following principles: (1) having a social mission that supersedes profit maximization, (2) being financially and economically sustainable, (3) paying back investments of investors without paying dividends, (4) using profits for expansion and improvement according to the social mission, (5) being environmentally conscious, (6) paying its workforce according to market wages but with better working conditions, and (7) doing it with joy (p. 3). What is not listed here is the participatory nature that is also central to Yunus's conception of social business. Taking Grameen Bank as an example, the borrowers of microcredits become owners of the social business and thus have a say.

Democratic Enterprise

One more topic must be added to the three social mission organizations already discussed. Defourny and Nyssens (2012) from the EMES network[4] constructed an ideal type of social enterprise covering nine indicators structured under three subsets, namely economic, social, and participatory governance. The economic subset consists of the indicators (1) continuous production, (2) some paid work, and (3) an economic risk. The social subset includes (4) an explicit social aim; (5) limited profit distribution, reflecting the primacy of social aim; and (6) an initiative launched by a group of citizens or a third sector organization(s). Finally, the participatory governance subset is covered by (7) a high degree of autonomy; (8) a participatory nature, which involves various parties affected by the activity; and (9) a decision-making power not based on capital ownership.

While some authors are critical of a blend of market forces and democratic participation (e.g., Edwards, 2008; Eikenberry, 2009), Defourny and Nyssens particularly recommend this blend. Empirically, a boom of organizations showing these features has been found at least in Europe (Borzaga & Defourny, 2004). The stakeholder inclusion can also be understood as a way to protect the social mission of an organization despite it being prone to market forces. Indeed, "[t]he degree to which a venture prioritizes the needs of stakeholders, the involvement and engagement of stakeholders in a venture, and the proactiveness with which it emphasizes value creation to stakeholders will move the venture toward a greater social mission" (Neck et al., 2009, p. 17). This democratic governance perspective therefore is a branch of its own and deserves specific attention in the context of social mission organizations. For this research perspective, this author suggests the term *democratic enterprise* to distinguish this form in the context of social enterprise research and to stress the main feature this body of research focuses on.

An Integrative Perspective on Social Mission Organizations

The four different concepts presented—social entrepreneurship, social enterprise, social business, and democratic enterprise—cover the range of organizations that can be labeled social mission organizations. Central to all these concepts is the creation of social value

[4] "EMES is a research network of established university research centres and individual researchers whose goal has been so far to gradually build up a European corpus of theoretical and empirical knowledge, pluralistic in disciplines and methodologies, around our 'SE' concepts: social enterprise, social entrepreneurship, social economy and solidarity economy" (http://www.emes.net).

FIGURE 2.1 Types of Social Mission Organizations and Their Overlapping Zones

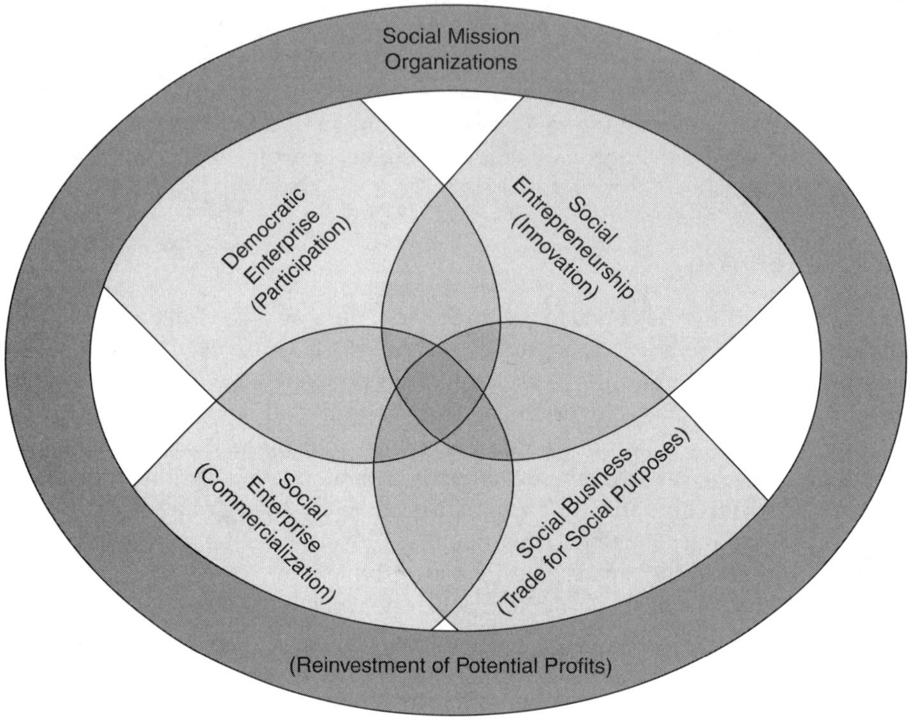

(e.g., Bacq & Janssen, 2011; Mair & Martí, 2006) or the addressing of a social need or problem (e.g., Dacin et al., 2011; Mort, Weerawardena, & Carnegie, 2003). This implies that the profit motive is secondary to the social mission and that potential profits are to be reinvested in the social cause the organization is addressing. When discussing the different concepts, it became apparent that the demarcation lines between them are—conceptually and empirically—all but clear (Chell, Nicolopoulou, & Karatas-Özkan, 2010; also Defourny & Nyssens, 2010). For instance, often enough organizations show an increase in revenue generation on the one hand and are innovative on the other hand at the same time. Is such an organization social enterprise or social entrepreneurial? This author suggests that these questions do not really help from a research perspective and add to the conceptual confusion. Instead it would be more fruitful to use the key feature of the concepts—participation, commercialization, trade for social purposes, and innovation—as different research perspectives and assume that these overlap heavily on an empirical level. Figure 2.1 shows the overlapping zones between the concepts introduced above. These overlapping zones indicate empirical cases with a mixture of the key features mapped to the concepts.

From an empirical perspective there are 13 possible cases, which are explicated in Table 2.3. The overlapping zones in Figure 2.1 are different in their size, but that does not

TABLE 2.3 Possible Empirical Cases of Social Mission Organizations

	Democratic Participation	Innovation	Commercialization	Trade for Social Purposes
Organization 1	YES	-	-	-
Organization 2	YES	YES	-	-
Organization 3	YES	YES	YES	-
Organization 4	YES	YES	-	YES
Organization 5	YES	-	YES	YES
Organization 6	YES	-	-	YES
Organization 7	-	YES	-	-
Organization 8	-	YES	YES	-
Organization 9	-	YES	YES	YES
Organization 10	-	-	YES	-
Organization 11	-	-	YES	YES
Organization 12	-	-	-	YES
Organization 13	YES	YES	YES	YES

indicate that empirically these cases occur in such proportions. It remains a question for future research which combinations of key features can be detected most often and to reveal possible reasons for these combinations.

Although the term social mission is primary for all social mission organizations, there is no systematic debate about how to distinguish social causes from nonsocial causes in relation to social mission organizations, or more precisely, social problems from nonsocial problems. This question is important because it is the ultimate distinction between social mission organizations and commercial organizations. Some scholars state that the social problems are often complex or wicked problems (e.g., Bornstein, 2004; Waddock & Post, 1991), which makes it necessary to take a long-term perspective, form networks, and include multiple stakeholders. Social innovations—the concept introduced next—address social problems and thus need to consider their complex circumstances. Maybe we can get a better understanding of what social problems are by analyzing the discourse on social innovation.

WHAT IS SOCIAL ABOUT SOCIAL INNOVATION?

German sociologist Wolfgang Zapf (1989) was one of the first to come up with a conception and typology of *social* innovations. Zapf characterized *social innovations* as "new ways to achieve goals, especially new organizational forms, new regulations, and new lifestyles, which trigger the direction of social change and solve problems better than former practices; therefore these practices are worthy to be imitated and institutionalized" (p. 177, own translation).

To define social innovation as a distinct field of practice and research, the addition of "social" needs to be qualified. A well-known, recent definition by BEPA (2011) stresses that social innovations are social both in their means and their ends. This point of departure corresponds to the distinction made by Nicholls and Murdoch (2012) that social innovation can be perceived separately as a social process or social outcome. But some other definitions define the social part of social innovation only by inputs (Mulgan, 2006; Mulgan, Tucker, Ali, & Sanders, 2007). Thus, this author arranges the discussion of social innovation according to input, means or process, output, and outcome-driven definitions. What is more, this author contends that a strong social innovation needs to be social in all these respects. This discussion then is followed by a clarification of different understandings of the social innovation process, which is related to the input, means, and output understanding and an important step toward linking social innovation discourse with social mission organizations.

Inputs of Social Innovation

Only a few definitions of social innovation focus solely on inputs such as motivations or desires. For these authors, social innovations are "innovative activities and services that are motivated by the goal of meeting a social need and that are predominantly developed and diffused through organizations whose primary purposes are social" (Mulgan, 2006, p. 46; Mulgan et al., 2007, p. 8). This motivation arises due to being confronted with groups of people who are excluded from the market system. These situations evoke the "desire to meet social needs which can be neglected by traditional forms of private market provision and which have often been poorly served or unresolved by services organized by the state" (Harris & Albury, 2009, p. 16).

The input definitions provoke two responses. First, they often link to organizations or activities of the nonprofit sector because a motivation or desire to resolve a social issue reflects a social mission, which is the core of nonprofit organizations as well as social mission organizations. Second, these definitions hint at the main difference between social innovation and social change, which is intentionality (Kesselring & Leitner, 2008). Implementing social innovation consists of "planned and coordinated actions" (Greenhalgh, Glen, Macfarlane, Bate, & Kyriakidou, 2004, p. 582) toward societal problems. In contrast, *social change* is defined as a more unplanned and uncoordinated process that might occur as a reaction to social innovations. More interesting, social change can also be a trigger for further social innovation. This might also be due to two reasons. First, social innovations are often investigated on a micro or individual level of analysis (i.e., analyzing the implementation of a specific innovation and its further diffusion), whereas social change is investigated on a macro level of analysis (i.e., analyzing changes and trends within society). Second, social innovation from a practitioner point of view is heavily linked to new products and services (material view), whereas social change deals with changes in values, norms, and attitudes (immaterial view). This author calls into question whether the materialistic view is helpful and covers all forms of social innovations. For instance, new forms of democratic participation would not qualify as social innovations in a materialistic sense because they are neither products nor services. The process view on social innovation is intertwined with this issue.

Means and Processes of Social Innovation

In his recent book on innovation, Steven Johnson (2010) stressed the importance of knowledge exchange and networks and that good ideas most often arise from circumstances in which there are no commercial interests prior to the innovation. These notions have to be underlined in the context of social innovations. *Social processes* refer to collaboration, the application of open source methodologies, and the reciprocal use of networks. Furthermore, social processes have to do with not producing any negative externalities during the process of solving a social problem (e.g., bad working conditions for nurses in a home for the aged or pollution from new products). Mulgan (2012) stated that social innovations require various actors to work together, such as social entrepreneurs, social movements, governments, foundations, and others. These various actors support each other collaboratively in processes "of collective idea generation, selection and implementation" (Dawson & Daniel, 2010, p. 16). Thus, governance issues gain importance in this perspective on social innovation.

Outputs of Social Innovation

Some authors stress the output dimension because input definitions of social innovations often lack a convincing approach to measure motivations and desires toward social outcomes or outputs. This is interesting insofar as there is a massive body of research on motivation in psychology. However, there has been no link made between motivational research in psychology and social innovation input definitions. A very prominent definition in the field of output-focused definitions comes from Phills, Deiglmeier, and Miller (2008). For them, a social innovation is "a novel solution to a social problem that is more effective, efficient, sustainable, or just than existing solutions and for which the value created accrues primarily to society as a whole rather than private individuals. A social innovation can be a product, production process, or technology (much like innovation in general), but it can also be a principle, an idea, a piece of legislation, a social movement, an intervention, or some combination of them" (Phills et al., 2008, p. 39).

This definition obviously builds on the innovation types introduced by Schumpeter (see the paragraph on social entrepreneurship) and adds four social qualifiers (efficient, effective, sustainable, just), which can also be found in other definitions (e.g., Salamon, Geller, & Mengel, 2010). Also it differentiates between products, principles, and social movements as types of social innovations. This approach opens the field of social innovation without narrowing it down to products and services alone. But for future research it seems useful to clarify whether these different types of social innovation relate to each other in a logical or chronological way.

Outcomes or Impacts of Social Innovation

Proponents of defining social innovations by outcomes or impacts are Eduardo Pol and Simon Ville. They stated that a criterion of social innovation is its "potential to improve either the quality or the quantity of life" (Pol & Ville, 2009, p. 881). Furthermore, they distinguish between micro and macro quality of life improvements. The former are quality of life improvements regarding particular individuals determined by personal characteristics and the set of valued options, whereas the latter are characterized by valued options a group of individuals can select from such as material well-being, education, job security, political freedom, or health. With this definition we touch the territory of values.

Finally, we can conclude that none of the presented definitions comes without limitations. But these different definitions and discussions help clarify the term *social innovation*. This author argues that a good and strong social innovation needs to be social in all four respects: inputs, means, outputs, and outcomes. That does not mean that innovations that are just social in only one, two, or three of the features are not social innovations. Instead, these are weaker types of social innovation. To qualify inputs, means, outputs, and outcomes as *social*, a normative discourse is necessary to test and/or generate legitimacy. But this issue has rarely been touched in the recent literature.

Legitimacy and Phases of Social Innovation

Social innovation is often presented as an inevitably positive thing. This thrust has to do with the promise that goes along with the definitions: Social innovation is laden with the burden of positive change and solving social issues in a more efficient, effective, sustainable, or just way. But where there is change, there are winners and losers, and often unintended consequences occur (Gillwald, 2000). In short, social innovation calls for evaluation to determine the positive effects that it claims. One could argue that those social innovations will gain legitimacy if they match with the values of at least a group of people who are affected and benefit through their introduction. Along with this, we can assume that—from a pluralistic point of view—each innovation and social change will cause negative effects for some group of people, while others may achieve an advantage (Kesselring & Leitner, 2008; Lindhult, 2008).

Gillwald (2000) distinguished five different benefit dimensions of social innovations: economic (efficiency), social (integrative), political (capability of action), cultural (satisfaction of higher needs), or ecological (protection of environmental goods) (p. 15). But this categorization again does not leave out the dilemma of setting priorities between different dimensions. Mulgan (2012) reformulated this dilemma as a positive consequence: "[W]hat counts as good, or a socially recognized need, is constantly contested, and this very contest provides some of the dynamic energy that drives the field" (p. 36).

As mentioned above, some authors link social innovation primarily to changes in attitudes, norms, perceptions, or behaviors (e.g., Neumeier, 2012). These changes can be discussed as preconditions of social innovation implementation. However, they can also represent diffusion. They serve as a necessary condition for acceptance and legitimacy of the social innovation. But also it can be the case that the social innovation itself may change people's attitudes, norms, and behavior. In their broader approach, Nicholls and Murdoch (2012) distinguished between three levels of social innovation: incremental (products and services that address market failures), institutional (reconfiguration of existing market structures and patterns), and disruptive (change of cognitive frames via politics and/or social movements).

Also, Mulgan et al. (2007) hinted to the importance of social movements that strive for larger social change. As a result, social movements may cause innovations in organizations and/or products and services and finally change lifestyles. Then the social innovation has to be accepted and adopted by the relevant groups (Kesselring & Leitner, 2008, p.10). In other words, social innovation does not come without a change in norms, habits, and attitudes (Gillwald, 2000; Seelos & Mair, 2012). These more soft changes are social innovations in their own right. What is more, these social innovations help accelerate the development and implementation of new services and products accordingly. For instance, one good example in this context is the proliferation of fair trade.

This discussion leads to the fact that social innovation does not occur at one specific point in time. It is better understood as a process. Compared to conventional process understandings in business or technical innovation, which distinguish between invention, implementation, and diffusion (Schumpeter, 1912), it should be clear now that for social innovation one phase is prior where social problems and social needs are articulated and discussed within society to generate legitimacy. Articulating social needs and social problems (e.g., through social movements or nongovernmental organizations) is a necessary ingredient for organizations to become active regarding new products and services. Thus, this author suggests a differentiation between four phases: claims, invention, implementation, and diffusion. The invention phase covers proposals as well as the generation of prototypes and pilots. Some authors (Murray, Caulier-Grice, & Mulgan, 2010) also add systemic change as a phase, but not every social innovation leads to broad systemic changes, and thus this author suggests to remove this phase. Figure 2.2 presents different approaches to phases of innovation and social innovation in their chronological order.

FIGURE 2.2 Phase Models of Innovation and Social Innovation

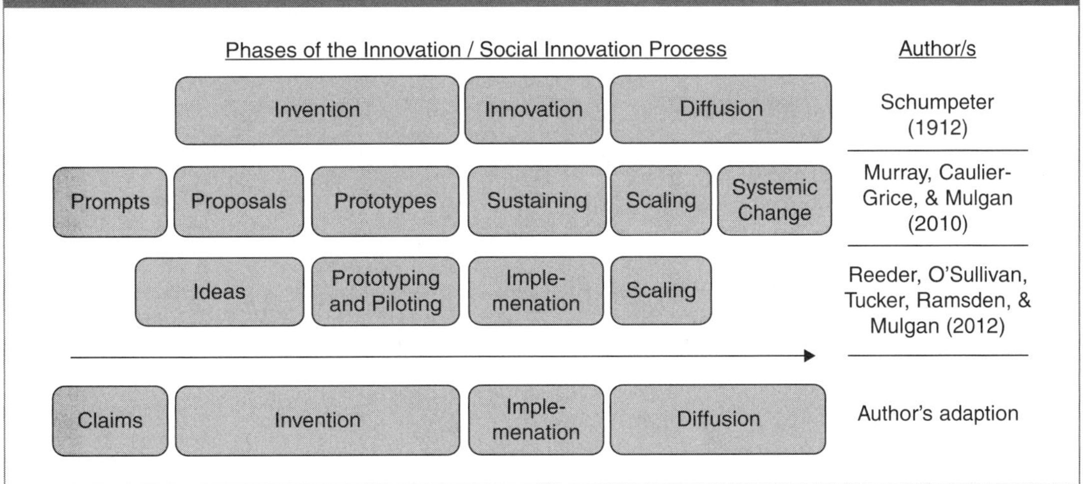

Differentiating Technical, Business, and Social Innovation

The social part of social innovation has been clarified so far. This author suggested a differentiation between four different types of definitions of social innovation according to their emphasis on inputs, means or processes, outputs, and outcomes. With this differentiation at hand, it is possible to compare social innovations empirically by their degrees of social innovativeness. Those social innovations that are social in inputs, means, outputs, and outcomes can be described as strong social innovations, whereas those social innovations that have only one, two, or three of the criteria classified as social can be perceived as weak social innovations.

Another way to describe degrees of social innovativeness lies in their comparison to technical and business innovations. "Business innovations are described as motivated by profit maximization and diffused through organizations that are primarily motivated by profit maximization" (Mulgan, 2006, p. 146). Often enough, business innovations are linked to technical innovations. "The substantive distinction between social and technical innovations can be found in their immaterial intangible structure. The innovation does not occur in the medium of technical artefact but at the level of social practice" (Howaldt & Schwarz, 2010, p. 26). Brooks (1982), for example, distinguished between pure technical innovations (e.g., new materials), sociotechnical innovations (e.g., telecommunication), and social innovations. Here again we see mixed forms of innovations, as well as pure forms.

Pol and Ville (2009) distinguished between (a) pure social innovations, which are social innovations without any business innovation blend; (b) pure business innovations; and (c) bifocal innovations, which are both business innovations and social innovations. Pure social innovations are those that are not addressed by the market because they do not have the potential to generate profits. Thus, other forms of financing need to be found. Borzaga and Bodini (2012) added a differentiation to that scheme. Pure social innovations can occur in organizations that are financially sustainable (social business) or in organizations that need to be subsidized.

FIGURE 2.3 Classes Of Innovations

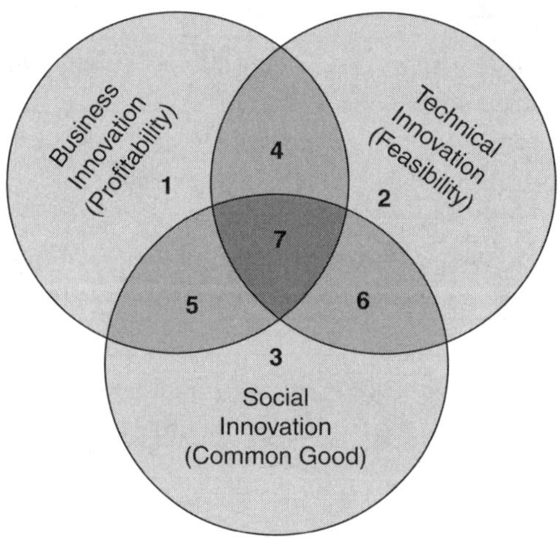

It remains a question whether the former is a bifocal social innovation or a pure type because the financially sustainable organizations are prone to market volatilities and forces.

However, this addition is important for supporters of social innovations, be they foundations, countries, or the European Union, and so on. Several authors express that social innovation and social entrepreneurship are filling the gaps generated by market failures (Goldenberg, Kamoji, Orton, & Williamson, 2009; Nicholls & Murdock, 2012; Wolk, 2007), although one could easily argue that there are organizations that create social innovations that are active in markets (e.g., Borzaga & Bodini, 2012). Phills et al. (2008), for example, addressed the question of whether social innovations are also those innovations that show both benefits for society and private, individual gains regarding profits. Without making a graduation between types of social innovations, they explicitly exclude lifesaving drugs from being a social innovation because of the private gains that go along with them (i.e., profits for pharmaceutical industries and their shareholders). Other examples are loans or investments for the poor by which some financial institutions gain tremendously (Froud, Johal, Montgomerie, & Williams, 2010).

As a result, combining technical, business, and social innovation results in a typology of seven different types of innovations. Pure technical innovations are motivated by feasibility. Pure business innovations are motivated by profit maximization. And pure social innovations are motivated by contributing to the common good (may it be happiness, quality or quantity of life, etc.). Then there are three bifocal types of innovations and finally a trifocal type of innovation blending technical, business, and social innovation. Figure 2.3 illustrates this classification and Table 2.4 explains the different types and gives examples.

TABLE 2.4 Types of Social Innovation and Their Empirical Correspondences

No.	Type	Explanation	Example
1	Economic innovation	Pure profit maximization	New advisory service, new financial instrument
2	Technical innovation	Pure feasibility	Particle accelerator
3	Social innovation	Pure common good	Social insurance
4	Economic-technical innovation	Technical innovation often appears as a means for profit maximization	Smartphone, washing machine, etc.
5	Social-economic innovation	Economic innovation appears as a means for social innovation, but this priority can change over time	Microcredit, Fair Trade
6	Social-technical innovation	Technical innovation appears as a means for social innovation	Verbavoice (verbavoiceserver.de)[5]; wheelmap (wheelmap.org)[6]
7	Social-technical-economic innovation	A blend of social, technical, and economic components	Lifesaving drugs that are sold at high prices (not everyone can buy), electric cars

[5] Verbavoice is developing software tools to enable deaf-mute people to communicate in everyday life situations, for example by connecting deaf-mute people with an interpreter via a smartphone in the post office.

[6] Wheelmap develops an online map for registering locations (cafés, restaurants, shops, etc.) and their status of accessibility for handicapped people (no access, access but no toilet, access and toilet available).

THE ROLE OF NONPROFITS IN THE SOCIAL INNOVATION PROCESS

Having said earlier that innovation is an integral part of the concept of social entrepreneurship, and also that the social enterprise and social business concepts have their traces of innovativeness, there is an ongoing discourse on which organizational types or sectors are best suited for bringing up social innovations. In 1987, Peter Drucker stated that the innovativeness of the public sector is outdated. They had their great times with, for instance, the implementation of social insurances; but today it is for business and the nonprofit (or third) sector to come up with solutions for the social problems of our times. Some others argue that the business sector is the primary source of social innovation. This perception is prevalent among some scholars in the social entrepreneurship field, but even more prominent in the concept of Creating Shared Value (CSV) (Porter & Kramer, 2011).

One might argue that the nonprofit sector is very well-suited to bring about social innovation. Arguing for this option, this author sees five promising points of departure:

1. Failure Theory: Early work in the field of nonprofits was concerned with the emergence of the sector, as the organizational discussions were focused on the dichotomy between state and market. Thus, they needed to argue that another, a third sector, is also detectable within society. Two main pillars of early argumentation can be distinguished here. First, market failure theorists argue that market asymmetries exist (i.e., when customers are unable to accurately calculate the price or are unable to pay for the product or service) (Titmus, 1973). In these kinds of situations, nonprofits have an advantage because of their trustworthiness (Hansmann, 1980, 1987). Second, government failure theorists argue that the state is unable to provide all citizens with public goods to their satisfaction. Weisbrod (1975) explained the existence of nonprofits by demand heterogeneity and the median voter. Nonprofit organizations emerge to fulfill these unmet demands. According to these failure theories, nonprofits are those types of organizations that provide people with important goods and services that neither private organizations nor the state are able to provide, such as special nursery services or community building. In many cases these goods and services address social needs in a very basic sense. Therefore, a promising link between nonprofits and social innovations lies in these early theories.

2. Social Mission: Related to failure theory, another interesting point of departure for theorizing the link between nonprofits and social innovation is the argument that because of their very social mission, nonprofits are fundamentally well-suited to bring about social innovation. It is their social motivation character and their orientation toward social outcomes that makes them address social problems and social needs in a better way than organizations of other sectors (Dees, 1998).

3. Governance Structure: When differentiating organizations matched to different sectors, it has often been pointed out that nonprofits are characterized by democratic governance structures, participation possibilities, and stakeholder governance approaches, whereas for-profits are more likely governed according to a stewardship model in a hierarchical way (e.g., Enjolras, 2009; Stone & Ostrower, 2007). In regard to bringing forth

social innovations, democratic governance structures can be an important feature; under these conditions, they seem more likely to produce solutions that address social needs more effectively due to the inclusion of the groups affected. They also reduce externalities to a maximum extent.

4. Recombination of Resources: Deriving from Schumpeter's work, social innovation is often referred to as the *recombination of resources*. More precisely, the recombination of resources from different sectors has been identified as most suited for powerful social innovations. This recombination becomes powerful in combination with the understanding of the third or nonprofit sector as an intermediate zone. For example, Adalbert Evers (2005) argued that nonprofits are acting in an intermediate zone between different sectors because they embrace resources and rationales from the three other sectors (state, economy, and community/families). Thus, organizations of this intermediate zone (nonprofits and also the hybrid types characterized above) are best suited for the recombination of different resources, which can result in social innovation (see also Goldstein, Hazy, & Silberstrang, 2010; Leadbeater, 2007).

5. Functional Roles: Another old reference point in nonprofit literature is the functional role model of voluntary organizations by Kramer (1981). He distinguished between four different roles of voluntary organizations, which are the service provider role, vanguard role, value guardian role, and advocacy role. Later, other scholars argued that these roles can also be applied to other nonprofit organizations (Anheier, 2005). Furthermore, others added roles to this initial scheme later, such as community building, expressive leadership, or social entrepreneurship (Neumayer et al., 2007; Salamon, Hems, & Chinnock, 2000). Starting from a social innovation process understanding, it might be interesting to reveal whether the functional roles that make nonprofit organizations unique are necessary for or within the social innovation process.

In the following section, this author elaborates on the fifth way to link social innovation with nonprofit organizations using the classical reference to the functional role understanding of nonprofit organizations by Kramer (1981). Primarily focusing on voluntary organizations as types of nonprofits, he distinguishes four different functional roles these organizations can incorporate. First, the *service provider role* describes organizations that deliver important collective—often specialized—goods and services for heterogeneous demands. These services are usually provided neither by business nor by government and can complement other offerings or differ in their quality. Second, nonprofits can perform a *vanguard role*, in which they develop and implement innovations, such as new approaches, processes, or programs in service delivery. Some organizations might serve as change agents within their fields of action. Their ideas and innovations might be adopted by government or by businesses if they prove successful. Third, the *value guardian role* expresses the promotion and guardianship of particularistic values of societal groups by nonprofits. This role contributes to heterogeneity in civil society, allowing the expression, maintenance, and fostering of diverse values that result in pluralism and democratization. Fourth, the *advocacy role* includes nonprofits that give minorities, particularistic interests, and underrepresented groups a voice in the political arena; furthermore, the *advocacy role* includes criticizing and watchdog functions related to government, aiming at changes or improvements in social and other policies.

Although these roles were introduced to express roles of voluntary agencies, Anheier (2005) believes that they can be applied to nonprofit organizations more generally. So do several successive authors, but they add some further roles to the model. Interesting for our context is that Salamon et al. (2000) highlighted the innovation role. The *innovation role* describes the high potential of nonprofits to bring in innovations because they are valued as more flexible and adaptable to changing needs and demands and because of their risk-taking potential. Neumayer et al. (2007) distinguished between eight different functions of nonprofits, of which the *social entrepreneurship role* is formulated as a specific, distinct function highly related to innovativeness. What is more, the authors criticize former attempts of role models because they were neither applicable to all nonprofit organizations nor did they show that empirically, organizations often perform more than one role. Further, with this expansion, we also find terminology used in the field of social mission organizations. Thus, this author suggests applying this role model understanding to these kinds of organizational types.

Linking these roles to an understanding of the social innovation process (see Figure 2.2), the roles presented can be rearranged in the way shown in Figure 2.4. Starting with bringing up claims within society, advocacy organizations and value guardians bring critiques against the status quo; they point to social problems and social needs and call for changes. When it comes to inventing, social mission organizations play a vanguard role because of their connection to marginalized and affected groups. The participative nature of social mission organizations allows them to search for the best solution to address their social hardships. Social entrepreneurs, often the same persons or organizations that have invented the solution, bring these inventions to implementation. They do not directly face the market pressure of economic usability and the pressure of profit making; this is especially important in cases where social needs are addressed that can be traced back to be market externalities and thus the capacity of the market to deal with these issues is relatively low. In the diffusion phase, service providers, especially mature organizations, are of importance. These organizations have the structures and the geographical knowledge to bring new solutions to many sides quickly. In cases where the social entrepreneur organization is growing, the organization switches its role to become a service provider without saying that the organization is losing its entrepreneurial spirit.

Finally, the dominant action modes indicate a switch in the course of the social innovation process. In the beginning, before a solution is implemented (often within markets), the discursive character is the dominant action mode, because the new solution is debated and participation for a good solution is necessary. When it comes to market implementation, the discourse is pushed to the back and the doing (i.e., the dealing with the market environment in a pragmatic way) gains the upper hand. That does not imply that feedback loops are not allowed; rather, these processes might be the start of another follow-up process. Innovations can never be understood in a smooth way; chaotic conditions of emergence and systemic influences are much more likely (Milbergs & Vonortas, 2004).

FIGURE 2.4 Model Linking the Social Innovation Process and Functional Roles

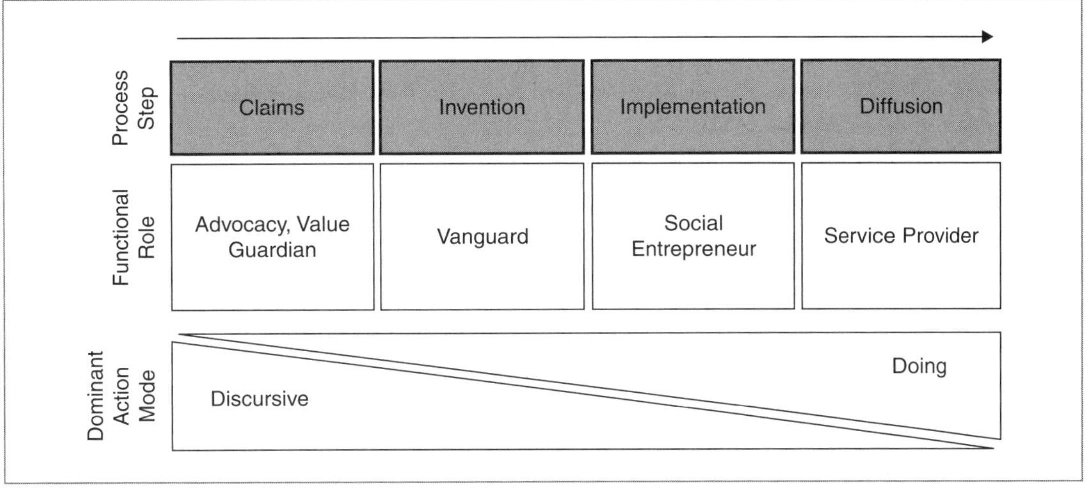

With this model at hand, this author is not arguing that there is no social innovation potential within the business or the public sectors. Rather, the purpose of this model is to understand what roles social mission organizations (covering also mature nonprofits, social entrepreneurs, social enterprises, or social businesses) can play within the social innovation process. Thus, it serves as a kind of orientation tool, so the contribution of an organization to a social innovation can be better understood with this model in mind. The model integrates the innovation types of Schumpeter, and it also stresses that awareness and normative changes within society are an important and integral part of social innovation. It seems that the diverse functional roles of nonprofit sector organizations cover the entire range of the social innovation process. However, it remains to theoretically and empirically underpin this process understanding and the underlying hypotheses. Two particular hypotheses that are explicitly included within the model are highlighted here.

1. The nonprofit sector and social mission organizations are not the exclusive originating space of social innovations. However, the functional roles that social mission organizations perform in the social innovation process cannot be replaced by organizations from other sectors. That is, business sector organizations would not develop social innovations without nonprofit organizations campaigning or putting pressure on specific social issues. When profit making is the dominant logic, social as well as environmental issues and reducing externalities will be pushed to the back unless these issues would result in a win-win situation (i.e., they would produce higher amounts of profit).

2. The discursive, participative character of social mission organizations is central in the beginning of a social innovation process for coming up with *good* and strong social

innovations, as the discursive character can best guarantee solutions that cause minimum externalities. However, claiming and the role of advocacy remain important in the course of the rest of the social innovation process.

SUMMARY AND CONCLUSIONS

In this chapter, this author tried to structure the debate around several new forms of organizations and social innovation. These concepts lack empirical grounding as well theoretical reflection. For further research progress, more theoretical underpinning is necessary, and the models and concepts developed here give a brief overview on the state of research of these topics. This author tried to give some valuable impulses for further research and theoretical development by also revealing some links between the arrays of concepts debated.

First, the landscape of social mission organizations has been differentiated into social business (financial sustainability), social entrepreneurship (innovativeness), social enterprise (earned-income strategies of nonprofits), and democratic enterprises (participatory governance structures). Instead of saying that one investigates a specific type of organizational form, like social entrepreneurship or social enterprise, this author suggested the use of key features (innovativeness, earned-income, etc.) as research topics. This differentiation might be fruitful ground to investigate social mission organizations. However, often enough we find blends of the different features in the same social mission organization. In such a case, a researcher might find it hard to clarify what concept he or she is investigating. Thus, the differentiation between different key features offers at least four different research perspectives that would help link research findings from different authors much more easily. However, this is just a starting point for further necessary operationalization and theorization.

Second, the concept of social innovation also lacks definitional clarity. It has been suggested to map the different concepts of social innovation according to whether their social aspect emphasizes inputs, means/processes, outputs, or outcomes. For qualifying as a strong social innovation, this author suggests that an innovation needs to be social in all four respects. And this question can only be answered satisfactorily by explicitly using a normative discourse among people affected. As a complement to this point of departure, to qualify social innovation, a differentiation between pure, bifocal, and trifocal forms of social, technical, and business innovation has been presented. Taken together, these approaches help structure the huge field of social innovation and hopefully contribute to more refined research within the field.

The drive for conceptual clarity regarding these concepts is fruitful from an analytical and research point of view. But these concepts also include a more political dimension from a practitioner and policy maker point of view. This is why recently both the concepts of social entrepreneurship and social innovation have gained increased attractiveness in the context of two major societal challenges in the global north. First, shrinking governmental funds make it harder for governments to care for the citizens' social needs. Thus, a remedy for meeting the social needs of society is to proliferate social entrepreneurship and social innovation to pass on the responsibility for solutions to others. Second, and this is a major issue, is the current economic crisis. The effect of this challenge is at least twofold in the context of social entrepreneurship and social innovation. On the one hand, the economic crisis causes the worsening of long-known social problems like youth unemployment and poverty; on the other hand, there is also a legitimacy crisis of capitalism going on, reflected in the calls for transformations in current business attitudes. The latter effect leads to the occupation of the positively laden concept of social entrepreneurship by the business world.

Social entrepreneurship here is used to show that the market approach can help in overcoming societies' worst problems, and thus it helps regain legitimacy for the capitalistic system. But this author would like to leave this claim open as a question about whether this is a convincing argument, because it seems dubious that the same logic (which is the business logic) that has caused most of the social problems we face today is also able to eliminate them.

This is why this author has put forth five possible theoretical starting points for arguing that social mission organizations play an integral part in the generation of social innovations. Here the functional roles have been taken as a point of departure for arguing that along the social innovation process there is no possible substitute for social mission organizations concerning the generation of strong social innovations. However, it needs to be clarified what conditions are relevant regarding the transition from one phase to another within the model. This is also an open question for future research.

From a pragmatic point of view, for this kind of battle among different logics and sectors to be the guiding force in generating social innovations is worthless because the ultimate test whether a social innovation is a good and strong one is about its potential to reduce social problems and pressing social needs to a maximum extent without causing externalities or other social problems somewhere else. Thus, collaboration between organizations from different sectors remains the major issue. This is why translation processes and a self-awareness of the various roles these different actors play within the process of social innovation are important factors in creating fruitful, solution-oriented collaboration. The models and classifications presented here are intended to serve as points of departure for research and practice in that direction.

REFERENCES

Albert, M. (1991). *Capitalisme contre capitalisme*. Paris, France: Edition du Seuil.

Alvord, S. H., Brown, L. D., & Letts, C. (2004). Social entrepreneurship and social transformation: An exploratory study. *Journal of Applied Behavioral Science, 40*(3), 260–282.

Andersson, F. O. (2012). *Social entrepreneurship as a fetish*. Retrieved from http://nonprofitquarterly.org/management/20140-social-entrepreneurship-as-fetish.html

Anheier, H. K. (2005). *Nonprofit organizations: Theory, management, policy*. London, United Kingdom: Routledge.

Anheier, H. K., & Then, V. (2004). *Zwischen Eigennutz und Gemeinwohl: Neue Formen und Wege der Gemeinnützigkeit*. Gütersloh, Germany: Verlag Bertelsmann Stiftung.

Bacq, C., & Janssen, F. (2011). The multiple faces of social entrepreneurship: A review of definitional issues based on geographical and thematic criteria. *Entrepreneurship & Regional Development, 23*(5), 373–403.

BEPA—Bureau of European Advisers. (2011). *Empowering people, driving change: Social innovation in the European Union*. Luxembourg: European Communities.

Billis, D. (2010). *Hybrid organizations and the third sector: Challenges for practice, theory and policy*. New York, NY: Palgrave Macmillan.

Bishop, M. (2006). The rise of the social entrepreneur: Whatever he may be [Special edition]. *Economist, 378*(8466), 11–13.

Bornstein, D. (2004). *How to change the world: Social entrepreneurs and the power of new ideas*. New York, NY: Oxford University Press.

Borzaga, C., & Bodini, R. (2012). *What to make of social innovation? Towards a framework for policy development*. Euricse Working Paper, N.036 | 12. Retrieved from http://euricse.eu/sites/euricse.eu/files/db_uploads/documents/1338304696_n2082.pdf

Borzaga, C., & Defourny, J. (2004). *The emergence of social enterprise*. London, United Kingdom: Routledge.

Boyd, B., Henning, N., Reyna, E., Wang, D. E., & Welch, M. D. (2009). *Hybrid organizations: New business models for environmental leadership*. Sheffield, United Kingdom: Greenleaf.

Brandsen, T., van de Donk, W., & Putters, K. (2005). Griffins or chameleons? Hybridity as a permanent and inevitable characteristic of the third sector. *International Journal of Public Administration, 28*(9/10), 749–65.

Brooks, H. (1982). Social and technological innovation. In S. B. Lundstet & E. W. Colglazier, Jr. (Eds.), *Managing innovation* (pp. 1–30). New York, NY: Pergamon Press.

Chell, E., Nicolopoulou, K., & Karatas-Özkan, M. (2010). Social entrepreneurship and enterprise: International and innovation perspectives. *Entrepreneurship & Regional Development, 22*(6), 485–493.

Cooney, K. (2006). The institutional and technical structuring of nonprofit ventures: Case study of a U.S. hybrid organization caught between two fields. *Voluntas: International Journal of Voluntary & Nonprofit Organizations, 17*(2), 137–161.

Dacin, T. M., Dacin, P. A., & Tracey, P. (2011). Social entrepreneurship: A critique and future directions. *Organization Science, 22*(5), 1203–1213.

Dart, R. (2004). Being "business-like" in a nonprofit organization: A grounded and inductive typology. *Nonprofit and Voluntary Sector Quarterly, 33*(2), 290–310.

Dawson, P., & Daniel, L. (2010). Understanding social innovation: A provisional framework. *International Journal of Technology Management, 51*(1), 9–21.

Dees, G. J. (1998). Enterprising nonprofits. *Harvard Business Review, 76*(1), 54–67.

Dees, G. J. (2001). The meaning of "social entrepreneurship." Retrieved from http://www.fuqua.duke.edu/centers/case/documents/dees_sedef.pdf

Dees, G. J. (2012). A tale of two cultures: Charity, problem solving, and the future of social entrepreneurship. *Journal of Business Ethics, 111*(3), 321–334.

Dees, G. J., & Anderson, B. B. (2006). Framing a theory of social entrepreneurship: Building on two schools of practice and thought. In R. Mosher-Williams (Ed.), *Research on social entrepreneurship: Understanding and contributing to an emerging field. ARNOVA Occasional Paper Series, 1*(3), 39–66.

Defourny, J., & Nyssens, M. (2010). Conceptions of social enterprise and social entrepreneurship in Europe and the United States: Convergences and divergences. *Journal of Social Entrepreneurship, 1*(1), 32–53.

Drayton, B. (2002). The citizen sector: Becoming as entrepreneurial and competitive as business. *California Management Review, 44*(3), 120–132.

Drayton, B. (2005). *Social entrepreneurs: Creating a competitive and entrepreneurial citizen sector*. Retrieved from http://www.changemakers.net/library/readings/drayton.cfm

Drucker, P. F. (1987). Social innovation: Management's new dimension. *Long Range Planning, 20*(6), 29–34.

Drucker, P. F. (2007). *Innovation and entrepreneurship: Practice and principles*. Amsterdam, The Netherlands: Elsevier.

Edwards, M. (2008). *Just another emperor? The myth and realities of philanthrocapitalism*. Retrieved from http://www.futurepositive.org/edwards_WEB.pdf

Eikenberry, A. M. (2009). Refusing the market: A democratic discourse for voluntary and nonprofit organizations. *Nonprofit and Voluntary Sector Quarterly, 38*(4), 582–596.

Eikenberry, A. M., & Kluver, J. D. (2004). The marketization of the nonprofit sector: Civil society at risk? *Public Administration Review, 64*(2), 132–140.

Emerson, J. (2004). *The blended value map: Tracking the intersects and opportunities of economic, social and environmental value creation*. Retrieved from http://www.blendedvalue.org/media/pdf-bv-map.pdf

Emerson, J., & Twersky, F. (Eds.). (1996). *New social entrepreneurs: The success, challenge and lessons of non-profit enterprise creation*. San Francisco, CA: The Roberts Foundation.

Enjolras, B. (2009). *A governance structure approach to voluntary organizations*. EMES Working Paper 09/01. Retrieved from http://www.emes.net/fileadmin/emes/PDF_files/Working_Papers/WP_09-01_Enjolras_WEB.pdf

Evers, A. (2005). Mixed welfare systems and hybrid organizations: Changes in the governance and provision of social services. *International Journal of Public Administration, 28*(9/10), 736–748.

Froud, J., Johal, S., Montgomerie, J., & Williams, K. (2010). Escaping the tyranny of earned income? Failure of finance as social innovation, *New Political Economy, 15*(1), 147–164.

Galera G., & Borzaga, C. (2009). Social enterprise: An international overview of its conceptual evolution and legal implementation. *Social Enterprise Journal, 5*(3), 210–228.

Gillwald, K. (2000). *Konzepte sozialer Innovation*. WZB paper: Querschnittsgruppe Arbeit und Ökologie. Retrieved from http://bibliothek.wzb.eu/pdf/2000/p00-519.pdf

Glänzel, G., & Schmitz, B. (2012). Hybride Organisationen: Spezial- oder Regelfall? In H. K. Anheier, A. Schröer, & V. Then (Eds.), *Soziale Investitionen* (pp. 181–203). Wiesbaden, Germany: VS Verlag für Sozialwissenschaften.

Goldstein, J., Hazy, J. K., & Silberstrang, J. (2010). A complexity science model of social innovation in social enterprise. *Journal of Social Entrepreneurship, 1*(1), 101–125.

Goldenberg, M., Kamoji, W., Orton, L., & Williamson, M. (2009). *Social innovation in Canada: An update*. Slater, Ottawa, Ontario: CPRN Research Report. Retrieved from http://www.cprn.org/documents/51684_EN.pdf

Greenhalgh, T., Glen, R., Macfarlane, F., Bate, P., & Kyriakidou, O. (2004). Diffusion of innovations in service organizations: Systematic review and recommendations. *Milbank Quarterly, 82*(4), 581–629.

Hansmann, H. (1980). The role of nonprofit enterprise. *Yale Law Journal, 89*(5), 835–901.

Hansmann, H. (1987). Economic theories of nonprofit organizations. In W. W. Powell (Ed.), *The non-profit sector: A research handbook* (pp. 27–42). New Haven, CT: Yale University Press.

Hasenfeld, Y., & Gidron, B. (2005). Understanding multi-purpose hybrid voluntary organizations: The contributions of theories on civil society, social movements and non-profit organizations. *Journal of Civil Society, 1*(2), 97–112.

Harris, M., & Albury, D. (2009). *The innovation imperative: Why radical innovation is needed to reinvent public services for the recession and beyond*. London, United Kingdom: NESTA Discussion Paper. Retrieved from http://socialwelfare.bl.uk/subject-areas/government-issues/social-policy/nesta/1516692009_innovation_imperative.pdf

Helm, S. T., & Andersson, F. O. (2010). Beyond taxonomy: An empirical validation of social entrepreneurship in the nonprofit sector. *Nonprofit Management & Leadership, 20*(3), 259–276.

Hill, T. L., Kothari, T. H., & Shea, M. (2010). Patterns of meaning in the social entrepreneurship literature: A research platform. *Journal of Social Entrepreneurship, 1*(1), 5–31.

Hjorth, D., & Bjerke, B. (2006). Public entrepreneurship: Moving from social/consumer to public/citizen. In C. Steyaert & D. Hjorth (Eds.), *Entrepreneurship as social change: A third movements in entrepreneurship book* (pp. 97–120). Cheltenham, United Kingdom: Edward Elgar.

Howaldt, J., & Schwarz, M. (2010). *Social innovation: Concepts, research fields and international trends.* Dortmund, Germany: Sozialforschungsstelle Dortmund. Retrieved from http://www.sfs-dortmund.de/odb/Repository/Publication/Doc%5C1289%5CIMO_Trendstudie_Howaldt_Schwarz_englische_Version.pdf

Huybrechts, B., & Nicholls, A. (2012). Social entrepreneurship: Definitions, drivers and challenges. In C. Volkmann, K. O. Tokarski, & K. Ernst (Eds.), *Social entrepreneurship and social business: An introduction and discussion with case studies* (pp. 31–48). Wiesbaden, Germany: Gabler.

Jäger, U. P. (2010). *Managing social businesses: Mission, governance, strategy, and accountability.* Basingstoke, United Kingdom: Palgrave Macmillan.

Johnson, S. (2010). *Where good ideas come from: The seven patterns of innovation.* London, United Kingdom: Penguin.

Kesselring, A., & Leitner, M. (2008). *Soziale innovationen in unternehmen.* Vienna, Austria: Unruhe Stiftung. Retrieved from https://www.zsi.at/attach/1Soziale_Innovation_in_Unternehmen_ENDBERICHT.pdf

Kramer, R. (1981). *Voluntary agencies in the welfare state.* Berkeley, CA University of California Press.

Leadbeater, C. (2007). *Social enterprises and social innovation: Strategies for the next ten years.* A social enterprise think piece for the Cabinet Office of the Third Sector. Retrieved from http://www.charlesleadbeater.net/cms/xstandard/social_enterprise_innovation.pdf

Lindhult, E. (2008). Are partnerships innovative? In L. Svensson & B. Nilsson (Eds.), *Partnership—As a strategy for social innovation and sustainable change.* Stockholm, Sweden: Satérnus Academic Press.

Mair, J., & Martí, I. (2006). Social entrepreneurship research: A source of explanation, prediction, and delight. *Journal of World Business, 41*(1), 36–44.

Mair, J., Robinson, J., & Hockerts, K. (Eds.). (2006). *Social entrepreneurship.* Houndmills, United Kingdom: Palgrave Macmillan.

Massarsky, C. W., & Beinhacker, S. L. (2002). *Enterprising nonprofits: Revenue generation in the nonprofit sector.* Englewood Cliffs, NJ: Yale School of Management and The Goldman Sachs Foundation Partnership on Nonprofit Ventures.

Milbergs, E., & Vonortas, N. (2004). *Innovation metrics: Measurement to insight.* National innovation initiative. 21st Century Innovation Working Group.

Murray, R., Caulier-Grice, J., & Mulgan, G. (2010). *The open book of social innovation.* Retrieved from http://ebookbrowse.com/murray-caulier-grice-mulgan-2010-the-book-of-social-innovation-pdf-d382057825

Mort, G. S., Weerawardena, J., & Carnegie, K. (2003). Social entrepreneurship: Towards conceptualization. *International Journal of Nonprofit and Voluntary Sector Marketing, 8*(1), 76–88.

Mulgan, G. (2006). The process of social innovation. *Innovations: Technology, Governance, Globalization, 1*(2), 145–162.

Mulgan, G. (2012). The theoretical foundations of social innovation. In A. Nicholls & A. Murdoch (Eds.), *Social innovation—Blurring boundaries to reconfigure markets* (pp. 33–65). New York, NY: Palgrave Macmillan.

Mulgan, G., Tucker, S., Ali, R., & Sanders, B. (2007). *Social innovation—What it is, why it matters and how it can be accelerated.* London, United Kingdom: Young Foundation.

Neck, H., Brush, C., & Allen, E. (2009). The landscape of social entrepreneurship. *Business Horizons, 52*(1), 13–19.

Neumeier, S. (2012). Why do social innovations in rural development matter and should they be considered more seriously in rural development research? Proposal for a stronger focus on social innovations in rural development research. *Sociologia Ruralis, 51*(1), 50.

Neumayer, M., Schneider, U., Meyer, M., Pospisil, M., Skarabelova, S., & Travickova, D. (2007). *Nonprofits' function in old and new democracies—An integrative framework and empirical evidence for Austria and the Czech Republic.* Working Paper 02/2007. Vienna, Austria: Institute for Social Policy.

Nicholls, A. (2006). Introduction. In A. Nicholls (Ed.), *Social entrepreneurship: New models of sustainable social change.* Oxford, United Kingdom: Oxford University Press.

Nicholls, A. (2010). The legitimacy of social entrepreneurship: Reflexive isomorphism in a pre-paradigmatic field. *Entrepreneurship Theory and Practice, 34*(4), 611–633.

Nicholls, A., & Murdoch, A. (2012). The nature of social innovation. In A. Nicholls & A. Murdoch (Eds.), *Social innovation—Blurring boundaries to reconfigure markets* (pp. 1–30). New York, NY: Palgrave Macmillan.

Office of the Third Sector. (2009). *Enterprising services.* London, United Kingdom: Cabinet of the Third Sector.

Phills, J. A., Jr., Deiglmeier, K., & Miller, D. T. (2008). Rediscovering social innovation. *Stanford Social Innovation Review, 8*(3), 34–43.

Pol, E., & Ville, S. (2009). Social innovation: Buzz word or enduring term? *Journal of Socio-Economics, 38*(6), 878–885.

Porter, M. E., & Kramer, M. R. (2011). Creating shared value. *Harvard Business Review, 89*(1), 62–77.

Powell, W. W. (1987). Hybrid organizational arrangements: New form of transitional development? *California Management Review, 30*(1), 67–87.

Reeder, N., O'Sullivan, C., Tucker, S., Ramsden, P., & Mulgan, G. (2012). *Strengthening social innovation in Europe—Journey to effective assessment and metrics.* Retrieved from ec.europa.eu/enterprise/policies/innovation/files/social-innovation/strengthening-social-innovation_en.pdf

Ridley-Duff, R. (2007). Communitarian perspectives on social enterprise. *Corporate Governance: An International Review, 15*(2), 382–392.

Salamon, L. M., Hems, L. C., & Chinnock, K. (2000). *The nonprofit sector—For what and for whom?* Working Papers of the John Hopkins Comparative Nonprofit Sector Project, No. 37. Baltimore, MD: The John Hopkins Center for Civil Society Studies.

Salamon, L. M., Geller, S. L., & Mengel, K. L. (2010). *Nonprofits, innovation, and performance measurement: Separating fact from fiction.* Communiqué No. 17. Baltimore, MD: Johns Hopkins University. Retrieved from http://ccss.jhu.edu/wp-content/uploads/downloads/2011/09/LP_Communique17_2010.pdf

Schmitz, B., & Scheuerle, T. (2012). Founding or transforming? Social intrapreneurship in three German Christian-based NPOs. *Journal of Social Entrepreneurship Perspectives, 1*(1), 13–36.

Schumpeter, J. A. (1912). *Theorie der wirtschaftlichen Entwicklung.* Berlin, Germany: Duncker und Humbolt.

Schumpeter, J. A. (1950). *Kapitalismus, sozialismus und demokratie.* Bern, Switzerland: A. Francke.

Seelos C., & Mair, J. (2012). Innovation is not the holy grail. *Stanford Social Innovation Review, 10*(4), 45–49.

Shane, S., & Venkataraman, S. (2000). The promise of entrepreneurship as a field of research. *Academy of Management Review, 25*(1), 217–226.

Short, J. C., Moss, T. W., & Lumpkin, G. T. (2009). Research in social entrepreneurship: Past contributions and future opportunities. *Strategic Entrepreneurship Journal, 3*(2), 161–194.

Spear, R. (2006). Social entrepreneurship: A different model? *International Journal of Social Economics, 33*(5/6), 399–410.

Stone, M. M., & Ostrower, F. (2007). Acting in the public interest? Another look at research on nonprofit governance. *Nonprofit and Voluntary Sector Quarterly, 36*(3), 416–438.

Teasdale, S. (2012). What's in a name? Making sense of social enterprise discourses. *Public Policy and Administration, 27*(2), 99–119.

Titmus, R. (1973). *The gift relationship: From human blood to social policy*. London, United Kingdom: Penguin.

Trexler, J. (2008). Social entrepreneurship as an algorithm: Is social enterprise sustainable? *Emergence: Complexity and Organization, 10*(3), 65–85.

Waddock, S. A., & Post, J. E. (1991). Social entrepreneurs and catalytic change. *Public Administration Review, 51*(5), 393–401.

Weisbrod, B. A. (1975). Toward a theory of the voluntary nonprofit sector in a three-sector-economy. In E. S. Phleps (Ed.), *Altruism, morality and economic theory* (pp. 171–195). New York, NY: Russell Sage Foundation.

Weisbrod, B. A. (Ed.). (1998). *To profit or not to profit: The commercial transformation of the nonprofit sector*. Cambridge, United Kingdom: Cambridge University Press.

Westall, A. (2007). *How can innovation in social enterprise be understood, encouraged and enabled?* London, United Kingdom: Office of the Third Sector think piece. Retrieved from http://webarchive.nationalarchives.gov.uk/+/http:/www.cabinetoffice.gov.uk/upload/assets/www.cabinetoffice.gov.uk/third_sector/innovation_social_enterprise.pdf

Wolk, A. M. (2007). *Social entrepreneurship & government: A new breed of entrepreneurs developing solutions to social problems*. Retrieved from http://community-wealth.org/sites/clone.community-wealth.org/files/downloads/report-wolk.pdf

Young, D. (1986). Entrepreneurship and the behaviour of non-profit organizations: Elements of a theory. In S. Rose-Ackerman (Ed.), *The economics of non-profit institutions* (pp. 161–184). New York, NY: Oxford University Press.

Yunus, M. (2006). Social business entrepreneurs are the solution. In A. Nicholls (Ed.), *Social entrepreneurship. New models of sustainable social change* (pp. 39–44). Oxford, United Kingdom: Oxford University Press.

Yunus, M. (2010). *Building social business: The new kind of capitalism that serves humanity's most pressing needs*. New York, NY: PublicAffairs.

Zahra, S. A., Gedajlovic, E., Neubaum, D., & Shulman, J. M. (2009). A typology of social entrepreneurs: Motives, search process and ethical challenges. *Journal of Business Venturing, 24*(5), 519–532.

Zapf, W. (1989). Über soziale Innovationen. *Soziale Welt, 40*(1/2), 170–183.

CHAPTER 3

Welfare Reform Liaison Project (WRLP)

From Job Training to Community Development

Robert J. Wineburg

University of North Carolina at Greensboro

Odell Cleveland

Welfare Reform Liaison Project, Greensboro, NC

INTRODUCTION

This is a case study of how a new faith-based welfare-to-work organization, the Welfare Reform Liaison Project, evolved during a dramatic change in Welfare Policy in the United States; it responded to new employment requirements that a recipient had to fulfill to receive assistance. Three innovations are noted. The first is that the nonprofit welfare-to-work program developed new partnerships with local nonprofits, churches, and occasionally the business where they obtained employment. Those partnerships provided help to assist the recipient through case management support with various services for up to a year. The students in the training program stayed for a year when the official requirement was 90 days. Ninety days was simply not enough time for people to make the transition from welfare to work and obtain transportation, child care, and afterschool care if their children were in elementary or secondary school, which finished at 3:00 PM.

The second innovation was that the CEO, the second author of this case study, developed an in-house training system that allowed students in the overall program to take what was learned in the classroom aspect and apply it on the job right under the supervision of the classroom teachers. Part of the training strategy was to tailor training for local business needs as well. So often students and teachers worked closely with businesses both in class and at the onsite training facility at the Welfare Reform Liaison Project, and as the students matured, they and teachers moved to the business site for specific training that the business needed. For example, the organization expanded into training for digital imaging. They would get basic training both in the classroom and at Welfare Reform Liaison Project and in its onsite training facility. As they matured, the students and teacher would move to a contracting business and work with business trainers to learn what documents needed scanning and the organizational protocols for systematic movement of millions of paper documents to the scanning process. That is only one of many examples of innovative collaboration that are built into the Welfare Reform Liaison Project.

The third innovation was that from the onset of the program the CEO and the first author, an academic researcher at a local university, worked together to obtain various kinds of data to inform the project's organizational development. Perhaps the two clearest examples were surveying the students to determine the major barriers they faced in obtaining work, and surveying churches to see which ones could provide service to help students overcome barriers. The organization learned that the trainees had multiple barriers like health problems, the lack of transportation, inability to read well enough to function on a job, and the need to tend to a sick parent, among others. So case management plans had to be coordinated with multiple agencies and churches. Combined, these three innovations form the story below.

WHY THE AGENCY CAME TO BE

In 1996, The United States Congress enacted the Personal Responsibility and Work Opportunity Reconciliation Act, fundamentally reshaping the welfare policy that had been in place in America since the New Deal legislation of the 1930s. Among its provisions, the new law took what had been an entitlement program with few stringent employment requirements, Aid to Families with Dependent Children, and turned it into Temporary Assistance for Needy Families, a time-limited welfare-to-work program with very real strings attached. The main constraint was if the students (participants) didn't get work in 12 weeks, they lost their assistance. For many of those on welfare at the time, the fear was that the new law would mean just one thing: find and keep a job, or else lose federal benefits. The Welfare Reform Liaison Project trained students in the program for skill development needed to evolve into careers, not just short-term jobs. So innovative and sustained case management, coupled with closely monitored onsite and collaborative business training positioned graduates of the program well for success.

The general fear among welfare recipients was palpable, and was made all the worse by genuine confusion among local service providers about how to adapt to Temporary Assistance for Needy Families, or TANF. Under the 1996 legislation, the administering of assistance programs for the needy shifted from the federal level to a block-grant system in which states followed overarching federal rules but could administer the program through self-designed guidelines. The new law devolved welfare policy to state and local administrators, based on the belief that because they presumably knew their own backyards better than Beltway bureaucrats (federal officials in Washington, DC), they could more efficiently and effectively operate the nation's social safety net.

In places like Greensboro, North Carolina, however, the policy shift led not to efficiency and efficacy, but to outright chaos. There was an incredible lack of information in the local system of services about the specific implications of Work First, as the TANF program is called in North Carolina. Confusion reached down to the most basic level of interaction between service providers and those they were trying to help. Welfare offices were being renamed "job centers," and caseworkers were now being called "job coaches"; but culturally those tasked with adapting to the new laws were still operating by the old rules and lacked the institutional memory to know how to guide welfare recipients through the policy changes. The confusion allowed an organization like Welfare Reform Liaison Project to arrive on the scene and thrive because it addressed workforce training and attending case management services in a way not imagined in the old system.

At the same time as local social service providers in Greensboro were struggling to adapt to Work First, North Carolina's economy was being transformed in ways that directly hit the state's economically vulnerable minority workforce. Low-wage, low-skilled jobs in North Carolina's manufacturing base were being shipped to China, vastly shrinking the employment opportunities for those now being forced to work or lose federal benefits.

Not knowing where else to turn, many in Greensboro began turning to the one local institution they believed they could count on when the going got really rough: Mt. Zion Baptist, the largest African American church between Washington and Atlanta. The church, which had long been active in the community, already had in place an emergency assistance program.

Bishop George W. Brooks, the leader of Mt. Zion, knew from experience that his church's emergency assistance program, already provided without government support, might very well be overwhelmed with requests for help if he and his church did not act quickly and decisively. He had seen what happened in the 1980s, when the Reagan administration devolved nearly five dozen federal programs to the states. Then, too, the guiding notion had been that locals know best, but with no implementation scheme in place, local confusion led to outright inertia in the delivery of services. Amid the confusion in the 1980s, churches had stepped in to help, and Brooks expected that Mt. Zion would again be called on for assistance.

There was, however, one significant difference between the 1980s and 1996, one buried in Section 104 of the 110,000-word Personal Responsibility and Work Opportunity Reconciliation Act: religious organizations delivering the kinds of welfare services Mt. Zion was already being asked to deliver could now receive taxpayer dollars for doing so. Known as Charitable Choice, the provision in the legislation meant that Mt. Zion could receive money directly from the federal government.

The expectation in the Greensboro system of social services was that local government agencies would get less money to run their operations, while churches would become official partners in local efforts to find solutions to social problems. Behind that expectation, however, there were no implementation systems in place to obtain Charitable Choice money or to actually deliver services.

Bishop Brooks knew that women and men in Greensboro who were being pushed off welfare rolls were not making enough money, if any, to feed themselves and their families. And he knew that in order to get the broader community to share responsibility with his church for dealing with these and other changes, he had to stimulate efforts to build a nonprofit organization that would become a central address for community support.

While Bishop Brooks was considering how to best prepare for the inevitable flood, he was approached for academic advice by a parishioner, Odell Cleveland, who was studying the Black church's response to the 1996 welfare reform legislation on the way to becoming ordained as a Baptist minister. That initial discussion led, within 5 months, to Cleveland—with the full blessing of Mt. Zion—founding an independent organization, the Welfare Reform Liaison Project, to take over and expand on the work of the church's emergency assistance program.

The Welfare Reform Liaison Project, or WRLP, began, as its name implies, as a "project" with the limited aim of helping low-income, low-skilled women and men make the transition from welfare to work through job training. Cleveland's approach to those who landed at WRLP's door seeking help—nearly all of whom lived below the poverty level, and more than a third of whom had recently been homeless—was to do more than merely prepare them for a job. He knew they needed a hand up, not just a handout, and he gave them that hand up by preparing them for careers in the business world. He succeeded in doing so in a way that the local Department of Social Services never could, even before the 1996 welfare reform slashed the funding it received from Washington, DC.

The Department of Social Services, or DSS, was staffed by well-intentioned and hard-working individuals, but it was not, and was never intended to be, a job development or job referral agency. Cleveland, on the other hand, had two decades of experience in the business world and had a deep understanding of what local businesses needed from their workforce. He paid substantial attention to those workforce needs while shaping the training program at WRLP, and it was that cooperation with the business world that transformed what could have been just another welfare-to-work program into a widely emulated career-building agency.

INNOVATION

Cleveland's innovative approach to involving the business world was what set graduates of WRLP's program apart from those who passed through the traditional job-training programs in Greensboro. Such programs usually focused on résumé development, how to dress for an interview, mock interviews, and things of a basic nature. Besides the basics, WRLP instilled and developed in the program participants a set of job skills matched to the needs of the local business community, and did this in the classroom at its onsite training facility, or sometimes at places of prospective employers. Close supervision and evaluation were ongoing. WRLP succeeded in producing graduates who not only landed jobs, but also kept them. Since its founding, more than 1,000 of Greensboro's most needy have gone through WRLP, and they have gone on to earn a total of at least $11 million in documented wages—$11 million in earnings for men and women who, before they started the program, were taking rather than adding to the community's resources.

Cleveland further set WRLP apart from other local institutions involved in job training like the Private Industry Council that brokered partnerships with for-profit job placement agencies, or the Employment Security Commission that linked prospective employees with employers by partnering with the first author, who was trained in evidence-based service development. Indeed, it was hard data culled from the first author's comprehensive examination of Mt. Zion's emergency assistance program that led to WRLP securing its all-important first grant. The field research-driven data not only gave guidance to building a welfare-to-work organization amid the institutional chaos that prevailed in the wake of the 1996 welfare reform, it also integrated data collection into all of WRLP's subsequent programmatic efforts. At the time, few local nonprofits in America, let alone in Greensboro, launched themselves into the community with strategic moves based on rigorously gathered data.

That WRLP was able to quickly achieve results was due in large part to Cleveland and the local scholar innovatively marrying academic methods and community outreach. At its founding, WRLP's main concern was potential resistance from churches in the African American community that might be considering establishing a similar welfare-to-work initiative, or that might be irritated that the Mt. Zion-affiliated WRLP was not sufficiently seeking out communal partners from other black churches who may have been considering similar efforts. The latter concern was particularly acute, given that Greensboro was a service community in which broad-based collaboration had evolved into a mainstream operational norm. Developing services in isolation is frowned upon in Greensboro's social service culture whether a program emerges from a church or a nonprofit or government agency.

The solution, designed by the first author and implemented by Cleveland, was to survey half the leaders of the 160 mainline African American churches in the area. The survey was for all intents and purposes a needs assessment, but was not described as such to those being surveyed, lest WRLP be tarred in the local African American community as little more than an academic project. The survey produced a number of invaluable results.

First, it provided field data on what competition WRLP was facing from established local institutions. Second, by conducting the survey himself, Cleveland—who had not yet been ordained as a reverend—gained an opportunity to meet face-to-face with dozens and dozens of his religious brethren. And by meeting with those leaders of the area's major African American churches, he started to establish the kind of relationships on which future partnerships were built. Four quick examples follow. First, a local neighborhood church where WRLP had a transportation ministry helped a trainee get to work. Odell's meeting the leader of the church eased the brokering of that connection. Second, literally thousands of volunteer hours have been logged at WRLP from over 40 local congregations. This happened because of the personal relationships Odell Cleveland built early in the program development, which was based on the noted research strategy. Third, such contact allowed WRLP to shape and mold its own story being told in the community rather than having its identity shaped by other players in the local service community. Fourth, besides idiosyncratic personal connections, the research provided hard data on the aggregate resources of a set of future community partners whose importance to WRLP would grow as the organization moved into subsequent phases of program and organizational development.

The survey was emblematic of WRLP's approach to its relations with other communal actors. Everything began with identifying the needs and resources of those involved with the organization, from fellow communal institutions to government agencies to the men and women who came to WRLP for help.

WRLP's provision of support services to the first enrollees in its job-training program in 1997 is illustrative of the approach that would transform the organization into a national model for workforce development. At the time, outside-the-office issues prevented many welfare-dependent women in Greensboro from holding on to jobs arranged through the DSS. Until WRLP came along, few bothered to ask why. The answer—and the solution—was surprisingly simple.

Under North Carolina law at the time, those who came to the DSS for help were required to be given up to 12 weeks of training before being placed in a job. The DSS was not a job-training center, at least initially, so it contracted with for-profit firms to handle the overwhelming demand, with the stipulation that contracts would only be paid after trainees had been employed for 90 days. The for-profit firms were well aware that two of the biggest obstacles trainees faced in holding on to jobs were getting to and from work and finding someone to watch the kids, and to ensure that their trainees stayed employed for the 90 days required under DSS contracts, the firms provided transportation vouchers and brokered childcare.

But on the 91st day of a trainee's employment, after the DSS had disbursed payment, the for-profit firms no longer had an obligation to continue providing such support services—and, not surprisingly, they did not. Without those support services, many trainees were simply unable to continue with their jobs. WRLP's solution was as simple as it was innovative: It committed to ensuring a base of support services until a student was securely employed, for as long as a full calendar year. The end result was job training built around the needs, limitations, and structural barriers of WRLP's trainees, and the results spoke for themselves.

WRLP had a similar approach in its dealings with communal partners, first identifying the needs and resources of area institutions and then structuring programs to match. It was one such partnership, with the local chapter of United Way, that led to the establishment of the program that would come to define WRLP's success—and more important, that would ensure that the fledgling organization had a steady revenue stream and would not be overly dependent on often-fickle grant money.

Through the first author, who had been advising WRLP, Cleveland met with a vice president at the local United Way, Nathan Cook. Cook was the point man in Greensboro for Gifts In Kind, a program run by Gifts In Kind International that used the national network of United Way chapters as a clearinghouse for unused corporate goods. Companies that had new goods that were unsellable for some reason had a vested financial interest in donating and offloading them, and Gifts In Kind was established to funnel those inexpensive and unwanted goods to local United Way chapters and then on to affiliated nonprofits.

As Cleveland realized during that initial meeting with Cook, United Way had neither the infrastructure nor the institutional know-how to fully take advantage of the Gifts In Kind program. Simply put, United Way was not a business, and was not run like one. As a 20-year veteran of the trucking industry who knew distribution systems inside and out, Cleveland knew he could obtain and distribute the goods in a far more efficient manner.

More important, Cleveland identified a tiny loophole in the Gifts In Kind program that would spark WRLP's meteoric growth: Excess goods obtained by a nonprofit through Gifts In Kind could not be sold outright, but could be redistributed to other nonprofits for an administration fee. Cleveland took that loophole and made it the centerpiece of WRLP's efforts, and within one year WRLP had become the nation's largest Gifts In Kind distributor. In 2001, WRLP earned a Federal Community Service Block Grant Designee status that has since supported the agency yearly at about $750,000, while the Distribution Center grew to where it yielded over $400,000 in discretionary income yearly.

In the years since, the redistribution program—with corporate partners including Wal-Mart, Men's Wearhouse, Radio Shack, and CVS—not only outgrew its original home in a two-car garage annexed to Mt. Zion, but it also outgrew a subsequent 16,000-square-foot warehouse and a 50,000-square-foot location after that, and now occupies an 80,000-square-foot industrial facility. Today those administrative and contracting fees earn WRLP nearly half a million dollars annually, accounting for more than one third of the organization's budget.

That was hardly the full extent of innovation at WRLP, however. In a stroke of entrepreneurship that would eventually earn Cleveland an invitation to the White House for a jobs summit, WRLP's job-training and redistribution efforts were pursued simultaneously in the organization's ever-expanding Job Training Distribution Center, all while helping Greensboro's neediest. The very same warehouse that housed the goods WRLP received through Gifts In Kind, and later from corporations directly, became a real-world classroom in which trainees were taught employable skills.

Trainees, all jobless and few with any sustained record of employment, became responsible for sorting and repackaging the goods, and then for stocking the shelves of the distribution center for steeply discounted sale to local poverty-stricken families. In addition to gaining experience in the kind of work needed by local businesses, trainees at the distribution center gained reinforcement of basic professional habits, such as showing up for work prepared and on time, paying attention to detail while performing tasks, and being able to work under supervision.

CONCLUSIONS

The job-training process at WRLP, one that combined onsite classroom, onsite training in the distribution center, and working with employers worked, again and again, well enough that it drew other North Carolina organizations to Greensboro to study Cleveland's brainchild. Among those studying WRLP's methods was an interfaith group of religious leaders from Durham, North Carolina, and in 2009, they established the Durham Economic Resource Center, explicitly modeling it on WRLP. The Durham Center's record since—70% of its trainees have either found a job or continued with further education—is evidence, albeit limited, that the success of WRLP's job-training programs can be replicated elsewhere.

That, on one level, is the main contribution of WRLP's rise. Cleveland may have been the innovating leader who showed the way, but the path he followed can be—and is being—followed by other organizational leaders. However, there are things that Cleveland employed even as the organization became a complex training organization that set WRLP apart. He interviewed every applicant and taught personal development courses in the classroom to every student. So his hands-on personal touch has been a key to success. Organizationally, there was an unwritten rule that anyone who calls for an appointment deserves at least one hour of time. Important partnerships emerged because Odell had time for any- and everyone. Odell saw himself as a man of the Lord and a business man and was positioned securely in both the religious world of Greensboro and its business world, giving WRLP dual legitimacy with two sets of important community institutions.

DISCUSSION QUESTIONS

1. We casually mentioned that we conducted a survey to assess whether other churches in the African American community were planning similar programs to ours. Explore why this evidence gathering is important in community-based program development.
2. Along those same lines, explore more fully, as a new CEO emanating from the church, why it was important that Odell conduct the survey instead of academic researchers. Include points about community building, controlling the narrative, and messaging.
3. What was the difference between a Department of Social Services retooling to become a workforce development agency and a new start-up like WRLP doing the same thing from scratch?
4. Explore what it meant for WRPL to have a long-term trusted academic researcher at Odell Cleveland's side.
5. What does a major policy shift like welfare reform do to the actors in human service at the point of implementation? Can you name major policy changes that have affected the design and delivery of services?
6. Are nonprofits more innovative than government programs?

ADDITIONAL RESOURCES

Cleveland, O., & Wineburg, R. (2010). *Pracademics and community change: A true story of nonprofit development and social entrepreneurship during Welfare Reform.* Chicago, IL: Lyceum Books.

CHAPTER 4

HelpHOPELive

Meeting Financial Needs in Medical Crises

Ram A. Cnaan
University of Pennsylvania and Kyung Hee University

Lynne Coughlin Samson
HelpHOPELive

THE PROBLEM AND THE RATIONALE FOR SOLVING IT

We all know it. . . . that unbelievably powerful feeling of helplessness when we find out someone we love has just received a heartbreaking diagnosis with lifelong implications. . . .What can we do to help?" Some pray, some call, many organize themselves to make a casserole. . . . a phenomenon HelpHOPELive calls *community empathy*. HelpHOPELive has spent 30 years mobilizing and organizing community empathy (turning casseroles into cash) to raise funds for transplant and catastrophic injury expenses not paid by insurance.

A lot has changed in 30 years regarding what expenses medical insurance will cover. For instance, at the time the organization was founded, the lifesaving power of heart transplantation was an experimental procedure that insurance would not cover. Today, seemingly daily, the lifesaving power of stem cell transplants is being harnessed to treat more and more terminal diagnoses. HelpHOPElive's sustainable model continues to assist families, friends, and neighbors to raise funds both for experimental treatments not paid for by insurance as well as the lifelong uninsured expenses associated with transplant and catastrophic injury. With its grassroots fundraising, HelpHOPELive sustains families during their worst health nightmares.

Other changes involve the way we help communities raise funds. Think of the 1980s firsts: the first PC, Cabbage Patch Kids, CDs from 8 track, and first Apple MAC, cell phones, Prozac, and Doppler radar. Stamps were $.25 and gas $1.07 per gallon. Leggings and leg warmers were in. People usually communicated with those far away through letters or by telephone. Most people owned a telephone but wrote letters. Most people had televisions with two to five channels. Very few people had computers, and virtually no one had a mobile phone. Now we have e-mail, Facebook, Skype, the latest "smart" phone—the list goes on and on.

Though the "context"—the cultural landscape—has changed dramatically, as well as the methods we use to help our families, two critical things have not: medical expenses not covered by insurance or families, and friends and neighbors wanting to help.

HelpHOPELive intends to continue to innovate with the times. Health care in America is expensive and not universally accessible. The cost of health care in the United States is rising yearly, consuming a larger and larger percentage of household budgets (Polsky & Grande, 2009). Many Americans (about 20%) have no health insurance, and many more have insurance that pays for only limited health-related problems (Kaiser Commission on Medicaid and the Uninsured, 2010). Many families, assuming that they have full coverage, find that they reach the limit with actual costs exceeding coverage.

We are a society geared toward cure, fixing our bodies, extending our lives and, most important, by providing a better quality of life for those with life-compromising chronic diseases or disabilities. This is especially the case when a family member faces the need for organ transplant or after a catastrophic injury. In such cases, most American families face major financial burdens and barriers, often having to make painful decisions related to enormous and unrelenting lifelong out-of-pocket costs.

It is not surprising that Himmelstein, Thorne, Warren, and Woolhandler (2009) found that "62.1% of all bankruptcies in 2007 were medically related; 92% of these medical debtors had debts over $5000, or 10% of pretax family income" (p. 741). Even more alarming is these authors' finding that medical debtors were well educated, owned homes, and had middle-class occupations. Three quarters had health insurance.

Sadly, many Americans cannot afford the health care they need or that will give them the best opportunity to live a productive life. This was true in 1983 when Jack Kolff, MD, and Patricia Kolff, BSN, founded the National Heart and Transplant Assistance Fund (NHATF), and it is still true today.

Dr. Kolff, a cardiothoracic surgeon at Temple University Hospital, sought to perform the first lifesaving heart transplant in the Philadelphia area. He was told that because the procedure was experimental insurance would not pay for the operation. Dr. Kolff knew heart transplant procedures could provide a healthy life for individuals otherwise limited to the slow but steady decline ensured by reliance on a ventricular assist device, a temporary "fix" for those with heart disease. Dr. Kolff and his wife felt strongly that "*no American should be denied health care due to lack of financial resources*."

To address the gap in funding for heart transplantation, the Kolffs established the National Heart Assist and Transplant Fund (NHATF) in 1983, predecessor to the National Transplant Assistance Fund (NTAF) in 1996, and later renamed HelpHOPELive in 2010. While the name changed, its core service remained the same—to raise funds for uninsured medical expenses.

The innovative premise was simple: The Kolffs believed that the "hope of a second chance" for a loved one would motivate communities to raise grassroots funds for heart transplants. Even if insurance companies were not willing to step up to the plate, the Kolffs believed the public would support those in need of costly and uninsured surgery if it helped their love ones thrive. The Kolffs were right. Within 2 years of its origin, NHATF had raised enough funding for three heart transplants.

The idea of community support for needy members is not new and was recently renewed by the communitarianism theory (Etzioni, 1996). Communities pull together in times of crisis to take care of each other, as was the case after the 9/11 attack and Hurricanes Katrina, Irene, and Sandy, to name a few. American reliance on neighbors, friends, and family (as opposed to government) is a long-standing tradition observed by Alexis de Tocqueville in 1835. Tocqueville (1835/2000) observed that, unlike Europe, where citizens turn to government to deal with social issues, Americans self-organize to help themselves and their neighbors.

Helping people recover offers opportunities for healthy and productive lives. Americans value economic self-sufficiency and self-reliance, assisting those whom they deem worthy (Handler & Hasenfeld, 1991). With the number of Americans without private health insurance on the rise, and fewer employers offering quality health insurance; Americans have become less able to meet their needs if encountering a serious health problem.

Americans are generous with their time and money (Anheier & Salamon, 1999; Bekkers & Wiepking, 2011). When disaster strikes, huge numbers of people donate funds and volunteer to help. Given this backdrop, it was quite logical that when lives could be saved through organ transplant, and it was not covered by medical insurance, there might well be a community willing to pitch in to help defray the cost.

While the inability to afford health care is a life-threatening crisis for many American citizens, it is particularly severe for those requiring a transplant or disabled by traumatic catastrophic injury because both face the challenge of lifelong medical expenses related to their conditions. While many solid organ transplant procedures (average cost: $650,000) are now covered by medical insurance, it is the ancillary lifetime costs that can cripple a family's finances. Moreover, stem cell transplants, particularly those being tried for the first time for a particular disease (average cost: $75,000–$100,000), are not covered by insurance until the medical efficacy of the procedure has been demonstrated (Steinberg, Tunis, & Shapiro, 1995). Likewise, first-year costs of a quadriplegic's care can exceed $500,000, with over $100,000 uncovered even by the best health insurance (e.g., house modifications $50,000+, accessible transport $50,000+, and home health care $70,000+).

Transplant patients and those disabled by traumatic spinal cord or brain injuries have two important similarities that make them prime candidates for grassroots fundraising:

1. Lifelong exorbitant out-of-pocket costs for medication co-pays, continued rehabilitation therapy, relocation and lodging expenses, and transportation, and
2. The hope of a second chance at an independent life. It is this *hope* that motivates family, friends, and neighbors to participate in fundraising. It is human nature to want to help a hopeful situation.

HelpHOPELive responds to families when they are most devastated, offering ongoing guidance and support to raise funds in the community through community volunteers. It also offers fiscal accountability that funds raised will be used for uninsured expenses of the patient, and offers tax-deductibility for donors. Funds raised do not jeopardize eligibility for government assistance (Medicaid) or eligibility for foundation, corporate, matching, and incentive grants.

THE INNOVATION: THE EARLY YEARS OF THE ORGANIZATION—TRIUMPHS AND CHALLENGES[I]

When the Kolffs started NHATF, they hoped to work as a program of another nonprofit but that proved a colossal disaster for the mission because the nonprofit with which they chose to affiliate was not trustworthy and misspent funds raised. It took about a year to untangle the web of commitments. When the dust settled, not only was no money recovered, but the Kolffs also owed $60,000 to vendors who had provided various goods and services. Lesson learned: work with a nonprofit that you can research and trust . . . or start your own! Today, there are endless ways to research those with whom you seek to partner to make sure they are reputable. These techniques (Charity Navigator, Google, etc.) did not exist in 1983.

With the help of a few friends and minimal support, Dr. and Mrs. Kolff recruited volunteers and worked at their dining room table for countless days and months to raise funds. Her approach and model were virtually identical to one employed by HelpHOPELive today. They had lots of volunteer experience fundraising for schools and other civic causes, and they understood the inherent generosity of Americans for causes about which they felt passionate. When it came to transplant, they knew the critical needs, the associated costs, and who in the country was performing heart transplant surgeries. NHATF first gathered information about all the transplant centers, determining which were willing to take in Philadelphia patients. Helping patients identify appropriate transplant centers was the first area of successful assistance, followed later by success in actual grassroots fundraising for individuals.

In the early years, NHATF received small grants from local benefactors and foundations, but these were neither large enough nor long-term enough to assure sustainability. When the NHATF model fully evolved—to help people fundraise for their relatives and friends—it also became clear that fundraising for transplants was not a "trendy concept" likely to engender sustaining financial support from foundations or corporations. It was much easier to raise funds for individuals from communities than for the umbrella organization dedicated to teaching fundraising strategies. Below are select core issues and innovations experienced since inception.

The Business Model

During the first 20 years, NTAF thrived because of the stability of its business model. Taking a small fee from each dollar raised (still 4% after 30 years), the organization then protected those funds for patients' medical expenses and invested them, generating interest and dividends to fund growth. NTAF later sought foundation and corporate grants—the challenge was helping funders understand the powerful leverage of community fundraising as a solution for uninsured medical expenses. HelpHOPELive's spectacular credentialing stemmed

[I]Data for this chapter were collected through in-depth interviews with the first executive director, through analysis of documents and annual reports, through interviews with current staff members, and through the personal experience of Lynne Coughlin Samson as the current executive director of HelpHOPELive. The authors are aware that their perception of the organization may be somewhat biased based on Ms. Samson's role in it. However, this involvement also allowed them intimate knowledge of the organization's challenges and tribulations that most researchers do not access.

from its long-term fiscal accountability. This evolved, in part, from its low overhead relative to program dollars. Staff members work with communities via telephone, computer, and fax, avoiding the expenses of travel to consult on fundraising.

The increase in patients served, funds raised, and assistance provided led to an increase in payroll and overhead expenses. This increase coincided with a decline in investment returns and grant funding related, in part, to a severely compromised American economy from 2008 to 2011. It became evident that innovations in the organizational model were needed for sustainability.

It also became clear that NTAF could start thousands of fundraising campaigns annually, but that only a percentage would raise enough funds to have a life-changing impact. While each campaign required the same administrative overhead, some required a great deal more "hand holding" than others, having unrealistic aspirations and few community connections for a successful campaign. These campaigns were not a beneficial solution for patients because they raised false hope regarding funds that never materialized. As such, these campaigns took more than their share of organizational resources.

In 2010, NTAF changed its approach to assess impact by assistance provided rather than the number of new campaigns initiated annually. This was a significant strategic and cultural shift—recognizing for the first time that the organization could not expand its impact trying to serve every patient who sought services.

While NTAF's long-term staff provided stability of administration, it was difficult for them to embrace the new strategies. However, at the end of the day, it is virtually impossible to predict with precision if a particular campaign will be spectacularly successful or a flop. Because HelpHOPELive is not *in* the community, it is difficult to precisely evaluate the impact of a campaign. However, the saved travel dollars are returned to the patients.

Funds Provide the Power to Negotiate With Hospitals for Treatment

As NHATF became known nationally, it had the funds to bargain with hospitals on behalf of the patients. If a hospital demanded $120,000 for a transplant, NHTAF could offer the funds raised, even if they were less than the "price tag" for the surgery. The hospitals had a choice—do the surgery, save a life, and be guaranteed a certain amount of compensation (the funds raised), or take a hard line on costs, lose the funds, and perhaps the patient as well. The organization effectively lowered the cost of transplant and enabled more people to benefit from the lifesaving operation. This was an unanticipated positive impact of the innovative model.

Early Expansion—New Organ Transplants

As organ transplantation expanded from hearts to include other organs such as kidneys and livers, the organization expanded as well. While initially experimental, each type of organ transplant needed to be funded through community-based fundraising until its medical success (efficacy) was demonstrated regarding increased quality of life and life expectancy. NHATF helped communities raise funds for these new experimental procedures. From solid organs to bone marrow and stem cells in the later 1990s, the organization continued to expand the constituencies it served to embrace all types of transplant. To represent its expanded role, the name was changed to the National Transplant Assistance Fund.

Early Human Resources Solutions

The organization was initially able to minimize human resources expenses by hiring people who did not need benefits and who wished to work part time but had passion for the cause. As the organization grew and full-time workers were required to meet increasing patient demands, the cost of human resources grew astronomically as benefits were built in to attract younger full-time talent. In this case the initial innovative human resources solution had a limited life expectancy.

Lynne Samson, the coauthor of this chapter, became the second executive director, following the retirement of Pat Kolff in 2003. Samson was a lawyer and activist with known leadership skills who could not have seen herself engaged in such an organization until her stepdaughter suffered a spinal cord injury. The support she and her family received from the community through NTAF made her aware of the importance of the organization's mission and services. When she was approached to become the executive director, she welcomed the opportunity to spread the word about community-based fundraising to help maximize recovery options. It was an opportunity to pay forward the humbling gift her family received regarding financial and psychosocial support.

Emergency Grant Program

In 2006, the organization also started an emergency grant program to provide direct financial support for life-threatening crises where fundraising was impractical. This was a meaningful milestone because the organization was financially stable enough to react to emergency needs and bypass the need for fundraising for those families with time sensitive needs.

The Emergency Grant Fund helped patients bridge the financial gap in coverage, filling a targeted need: to pay for time limited expenses with a clearly defined cost (Examples: medication expenses between coverage and unexpected hospital lodging related to organ rejection. The growth of the Emergency Needs Fund has been dramatic. In just 5 years (2008—2012), HelpHOPELive gave nearly 500 grants (totaling $412,653). In 2012 alone the organization gave 70 grants, totaling $63,735.

Challenge of an IRS Audit and the Positive Outcome

Another challenge came when the Internal Revenue Service audited NTAF and questioned its fundraising model. The IRS realized that the organization was providing enormous financial assistance for medical expenses not covered by private insurance or government aid (Medicaid). The outcome required the organization to change its procedures to pool funds from the individual campaigns into regional funds to which the families would apply for assistance. The IRS liked the fact that NTAF provided grants in addition to the funds raised and provided some assistance to those who could not fundraise.

While the audit, which spanned 4 years, was initially extremely stressful for the staff and board, the outcome validated the organization's approach. It provided a regulatory endorsement of the organization's model.

Evolution in the Board of Directors

The growth in capacity of the NTAF Board of Directors has allowed for important visioning and strategizing as the interplay between health care and insurance has become increasingly complex. The founders were both Executive Director and Board Chair for over 20 years. When Kolff and Samson retired, several board members resigned, leaving Samson with a small "founder's board," comprised of the founders' friends, and the opportunity to make board development a priority. Recognizing the importance of fiscal accountability, Samson established a Finance Committee in 2004 to oversee investment management since investment returns provided critical capital for operating expenses and growth. The establishment of board committees came just as the federal government increased scrutiny of nonprofit finances as the result of corporate and nonprofit scandals involving taxpayer funds. The *Sarbanes-Oxley Act* and expansion of IRS compliance requirements significantly increased requirements for board oversight and reporting. Samson had the pieces in place before they were required—perhaps not innovative but staying ahead of the compliance curve (despite the huge increase in administrative resources required) allowed NTAF to move ahead with mission-focused growth rather than worrying about responding to IRS inquiries. Samson also sought to recruit board members with skill sets to help with organizational growth issues such as accounting, finance, communications, and human resources.

OPPORTUNITIES, CHALLENGES, AND INNOVATION IN THE LAST 10 YEARS

Strategy for Growth

Unfortunately, there will never be a shortage of patients lacking funds to pay for the medical care they desire. Thus, HelpHOPELive has a virtually inexhaustible supply of potential clients whom it could serve. In the past 10 years, many patients outside the organization's mission have sought help from HelpHOPELive; cancer patients are one such example. Typically, cancer patients have been referred to other organizations that provide modest direct support.

While there is no shortage of patients in need, it is a unique combination of factors that make fundraising successful.

1. There must be realistic and emotionally moving *hope* in a future quality of life that will be afforded by the raised funds.
2. The disease, condition, or treatment must be relatively unusual, or it has been the HelpHOPELive experience, otherwise, the community will not be moved.
3. "Survivor's guilt" (e.g., "why them and not me"), which may follow a traumatic or surprising event, often inspires significant generosity.

Cancer patients may have a difficult time raising funds. Most Americans believe (rightly or wrongly) that insurance will pay for cancer treatments because virtually everyone knows someone without resources who has received cancer treatment. While it is far from an exact science, the organization's experience has been that fundraising often fails if the diagnosis is common, if there is poor prognosis, or if donors feel as if the situation is so bad that their modest donation will not make a difference.

In visioning for its future, HelpHOPELive will seek to serve additional constituencies who can benefit from its services because they have (1) a hope-inspiring prognosis, (2) the connections to benefit from community-based fundraising, and (3) the understanding that a nonprofit offers advantages over web-based solutions. Initially, HelpHOPELive intends to run a pilot program to assist those with degenerative diseases where the prognosis often requires significant home modifications to stay in the community (e.g., Lou Gehrig's Disease, Multiple Scleroses, etc.). It is believed that communities will support the desire of these families to stay at home with the financial support to do so through fundraising.

In addition HelpHOPELive is branching out into a completely new solution for small companies with limited benefits for their employees—Corporate Compassion Funds. HelpHOPELive is working with small businesses to allow them to establish HelpHOPELive campaigns to provide funds to supplement health insurance in times of crisis. Campaigns would be funded through corporate events with vendor sponsorship or through direct contribution (like the United Way asks). The demand for this type of fundraising is seen as health benefits coupled with corporate social responsibility.

In addition, HelpHOPELive will expand its services to returning combat warriors with catastrophic injuries. While this population is served by the Veteran Administration (VA), there are many aspects of care that are costly and are not reimbursable. While this constituency has a willing community, the Department of Defense and service-related organizations have been major barriers, believing that the military "takes care of its own." With the United States at war in Iraq and Afghanistan for over 10 years, communities looked for ways to thank the brave men and women who have sacrificed so much. What better way to say thank you than to help friends or neighbors, injured while serving, return to their communities to lives of purpose—by affording them choices in treatment and tools for independence to provide the best quality of life in their community. Though the VA system cannot offer these choices, it has manifested a resistance to letting other systems of assistance step in and help.

Impact of Social Media

Social media has increased the organization's reach because families share their stories via Facebook, Twitter, and other outlets. In 2005, the organization was way ahead of the curve in establishing personalized patient fundraising pages for each campaign. These pages allowed families to easily raise funds across geographical boundaries, permitting the patient's story and plea to be shared electronically, with online donations securely received by HelpHOPELive into the patient's campaign. Online donations have grown to comprise 28% of all donations annually and mobile donations were 10% of all online donations for the first 3 months after launching a mobile website.

Technology Challenges

As HelpHOPELive moved forward with its new strategy, it also has had to consolidate databases to build capacity for sustainable, scalable, and efficient service. As families demanded more and faster assistance, HelpHOPELive built an intricate web of connections between its patient records and donor management software systems. This complex and fragile system became unwieldy and unsustainable as upgrades to one system crashed system connections, slowing service delivery and requiring a greater percentage of operating expenses to be spent on technology costs, including hardware, software, maintenance services, training, outside consultants, and upgrades.

During the next 2 years, HelpHOPELive plans to construct an "open source" system that will allow patients to access all HelpHOPELive services through web-based solutions. This project will allow scalability, the ability to serve more patients and raise more funds, and provide more efficient financial assistance, all without a relative increase in staff and other overhead costs.

While visioning for the future, the organization remains mindful that its fragile patients often do not have computers or are not tech savvy. These patients will continue to rely on the organization for additional help with technology. The organization will meet fundraising volunteers and families "where they are," technologically speaking—spanning the range from handholding to streamlined web-based solutions. While technology is always a moving target, the organization will continue to be personal, because it is the personal relationships that are the core of fundraising success, ensuring patient families get the help they need.

Branding

Branding became an organizational priority in 2010. Due to the lackluster economy, NTAF needed to raise additional organizational funding but had no *image* as an organization, only perceived by the public as a group of "silos" for patients. The name NTAF did not accurately reflect the constituencies served. It was not easily communicated, and few people felt affinity toward it. Communicating the mission and impact to the public had been a major challenge since inception.

Many funders viewed NTAF as a regranting agency (providing individual assistance), precluding it from funding eligibility. This limited view made grants hard to solicit and obtain. Foundations and corporations saw little reason to support an organization that redistributed funds to individuals. They failed to understand the essential service of organizing community-based fundraising. The work of teaching communities to fundraise was not communicated by the name or the organization material. This realization forced Ms. Samson to consult marketing and branding experts for advice. After an extensive examination, including inside and outside focus groups, the decision was made in October 2011 to change the name to HelpHOPELive to better reflect what community volunteers and donors accomplish when they work with the organization.

ASSESSMENT OF SUCCESS

What started 30 years ago as a community effort to address health-care needs in the greater Philadelphia area has grown into a national organization serving more than 6,000 patients and families. Since its inception, HelpHOPELive has paid more than $76 million for clients' uninsured medical expenses through grassroots fundraising. In just 6 years, the amount of assistance provided per year has almost doubled, from $3.5 million in 2005 to $6.7 million in 2012. The number of new patient campaigns has grown at an even faster pace, more than doubling from 308 in 2005 to 643 in 2011. The immense growth in these years was due to an ever-increasing number of catastrophic injury families discovering HelpHOPELive services. In 2012, funds raised for catastrophic injury families comprised more than 50% of all funds raised, more than doubling from 22% in 2005.

In 2008 and 2012, HelpHOPELive commissioned an independent study to evaluate its impact—how effectively the organization was accomplishing its mission. In each of 23 categories of life quality (stress, financial health, hope, independence, etc.), the study found that families felt better about their circumstances after working with HelpHOPELive than beforehand. The favorable change was statistically significant in each category.

In 2012—for the 9th consecutive year—HelpHOPELive earned a four-star rating from Charity Navigator, the nation's premier independent charity evaluator, demonstrating its effectiveness in pushing funds back into assistance instead of overhead. The BBB WiseGiving Alliance has found that HelpHOPELive meets its 20 Standards for Charity Accountability. Only 1% of nonprofits rated have earned four Charity Navigator stars for 9 consecutive years.

FIGURE 4.1 Demonstrates Where the Funds Distributed by HelpHOPElive Are Used

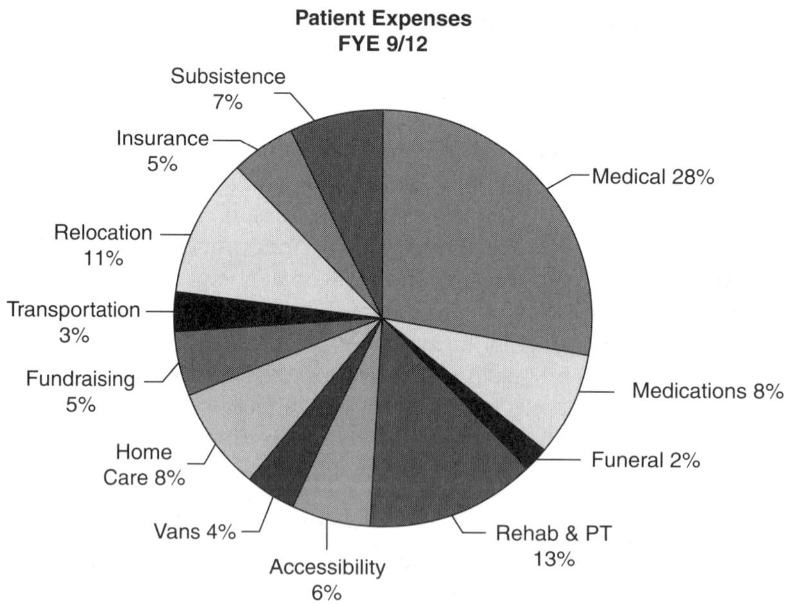

CONCLUSIONS

HelpHOPELive is a creative and innovative response to the needs of the uninsured and has shown great flexibility and adaptability over time. The core goal of the organization (funds for uninsured medical expenses) has remained the same; the means of achieving the goal and the populations served have changed. HelpHOPELive was an innovative response to a new target population. The Kolffs, thanks to Jack Kolff's exposure to heart transplantation, identified a new group of unserved clients. Through trial and error, they developed an innovative method of assisting those in need and in the process started a new nonprofit organization. Similar organizations were established in other regions but many of them failed to mature and either closed shop or merged with other organizations. While the need and the implementation are American in nature, this model can be replicated for other needs and in other countries where similar needs exist.

HelpHOPELive has continued to extend its reach to new constituencies who could benefit from its model. A recent focus on branding and diversifying revenue streams for sustainability kept the organization looking forward to effectively achieve its goals. In this spirit, the leadership is currently focusing on "successful planning" in an effort to ensure smooth transitions for board and management leadership.

As HelpHOPELive turns 30, it has provided over $76 million in medical assistance for uninsured medical expenses related to transplant and catastrophic injury. Over the course of the organization's history, as various natural disasters have occurred, one would have expected the organization to experience a decline in support because philanthropic dollars were diverted to these worthy causes. Yet HelpHOPELive has not seen this effect and has grown to serve more patients with more financial assistance in each consecutive year.

In *The Times of Our Lives*, Tom Brokaw (2011) observed "There is a long and rich national history of Americans finding common cause and responding with a common effort" (p. 148). This effort goes back to our founding fathers, who gathered with diverse beliefs they were able to put aside to come together bound by the determination to establish free will as a governing principle of the Constitution (Brokaw, 2011). HelpHOPELive capitalizes on that spirit and helps neighbors, friends, and relatives come together to participate in a common effort to help a patient in time of need.

The biggest current challenge for HelpHOPELive, and its communities and societies at large, is the threat of social media to narrow the opportunities and responsibilities that "in person" relationships provide. There are many wonderful aspects of social media. Old and broken relationships can be restored. But at the end of the day, during the holiday season, during a crisis, people do not want to curl up and receive a hug from their computer or telephone. People want the tangible, emotion filled, even volatile, impact of in-person relationships, where times and experiences are shared. People seek the psychic and spiritual connection these experiences provide. It is these personal relationships that will continue to be at the core of the fundraising success that ensures financial assistance for medical care.

DISCUSSION QUESTIONS

1. What are the innovative aspects in HelpHOPELive? Is it still innovative, and should it attempt to be more innovative?
2. The success of HelpHOPELive came through much trial and error; what lessons should new similar organizations take into account?
3. Is the model used by HelpHOPELive replicable? If so, to which populations and how? If not, why?
4. The core personnel of HelpHOPELive is comprised of women who have been working there for many years. What are the advantages or disadvantages of this unique workforce?
5. If you were to be named the next executive director of HelpHOPELive, where would you put your energy and what changes would you seek to make?

REFERENCES

Anheier, H. K., & Salamon, L. (1999). Volunteering cross-national perspective: Initial comparisons. *Law and Contemporary Problems, 62*(4), 43–65.

Bekkers, R., & Wiepking, P. (2011). Who gives? A literature review of predictors of charitable giving, Part I: Religion, education, age, and socialization. *Voluntary Sector Review, 2*(3), 337–365.

Brokaw, T. (2011). *Times of our lives: A conversation about America*. New York, NY: Random House.

Etzioni, A. (1996). *The new golden rule*. New York, NY: Basic Books.

Handler, J., & Hasenfeld, Y. (1991). *The moral construction of poverty: Welfare reform in America*. Newberry Park, CA: Sage.

Himmelstein, D. U., Thorne, D., Warren, E., & Woolhandler, S. (2009). Medical Bankruptcy in the United States, 2007: Results of a National Study. *American Journal of Medicine, 122*(8), 741–746.

Kaiser Commission on Medicaid and the Uninsured. (2010). *Medicaid beneficiaries and access to care*. Washington, DC: Author.

Polsky, D., & Grande, D. (2009). The burden of health care costs for working families: Implications for reform. *New England Journal of Medicine, 361*(1), 437–439.

Steinberg, E. P., Tunis, S., & Shapiro, D. (1995). Insurance coverage for experimental technologies. *Health Affairs, 14*(4), 143–158.

Tocqueville, A. D. (2000/1835). *Democracy in America* (H. C. Mansfield & D. Winthrop, Eds. and Trans.). Chicago, IL: University of Chicago Press.

CHAPTER 5

Café au Play

Creating a Family-Centered Social Space in Portland, Oregon

Charles Heying

Associate Professor, Nohad A. Toulan School of Urban Studies and Planning, Portland State University

THE PROBLEM

When Kristin Heying[1] moved to Portland, Oregon with her toddler daughter, she was in the process of becoming a single mom. Recognizing the need to build relationships in their new community, Kristin and her daughter began participating in Parks and Recreation classes, one of the few affordable options for child-centered activities. Through these classes, Kristin became close friends with two other mothers. But when they tried to get together outside class, they discovered that few cafés or coffee shops were designed to accommodate moms with active kids in tow.

THE INNOVATION

Kristin and her friends began discussing what could be done to change the situation. One of the moms, who had worked as a barista, suggested they start a family-friendly coffee shop; another suggested a membership-based play space. But they soon realized that they were looking for something more than a traditional business with a nice play area. They had a larger vision for a place where caregivers could find community and support while their children played together. They envisioned a drop-in gathering place, open regular hours,

[1] Kristin Heying is the author's daughter and Executive Director of Café au Play.

that offered interactive children's activities like daily story times, live music, or puppet plays. For adults, they imagined volunteers providing classes on a variety of topics from parenting challenges to nutrition and health. While such a community center model would fit less well within a for-profit framework, they believed it might work as a nonprofit where the coffee shop would generate revenues while also providing a reason for caregivers to get together. As this model was taking shape, Kristin began graduate study in nonprofit management at Portland State University and assembled a board of directors who laid the groundwork for the organization. Because of my professional interest in the project, I was invited to join the board.[2] In December, 2004, the first Café au Play organizational meeting was held.

A formative influence in our early board discussions was Ray Oldenburg's (1999) *The Great Good Place: Cafés, Coffee Shops, Bookstores, Bars, Hair Salons, and Other Hangouts at the Heart of a Community*. Ultimately, the concept of a *third place* that Oldenberg develops in his book, provided an important frame for the mission of Café au Play that was evolving from the experiences of Kristin and her friends. Oldenburg joined other critics (Bellah, 1986; Jacobs, 1961; Putnam, 2000) who decried the loss of community, declining sense of place, and the excessive privatization of American life. Oldenburg focused particularly on the loss of local hangouts operated and patronized by people who lived in a neighborhood. For Oldenburg, these *third places* were the glue that held communities together. These were places where you could drop in to meet the regulars, to establish connections outside home and work. The open unscheduled characteristic of *third places* was especially appealing to these young mothers who found the play-date model clumsy and cliquish. They valued the flexibility of a drop-in space, the potential to enjoy programs and learn about resources, and the possibility of broadening their network of friends. Creating a *third place*, a community anchor welcoming for all ages but especially for children and caregivers, became the defining mission of Café au Play.

Over the next 2 years, the now expanded board began to build community support for the Café au Play idea. Volunteers provided information and solicited support through community workshops and street fairs. By spring 2005, we completed our first major fundraiser, *A Love Affair with Chocolate*, a desert and wine extravaganza held in an upscale gallery that netted close to $2,000 and some substantial media recognition. Café au Play also began to build its online presence and brand identity, soliciting members for our listserv and posting online notices of activities. We also recruited a graphic arts student to design our first logo and launch a basic website with a coherent graphic identity.

On the procedural side, the board secured fiscal sponsorship from Southeast Uplift, one of Portland's official Neighborhood Coalitions, so Café au Play could accept tax deductible donations (Southeast Uplift, 2014). Bylaws were adopted and an official board recruitment process developed. The board also began the process of applying for 501(c)(3) status, obtaining final approval in 2007. During this formative period, the board developed a long-term strategic plan, including a detailed timeline that, in hindsight, was wildly optimistic.

By late summer 2006, with confidence growing in our ability to stage events, the board determined that our next step was to develop a pilot program to demonstrate the kind of

[2] I continue to serve as a board member and active volunteer.

experiences we hoped to offer families year round. Over the next 6 months, *On the Road with Café au Play* held events at six local coffee shops and community spaces (Cermak & Thomas, 2006). We mobilized dozens of artists, entertainers, and family resource providers to offer patrons a taste of the Café au Play experience. The response to *On the Road* was tremendous. Several events attracted over 100 participants. Our most attended event, at Haven Coffeehouse, was covered by a full-page article in *The Oregonian* (Williams, 2006), the state's largest newspaper.

A PARTNERSHIP IS FORMED

Café au Play now inhabits the former Drive Thru Wake-Up Deli site on 57th and Division Street. The location is roughly central to Inner Southeast Portland, bordering both Mount Tabor and South Tabor neighborhoods and across from Atkinson Elementary School. The Deli site, now called Tabor Commons, consisted of a nondescript 1,000 sq. ft. building surrounded by a 13,000 sq. ft. asphalt parking lot. The site was infamous in the neighborhood with a long and checkered history including drug dealing, laundering of food stamps, gang violence, and vandalism. The one-time gas station had also been a used car dealership, a convenience store, and most recently a deli that was seized by the federal government for the owner's role in selling ingredients to local methamphetamine makers (De Sousa, 2012).

In June 2006, U.S. Marshals transferred the property to the Southeast Uplift Neighborhood Coalition on behalf of the Tabor Commons partners consisting of the Mount Tabor and South Tabor Neighborhood Associations and the Atkinson PTA. It had taken 3 years of hard work by community members to obtain the property. Paul Leistner, a community activist who lives next to the site, was the prime mover in effecting the changes. In addition to negotiating federal, state, and local regulations and paperwork, he helped raise nearly $50,000 to cover the costs of acquiring the property and to begin its transformation from a brownfield to a community space (De Sousa, 2012).

The property was transferred to the Tabor Commons partners under a new U.S. Justice Department program, Operation Goodwill, that encouraged drug-seized properties to be turned over to nonprofit groups who could demonstrate a community serving function. To build support for their application, Leistner organized a series of well-attended community meetings where the future use of the Tabor Commons site was considered (Ashton, 2006). In the first of these meetings, Café au Play presented its vision for a nonprofit family-oriented coffee shop to a receptive audience. By the third meeting, a design charrette, Café au Play was identified as the tenant in Opsis Architect's animated video of how the site could be built out (Cermak & Thomas, 2006). The partnership with Tabor Commons was solidified when Café au Play was invited to join the Tabor Commons board.

After obtaining control of the property, Leistner worked closely with local, state, and federal partners to creatively package a cluster of grants that funded (a) the removal of the buried oil tanks and over 200 tons of contaminated soil, and (b) a green job curriculum that supported the nonprofit Women in the Trades program to deconstruct the interior of the building, remove and recycle the parking lot asphalt, and begin the reconstruction of the building (De Sousa, 2012).

As the process of remediation and reconstruction was under way, Café au Play, now assured that it would be the Tabor Commons tenant, continued its efforts to raise startup funds to outfit the coffee shop. But Café au Play was also being drawn into the process of redeveloping the building and site, something that was technically the responsibility of the Tabor Commons partners. This was the beginning of the blurring of roles that has continued to the present.

Café au Play and Tabor Commons were joined by necessity, shared goals, and personal trust to work with each other and merge our efforts. Leistner, whose Tabor Commons partnership essentially ceased to meet after the property was transferred, continued to be personally effective in articulating the vision of Tabor Commons, attracting resources to the project, and steadfastly volunteering throughout project development. Kristin Heying of Café au Play brought the resources of a strong and growing organization with diverse linkages among a younger cohort interested in the Café au Play concept. Café au Play board members, spouses, and volunteers became deeply involved in renovating both the building and site. For example, all the electrical wiring services were donated by Café au Play board member Tracy Sullivan, a union electrician. Other board members or spouses with professional skills built the interior cabinetry, poured and polished the concrete coffee bar, and tiled the bathroom.

Café au Play and Tabor Commons jointly applied for grants for site renovations and build out. Josh Lighthipe, civil engineer and current Café au Play board president, worked with Leistner to secure grants for our award winning sustainable design features such as rainwater swales, a permeable parking lot, and ecoroofs (Homolac, 2012). Café au Play took a lead role in securing funds for building materials and working with professional muralists, John Early and Laura Bender, to obtain a Regional Arts Council grant for the exterior mural (Ashton, 2008).

With a level of perseverance that, in retrospect, seems remarkable, by summer 2010, Café au Play at Tabor Commons held its Grand Opening Celebration. Café au Play's goal had been to open debt free with a functional landscape, renovated building, a fully outfitted coffee shop, no-cost lease, and a reserve fund to carry us through the first year. We did all that. But it would take another summer before we were able to redo the parking lot with permeable pavers, and the summer after that for the new street frontage sidewalks to be installed with bike racks and a curb bump-out at the school crossing. And our patrons would endure dripping condensation for a year before we used the last of the Tabor Commons fund to insulate the roof.

By fall of 2010, we had completed our soft opening and were fully operational. The 1,000 sq. ft. Café au Play building, once a nondescript white box, now boldly displayed a wraparound mural. The site, once a wall-to-wall parking lot of crumbling asphalt was now lush with plants, trees, and rain gardens studded with basalt rock outcroppings. A faux stone sidewalk bordered the building on two sides with an all-glass garage door opening to the back patio. The deli, with its disreputable activities, was now replaced with a family-friendly community space (Griffin, 2010).

FIRST CRISIS

No organization succeeds without encountering both minor and major crises. A resilient organization manages the crises and learns from them; a brittle organization will stumble and possibly fail. Café au Play has encountered two major crises: the first was an event that precipitated a change in board procedures; the second has been an ongoing financial struggle that became a full-blown crisis in the summer of 2012. From the second crisis, we learned the limits of our revenue model and the need, even for a social enterprise, for effective fundraising strategies that build on organizational strengths. The challenges of both crises have demonstrated the resilience of Café au Play and the strengths of the social enterprise model.

In the fall of 2006, Café au Play was wrapping up its *On the Road with Café Play* tour where we presented our vision to the community of what Café au Play could become. Simultaneously, we were promoting that vision in the community meetings that would determine the use of the Tabor Commons site. As we participated in these events, we began planning on our first auction with the intention of making a significant dent in our fundraising goal of $70,000. We staged the auction by late November, and it was both a major success and a crushing failure.

On the surface, the auction appeared to go extremely well, raising nearly $12,000, but it revealed deep fractures in our organization. The clash of working styles and the pressure to get everyone to follow through on commitments led to a falling out, with half the board leaving in the weeks after the event. It was not Café au Play's finest hour. With the demise of the board following the event, the remaining members reconsidered the method of recruiting board members. Before the event, the pressure to grow the board led to an open-door policy. Anyone who expressed an interest was invited to join the board. While we did utilize all the traditional vetting procedures, forms, and interviews, these turned out to be of little use in helping potential board members know what they were getting into or helping the existing board understand what level of commitment the potential board member was bringing.

The solution to the crisis seems to have worked well. We dropped all the formal application procedures, no more forms, interviews, or recommendations. These all seemed cumbersome and unhelpful. Instead we created a new board role for potential board members. For the first 6 months, the potential board member served as an ad hoc participant, attending meetings, and doing everything a working board member would do. After 6 months, the board and the candidate mutually decided whether to proceed to full board status.

The first 6 months are eye opening for some candidates who have good intentions but are unaware of the considerable commitment required. It is also helpful for the existing board to understand the motivations, capacity, and follow through of the potential recruit. Over time, we have learned to live with a variety of working styles, but the real determinant is whether the board member can work effectively in the organization. As a result, we have seen quite a number of board candidates come and go during the probationary period. What seems to influence some of them to leave is coming to terms with the tenuous financial situation of Café au Play and what that means regarding fundraising.

Each board meeting begins with an update of the finances and an estimate of how many months our reserve will last. It is a surprise to new recruits that the café is not self-supporting and may never be. Being so open may seem a strange way to recruit board members, but financial honesty plus the recognition that we have a well-earned reputation for resourcefulness in meeting our financial goals seems to help. Openness effectively discourages the casual volunteer who is not deeply committed to the mission of the organization, those who realize they do not have the time to give, or those who are coming with their own personal agenda.

On the downside of the Café au Play model of honesty and high work expectations is that it limits our ability to recruit professionals with links to corporate and foundation funding. These professionals come with a different model of board engagement, usually involving the donation of pro bono work, offering policy advice or fiduciary oversight, or simply serving as a link to corporate donations. With some exceptions, potential board members with these expectations are usually unable or unwilling to engage in the real nitty-gritty of keeping a social enterprise afloat.

SECOND CRISIS

In the process of raising start-up funds, Café au Play seemed to try everything: an auction, children's clothing sales, a yard sale, hazardous material collections, revenue partnerships, holiday parties, and so on. All were successful financially and, with the exception of the auction, all contributed to enhancing board commitment and building organizational competence. It was through these experiments that we discovered the holiday tree sale, which has become our signature event and bread-and-butter fundraiser. Our willingness to experiment and our competence in staging events would serve us well when we encountered our second major crisis, a funding shortfall in the summer of 2012 that threatened our continued operation.

When we opened in September 2010, we knew that we did not have adequate financial reserves, but we trusted that the holiday tree sale, to commence 3 months after our opening, would help us get through the first year. Unfortunately, we did not expect that the café would be so costly to sustain for so long. Over the first 3 years, we estimated that on average we lost about $2,000 per month. Our location is ideal, our construction phase is now largely behind us, we have adequate parking, we are very busy, we have daily events that produce standing-room-only audiences, we are a fixture in the community, and yet we lose money. Hard to explain unless you have attempted to launch a social enterprise and, in particular, have run a coffee shop that caters to families.

There are good reasons why we lost money. Of course, there is the expected steep learning curve of the first years of operation, a uniquely challenging task for a manager/executive director who must not only run a traditional business but also integrate the mission and sustain a nonprofit organization. On the business side, we soon discovered that we had some intractable structural issues. While our outdoor space is expansive and inviting, our indoor space is small, with a seating area less than 500 sq. ft. Our dedicated play area effectively reduces this even more. Add to that a show like that given by Red Yarn, a popular red-bearded performer of children's songs, and it becomes standing room only. In essence, we have created a space that is not appealing to the typical coffee shop patron. While parents and kids seem to like the hang-out ambience, to nonparents, it is noisy, crowded, and messy.

And parents do not buy their coffee and go. With all the energy expended to transport and settle children, parents are not about to get up and leave. This is their adult moment to sip their latte, visit with a friend, or just kick back. If things are going well, they could be there for hours. Café au Play should be thrilled; it's become the great *third place* we had imagined. Except it's hard to make money on that model, as we eventually learned. In addition, kids and families establish a unique rhythm for the shop—slow early morning, busy from 9:30 AM to 1:00 PM, slow during nap time, with some pick up again from 2:30 PM to 5:00 PM. It is difficult to schedule efficiently for this routine.

Given these structural limitations, it's surprising that Café au Play did not hit the financial wall sooner than we did. Our $20,000 reserve and revenue from our holiday tree sale sustained us through our first year and into the spring of 2011. But the writing was on the wall that something more would be needed. Our solution was to develop a Farmers Market to be rolled out in the summer of 2011. The Market seemed to have good synergies with our site, operation, and community mission. Although we were behind the curve launching our first Market season, our success was sufficient to encourage us to try again. We made a real commitment to the 2012 season, but it proved less successful that the first.

Timing and construction did us in. We opened our Farmers Market at a time when it was difficult to secure reliable vendors. New markets were opening all over Portland, and we were competing with several within our retail trade area that had more experience, space, and foot traffic. Hopes for a better second season were dashed when construction to replace our frontage curb and sidewalk, which was planned to be completed before market season, dragged on for 2 months into the summer. Construction fencing blocked visual access, restricted pedestrian flow, and eliminated side and front parking.

By mid-summer 2012, it was obvious that the Market would not provide the revenues needed to sustain operational shortfalls. Kristin Heying alerted the board that without a substantial fundraising effort, Café au Play would not make payroll within 2 months. As a stopgap measure, the board decided to reactivate the annual appeal we had initiated the previous summer. Its original purpose was to build a repeat donor base from the families who most benefited from our services. Despite our recognition that first year results were limited, we hoped that a more organized effort would produce better results. We rolled out our campaign, added a phone-a-thon, and encouraged board members to make personal appeals to people they knew.

The results were not encouraging, but the process taught us something about ourselves, our clientele, and the limits of this type of appeal. We learned that the art of the direct ask is something we do not excel in. Our organizational history, where we solicited hands-on community support and built partnerships with other organizations, did not prepare us for the very different type of relationship building it takes to establish a committed donor base. We also discovered the obvious; our board is not well connected to those with deep pockets in the community and ultimately our "big donors" turned out to be ourselves, family, and friends. We also learned the limits of our ability to tap into the young families who use our services. They are cash strapped and have not yet developed the habit of giving nor matured in their understanding that they are the adults responsible for organizational survival. And we discovered a generational lesson. Younger people have now experienced a lifetime of intrusive solicitation through every available media, so it is difficult to break the barrier of inattention and negativity such an approach generates.

Despite the less than overwhelming success of our several fundraising efforts, the revenue they produced added up to something substantial enough to keep us afloat and opened a space to try something else. And that something else, turned out to be a real winner.

Strangely enough, given the crisis that followed our first attempt, it was an auction. It didn't start out that way. It started off as a Harvest Sunday Supper that would raise money through ticket sales. Cory Schriber, a neighbor, former owner and chef of the Wildwood, one of Portland's pioneer locavore restaurants, and now an instructor at Portland's Culinary Institute, agreed to help organize the event. Not only would he be chef, but he would also enroll his students to cater the Harvest Supper as their final project. This meant that they would provide all the food and preparation on site. Schriber's contacts in the spirits industry also helped us obtain substantial wine and beer donations (Ashton, 2012).

With such a boost in support, we were free to be creative with the rest of the event. And the board responded. Beginning with the idea of having a small silent auction, it grew organically to include over 90 items. We added a raffle, a professional to host the event, performers, and music groups, including an amazing Irish traditional ensemble founded by one of our baristas. Using funds from anonymous donors, we were able to distribute free tickets to the long list of donors and volunteers who had supported us over the years. If we were going to fail, we would at least end with a grand gesture to our community.

The day was perfect, the music inspiring, the spirits flowed freely, and the food was beyond excellent. There was an authentic essence of appreciation and celebration. And it worked, the nearly $9,000 we netted from the event got us through the summer to our best ever holiday tree sale. Our crisis was averted, and our organization was stronger and more committed.

FINDING THAT RELIABLE FUNDRAISER

Only time will tell if the Harvest Sunday Supper becomes an annual event. Our many years of experimentation taught us that successful fundraising strategies draw on resources and connections in our networks, fit our organizational strengths, and are responsive to preferences and capacity of our base. The Harvest Supper seems to be a good fit, but it is also possible the stars came into alignment just this one time. In any case, our fundraising experiments reminded us of how dependent Café au Play has become on our signature fundraiser, the holiday tree sale.

Without our experience operating the tree sale prior to opening Café au Play and without the revenues it produced, Café au Play would not have survived. In 2008, our first year running the sale, we netted $6,000; by 2012, our fifth year, we had nearly tripled that to $16,000. The tree sale provided over $18,000 toward startup funding and, since Café au Play has opened, has provided $43,000 to cover operating losses.

It is nearly an ideal fundraiser for us. We have plentiful outdoor space and adequate street and lot parking. The trees are an amenity during the holiday season, increasing café revenues on the weekends. Café au Play benefits from our location on Division Street, a narrow arterial with pedestrian-friendly design that provides bike and pedestrian access to both Mount Tabor and South Tabor neighborhoods.

Besides our location, the holiday tree sale works very well for episodic volunteers. Many of our volunteers return every year just for this event. We have also developed a good working relationship with Warner Pacific College, four blocks east of Café au Play, and with Hands Around Greater Portland, an organization whose purpose is to connect volunteers with nonprofit organizations.

Over the years, we have routinized most of our activity and volunteers pick up skills quickly and seem to enjoy it. Many who buy trees are neighbors and repeat customers who see this as an opportunity to get a great tree, excellent service, and contribute to a community-oriented nonprofit. Trees leave the lot by auto, stroller, wagon, bike, and wheelbarrow. It is a great bonding event with the community.

WINDS OF CHANGE, TIES THAT BIND, SUPPORT THAT STAYS

Winds of Change: In trying to identify why some social enterprises are successful, it seems clear that the organization must operate within the context of its environment. Café au Play was started on the cusp of the move to Portland by young people who were attracted by the urban vibe and later decided that the city rather than the suburbs was the right place to raise families. Café au Play identified a mission niche that served this client base. The Café au Play and Tabor Commons partnership has been remarkably successful in obtaining grants for building and infrastructure improvements. We caught the wind of Portland's tack toward pedestrian-friendly neighborhood design, sustainable development, and bioremediation. We also benefitted from a new Justice Department initiative, Operation Goodwill, that encouraged the U.S. Marshall service to turn over drug-seized properties to community groups and nonprofits. Our timing was also right with the election of Mayor Tom Potter, who initiated a citywide visioning exercise that identified support for local neighborhood serving enterprises as a priority and then supported this initiative with neighborhood Vision into Action Grants from which we secured $12,000 in building funds.

Ties That Bind: Every successful business, nonprofit, or social enterprise knows that their survival depends on their personal and organizational networks that can be mobilized for information and support. We have learned that the embeddedness of an organization in these networks increases with the number of times they are activated and the trust that is built from successful engagement and visible accomplishment (Granovetter, 1985). We have learned that the most powerful relationships are those that evolve over time into multistranded linkages of mutual support. In previous sections, I described how some of these networks are activated as board members drew their family, friends, and affiliates into our projects. What follows are several more examples that show the dimensionality and activation of these networks.

Paul Leistner, the neighborhood activist who created the Tabor Commons project, lives next to Café au Play. He received his PhD in from the Nohad A. Toulan School of Urban Studies and Planning, where I am a faculty member and served on his dissertation committee. We have jointly served on the Southeast Uplift Board of Directors, which was the fiscal sponsor for Café au Play as well as the titular owner of Tabor Commons. Leistner was former president and board member of the Mount Tabor Neighborhood Association, was one of the three key Tabor Commons partners. The Mount Tabor Neighborhood association donated over $8,000 toward building renovation of Tabor Commons and Café au Play. Leistner also recruited Master of Urban and Regional Planning students from the Toulan School to undertake their Planning Workshop project for Tabor Commons (Buckley, Henry, Shane, & Wolter, 2005). The students developed a consultant report that outlined the resources for brownfield remediation. Clark Henry, a student member of that Planning Workshop team, was also the City of Portland, Brownfield administrator at the time. He was instrumental in securing the local, city, and state funds for removing the buried storage tanks on the site.

Multistranded relationships can grow from professional affiliations as well. Josh Lighthipe, who lived in the neighborhood and was a parent of a toddler, learned of the Café au Play project through a neighbor and professional colleague involved in the master planning of Tabor Commons. Lighthipe, a civil engineer whose expertise is green infrastructure design, volunteered at Tabor Commons because of the opportunity to do hands-on work in bioremediation. Through involvement with Café au Play board members on these work parties, Lighthipe was eventually recruited to serve on the Café au Play board and later became its president. Lighthipe's professional affiliations were beneficial in identifying and securing the green infrastructure grants for site renovation (KPFF Stormwater Cinema, 2013).

Kristin Heying maintains linkages to other entrepreneurs who were involved in similar ventures. During the development of Café au Play, Heying worked with the owner of Bipartisan Café who provided insights on startups, marketing, and management. Later he helped Heying and Charlotte Krayenbull, our volunteer designer, outline the café layout and function.

Anyone who has worked in nonprofits will recognize the pattern; nonprofits are built and survive based on these relationships. The more connected you are, the more resilient will be your organization. Relationships wax and wane, but connections always remain to be reactivated both intentionally and serendipitously. But there are distinct types of networks—people travel in different circles representing different access and resources. Café au Play seems connected to supportive friends and neighbors, many of whom are connected to professional and entrepreneurial networks. However, we are not connected to networks of those with deep pockets or those who have access to foundation and corporate networks.

Support That Stays: With the many events and construction projects we engage in, we have ample opportunities to work with volunteers. We have developed a working style that seems to help us retain volunteers and develop long-term relationships with organizations like Warner Pacific College that encourage a culture of civic engagement in their students. We model behavior, provide training and direction, give responsibility, expect performance, engage in activities that lead to a sense of accomplishment, and give back through incentives and recognition.

During our tree sale, at least one board member must be present for every shift during the 4 weeks of the sale. This is a real commitment, but it pays off. Volunteers who see us working for hours in the ever-present Portland rain till we are bone weary and soaked through are more willing to do their part. For all work parties, board members work alongside volunteers. Our mode of operation has been to provide good direction, hand off responsibility, and expect performance. Working at Café au Play is never a casual outing, and there is a certain respect for that. Volunteers leave with a sense of something being accomplished, some visible progress being made, and something of worth they can feel a part of.

We also reciprocate in small and symbolic ways. As an incentive, we provide free drinks and sandwiches for all volunteers. At the end of the work period, we personally thank them for their work and recognize their contributions by posting photos and affiliations on our social media sites. All this creates a sense of ownership that further embeds our organization in the local community.

STRENGTHS AND WEAKNESSES OF THE SOCIAL ENTERPRISE MODEL

When the founding board first envisioned a social enterprise, it seemed a close fit with mission and need. The coffee shop would be a family-friendly *third place* and a revenue generating operation that, after a few lean years, would be self-sustaining. But reality suggests otherwise. Not only has our major fundraiser been used to backfill substantial revenue shortfalls, but we also have needed to experiment with other funding schemes to save the organization from what seems an ever-present threat of closing our doors.

Why did it not work out as we expected? Part of it was our blissful ignorance of what it would take to create and sustain an organization, much less a new and innovative one. In our optimism, we focused more on the potential strengths of the social enterprise model rather than the weaknesses.

High on the list of potential weaknesses is the unrealistic expectations of leadership. The executive director of an earned income social enterprise like Café au Play must excel in two realms. She or he must be skilled in the usual nonprofit kitbag from event planning and fundraising to board and volunteer engagement. But she or he must also be an excellent business manager, skilled in personnel management, intimately aware of cost leakages and revenue opportunities as well of new industry service trends. The list of expected competences is long indeed, especially in a new enterprise where resources are severely constrained

Another potential weakness is public perception. For newcomers and some regulars there is a lack of understanding that Café au Play is a nonprofit service organization. On the surface it looks like a successful business, so they are likely to treat it as such, unaware of the significant community investment it takes to sustain it.

Café au Play is also disadvantaged regarding our ability to seek external support for our programming. Since we generate a revenue stream and our mission is not considered a critical social need, we have a more difficult task selling ourselves to grant-giving organizations. While we believe we provide a critical and valued service, it is not so viewed by foundations and government agencies whose mission and funding sources often constrain their grants to organizations that serve the most marginalized citizens. Because the list of funders willing to consider smaller organizations operating outside mainstream social service models is short, we have so far been unsuccessful in obtaining program grants.

But the social enterprise may have provided important advantages, given that we are succeeding where nearly all for-profit family-centered establishments have failed. In the years that Café au Play has been in development, we have seen six for-profit family-friendly coffeehouses either close (4) or substantially rebrand their operation away from a family-centric focus (2). Because we can fundraise and solicit support from the community in a way that a private for-profit venture cannot, we can operate at a loss and still fulfill our community-serving mission. There is no question that we are constrained by market logic, but we are not bound by it. And because we have a profit side, we can share the overhead costs between the revenue generating and mission-oriented sides of our enterprise.

IS CAFÉ AU PLAY A SOCIAL INNOVATION?

In many ways, Café au Play fits the criteria for social innovation identified by Cnaan and Vinokur-Kaplan in this volume. Café au Play was transformative for its community—supporting the visioning process that led to its partnership with Tabor Commons, building collaborations with other nonprofit organizations, and combining diverse sources of funding with volunteer initiative to transform a former drug house into a community institution.

Café au Play developed a novel solution to social problems encountered by its entrepreneurial founder and her friends—the isolation of parenting and the lack of public spaces that welcomed children and families. Café au Play provides a place to go for parents, grandparents, and caretakers to be in the presence of others—a simple act that helps them overcome the isolation of caring for children in the private space of home. At Café au Play, caregivers can have some adult time while their children interact in a creative and social play environment. It sets the stage for casual interactions that can lead to networks of friendship and support.

Café au Play also developed an innovative revenue model. Because it wanted to be a resource open to all families, we rejected the pay-to-play model of kids clubs and play spaces. Instead, we developed a hybrid model that combined coffee shop revenues with nonprofit fundraising and volunteer support. Our social enterprise approach seems to be more resilient, succeeding where for-profit ventures failed.

Café au Play has taken an innovative approach to the design of our outdoor spaces. By using high tolerance greenscaping, creekbed-type water runnels, and basalt boulder outcroppings, we combined the latest techniques in green infrastructure design with the best models for natural play areas.

Café au Play has also changed the ecology of social spaces for children and families in Portland by creating an audience for new performance occupations and family service providers. Magicians, puppeteers, and artists have all found a home at Café au Play. Two of our regular performers, Red Yarn and Oliver Rootbeer and Dingo, now make their livings from free-will donations on a kids-performance circuit anchored by Café au Play. Café au Play has also created a new space for educators and therapists to introduce services to clients. We regularly provide outreach in family health, breast feeding, healthy eating, natural healing, and nearly any topic that has someone willing to promote it without a fee. Sam Stevens, a family therapist who offers a monthly New Fathers Meet Up Group, was recently featured in an *Oregonian* (Muldoon, 2013) article on the mental health needs of new dads.

CONCLUSION

Is the Café au Play replicable? Yes, something like it will be done elsewhere, but the particular form it takes will depend on its ability to tack with the *winds of change* that drive it, the degree to which it becomes deeply embedded in the network of *ties that bind*, and the skill of its entrepreneurial founder and board to engender *support that stays.* While all these will alter form and outcomes, there is only one constant that will ultimately determine success—sheer dogged persistence, a persistence first generated by adventure, then vestedness, and finally a sense of responsibility to staff, families, and community who depend on the service you provide.

When we developed our timeline in the formative years of organizational founding, we estimated that we would open in 2 years. We substantially missed that target, but given where we started, with no money, an inexperienced board, a challenging site, and a grand vision, our delay seems understandable and our survival surprising. Café au Play proceeded with the implicit understanding that we would get this done when it got done, and that we would move no faster than the community that supported us.

That support has carried us forward to a more optimistic present. Our average daily revenues are closing in on breaking even. We have increased staff wages and overlap coverage. We have begun to produce our own line of baked goods. Our barista training program, which is so popular among high schoolers we cannot meet demand, may soon open Night Grounds, an evening coffee shop for teens. Our last major construction project, the canopy over our back patio, is complete, essentially doubling our three-season seating capacity. Our loyal patrons, who have tolerated a crowded space, repeated construction events, and the missteps of our first years, continue to support us and spread the word. It's a hopeful sign.

DISCUSSION QUESTIONS

1. Café au Play has succeeded where for-profit enterprises with similar missions did not. To what extent was this attributable to Café au Play being a social enterprise? What other factors were important to its success?

2. Café au Play began with the vision that coffee shop revenues would eventually allow the organization to be self-sustaining. However, Café au Play founders soon learned that traditional nonprofit revenue strategies (fundraisers, grants, donations) would be critical to its survival. What does this reveal about the strengths and weaknesses of the social enterprise model?

3. The social enterprise model puts heavy demand on its leadership because it requires entrepreneurial vision as well as excellence in both business and nonprofit arenas. What are the implications for Café au Play as it transitions to a second generation of leaders and managers? Given its small size, unique history, and mixed revenue stream, will it be able to find people with the appropriate vision and skills to carry the organization forward? How should Café au Play plan for this transition? What aspects of this situation are unique to social enterprise organizations, and what are universal for all organizations during periods of transition?

4. Café au Play actively developed partnerships with other organizations and individuals. While most were successful, all involved tensions and risks. Was Café au Play strategic, opportunistic, or simply lucky in the partnerships it formed? Drawing on your own organizational experience, discuss how you have negotiated the potential problems of partnerships and whether the benefits of collaboration outweigh the risks. Consider how this calculus changes with the vision, developmental stage, and resources of an organization.

5. Café au Play was very successful getting grants for green infrastructure (rain gardens, permeable pavers, ecoroofs) and other capital improvements, but it has not been successful in getting programming grants. This experience is contrary to that of many small nonprofit social service organizations that are more successful obtaining grants for innovative programs. What lessons did Café au Play leaders take from their experience? Do you think their assessment of the situation was accurate? Should they have been more persistent in pursuing programming grants, or did they use their resources efficiently by seeking grants in areas of past success? In what way did the grants jointly pursued by Tabor Commons and Café au Play shape Café au Play's development?

6. Café au Play has a foundational myth—a single mom with limited resources discovers there are few restaurants or coffee shops that are welcoming to children and families. With the help of friends and community partners, she leads an effort to transform a former deli with a history of disreputable activities into a self-sustaining community space where adults can interact while their children play. Discuss the role and importance of foundational myths. How important are they in attracting volunteers, media attention, and other resources? To what extent did Café au Play's foundational myth help it define its mission and promote its goals? Can a foundational myth prevent an organization from pursuing new areas of development, or is it an important touchstone preventing mission drift? Does a foundational myth distort the real story of how an organization learns and succeeds?

7. At the outset, the founders of Café au Play were wildly optimistic about how quickly they would become operational and self-sustaining. Is this typical of innovative enterprises, or were the founders particularly conservative in moving the project along? Do you think that organizational founders are typically aware of the commitment it takes to get a new organization off the ground? Is this blissful ignorance a good thing? Have you started a new organization that required more time and resources than expected? If you had known what a commitment it would take, would you do it again?

8. Café au Play managed several crisis situations that could have led to organizational failure. How would you evaluate their responses? Is there a one-best-way to respond to an organizational crisis or does the response shape the organization in a way that makes it seem appropriate in retrospect? What general attitudes did Café au Play leaders bring to the situation that allowed them to respond in a way that helped the organization move forward? Can organizational leaders be taught crisis management, or is it something learned by doing? Does crisis management depend on a skill set, or does it derive from a deeper knowledge of human behavior?

9. In the section "Ties That Bind," the author comments on the different types of networks in which organizations and their leaders are embedded and the benefits and limitations of these network affiliations. Did the author's description resonate with your experience? Describe the network affiliations of an organization you know. How do they affect the organization?

10. As Café au Play begins its third year of operation, it seems to have proven its ability to survive and thrive. Its major building projects are complete, it is debt free, has a stable revenue base, good leadership, an active board, and strong community support. Most important, it is fulfilling its mission of being an accessible *third place* for children and families. Why did it succeed? Was it luck, pluck, the right idea at the right time, or something else entirely? Identify five possible reasons for its success and discuss which you think was most critical. If you were on the board of Café au Play, what are some future opportunities and threats it should be anticipating and what recommendations would you make for action?

REFERENCES

Ashton, D. (2006). National Drug Czar treks to SE Portland; lauds 'meth store' makeover. *East Portland News*. Retrieved from http://eastpdxnews.com/community-resource/national-drug-czar-treks-to-se-portland-lauds-meth-store-makeover/

Ashton, D. F. (2008). Public art transforms look of former 'meth store.' *East Portland News*. Retrieved from http://eastpdxnews.com/general-news-features/public-art-transforms-look-of-former-meth-store/

Ashton, D. F. (2012). "Harvest Dinner" supports café in former drug house. *East Portland News*. Retrieved from http://eastpdxnews.com/general-news-features/harvest-dinner-supports-cafe-in-former-drug-house/

Bellah, R. N. (1986). *Habits of the heart: Individualism and commitment in American life* (1st Perennial Library ed.). New York, NY: Harper & Row.

Buckley, B., Henry, C., Shane, S., & Wolter, S. C. (2005). *57th & Division Street Community Ownership Project*. Master of Urban and Regional Planning Workshop Projects, Paper 54. Portland, OR: Portland State University. Retrieved from http://archives.pdx.edu/ds/psu/8647

Cermak, A., & Thomas, L. (Producers). (2006). *A home for Café au Play*. Retrieved from http://www.youtube.com/watch?v=qJb6jgy5xH4

De Sousa, C. (2012). *Tabor Commons to Café au Play, Portland, Oregon: A U.S. EPA Brownfields Sustainability Pilot*. University of Illinois at Chicago, Insitute for Environmental Science and Policy, Sustainable Brownfields Consortium. Retrieved from http://www.uic.edu/orgs/brownfields/research-results/documents/TaborWebpostFinal-12-9-11_000.pdf

Granovetter, M. (1985). Economic action and social structure: The problem of embeddedness. *American Journal of Sociology, 91*(3), 481–510.

Griffin, A. (2010, September 11). Café au Play succeeds at site of former Portland drug-plagued property, *The Oregonian*, pp. B1–B2. Retrieved from http://www.oregonlive.com/news/oregonian/anna_griffin/index.ssf/2010/09/cafe_au_play_a_successful_port.html

Homolac, K. (2012). *Brownfields Conference recognizes redevelopment success in Oregon*. Salem: Business Oregon. Retrieved from http://www.oregon4biz.com/news.php?a=83

Jacobs, J. (1961). *The death and life of great American cities*. New York, NY: Random House.

KPFF Stormwater Cinema (Producer). (2013). *A garden to play in*. Retrieved from http://vimeo.com/64325688

Muldoon, K. (2013, February 20). Post-partum depression among new dads inspires support groups, helplines and more. *The Oregonian*. Retrieved from http://www.oregonlive.com/health/index.ssf/2013/02/post-partum_depression_among_n.html

Oldenburg, R. (1999). *The great good place: Cafés, coffee shops, bookstores, bars, hair salons, and other hangouts at the heart of a community*. New York, NY: Marlowe.

Putnam, R. D. (2000). *Bowling alone: The collapse and revival of American community*. New York, NY: Simon & Schuster.

Southeast Uplift. (2014). *Fiscal sponsorship*. Retrieved from http://www.seuplift.org/what-we-do/administrative-support/

Williams, L. (2006, April 20). Dream blends lattes, little ones. *The Oregonian*, E1–2.

ADDITIONAL RESOURCES

Café au Play social media

Website blog: http://www.cafeauplay.org

Facebook: https://www.facebook.com/Cafeauplay

Picassa web album: http://picasaweb.google.com/cafeauplay.photos

Café au Play videos

On the Road with Café au Play. (2007). https://www.youtube.com/watch?v=qJb6jgy5xH4 Story of Café au Play, Tabor Commons and On the Road with Café au Play.

CAP Giving Video. (2010). http://vimeo.com/30254574 Edited by Mitchell Frister. Fundraising video that updates the Café au Play story to 2010.

A Garden to Play In. (2013). http://vimeo.com/64325688 Professional video produced by Café au Play corporate partner KPFF Consulting Engineers. Focuses on the green infrastructure projects and their contribution to Café au Play mission.

CHAPTER 6

The Mind Trust

Innovations in Urban Education

Wolfgang Bielefeld

Professor Emeritus School of Public and Environmental Affairs, Indiana University

INTRODUCTION: PUBLIC EDUCATION IN THE UNITED STATES

Since its inception to the present, the U.S. public education system has been subject to differing opinions, and often outright controversy, about issues such as the goals of public education, funding, and the relationship between public and private schools (for a history of U.S. education, see Mondale, 2002). This makes education one of the United States' most contentious public services. Concerns about public education were heightened by a 1983 report published by the National Commission on Excellence in Education. *A Nation at Risk: The Imperative for Educational Reform* concluded that the average graduate of U.S. schools was not as well educated as the average graduate of 25 years ago. The most famous line of the widely publicized report declared that "the educational foundations of our society are presently being eroded by a rising tide of mediocrity that threatens our very future as a Nation and a people" (p. 9).

The report recommended that schools adopt more rigorous and measurable standards, have higher expectations for student performance and conduct, devote more time to teaching a set of new basics, and improve teacher quality. The report caused great public concern and a vigorous debate in the education policy community. It led to comprehensive school reform efforts, was the impetus for the academic-standards movement, drew attention to the importance of education policy, and led to a focus on school accountability (Weiss, 2003). Following this, the basic question that has been examined and debated over the subsequent years is whether public school student performance has or has not improved. A second issue developed later, when student achievement data and public school reform efforts were interpreted as not showing adequate results. This issue was the viability and efficacy of educational alternatives to public schools. These included home schooling, charter schools, private contracting, and education vouchers as well as assistance through tuition tax credits, scholarship tax credits, and education deductions.

The performance of urban schools has been particularly problematic. A 1998 policy brief on urban education by the Brookings Institute (Ravitch, 1998) concluded that student performance in the nation's urban schools was low in general and appallingly low in urban schools that enroll high proportions of poor students. The brief cited a massive survey of urban education (*Education Week,* 1998) as well as tests administered by the federally funded National Assessment of Educational Progress (NEAP). While urban schools enrolled 24% of all public school students in the United States, they enrolled 35% of poor students and 43% of minority students. The survey found that in about half the states with large cities, a majority of urban students failed to meet even minimum standards on national tests. Moreover, in urban schools where most of the students were poor, two thirds or more failed to reach even the basic level on national tests. For example, data showed that 63% of fourth-grade students in nonurban schools across the nation reached the basic level in reading as compared to 43% of students in urban schools. Worse yet, in high-poverty schools in urban districts, only 23% of fourth graders met that minimal standard. Overall, slightly more than half of big-city students were unable to graduate from high school in the customary 4 years. Finally, there were large differences between students in high-poverty schools in urban and nonurban districts. Poor children in city schools were far less likely to meet the basic achievement level on NAEP tests than poor children who did not live in cities.

THE PROBLEM: INDIANAPOLIS PUBLIC SCHOOL (IPS) SYSTEM PERFORMANCE

To address increasing concerns about public education in the state, Indiana passed Public Law 221 in 1999 (Indiana Department of Education, 2013a). P.L. 221 is Indiana's comprehensive accountability system for K–12 education. The law aims to establish major educational reform and accountability statewide. To measure progress, P.L. 221 assigns Indiana public and accredited nonpublic schools A–F letter grades based on student performance on standardized tests and on student improvement.

In February of 2012, Indiana was granted a waiver from key requirements of No Child Left Behind (NCLB), a federal education program (Stokes, 2012). The state replaced NCLB's accountability standard with a requirement that every Indiana school must earn a state letter grade of an A—or failing that, improve two letter grades to earn no worse than a C—by 2020. Schools classified in the lowest category of performers in the state for 6 consecutive years could be taken over by the Indiana State Board of Education. The Board could also take a number of remediation efforts, including turning over administration of failing schools to an outside manager or charter school operator.

As in other urban areas across the country, schools in Indiana's major metropolitan areas (Indianapolis and Gary) have struggled. In terms of the Indianapolis public school system (IPS), Hughes (2010) notes,

> "As IPS continued to grow into the latter half of the 20th Century, many of the social issues which affected the nation at-large came front and center to face the district's leaders. Chief among these, of course, was the issue of desegregation and the concomitant busing issue which evolved as officials sought to integrate schools in the 1960s and 1970s. Resistance from all corners and the general economic

downturn of the seventies led to a dark period for IPS, featuring dropping student achievement and rising violence in the schools themselves" (para. 5).

IPS's 2010–2012 strategic plan provides information about student performance (Indianapolis Public Schools, 2013). These figures show that 2010 expectations for high school graduation and passing performance on standardized tests were rarely above 60% (and sometimes as low at 42% on some tests). These figures can be compared to statewide figures that show an 85% high school graduation rate and 80% pass rates on most standardized tests (The Mind Trust, 2011). In 2012, 17 IPS schools fell into the F category, including about half of the district's high schools. In August of 2011, the State Board of Education took action on six failing schools in IPS (Stokes, 2011). This included bringing in new management for five of them. In February of 2013, the Board voted to hand oversight of four of those schools to the office of Indianapolis Mayor Greg Ballard ("Mayor to Take Control," 2013).

THE INNOVATIONS: THE MIND TRUST INITIATIVES

The Mind Trust is a nonprofit organization established in Indianapolis in 2006. Its goal is nothing less than the transformation of the educational landscape in Indianapolis through initiating and promoting innovative educational initiatives. By providing fellowships and other resources, initiating public discussions, and creating networks, The Mind Trust has cultivated a climate conducive to creativity and new ideas in public education. It has attracted entrepreneurially minded, innovative people to Indianapolis and provided them with a culture of educational innovation as well as the resources to develop and implement new programs to change the public education system. To accomplish its goals, The Mind Trust has utilized a number of strategies. These are briefly described below (The Mind Trust, 2012, 2013a). More information is presented in the Impact and Effectiveness section of this chapter.

Recruiting National Organizations

The Mind Trust invests in attracting established education-reform organizations to Indianapolis and providing them with ongoing support. These programs have proven national track records of making a dramatic impact on student outcomes, whether by increasing college attendance or putting excellent teachers in classrooms. Organizations brought to Indianapolis by The Mind Trust include

- Teach for America: Recruits top college graduates who commit to teach for 2 years in underserved public schools.
- Indianapolis Teaching Fellows (TNTP): Draws talented professionals from noneducation backgrounds to become teachers in subjects such as math, science, foreign language, and special education.
- College Summit: Increases college attendance rates among low-income students by fostering a college-going culture in high schools.

- Diploma Plus: Boosts outcomes among at-risk students through a school model that includes a performance-based system and a supportive school culture.
- Stand for Children: A leading grassroots education advocacy organization that empowers families and educators to have a voice in education policy.

Fostering New Initiatives—Education Entrepreneur Fellowship

The Mind Trust empowers talented people to transform K–12 education by starting innovative programs to address some of its most pressing problems. During the 2-year fellowship, The Mind Trust provides its Education Entrepreneur Fellows with a $90,000 annual salary, full health care and benefits, and a $20,000 startup stipend. In addition, The Mind Trust supports the fellows as they launch their new ventures in Indianapolis. Since The Mind Trust began receiving applications for the fellowship in 2008, more than 3,000 individuals from 48 states and 36 countries have applied. From that pool, The Mind Trust has selected seven fellows who have started initiatives tackling needs ranging from summer learning loss to teacher attrition. Those initiatives have been featured in national media. They include

- Summer Advantage USA: Provides rigorous academic and enrichment programs during the summer months for underperforming, low-income students.
- Teach Plus: Helps retain great teachers in urban schools by training them to become education-policy advocates and providing leadership incentives for high-performing teachers.
- FosterEd: Combats the academic achievement gap among foster children by providing them with trained experts to serve as education advocates.
- The Expectations Project: Mobilizes faith leaders and churchgoers to advocate for education reform policies designed to ensure all children have access to high quality public education.
- Seton Education Partners: Helps struggling urban Catholic schools avoid closure by launching new, secular charter models and providing technical assistance and guidance to parishes.
- Youth Music Exchange: Empowers students to start and manage their own record labels at schools, afterschool programs, and community centers to keep them engaged in school and motivated about learning.
- Global Citizen Year: Recruits, trains, and supports a diverse corps of emerging leaders as they work as apprentices in nongovernmental organizations in developing nations during a "bridge year" between high school and college.

Charter School Incubator

The Mind Trust awards $1 million grants—the largest award of its kind nationally—to entice talented teams to start networks of charter schools in Indianapolis.

Scaling Up

To help expand the most successful of these national and Indianapolis-grown organizations, The Mind Trust launched a 3-year, $18 million fundraising campaign, Grow What Works, in May 2011. The fundraising goal was exceeded ahead of schedule and raised $19.2 million. By growing the most successful organizations in The Mind Trust's network and supporting the Education Entrepreneur Fellowship and Charter School Incubator, Grow What Works increased the scope of organizations The Mind Trust can incubate in Indianapolis, as well as the pool of talent these organizations can attract and the number of students they can serve

Creating Excellent School Conditions—Opportunity Schools Report

In December 2011, The Mind Trust released a report proposing a dramatic overhaul of Indianapolis Public Schools. Since then, the report, *Creating Opportunity Schools: A Bold Plan to Transform Indianapolis Public Schools* (The Mind Trust, 2011), has sparked significant conversations, including coverage in local and national media outlets.

Cities for Education Entrepreneurship Trust (CEE-Trust)

In 2010, The Mind Trust recruited several peer organizations from other cities to join a new network that the organization founded called the Cities for Education Entrepreneurship Trust (CEE-Trust). CEE-Trust is a growing national network of 27 city-focused foundations, nonprofits, and mayors' offices that work together to promote education innovation and reform.

THE ESTABLISHMENT OF THE MIND TRUST

In 2001, at the urging of then Indianapolis Mayor Bart Peterson, the Indiana Legislature passed a law making Indianapolis the only city in the nation where the mayor had the ability to authorize charter schools (The Mind Trust, 2013a). After the law passed, Mayor Peterson entrusted David Harris, one of his policy advisors, with the task of building a new city office that would authorize charter schools. David Harris began the effort by examining best practices in charter school authorization across the country and building a roster of outside experts from academia, the private sector, and leading nonprofits to advise him. Five years later, in 2006, Bart Peterson and David Harris accepted Harvard's prestigious Innovations in American Government Award for the Indianapolis Mayor's Charter Schools initiative that they established.

Based on this experience, David Harris believed that for Indianapolis's charter sector and public education system to advance further, the city needed a critical mass of talented and innovative teachers and school leaders. To bring this about, it would be necessary to provide the right support and incentives for talent to thrive in Indianapolis and to create an attractive culture of education innovation. In 2006, David Harris started a nonprofit, The Mind Trust, to accomplish these goals.

THE MIND TRUST TODAY

Since its inception, The Mind Trust has developed and refined its strategic approach and grown steadily. Table 6.1 below shows The Mind Trust's income and expenditures for 2012.

As the table shows, The Mind Trust is not a large organization. To accomplish the mission that The Mind Trust has set and the changes it has envisioned, The Mind Trust has worked with and through others in an entrepreneurial way to become a catalyst for change. The Mind Trust programs harness and empower the creativity and energy of those seeking to improve the public education system. In this way, The Mind Trust can leverage its resources and magnify its impact. The Mind Trust is strategically advancing three agendas:

1. Empower entrepreneurs and change makers to start and improve schools and programs
2. Build networks to create and sustain local and national public education change
3. Initiate public dialogue to establish priorities and parameters for public education

TABLE 6.1 The Mind Trust 2012 Income and Expenditures*

Source of Income	FY 2012 Amount	Percentage of Total
National Foundation Giving	951,210	23%
Local Foundation Giving	1,882,568	46%
Corporate Giving	626,200	15%
Individual Giving	288,243	7%
Government Grants	250,000	6%
Nonprofit Grants	84,344	2%
Miscellaneous Income	14,118	0%
Total Revenue	4,096,683	100%
Expenditures	**FY 2012**	**Percentage of Total**
Core Operations Expenses	583,267	14%
TMT Programs and Initiatives	1,551,860	38%
Grants and Awards to Partner Organizations	1,961,556	48%
Total Expenditures	4,096,683	100%

*Money received and expended in 2012.

Source: The Mind Trust

IMPACT AND EFFECTIVENESS

The Mind Trust has compiled an impressive array of accomplishments in a short period of time. This can be attributed to the entrepreneurial way that The Mind Trust has approached the initiatives it has launched. While the ideas about educational reform that underlie The Mind Trust's work are broadly available, The Mind Trust's success has been due to the scope and scale of the initiatives it has launched, the degree to which they have reinforced each other, and their focus on one geographic area. As a result of this approach, The Mind Trust has been able to strategically influence the Indianapolis urban education ecosystem.

CONCLUSIONS

The Mind Trust's Approach to Educational Change Using a Social Entrepreneurial Approach

Bloom and Dees (2008) describe how significant problems in social systems can be addressed: "[S]ocial entrepreneurs must understand and often alter the social system that creates and sustains the problems in the first place. . . . To understand and change these social systems, social entrepreneurs should borrow insights from ecology and use an ecosystems framework" (p. 47). The social ecosystems of a service area include resource providers, service organizations (in cooperation or competition), beneficiaries or customers, opponents and problem makers, affected or influential bystanders, and the larger environment within which interactions take place (laws, policies, social norms, demographic trends, and cultural institutions).

According to Bloom and Dees, there are two ways to create systemic change in ecosystems. The Mind Trust has utilized both approaches. The clearest way is to change one or more of the environmental conditions that shape the behavior of players. The Mind Trust initiatives have engaged public policy on education, influenced the way that educators and educational organizations interact, contributed to the creation of a culture of innovation in education, and bolstered the educational infrastructure. Bloom and Dees's second way to create change is to introduce an innovation that spreads well enough to establish new and stable behavior patterns. The Mind Trust has contributed to the development and spread of significant innovations through its support of educational entrepreneurs and charter schools.

In a study of nonprofits that have had significant impacts on their environments, Grant and Crutchfield (2007) describe the characteristics of what they call high-impact nonprofits. The Mind Trust exemplifies these characteristics. They include the five characteristics discussed below.

1. Serve and advocate: Large-scale change cannot be accomplished through service delivery alone. Policy advocacy is necessary. The Mind Trust through its own activity and the networks it has created has been a vigorous proponent of policy change.

2. Make markets work: Large social problems often involve both market and nonmarket dimensions. Market dynamics can be used to mobilize behavior in efficient and effective ways. Through its support of charter schools, The Mind Trust initiatives have enhanced the competitive aspects of public education.
3. Inspire evangelists: The Mind Trust has built a strong community of supporters who help it advance its goals. These include volunteers, donors, and advisors. The far-reaching nature of The Mind Trust's initiatives has created strong commitment among supporters.
4. Nurture nonprofit networks: This has been a hallmark of The Mind Trust since its inception, and a number of influential networks have been established.
5. Share leadership: The Mind Trust has been instrumental in bringing leadership to Indianapolis as well as creating opportunities for additional local leaders to develop.

Program Impacts

The Mind Trust has created a robust network of organizations and talented people. Because of this network's scale and effects, education innovators, excellent teachers, policy experts, and reform advocates from across the country have come to Indianapolis and made impacts on the city's education system. *The Indianapolis Star* (Tully, 2012) wrote that The Mind Trust

> has singlehandedly changed the tenor of the debate surrounding the city's schools and brought an army of education talent to Indianapolis in recent years . . . has done what might have seemed impossible not so long ago: convinced people that while it won't be easy or fast, the potential to turn around an urban center's struggling education system is real. (para. 2)

In 6 years, The Mind Trust has impacted the lives of 77,417 Indianapolis children and their families. Table 6.2 below shows the impacts of selected programs that The Mind Trust has initiated and supported (The Mind Trust, 2012).

In addition to these impacts, over the next 5 to 10 years, the *Charter School Incubator* is expected to help to start 15 to 20 charter schools serving up to 10,000 students in Indianapolis. The Mind Trust selected its first two recipients in summer 2012 from among 35 applicants from 18 states. The winners include the George & Veronica Phalen Leadership Academies and Christel House (The Mind Trust, 2013a).

- George & Veronica Phalen Leadership Academies: Started by Education Entrepreneur Fellow Earl Martin Phalen, these K–8 schools incorporate rigorous standards, an innovative instructional approach, and strong parent engagement to help students excel. Classrooms are organized in pods around computer labs, allowing students to rotate from large-group instruction into individualized tutoring, small-group project work, online learning and independent study. The first school was launched in 2013. A total of five schools will be established over the next 7 years to serve at least 3,000 students annually.

TABLE 6.2 Impact of Selected The Mind Trust Programs

Program	Description	Impact
Teach for America	Recruits top college graduates who commit to teach for 2 years in underserved public schools. Through the process, they often become lifelong leaders in the pursuit of educational equity.	Placed 577 teachers in Indianapolis classrooms. The average improvements of their students are in the top quarter of Indiana students.
Indianapolis Teaching Fellows (TNTP)	Draws talented professionals from noneducation backgrounds to become teachers in subjects such as math, science, foreign language, and special education.	Three quarters of Indianapolis Teaching Fellows are rated better than other first-year teachers by their supervisors.
Teach Plus Teaching Policy Fellowship	Engaged Indianapolis public school teachers as education policy experts and advocates. Helps stem the exodus of highly effective urban teachers from classrooms in their initial years of teaching.	Engaged about 40 Indianapolis public school teachers.
Summer Advantage USA	Provides rigorous academic and enrichment programs during the summer months for underperforming, low-income students to combat the learning regression that takes place during those months.	Enrolled 6,700 mostly low-income students. Students progressed by an average of 2.5 months in reading and math during the 5-week program.
College Summit	Increases college attendance rates among low-income students by fostering a college-going culture in high schools and helping students to navigate the application process.	Assisted 8,510 students in Indianapolis. On average, these participants are three times more likely to enroll in college than their nonparticipant peers.
Stand for Children	Built grassroots support for transformative education policies and spread critical awareness of school options among parents and key stakeholders.	Engaged more than 300 parents, teachers, and students as education reform advocates in Indianapolis.
FosterEd	Provided foster children with educational advocates who work on the students' behalf to improve their academic outcomes.	Served over 2,500 foster children in Indianapolis. Because of the program's success, the Indiana Department of Child Services funded the expansion of FosterEd throughout the state.

- Christel House: This well-regarded local nonprofit created a five-school network with two types of schools. The first type is a K–12 model that replicates the existing Christel House Academy, which has produced among the best results in the state among low-income students. The first Christel House Academy expansion school, slated to serve 750 students, opened in 2014. A second school model is called Dropout Recovery Schools (DORS). The first DORS (Christel House DORS), which prepares former high-school dropouts for college and career success and serves about 300 students, was launched in 2012.

In addition, The Mind Trust's efforts have made Indianapolis an attractive place to launch new schools and education initiatives. As a result, talented people from across the country have come to and remained in Indianapolis. They are continuing to improve public education. The Mind Trust's network has produced

- 499 high-quality classroom teachers
- 40 world-class school leaders
- Two reform-minded members of the Indianapolis Public Schools Board
- 22 education policy and advocacy leaders
- The city's first deputy mayor of education

The summary numbers above are ample evidence of the utility of The Mind Trust's strategy and its significant impact. Each program, however, has a compelling story to tell about how innovative change can be made. Below we present more details on a program in line with one of The Mind Trust's three approaches.

Summer Advantage: Empower Entrepreneurs and Change Makers

On average, students from low-income communities lose 3 months of learning during the summer because of limited academic opportunities. Summer Advantage USA reverses that trend by providing students with academic programs and enrichment opportunities such as art, music, field trips, and guest speakers (http://www.summeradvantage.org). Earl Martin Phalen, a Harvard Law School alumnus and founder of two other education-focused nonprofits, started Summer Advantage in 2009 through The Mind Trust's Education Entrepreneur Fellowship.

The program has been successful. In 2009, 863 students were served, and by 2012 this figure had risen to 1,800. In total, 6,699 children in Indianapolis have been served. After 5 weeks of Summer Advantage, students experience 2.9 months' gain in mathematics and 2.5 months' gain in reading and language arts. In addition, parents and students are satisfied (http://summeradvantage.org/impact).

- 95% of Summer Advantage parents would recommend Summer Advantage to other parents and 91% of them would sign their children up for the program again.
- 91% of students attended the program daily, 95% reported that they like to learn, and 96% said that they felt like the adults at Summer Advantage care about them.

The founder, Earl Martin Phalen, exemplifies the type of entrepreneur and creative leader that The Mind Trust seeks out and supports to leverage its impact and spread innovation in the public education system (The Mind Trust, 2013b). Earl Martin Phalen was born into the foster care system in 1967, a time when 70% of his African American male peers in foster care would end up in jail. He was adopted by George and Veronica Phalen, and their passion for education propelled him to success. Phalen graduated from Yale University and Harvard Law School. Having witnessed the transformative power of education, Phalen has dedicated the past 20 years of his life to expanding the life opportunities of children through learning and academic engagement. As a Harvard Law School student, Phalen cofounded Building Educated Leaders for Life (BELL, http://www.experiencebell.org), which grew from a community service project educating 20 children to a national nonprofit annually educating 15,000 scholars with a budget of $27.5 million.

Phalen's work has been noted by the *New York Times*, *Parents Magazine*, *Education Week*, ABC World News, and recognized by the entertainment industry at the BET (Black Entertainment Television) Awards. Summer Advantage USA has been recognized by the White House, *Time* magazine, and MSNBC. Based on the high achievement of Summer Advantage scholars, in 2012 the Indiana Charter School Board granted approval to the George and Veronica Phalen Leadership Academies to open 10 new Academies. The Mind Trust also provided support for this initiative. Named after Earl's parents, the Academies will provide a high-quality, academic, and enriching blended learning curriculum to over 10,000 children.

CEE-Trust: Building Networks to Create and Sustain Change

In 2010, The Mind Trust recruited a number of peer organizations from other cities to join a new network that the organization founded called the Cities for Education Entrepreneurship Trust (CEE-Trust). CEE-Trust is a growing national network of 27 city-focused foundations, nonprofits, and mayors' offices that work together to promote education innovation and reform. CEE-Trust is broadly focused on helping members create ecosystems for education innovation and reform in their cities. CEE-Trust facilitates the growth of entrepreneurial education initiatives, shares high-impact reform strategies between cities, and helps communities design and launch city-based initiatives that champion education innovation and reform (http://www.cee-trust.org).

Acting as a convener, collaborator, and consultant, CEE-Trust helps cities across the country establish strong conditions for education reform

- Convening: The CEE-Trust network gathers annually and leads working groups on individual topics like charter school incubation, school governance reform, and blended learning. Through various convenings, CEE-Trust shares lessons learned, fosters communication, documents best practices, and helps cities improve their efforts to drive the education reform agenda forward.
- Collaborating: CEE-Trust helps members explore new reform strategies, develop and execute collaborative projects, and partner with education entrepreneurs looking for opportunities to expand their programs.

- Consulting: CEE-Trust provides members with limited consulting support as they explore or implement new reform projects. It also offers more in-depth consulting services to city-focused groups that are interested in developing education reform strategies informed by lessons learned through CEE-Trust's work with its members.
- CEE-Trust member organizations have the opportunity to participate in smaller working groups that convene a few times per year (http://www.cee-trust.org/about/workinggroups.aspx). Each of the working groups increases members' understanding of a given topic in education reform, helps members overcome specific challenges, and explores new connections and collaborations between cities. They include:
  - School Governance Reform Working Group: Focuses on exploring ways in which CEE-Trust member organizations are driving major changes to the structure and governance of their school systems.
  - Charter Incubation Working Group: Explores strategies for growing the charter sector by investing in the recruitment, selection, training, and support of school leaders as they develop and launch new schools.
  - Blended Learning Working Group: Focuses on building members' understandings of the emerging blended learning field. This group makes site visits to blended learning schools, meets with national thought leaders, and has special access to winners of the Gates Foundation's Next Generation Learning Challenges—a business plan competition for emerging blended learning school leaders.
  - Funding for Ed Reform Working Group: Explores issues relating to how city-focused funders can play a leading role in education reform, including questions around risk (how to help foundations and boards be more open to risk in their decision making), developing common metrics and accountability goals as a sector, establishing best practices in grant making, and building community support for change.

Opportunity Schools Report: Initiating Dialogue to Change Systems

In December 2011, The Mind Trust made policy recommendations with the release of a 155-page report, *Creating Opportunity Schools,* which presents a comprehensive vision for restructuring IPS. The Center on Reinventing Public Education's Paul Hill told *Education Week* it puts Indianapolis "on the leading edge of . . . efforts to redefine the school system" (Samuels, 2012). The plan's key components include

- Shift control of key decisions and most resources from its central office to individual schools.
- Invest millions in existing funds to attract talented teachers and school leaders to the district.
- Launch new, world-class schools to replace failing programs. Redirect existing resources to provide pre–K for all 4-year-olds in IPS.
- Allow all parents to choose schools that best meet their children's needs.

Since its release, the plan has received more than 90 media mentions in outlets ranging from *The Indianapolis Star* to *Education Week*. *Creating Opportunity Schools* presented a detailed analysis of the way IPS currently operates and specific recommendations for altering those operations in a way designed to maximize district effectiveness. The specificity and thoughtfulness of the plan gave the community tangible ideas to discuss in a series of community conversations as well as the 2012 IPS Board races.

Several other groups have offered their own district-overhaul plans. Key organizations convened a series of 24 community conversations attended by more than 600 people to get public input on The Mind Trust's and other groups' plans for improving IPS. As *The Indianapolis Star* editorialized in December 2011, "The Mind Trust has done this city a tremendous favor with today's release of its dramatic plan to overhaul Indianapolis Public Schools. . . . This is the start of what needs to be a long conversation" (Murray & Berggoetz, 2011).

In addition, it has been widely reported that The Mind Trust's plan catalyzed a turnover in IPS board leadership in the 2012 election. Four reform-minded candidates who, it was reported, embraced significant elements of The Mind Trust's plan, were elected to the board, leading *The Indianapolis Star* and other observers to conclude that change in IPS is likely and that such change could include some of the elements of the *Creating Opportunity Schools* report (Elliot, 2012).

DISCUSSION QUESTIONS

1. Social entrepreneurship begins with the recognition of an opportunity to create social value. The opportunity David Harris recognized lead eventually to The Mind Trust. What was the opportunity Harris recognized? What social value did he envision creating? Why was this social value not being created before?

2. What factors might have led David Harris to see and pursue the opportunity when others did not? To what extent were the factors person or situational? Consider the role that prior experience might have played. How useful were social networks? Did the availability of assets play a part?

3. The Mind Trust's programs involved supporting and working with other organizations and individuals rather than providing direct services. What are the advantages and disadvantages of this "support" model? Could The Mind Trust have had the degree of impact it did using the "direct service" model? Why or why not?

4. To what extent did The Mind Trust use networks to accomplish its goals? Why was The Mind Trust successful in establishing and using these networks?

5. Who are The Mind Trust's major stakeholders? Consider both public and private sector actors. How might these different stakeholders assess the effectiveness of The Mind Trust? Might these assessments differ? If so, how could or should The Mind Trust respond to these differences?

6. Scaling (increasing the impact) of a venture can entail more extensive local activity (scaling deep), expanding operations to other geographic areas (scaling out),

or providing information, technical assistance, or advocacy (indirect). Which technique(s) did The Mind Trust employ? Why do you think they used this/these?

7. Could an organization like The Mind Trust be established in other communities? How transferable to other communities is The Mind Trust's model? What factors might facilitate this and what factors might inhibit the establishment?

REFERENCES

Bloom, P., & Dees, G. (2008, Winter). Cultivate your ecosystem. *Stanford Social Innovation Review*, 47–63.

Education Week. (1998, January 8). Quality counts '98: The urban challenge, public education in the 50 states. *Education Week, 17*.

Elliott, S. (2012, August 26). Our children, our city: Election may step up IPS reform. *The Indianapolis Star*. Retrieved from http://www.indystar.com/article/20120826/NEWS04/208260353/Our-Children-Our-City-Election-may-step-up-IPS-reform?nclick_check = 1

Grant, H., & Crutchfield, L. (2007). Creating high-impact nonprofits. Stanford Social Innovation Review, Fall: 32–41.

Hughes, A. (2010, July 10). A brief history of the Indianapolis Public School System (IPS). Retrieved from http://voices.yahoo.com/a-brief-history-indianapolis-public-school-6460956.html?cat = 8

Indiana Department of Education. (2013a). PL221. Retrieved from http://www.doe.in.gov/accountability/pl-221

Indiana Department of Education. (2013b). *2012 A–F statewide totals—Percentages and total schools*. Retrieved from http://www.doe.in.gov/sites/default/files/accountability/statewideonepagerfinal.pdf

Indianapolis Public Schools. (2013). *Indianapolis Public Schools 2010–2015 strategic plan*. Retrieved from http://schoolboard.ips.k12.in.us/files/2012/12/2010-15StrategicPlan-copy.pdf

Mayor to take control of four struggling Indy schools. (2013, February 6). *Indiana Business Journal*. Retrieved from http://www.ibj.com/mayor-to-take-control-of-four-struggling-indy-schools/PARAMS/article/39478

The Mind Trust. (2011). *Creating opportunity schools: A bold plan to transform Indianapolis schools*. Indianapolis, IN: Author.

The Mind Trust. (2012, October). *A landscape transformed: A report on the impact of the Grow What Works Campaign*. Indianapolis, IN: Author.

The Mind Trust. (2013a). *The Mind Trust*. Indianapolis, IN: Author. Retrieved from http://www.themindtrust.org/files/file/tmt-overview-2013.pdf

The Mind Trust. (2013b). *Summer Advantage USA*. Indianapolis, IN: Author.

Mondale, S. (2002). *School: The story of American public education*. Boston, MA: Beacon Press.

Murray, J., & Berggoetz, B. (2011, December 25). Top 10 local stories of 2011. *The Indianapolis Star*. Retrieved from http://www.indystar.com/article/20111225/NEWS/112250342

National Commission on Excellence in Education. (1983). *A nation at risk: The imperative for educational reform*. Washington, DC: U.S. Department of Education.

Ravitch, D. (1998, August). *A new era in urban education?* (Brookings Policy Brief Series #35). Retrieved from http://www.brookings.edu/research/papers/1998/08/education-ravitch

Samuels, C. (2012a, January 24). Bold remake proposed for Indianapolis schools. *Education Week*. Retrieved from http://www.edweek.org/ew/articles/2012/01/25/18indy.h31.html

Stokes, K. (2011, August 25). What happened to six Indianapolis public schools Thursday? *StateImpact*. Retrieved from http://stateimpact.npr.org/indiana/2011/08/25/what-happened-to-six-indianapolis-public-schools-today/

Stokes, K. (2012, February 9). Feds approve Indiana's "No Child Left Behind" waiver. *StateImpact*. Retrieved from http://stateimpact.npr.org/indiana/2012/02/09/report-feds-approve-indianas-no-child-left-behind-waiver/

Tully, M. (2012, October 10). The Mind Trust continues to be dynamic force for education reform. *The Indianapolis Star*. Retrieved from http://www.themindtrust.org/files/documents/october2012tullycolumnwebversion-1.pdf

Weiss, S. (2003). *Nation at risk continues to affect education system*. Presented at the National Forum on Education Policy, July 13–16, Denver, Colorado. Cited in *Education Week* (2004, August 3). A nation at risk. Retrieved from http://www.edweek.org/ew/issues/a-nation-at-risk/

CHAPTER 7

GiveIndia

Web Donations in an Emerging Philanthropic Market

Micheal L. Shier
Factor-Inwentash Faculty of Social Work, University of Toronto

Femida Handy
School of Social Policy and Practice, University of Pennsylvania

INTRODUCTION

This case study provides an overview of an innovative approach undertaken by the nonprofit organization, GiveIndia, which acts as an intermediary organization linking donors with nonprofit organizations and their service recipients through a web-based donation platform. Since that process has been going on for years, GiveIndia is innovative in three respects. First, it is because of its use of technology and its successful adaptation of philanthropic giving to a changing technological environment. Second GiveIndia's model of operation is innovative in reducing overall administrative costs. And third, the general structure of GiveIndia's program is innovative in its ability to assure donors that their money is being spent as they directed. Each of these innovations is discussed along with the organization's development and the problem and context in which the innovations emerged.

THE PROBLEM

Indigenous nongovernmental organizations (NGOs) existed throughout India prior to Independence (1947). Many of these initial organizations focused on gaining freedom and political rights, in addition to providing services to the poor. Since Independence, NGOs have been more active in providing direct services and advocating for lower castes, women, and the environment. An increasing emphasis has been placed on not only specialized services for specific population groups but also local challenges and needs. This network of NGOs has been central to addressing the persistent and emerging challenges within local communities in India, where many direct human services are not directly funded by the national government as they are in most western developed nations (Handy, Kassam, Feeney, & Ranade, 2006; Sen, 1993, 1999). Thus, due to India's political and social context, NGOs are especially important for advocating and providing direct services to this nation's vulnerable populations. This chapter focuses on how Indian NGOs, which must survive in a climate of bureaucracy, corruption, and a lack of philanthropic culture, successfully secure sufficient financial resources for human services.

Currently in India (like elsewhere), NGOs have been seen as agents of development, especially in rural areas where the government lacks resources or is inefficient and overly bureaucratic (Datta, 2000). The Indian government does provide some support for NGOs, but it is limited and often only given to NGOs that have political connections. Another source of funding is international entities. While foreign funders (government and private) provide direct funding to many locally based NGOs, such funding is difficult to attain due to the many political constraints on NGOs receiving foreign funds, notwithstanding the legal restrictions qualifying organizations to receive international donations. However, this funding is not sufficient to address the plethora of social, environmental, and health-related issues experienced by the Indian population. Thus, NGOs are increasingly finding new ways to raise funds from domestic sources. With India's economic prosperity in the last decade, more domestic funds are becoming available for social and environmental causes. With Internet technology booming in India, NGOs have thus gone online to generate donations from the public (locally, nationally, and internationally). This method has gained popularity because it remains a relatively inexpensive way to reach multitudes.

Current levels of prosperity among higher income earners in India have resulted in increased annual private charitable giving, ranging from $5 billion to $6 billion (Sheth & Singhal, 2011). As such, the following questions arise: How do NGOs in local communities gain access to these private charitable resources? And given that there are individuals willing to make donations, how do they access these locally based organizations from which they are at geographic distances?

In India, and elsewhere throughout the world, NGOs are increasingly challenged to make meaningful connections with the general public. This includes those within and beyond their local communities, the business sector, local and national governments, and international entities. A further challenge for NGOs in India is their ability to create a positive perception in the public sphere about their legitimacy and trustworthiness. NGOs must find a way to inspire trust within the general public and convince potential donors that they are above corruption. Generating trust in a highly corrupt society is no easy task, and India's NGOs face an uphill battle doing so; India is ranked 94 among 174 countries in the Corruption Perceptions Index 2012, by Transparency International. Such corruption exists at all levels of society and impacts the daily lives of its citizens.

Furthermore, NGOs in India exist within a highly competitive nonprofit sector that further inhibits access to sufficient financial resources. According to one government report, an estimated 3.3 million nongovernmental organizations exist in India (Government of

India, 2009). Based on current population estimates, this figure represents one organization for every 400 people in the country. With so many NGOs competing for financial resources, the ability of an organization to meet its financial targets can be difficult and impair its mission.

This chapter examines an innovative fundraising tool developed and used by one Mumbai-based NGO, GiveIndia. Using the Internet to secure online donations, GiveIndia took on the challenge, in an inexpensive manner, of how to establish donor trust in legitimate NGOs who want to raise money from domestic and international donors. In the social and political climate where newspapers report daily on the local corruption in the public, for-profit, and NGO sectors, this effort was a daunting challenge: to convince potential donors that their hard earned donations would not be lining the pockets of corrupt NGO staff members, but rather would reach the intended beneficiaries.

In response to this challenge, GiveIndia was developed in 2000 as an online donation platform with a mission to transfer funds from private donors (both individuals and businesses) to grassroots (or community-based) organizations that provide health, environmental, educational, and social services in India.

GiveIndia acts as an intermediary between local NGOs and those wanting to donate money to a specific cause or organization. Taking on this role as intermediary was not necessarily unique at the time of GiveIndia's development. There were other nonprofit organizations in India acting in a similar capacity, such as Child Rights and You (CRY). The latter organization was developed in 1979, and it took on the role of intermediary between donors and NGOs providing services to children living in poverty. It relied primarily on direct mail campaigns, thus not tapping into the efficiency of the Internet to make connections between organizations and donors. The innovative quality of GiveIndia's online donation platform is based on its use of technology, the structure of the program, and the connections that are made between donors and recipients; these aspects are discussed in the following section.

Before moving to the case study of GiveIndia, however, it is important to highlight our understanding of the concept of innovation among NGOs. Scholarship on the phenomenon of innovation and change in and among nonprofit organizations has been somewhat void of metatheoretical perspectives. A metatheoretical perspective about innovation and nonprofit organizations is a theory that acts to explain why—and under what conditions—these organizations undertake innovative programs and initiatives. Instead, this area of scholarship has predominantly been informed by an empirical generalization (i.e., a relationship among variables that has been witnessed repeatedly though empirical analysis).

This dominant empirical generalization in the organizational theory literature is that internal operations of organizations are directly impacted by, and respond to, external environmental factors (Drori, Meyer, & Hwang, 2006; Jones, 2006; Mulroy, 2004)—a realization culminating in a perspective that has been termed *contingency theory* (Lawrence & Lorsch, 1967, and Thompson, 1967, cited in Hasenfeld 2010). The generalization is that the changing economic, political, cultural, social, and technological landscapes create a dynamic where organizations are challenged to evolve, restructure, and change. Innovation within nonprofit and nongovernmental organizations can be conceptualized around this empirical generalization (Shier & Graham, 2013).

But instead of viewing innovation only in a reactionary sense, where organizations are viewed as reactionary agents to changes in the external environment, we prefer to view organizations in more of a reciprocal relationship with their environments. People leading nonprofit organizations develop new organizations (or programs and initiatives within those organizations) that are in direct response to the needs emerging from their economic, political, cultural, social, and technological environments. These adaptations, in turn, influence the surrounding environment. Certainly this was the case for GiveIndia; it not only responded to the emerging needs and challenges of the developing nonprofit sector in India, but also addressed the conditions of corruption and poverty, as well as the technological and economic changes occurring simultaneously with emerging donating trends. GiveIndia's practices have helped change general public perceptions toward donating to local NGOs. More generally, GiveIndia has helped enhance the giving culture within India and has created interconnections locally, nationally, and globally to address issues directly impacting Indians.

THE INNOVATIONS

GiveIndia (www.giveindia.com), headquartered in Mumbai and founded by Venkat Krishna, is a nonprofit online fundraising platform. Venkat Krishna is a graduate of the country's premier business school: Indian Institute of Management Ahmedabad. This educational background had an influence on the particular development of GiveIndia. Beyond his business school education background, Venkat Krishna also cites several other reasons for creating GiveIndia, including ideological and spiritual beliefs; moreover, he mentions his practical observations about the disconnect between organizations and donors within India. People like him who develop organizations—some of which are seen as innovative—are influenced a great deal by their histories because those histories influence their perspectives of the present (Shier, Graham, Deane, & Jones, 2013). Venkat Krishna's experiences and history have greatly influenced the mission, goals, and day-to-day operations of GiveIndia.

GiveIndia's mission is "to promote an efficient and effective giving culture that provides greater opportunities to the poor in India." Its vision is to have "a strong 'giving' culture where Indians donate 2% of their income every year to give the poor a chance and a vibrant 'philanthropy marketplace' to ensure that the most efficient and effective nonprofits get access to the most resources" (GiveIndia, 2011). Its operating model, influenced by the business school's return on investment model, perceives each potential donor as an investor in promoting social good, with this investor looking for social returns regarding bettering the life of the poor through education, health, and other means (GiveIndia, 2011).

This vision is manifested in the program focus and structure of GiveIndia. By making connections between donors and NGOs, GiveIndia helps support the development of a giving culture within India. Also, in auditing and evaluating organizations that are the recipients of funds donated through GiveIndia, the organization acts as a regulatory mechanism to ensure that funds are used appropriately. This is an important point when understanding the unique nature of GiveIndia. People do not give to GiveIndia, they give *through* GiveIndia. It only acts as a web-based platform for receiving donations on behalf of 200 NGOs that are providing community-level services. What is also unique is that approximately 90% of the money that is channeled directly through GiveIndia reaches the organization or individual for whom it was intended. The overhead administrative costs only account for approximately 10% of all directly channeled donated money (GiveIndia, 2012). Many other organizations that act as intermediaries between donors and organizations (but utilize different linking techniques) utilize 30% to 50% of funds intended to be directly channeled to a particular cause or organization for administrative or other overhead-related costs.

Beyond creating a new organization to address emerging challenges (as we have described in the case of GiveIndia), *innovation* has also been defined within the literature as new, within-organization initiatives created to meet changing administrative and technological needs, including fundraising, resource sharing, and technological improvements (see, for example, Mano, 2009; Sargeant, 2001); direct practice innovations, including implementation of evidence-based practices and changing methods of intervention (see, for example, Cook & Sabah, 2009; Murray, 2009; Simpson, 2009); and program implementation, that includes the structure of the programs and the procedures utilized in the way services are provided (see, for example, Blue-Howells, McGuire, & Nakashima, 2008; Prince & Austin, 2001; Shier & Graham, 2013; Wood, 2007). In this order, Jaskyte and Lee (2006) refer to these three types of innovative programs or initiatives as administrative, product, and process innovations. GiveIndia's model of operation is an example of a process innovation. For instance, GiveIndia's organizational structure was developed to minimize administrative costs. In part this is achieved by the way GiveIndia interacts with donors through the online platform. However, further research is needed to investigate the specific ways in which GiveIndia is able to keep their costs of managing the donations so low. The findings could have practical implications for other similar programs struggling with sustainability.

In general, the structure of GiveIndia's program is an example of a product innovation. For instance, to maintain integrity and to provide assurance to donors that their money is going to be used for intended purposes, GiveIndia undertakes an extensive screening process, sometimes lasting up to 12 months, to determine the legitimacy of the NGOs they work with. GiveIndia scrutinizes annual reports and financial records from the local NGO's receiving funds, conducts audits, as well as visits NGO sites to ensure that the organization affiliated with GiveIndia is legitimate, efficient, and not corrupt (for further information see http://www.giveindia.org/t-certified.aspx). The unique aspect of this structure is that GiveIndia considers not the NGO but rather the donor as its client. Donors need to be assured that the money they donate is going to be utilized in the way that they had intended it to be spent, and that the feedback reports from the NGO are authentic. Through these process innovations, GiveIndia provides a framework in which donors can feel confident about how their money is spent.

How this process works in practice is that potential donors go to the GiveIndia website (www.giveindia.org), have the opportunity to conduct an online search for various donation options, and select a particular cause or organization in India to which they want to donate. With GiveIndia, donors learn about the charitable organizations related to the cause they are interested in and can target their donations with accuracy; they can choose the cause and the target recipients and assemble a donation to suit their interests (e.g., providing free medical checkups for 12 women over the age of 70, in a particular village, and the donation can be structured as a one-time gift, a series of multiple gifts, or as part of a monthly giving program). Furthermore, the donors also receive updates about who was helped and how the money they donated has helped. The feedback is given to enhance the donor's satisfaction, reinforce the NGO's credibility, and promote transparency for GiveIndia.

GiveIndia provides two other programs that engage donors in different ways than this online giving program: the payroll giving program and the high net worth individual program. The payroll giving program allows for employees of participating companies to provide a monthly donation that is directly withheld from employee earnings. Employees still follow the tailored approach described previously to direct their donations. The high net worth individual program seeks to target wealthy individuals or corporations in creating tailored donations that are larger sums of money. In the fiscal year ending in 2012, Rs. 270,922,000 were raised in donations. Of this total, 30% was raised through the Online Giving and Retail Program (23% was donated through GiveIndia by offline channels), 35% was raised through the Payroll Giving Program, and 12% was raised through the High Net Worth Individuals Program (GiveIndia, 2012). As these numbers demonstrate, the payroll giving program represents the greatest proportion of the total donated through GiveIndia, but the amount donated through the online retail giving program is nearly as substantial.

In 2011, the authors conducted a study involving GiveIndia donors (Shier & Handy, 2012) and found that of the approximately 735 respondents (approximately a 12% response rate of those who had donated through GiveIndia during the time period of data collection), 67% had donated money online through GiveIndia in the last 12 months, but only 28% had donated money online to some other program in the same time period. In comparison, 56% reported donating money offline within the last 12 months. From these results we speculate that there is an emerging market for donating online if the approach is appealing to the needs of the donor. Their study also found that people on average donate more offline than they do online (but the gap between those who donate online through GiveIndia and offline is shrinking). For instance, those who donated money online through GiveIndia donated on average approximately Rs. 5,700, while those donating offline reported donating on average Rs. 6,200. Those respondents who donated online to some other organization, on average only donated approximately Rs. 3,500.

Furthermore, the study found that potential GiveIndia donors were satisfied with the use of the Internet technology in making their donations. Only 12% of the sample reported being less satisfied with online donating than offline donating. Forty-two percent of respondents reported being more satisfied with online donating, and 45% reported being equally satisfied with online donating and offline donating. Also, many respondents (62%) reported that they did not perceive online donating to be any riskier than other methods of donating money. The extent to which GiveIndia helps foster these positive attitudes toward online donating requires further empirical investigation. However, as it stands, individuals are willing to engage in online donating at the same level of giving as they do with offline donating. GiveIndia has successfully established an innovative platform by following an umbrella fundraising approach on behalf of NGOs.

GIVEINDIA'S DEVELOPMENT

In early 2000, Venkat Krishna proposed the idea to develop the organization of GiveIndia. He received financial support through a network of connections; in particular, he received Rs. 1 million from ICICI Bank to fund his initial business plan. This allowed GiveIndia to register as a nonprofit organization in April of 2000. Venkat Krishna initially planned that GiveIndia would be developed and taken over by the ICICI Bank as part of an internal department of the bank that was newly developing, called the Social Initiatives Group. The intention was to develop an e-commerce platform to facilitate and transfer donations to local NGOs. In its early inception, there was a close relationship between the operations of GiveIndia and the ICICI Bank. The bank provided legitimacy for the development of the GiveIndia organization, and it also provided contacts through customer and employee lists. The initial website was also developed by information technology staff at ICICI Bank. Eventually, after 2 years of fostering this relationship with ICICI Bank, GiveIndia became independent, although it still maintains a working relationship with ICICI Bank, particularly with its payroll donor program.

The development of GiveIndia was based on a conceptualization of its founder, but to build the organization, a lot of resources were required and social network connections were instrumental. Furthermore, in the formative years of the organization as a result of its connections with the ICICI bank, GiveIndia was granted permission to receive foreign contributions to the relief efforts after the Gujarat earthquake in June 2001. This is an important institutional aspect to consider, because the current legal framework is heavily bureaucratic with many barriers to NGOs receiving international donations, thus restricting transnational giving to India (Jalali, 2008). The fact that GiveIndia was granted general registration under the Foreign Contribution Regulation Act very early in its existence is unique and not something that generally happens until years after formation.

CONCLUSIONS

GiveIndia is an innovative nonprofit because of the development of its program in response to changing aspects of its technological and economic environment. Likewise, after the organization's establishment, GiveIndia's staff developed the structure and day-to-day operations in such a way that their model became innovative, particularly regarding both product and process innovations. At present, there are no studies about the effectiveness and efficiency of GiveIndia's program; however, the study conducted by Shier and Handy (2012) on donor perspectives about GiveIndia (and the factors that contribute to whether or not individuals are willing to donate online) provides some evidence that donors are comfortable with donating through GiveIndia. GiveIndia's program has also helped develop a giving culture within India, which was one of its stated intentions. In Shier and Handy's study, 86% of respondents reported they were from India. Moreover, GiveIndia is reaching donors in villages and small, medium, and large cities throughout India.

While there has not been any evaluation research conducted on GiveIndia, we do believe that, based on the historical development of the organization, its model is replicable. To some extent, it has been replicated. Since GiveIndia's inception, similar online donating platforms have emerged. Developed around the same time as GiveIndia in April 2000, DonorsChoose.org was developed in the United States and acts as an online donor platform to fund educational projects in the United States. Likewise, in 2002, GlobalGiving.org was launched and acts as an intermediary between donors and local development projects throughout the world. Other similar donation platforms have developed in India (such as the Karmic Foundation). Thus, the use of online platforms through which to donate has grown considerably in recent years. This is evident in the increasing amount of money donated through these online organizations or programs. For instance, Vanderkam (2010) points out that, between 2004 and 2008, the online programs "Modest Needs grew from $194,379 to $2.7 million in revenue, GlobalGiving grew from $508,653 to $7.4 million and DonorsChoose.org grew from $2.8 million to $18 million" (p. 11A). Likewise, GiveIndia has grown considerably since its inception. In its first year of operation (2000–2001) it supported the transfer of Rs. 9.7 million, and from 2011 to 2012 it raised approximately Rs. 240 million (see http://www.giveindia.org/t-abtus_achievements.aspx) for 245 NGOs across India. Furthermore, within GiveIndia's payroll giving program, there are 110 participating companies with 38,000 active employees (GiveIndia, 2012).

In sum, GiveIndia has been a success. However, one final point is important to consider. In many attempts to describe innovation, the sky is perceived as the limit, and individual leaders are described as the source of innovation. This certainly has been the case among scholars writing about entrepreneurial leadership (see, for example, Rose-Ackerman, 1996; Ruvio, Rosenblatt, & Hertz-Lazarowitz, 2010; Weerawardena & Sullivan-Mort, 2006). Nevertheless, we also should ask: Are there constraints on what innovation can occur or be undertaken? Based on this case study, we would certainly argue that the political, legal, economic, and technological context of the organization has contributed to the type of innovation that can occur. This is evident in the description provided of how GiveIndia developed. Like elsewhere in the world, Indian nonprofit organizations exist in a particular rational-legal framework, developed through legislation and other public policy that provides the organization the legitimacy and authority it needs to exist. When trying to understand change and innovation (and limits placed on innovation), this context becomes particularly important. To believe that nonprofit organizations exist distinctly from the public sector (or the administrative bureaucracy of the state) as autonomous actors within the social environment disregards these dynamics of organizational development that have taken place in relation to the bureaucracy of the state. Instead, we believe these relationships define the interorganizational context in which nonprofit organizations play a part. Likewise, the problem and the innovative solutions are in part defined by this context, as in the case with GiveIndia.

DISCUSSION QUESTIONS

1. GiveIndia provides a useful case example to understand how a nonprofit organization is developed—in this particular case, developed within India. What is the process in which organizations are developed in other country contexts? Comparatively, are these processes similar?

2. When thinking about some innovations in your area of work or study, can you identify the different types of innovation that are undertaken (i.e., administrative, product, and process innovations)? In what ways is it useful to think about different types of innovation? What are some different outcomes that can be expected based on the type of innovation that is being undertaken?
3. Nonprofit organizations exist in a particular rational-legal context, typically defined by the legal structure of a given state. How is this understanding of context incorporated in theories of innovation? And in what ways can this context impact the types and nature of innovation that are developed?
4. In the case of GiveIndia, why did the fundraising Internet platform succeed? Can this be duplicated in another social or political context?

REFERENCES

Blue-Howells, J., McGuire, J., & Nakashima, J. (2008). Co-location of health care services for homeless veterans: A case study of innovation in program implementation. *Social Work in Health Care, 47*(3), 219–231.

Cook, P. G., & Sabah, Y. (2009). The role of virtual communities of practice in supporting collaborative learning among social workers. *British Journal of Social Work, 39*(4), 725–739.

Datta, R. (2000). On their own: Development strategies of the Self-Employed Women's Association (SEWA) in India. *Development, 43*(4), 51–55.

Drori, G. S., Meyer, J. W., & Hwang, H. (Eds.). (2006). *Globalization and organization: World society and organizational change.* Oxford, United Kingdom: Oxford University Press.

GiveIndia. (2011). *Our mission.* Retrieved from http://www.giveindia.org/t-abtus_mission.aspx

GiveIndia. (2012). *Annual report, 2011–2012.* Retrieved from http://www.giveindia.org/images/document/ar-final-2011-12.pdf

Government of India. (2009). *A survey on non profit institutions in India: Some findings.* New Delhi, India: Central Statistical Organisation, Ministry of Statistics and Programme Implementation.

Handy, F., Kassam, M., Feeney, S., & Ranade, B. (2006). *Grass-roots NGOs by women for women: The driving force of development in India.* New Delhi, India: Sage.

Hasenfeld, Y. (Ed.). (2010). *Human services as complex organizations.* Thousand Oaks, CA: Sage.

Jalali, R. (2008). International funding of NGO's in India: Bringing the state back in. *Voluntas, 19*, 161–188.

Jaskyte, K., & Lee, M. (2006). Interorganizational relationships: A source of innovation in nonprofit organizations? *Administration in Social Work, 30*(3), 43–54.

Jones, J. M. (2006). Understanding environmental influence on human service organizations: A study of the influence of managed care on child caring institutions. *Administration in Social Work, 30*(4), 63–90.

Mano, R. S. (2009). Information technology, adaptation and innovation in nonprofit human service organizations. *Journal of Technology in Human Services, 27*(3), 227–234.

Mulroy, E. A. (2004). Theoretical perspectives on the social environment to guide management and community practice: An organization-in-environment approach. *Administration in Social Work, 28*(1), 77–96.

Murray, C. E. (2009). Diffusion of innovation theory: A bridge for the research-practice gap in counseling. *Journal of Counseling and Development, 87*(1), 108–116.

Prince, J., & Austin, M. J. (2001). Innovative programs and practices emerging from the implementation of welfare reform: A cross-case analysis. *Journal of Community Practice, 9*(3), 1–14.

Rose-Ackerman, S. (1996). Altruism, nonprofits, and economic theory. *Journal of Economic Literature, 34*, 701–728.

Ruvio, A., Rosenblatt, Z., & Hertz-Lazarowitz, R. (2010). Entrepreneurial leadership vision in nonprofit vs. for-profit organizations. *Leadership Quarterly, 21*(1), 144–158.

Sargeant, A. (2001). Relationship fundraising: How to keep donors loyal. *Nonprofit Management and Leadership, 12*(2), 177–192.

Sen, S. (1993). Defining the nonprofit sector: India. In L. M. Salamon & H. K. Anheier (Eds.), *Working Papers of the Johns Hopkins Comparative Nonprofit Sector Project*, no. 12. Baltimore, MD: The Johns Hopkins Institute for Policy Studies.

Sen, S. (1999). Some aspects of state-NGO relationships in India in the post-independence era. *Development and Change, 30*, 327–355.

Sheth, A., & Singhal, M. (2011). *India philanthropy report 2011*. Mumbai, India: Bain & Company. Retrieved from http://www.bain.com/publications/articles/india-philanthropy-report-2011.aspx

Shier, M. L., & Graham, J. R. (2013). Identifying social service needs of Muslims living in a post 9/11 era: The role of community-based organizations. *Advances in Social Work, 14*(2), 379–394.

Shier, M. L., & Handy, F. (2012). Understanding online donor behavior: The role of donor characteristics, perceptions of the Internet, website and program, and influence from social networks. *International Journal of Nonprofit and Voluntary Sector Marketing, 17*(3), 219–230.

Shier, M. L., Graham, J. R., Deane, L., & Jones, M. E. (2013). Leadership in a Chinese advocacy focused non-profit organization: Adaptability to context for leadership success. *Social Development Issues, 35*(3), 96–108.

Simpson, D. D. (2009). Organizational readiness for stage-based dynamics of innovation implementation. *Research on Social Work Practice, 19*(5), 541–551.

Transparency International. (2012). *Corruption Perceptions Index 2012*. Retrieved from http://www.transparency.org/cpi2012/results

Weerawardena, J., & Sullivan-Mort, G. (2006). Investigating social entrepreneurship: A multi-dimensional model. *Journal of World Business, 41*(1), 21–35.

Vanderkam, L. (2010, November 17). Charity will never be the same. *USA Today*, 11A.

Wood, S. A. (2007). The analysis of an innovative HIV-positive women's support group. *Social Work With Groups, 30*(3), 9–28.

CHAPTER 8

Personal, Societal, and Political Conditions of Successful Innovations

A Case Study of the Difficult Survival of the Social Innovation Foundation (Hungary)

Gábor Hegyesi

University of Jewish Studies and ELTE University, Budapest

Katalin Talyigás

University of Jewish Studies, Budapest

Jon Van Til

Rutgers University, USA

INTRODUCTION: SOME THEORETICAL CONSIDERATIONS OF SOCIAL INNOVATION

In a prescient act of social innovation, two of the authors, Katalin Talyigás and Gábor Hegyesi (each a social worker, social scientist, and long-time activist in Hungarian civil society), and other colleagues chose the name Social Innovation Foundation (SZIA as it is known in Hungary) when they established their new nonprofit organization in 1997. Since that time, the idea of social innovation, together with its related concepts, social enterprise and social entrepreneurship, has entered the lexicon of citizens and public policy on a global scale.

The idea of social innovation is, however, like so many terms in the field of applied social study, both slippery and polysemic: Slippery in that it contains normative implications, both elusive and hidden, behind its "scientific" front; polysemic in that it used to encompass a wide range of meanings.

The term social innovation, of course, implies originality, or the presence of some sort of newness. It suggests a creative process by which individuals and organizations bring new, and presumably better, ideas into application. The ideas themselves need not be new—after all, there are not many ideas that can truly be characterized as being new, as Ecclesiastes reminds us—but it is their application in solving tough and often enduring social problems that counts.

Westley and Antadze (2010) usefully observe that social innovation differs from its related processes—social enterprise and social entrepreneurship—in that its focus is on systemic or interorganizational activities, while social enterprise is an organizational concept, and social entrepreneurs tend to be individuals. But like the entrepreneurial activities, as Schumpeter classically observed, social innovations are creative processes (cf. Dodgson, 2011). Each of the five forms of innovation identified by Schumpeter (1934)—product, production, market, supply, and organization—may be seen as elements for potential social innovation. Moreover, each form of innovation may, of course, contain implications that both advantage and disadvantage certain actors and interests in society.

Social innovation differs from technical innovation; when classifying a case of a technical innovation, the major question is: Who was the first to invent it? The person's first step is to get a patent, because it has enormous financial advantages in the market. Those who want to use it must pay for the description of the patent. In the case of social innovation, the system is very different. To be the very first in a global sense is not an issue, because there is no patent system to collect such data, nor are there legal claims to defend the interests of the first.

Social innovations are novelties developed within communities in an effort to solve social problems. They are very often innovations only when viewed from the local perspective, because similar forms may have already been discovered in another community. From this point of view, one could say that a very important dimension of social innovation is the introduction of a new solution for an old problem in a local community; a solution that is not necessarily completely new but that was previously unknown in the local context.

The gods of innovation both give and take within the complex structures of society. This may explain another dimension of innovation; for example, the surrounding societal environment does not always respond positively to innovative suggestions. The success of an innovation does not only depend on the quality and novelty of the innovation itself, but it also very much depends on the currently dominant values and interests of the community where the innovation is introduced.

This approach is true for SZIA. It provides an explanation for the ups and downs that this organization has encountered. The work of SZIA, described in this chapter, distinguishes between successful and unsuccessful implementation of particular social innovations regarding community acceptance.

This phenomenon could be better understood had there been established a "sociology of innovations." This chapter could be seen as an early attempt by the authors to reflect on their experiences within SZIA regarding this issue.

THE PROBLEM

In 1990, following political changes, Hungary became a capitalistic society. Politically this change was greatly supported, but the consequences were many and not always positive. Hungary went through an enormous economic and social crisis. The introduction of governmental price supports brought on 30% to 40% inflation between 1989 and 1991. Moreover the introduction of strong market measures to enhance the efficiency of firms caused a loss of approximately 40% of jobs, mainly among uneducated workers. As a consequence, the unemployment rate went up from 30% to 35%. Unemployment was the highest among Hungary's largest minority, the Roma, and they became the greatest losers from the political change. A second group that was greatly affected were the pensioners. Their incomes were no longer raised according to rates of inflation. Other well-known social problems of capitalist societies that have less-developed welfare systems emerged as well, including homelessness, poverty, growing inequalities, and so on. Therefore, the newly democratic Hungary faced not just a single problem but rather a whole raft of them that cried for solutions.

It is not accidental that one of the first reactions of the new political regime was the reform of the Social Law in 1993. The new law lay down a new concept for dealing with social problems, seeking to break the monopoly of the state—imposed during the pre-1990 period—in providing social services. A mixed system was introduced, ensuring the representation of churches, nonprofit organizations, and even profit-oriented institutions, along with state-owned ones, in the provision of social services. The law detailed compulsory services to be provided to different categories of the needy, such as home care for the elderly, the provision of kindergartens for children, and the development of institutions for handicapped children. Also provided within the law was the amount of money allocated to providers, independently from their organizational form.

As the new mixed social welfare system was set up, it became apparent to those who had been working in the social field for decades that at least two new and very important problems had arisen. One problem was the missing knowledge, trust, and experience as to how professionals in the three sectors (state, nonprofit, and market) should work in partnership with each other providing services within the new mixed social political system. It should also be noted that the authors had very little knowledge about how the mixed system would work. Hungary had very little experience with or knowledge about nonprofit organizations, profit-oriented social services, or even the work of professionally trained social workers, because these categories simply did not exist before 1990.

The other big issue was that of *quality*. In the socialist era the major issue had been *quantity*—in other words, shortage. As the leading economist of Hungary from the 1970s, János Kornai (1980), stated in his influential book, *Economics of Shortage*, the socialist economy was not able to meet the needs of people because it lacked the indicators of demand provided by the market. It was apparent that the state alone was not enough to provide sufficient services to people in need (see Weisbrod, 1975, pp. 171–195). The socialist state, however, had not allowed other organizations in other sectors to provide social services, because it was crucial to the system to prove that the state itself was able to meet all needs without outside assistance. As a consequence of the political change, many services in the nonstatutory sectors (the market and nonprofit sectors) began to emerge. Although there were regions in Hungary where quantity remained a problem, in many fields, services began to compete with each other and quality became a very important phenomenon. Thus it became an important issue to establish and measure good social work and identify good social services.

THE INNOVATIONS

One of many initiatives from those years to overcome the great number of social problems was the establishment of SZIA in 1997. The establishment of SZIA also represented an attempt to continue a 3-year cooperation with the British Council and the National Institute for Social Work, the title of which was "Progress Through Partnership." Those who participated in the program later became the founders of SZIA (officially founded by Gábor Székely). Each of the eight other founders was a social scientist, representing various social, educational, political, and scientific organizations. They were Dr. Vera Gáthy, Hungarian Academy of Sciences; Dr. Gabor Hegyesi, Eötvös Loránd University of Sciences; Eva Kárpáti, The Jewish Social Agency, the JOINT; Dr. Katalin Lévai, Kossuth Lajos University of Sciences; Dr. Zsuzsa Szémann, Hungarian Academia of Sciences; Dr. Katalin Talyigás, Executive Director of JOINT; and Dr. Erzsébet Visy, Research Institute on Urban Studies. The National Institute for Social Work was represented by its international director at the time, Dr. John Warwick.

The members of this team of experts had previously worked together on various projects from time to time, but it was a great challenge and opportunity to be selected to work together on an international project together with the National Institute of Social Work and the British Council. The topic was based on the aforementioned two big issues, and, after a long planning process, it was very well articulated in the Preface of the Report on the project by Dr. Paul Dick, who was the director of the British Council in Hungary at that time. "The aims of the project were to improve the quality and effectiveness of Hungarian social welfare services. The approach was to establish a network to develop and introduce standards in the provision of social care and to demonstrate the value of partnership, co-operation and sustainability. One key to success has been the involvement of decision makers, especially from local government, in the process" (Lévai, 1999, p. 7).

During the very successful international closing workshop in London in 1996, the Hungarian team decided to establish a nonprofit organization to continue the work. The members of the team were very much dedicated to the democratization of Hungary and involved in the political processes that followed the 1990 changes. They were closely concerned with those groups in society whom they saw as losing ground in the new situation and with the social consequences of the emerging crisis of uneven development. These consequences proved to be devastating.

At this closing workshop in London, all interested partners were very satisfied with the results. Still, there were more questions at the end of the project than answers. They learned that this would be a never-ending task and that new innovations are needed all the time! At a great pub in London, being helped by some fantastic British beer (what a great innovation!), they wrote down the name of the foundation on a little cardboard coaster: Social Innovation Foundation for the Development of Central-Eastern Europe. This name managed to express very well the mission of the organization, while the founders hoped that the organization would be an innovation in itself. Also, the products of the organization would offer innovative solutions to difficult social problems in the future. The authors of this chapter hoped to prove this statement. Naturally, it is not possible to describe all the details. The authors concentrate on some of the most important and most characteristic features of SZIA.

Soon after its official incorporation, the Foundation won its first application. Recognizing their experience in quality and partnership issues, the authors were selected to participate in an international Gerontology-Geriatric service program, together with groups and individuals from 17 other Central-Eastern European countries. The goal of the program was to create and organize an interdisciplinary curriculum for further education of professionals working in the social sector. They would be trained to work for the elderly in their homes, offering them both social and health services. While many other countries, such as the United States, have had much experience with these approaches, this type of service was quite an innovation in Hungary and in the region. That is why the program worked together with Professor Terry Hokenstadt, a well-known American expert from Case Western Reserve University in Cleveland, Ohio. The Foundation, in collaboration with Professor Hokenstadt, organized four regional trainings in Budapest, Ljubljana, Tallin, and Cluj-Napoca.

The program was based on the following conceptual prerequisites and goals:

- Needs-centered services
- Client- and community-centered services
- Lessening of inequalities
- Local decisions and civil solutions
- Use of funding system
- Capacity development in administration, economy, and quality assurance
- Creation of a complex welfare system, constantly being improved at the local level

After the implementation of this project, approximately 100 projects began in the region, providing home care, daily provision, and hospice services, but with great sustainability problems. Unfortunately, only some of these were able to survive after the end of the project. Another goal of the project was to disseminate professional standards in the field of care for the elderly, especially in the areas of institutional care, home care, and general social provision for the elderly. This goal was basically reached through the project's international seminars.

By this time, the structure of the leadership of the foundation was cemented. The aforementioned founding members were asked to serve on the Board of Directors, with Katalin Talyigás becoming the executive director and Gábor Hegyesi serving as president of the board. A small administration was also set up with four full-time staff members to run the organization and to seek out new applications.

The next major step in working out the strategy and character of the Foundation was our active participation in a European program won by the National Association of Nonprofit Human Services of Hungary (NANHS). The NANHS, as an umbrella organization founded in 1992, became one of the largest and most important professional associations in Hungary, offering more than 250 nonprofit social human services. Each of the present authors was actively involved in the life of the association. Katalin Talyigás acted as vice president, Jon Van Til served as chair of the International Advisory Board, and Gábor

Hegyesi was elected as president of the association, all serving as volunteers. The Social Innovation Foundation joined the association immediately after its incorporation and set about its work. The representatives of the member organizations of the 1997 Annual Meeting of the Association accepted the new strategic plan of the leaders of the association (written by the Social Innovation Foundation) to play a leading role in Hungary in developing quality standards for social services, offered by statutory, local governmental, and nonprofit organizations.

After a successful bid at the European Union in Brussels, the Foundation's task was to develop professional quality standards of services in the following six fields through an action research:

- Child welfare
- Unemployment
- Homelessness
- Rehabilitation
- Drugs and alcohol dependency
- Care for the elderly

The action research began in 1998. During the framing of this action research process, first the participating organizations accepted standards of services among themselves in a structure offered by the leaders of the project, and then introduced them into practice in their own organizations. After 3 months, the standards were reevaluated based on the monitoring experiences of the organizations. The standards were then changed again on demand and put into practice again for another 3 months. After a year, the lists of standards were ready and accepted, and the association made them accessible to every organization interested (Hegyesi & Talyigás, 2000, pp. 47–138).

By 2000, SZIA had become quite well known, with quality being its major brand in the nonprofit world. A sponsor wanted to contribute to developing a methodology that would give guidance to funders who were making decisions about which nonprofit organizations to support. SZIA staff began to work out a qualifying methodology and produced what became known as the Societal Justice Index (Hegyesi, Talyigás, & Fekete, 2005, pp. 1–60), an innovative methodology that was not previously known in Hungary.

The aim of the index was to evaluate nonprofit organizations that wanted voluntarily to be on the list of service providers, hoping that sponsors would select them based on their quantitative and qualitative measures. The pilot research was done in 2003 and was repeated in 2005. SZIA began to experience, as an unexpected surprise, that participating in the process was not very popular among organizations. It was perceived by some as a tool that allowed funders to really measure the activities of the organizations they supported. SZIA published the methodology (Hegyesi, Fekete, Kasziba, & Talyigás, 2006), but it has not yet been widely used in the sector. It rather stands as a theoretical achievement and is now taught at nonprofit trainings and in university courses.

The index also generated criticism among some competitors in the field who were also working on qualifying systems. It was an interesting experience to learn that there was already in existence a market of innovations. This not only showed the growth of the sector on the one hand, but also the fear that organizations had of being measured and analyzed from the outside, possibly letting others know their weaknesses besides, of course, their strengths. Many thoughtful professionals entering the field remain interested in learning the model, which the authors take as a hopeful sign that this much needed innovation will eventually win acceptance.

As developers of this index, we still believe that it is a genuine innovation that can help sponsors find an organization they can trust and help nonprofits provide their services in a better and more cost-effective fashion. In addition to demonstrating organizational efficiency, the index also provides important information about the ethical quality of the organization. SZIA persists in its efforts to expand the use of the Social Justice Index throughout the nonprofit sector, as an important tool in the decision-making processes of funders.

In 2004–2005, SZIA once again participated in a European project: I. Transnational Exchange Programme. The aim of the project was to work out a European system of quality standards for social services for disabled people. The project consisted of organizations from Greece, Austria, Belgium, Denmark, Portugal, and Hungary. In addition to SZIA, the National Association of Nonprofit Human Services and the Motivation Foundation also participated in the project. The latter organization specialized in employing disabled people and giving advice to other people with various disabilities. The result was a new model that was introduced into many organizations working with disabled people or offering services to them.

Parallel with this international work, SZIA took on a very important task in Hungary as well. For the first time, the Ministry of Social and Family Affairs initiated a reform in social policy and, as a part of it, suggested the introduction of quality assurance policies into social services. A team was set up, and SZIA was asked to coordinate the work. Gábor Hegyesi became the chair of the Quality Committee, and Katalin Talyigás was also involved. After an intensive project lasting more than a year, a report was presented (http://www.szmm.gov.hu/main.php?folderID = 872&articleID = 6206&ctag = articlelist&iid = 1). Its major recommendation was that an accredited quality assurance model should be introduced to every social service; however, it would be their right to choose among the models. And because the recommendation was to make this process compulsory, the state might have been expected to contribute to the costs of this introduction. Yet the Ministry of Finances did not approve the amount of money needed for the introduction of a compulsory system, and thus the provision of a quality system in Hungary has yet to be mandated.

Despite the failure to implement their recommendation, the sector still showed increasing interest in the work of the Quality Committee and its suggestions. The "Quality Revolution" had only slowly reached the social sector, as it was the last of society's major sectors to adopt such procedures, and it did not want to lose more time. Many industrial firms had introduced ISO models decades ago—and a number of multinational firms brought this new culture to Hungary after the political change, when privatization was implemented. Then hospitals and schools followed the trend. In the social sector, the Social Innovation Foundation and the National Association of Nonprofit Human Services played leading roles in drawing the attention of decision makers and social professionals to the importance of quality assurance and quality management systems with the already mentioned action research.

While there was still a growing interest in developing quality systems, contrary to the official statutory opinion that would not financially support their introduction into social services, some competition started between nonprofit and local governmental social services. SZIA made another important strategic decision. It decided to develop its own quality system based on the critical points of the already existing models and with special attention to the needs and specializations of nonprofit social services.

To reach this goal, SZIA had to introduce a quality system. In 2005, it began a joint developmental effort with one of the leading organizations in the market, CERTOP Ltd., to certify a SZIA quality assurance program. It was hard work but was successful, and SZIA was awarded the Certificate of ISO 9001:2001 in December of that year. This gave the Foundation the official authority to build quality systems in social innovation, research, and organizational development in other organizations.

The next phase started immediately after this. In January 2006, a team was established to work out a completely new product, the SZIA Quality Model. By that time Gábor Hegyesi had finished his studies and was awarded a university diploma as a Quality Manager. He and another professional, Zsuzsa Kasziba, were the leaders of this work, with Katalin Talyigás and Orsolya Fekete also playing important roles. The first task was to analyze the major existing quality systems, such as ISO and TQM.

The major conceptual novelty of the model is that the quality standards are set up by the management staff rather than by an external model or expert. They are based on the capacity of the organization and can be developed further anytime. Also, the introduction of the model is nonprofit-friendly. The training consists of five modules (from mission statement through efficient resource management), and it can be scheduled and delivered according to the financial and other considerations of the nonprofit organization. Along the way, the participants create their own quality handbook, determine the way they want to run and constantly develop their quality system, and prepare for the control necessary to receive certification from a third-party expert.

The work was successful; the SZIA Model was introduced (see www.szia.org) and became well accepted. Also—and this is important in the nonprofit world—it was not expensive. Low cost was a major goal of the innovation, because lack of resources forms a very important problem for nearly every nonprofit organization. In the last years, SZIA worked with approximately 60 organizations and found that the model worked well. There would have been more invitations had there not been the economic crisis of 2008 that ravaged most organizations within the sector. But those organizations that had a SZIA Model in place are clearly weathering the crisis better than those that did not use the new organizational tool.

The economic crisis had further effects on the work of SZIA. The Hungarian government—with financial support of the European Union—started a second round effort to set up some kind of quality standards after the failure of the first project called SZOLID. SZIA was again invited to work on the project, and its task was to work out the standards of social and child welfare services and those of good management. The work was done (Hegyesi, 2006), but again the outcome was the same: official support was not provided at the end of the project. SZIA suggested the quality assurance policy be introduced into the governmental work, but this idea was also refused.

In 2010, an even bigger problem occurred: the previous government lost the election, and the new government gained a two thirds majority in the Parliament. This in itself should not be seen as a problem; however, in this case, the policies of the new government had dramatic effects on many parts of society. SZIA found itself among the losers in light of the new regime's policies.

Here are just some relevant implications of these policies (Krasztev & Van Til, 2013; Sheppele, 2011; Tavares, 2013):

- The new government prefers to support the middle class rather than the poor, and thus a lot of money was withdrawn from social policy; poverty has grown a great deal.
- The new government is not friendly to an independent civil sector and has provided few resources for the support of nonprofit organizations.
- The new government prefers centralization and has not been friendly toward the democratic representations of various interest groups.

Here are some ways in which these policies affected the position of SZIA:

- The growth of social problems might be thought to require a lot of work from SZIA, because new challenges require new social innovations.
- But even in times of increasing poverty and social distress, it is has proven very difficult to raise funds from the state or other sources in Hungary.
- The government does not support any organization that does not openly support the government itself. SZIA is a nonpolitical organization, but its work is based on democratic values, and the organization believes in and supports political neutrality. SZIA feels that the organization has been placed on a kind of "black list."

To summarize the outcome of 2010: After a very successful decade of professional development, SZIA prepared to close itself down in 2012. While much of its activities have always been provided on a voluntary basis, there were expenses that had to be paid. Without at least the toleration of the state, it appeared that SZIA would be part of a governmental approach aimed at restricting the work of what no longer could be called an "independent sector."

In the final part of the chapter, you can read about a more general question: What strategies remain for an innovative yet troubled nonprofit organization to survive hard times and continue in its efforts to fulfill its mission?

A SUCCESSFUL STRUGGLE FOR SURVIVAL FOR THE TIME BEING

In the nonprofit world, program success does not necessarily ensure financial success. While many meritorious organizations succeed both in advancing their mission and funding their programs, others, like SZIA, hold firmly to their visions and goals but do not achieve fiscal viability. (There are also nonprofits whose missions and programs are dubious, but who nonetheless meet their financial goals, but that is another story: Cf. Van Til, 2008, chap. 6.)

The literature (Pratt, 2006) advises the struggling nonprofit to explore six strategies in its efforts to maintain fiscal viability in the face of absent or dwindling revenues:

1. Self-funding
2. Locating independent sources of revenue
3. Diversification of program
4. Utilization of submarket economies
5. Establishment of influence over funders
6. Establishment of shared purpose with elite networks

SZIA has attempted each of these strategies and has found some success with some of them. Beginning the discussion with the second listed strategy: SZIA has diligently explored the few and limited sources of independent revenue available to it in the context of a weak philanthropic scene and a dominant one-party state determined to extirpate organizations like it from the Hungarian scene. It has found some sources of support still independent from central control within the Hungarian social and political economy. These sources have offered contracts for staff training or Roma development in several far-flung locations throughout the vast Hungarian countryside. Also, SZIA has generated a large amount of professional social capital (albeit noncash) (e.g., Coleman, 1988) over the past few years that now gives indication of returns in the form of interesting potential contracts.

By delivering programs in the 13th District of Budapest as well as in such wide-ranging sites of northeast Hungary as Encs and Nyiregyháza, SZIA has both diversified its offerings and adjusted its program to the declared needs of a submarket political economy: those few constituencies throughout Hungary not under the majority control of the governing conservative Fidesz political party (or its cousin even farther to the right, the Jobbik Party). And within Budapest's 13th District (one of three not under Fidesz control), SZIA has received use of offices in return for the barter of consulting services, through its shared purposes with the elite network represented by the district's social service department.

It is also interesting to stress that both programs deal with partnership and quality issues. In Northeast Hungary, which is one of the poorest areas of the country, the staff has faced the task of introducing the SIF Quality Model into six newly established community centers. Monthly supervisory meetings with social workers from various social services are held to make sure that they do "good social work."

In the 13th District, SZIA's task is to participate in the development of a new partnership model between local government and civil society/nonprofit organizations. SZIA has much experience with the British model, called COMPACT (http://www.compactvoice.org.uk/about-compact), which was introduced into Hungary as part of the Progress Through Partnership project. Its leaders also hold vivid memories about failures of ministerial officers of the years between 1998 and 2002 (with the same conservative party in power as today) to work out partnership contracts in Hungary, instances marked by the absence of trust and information. With this knowledge and (sometimes) painful experience, SZIA aspires to continue to contribute to the healing of the wounds that governmental policy and action can inflict.

Above all, however, SZIA's survival is based on the basic power of any dedicated voluntary organization: by the volunteers' energy and the commitment of its board and, in this case, its staff as well. Its senior staff and consultants, like the three authoring this paper, receive their personal incomes from pension sources. Staff are paid from SZIA sources only when contracts allow, and they continue their efforts on a voluntary basis during the long unpaid stretches in between. Consultants are compensated only when the proposals they write are actually funded. Junior staff associates are recruited from the ranks of students and other volunteers.

SZIA's determination to persist represents one of the greatest strengths of the nonprofit sector—the ability to continue to be active even when the financial coffers appear to be entirely drained of coin. In such circumstances, when businesses close their doors and declare bankruptcies and governments turn to the printing of bills, the nonprofit organization has another option: to draw on the commitment of its staff and supporters and find ways to persist. Such is the lesson to be drawn from little SZIA in far-off Budapest: for the best in the voluntary sector, a way will be found.

CONCLUSIONS

Finally, one can say that even such a small organization as SZIA can meet at least two traditional criteria for innovation (Schumpeter, 1934). SZIA has been an innovation as an organization, and it is still one of the leading organizations in the field. Also, it developed various innovative products, many of which proved to be lasting. Of course, this chapter could deal only with a small part of the activities of SZIA. Here are a few additional things SZIA has accomplished:

- It published 12 books in English and in Hungarian that support the activities described above.
- In partnership with the General Business School, Budapest, it established a competition called Pro Bono that has awarded annual prizes to outstanding social entrepreneurs every year since 2007. Thirteen organizations have received this award.
- It has developed and put into practice 32 social innovations (products, programs, written strategies, etc.) during the period of 1997 to 2013.

The case study of SZIA shows that no innovation can be envisaged without the dedicated efforts of innovative, committed persons. At the same time, unfavorable societal conditions (financial, social, political, etc.) may dramatically hinder or even prevent innovation from taking shape. These challenges, however, may contribute to finding new, innovative paths that force the organization to redefine and rethink the meaning and borders of the nonprofit/civil sector.

The nonpolitical status of civil organizations is under direct attack by the governing Fidesz party in Hungary (Van Til & Krasztev, in press). The policy of that party is simple: If you are not with us, you are against us. To be a neutral and nonpartisan civil organization is seen as being against the government, according to its terminology. And to be categorized as such means that there will be no state support for the organization—only antagonism and opposition.

This is a dilemma for civil organizations. Also, it is a trap for SZIA from the point of view of its mission, because its goal has always been to work out innovative solutions for complex social problems and to disseminate them through partnerships with governments and other organizations. While SZIA has always been politically neutral, at the same time the values its board chose—democracy, equality, liberalism, human rights, and social justice—were not at all neutral. SZIA's members oppose some values often exhibited and supported by the governing regime in Hungary: hyper-nationalism, homophobia, discrimination, and racism—just to mention a few. SZIA works together with those parties and civil organizations that follow its chosen values and struggles against the policies of parties and organizations that hold views it cannot support.

Today this organizational choice is not an easy one in Hungary. Sometimes it results in failures, but sometimes it succeeds, if only by standing up for, and giving voice to, core values of independent civil and citizen action in its society.

DISCUSSION QUESTIONS

1. What kinds of relationship can be established between political and civil organizations?
2. Did the actions involved in founding SZIA actually represent an innovation, in that it was a totally new creation? Or do social innovations rather involve putting together many ideas, some old and some new, into new patterns of action and organization?
3. What are some main challenges that Hungary faced as it moved from a centralized socialist system to one that was designed to be more democratic and more capitalistic?
4. How important do you think networking is in the social innovation process?
5. Of all SZIA's innovations described in this chapter, which seems to you to be the most significant? Does it matter that this innovation has not been rapidly picked up by other nonprofit organizations?
6. How do you feel about SZIA's decision to keep itself going, even after it lost most of its financial support?
7. What advice would you give to anybody who wants to be a social innovator?

REFERENCES

Coleman, J. (1988). Social capital in the creation of human capital. *American Journal of Sociology, 94*, S95–S120.

Dodgson, M. (2011). Exploring new combinations in innovation and entrepreneurship: Social networks, Schumpeter, and the case of Josiah Wedgwood (1730–1795). *Industrial and Corporate Change, 20*, 1119–1151.

Hegyesi, G. (2006). *Report on quality assurance policy in social services*. Retrieved from http://www.szmm.gov.hu/main.php? folderID = 872&articleID = 6206&ctag = articlelist&iid = 1

Hegyesi, G., Fekete, O., Kasziba, Z., & Talyigás, K. (2006). *The SIF Quality Model Programme*.

Hegyesi, G., & Talyigás, K. (Eds.). (2000). *Professional standards in the fields of human services*. Budapest, Hungary: National Association of Non-profit Human Services.

Hegyesi, G., Talyigás, K., & Fekete, O. (2005). *The "societal justice index": To the attention of donors and money distributors*. Budapest, Hungary: Social Innovation Foundation (SZIA).

Kornai, J. (1980). Economics of shortage. *Közgazdasági és Jogi Kiadó*. Budapest, Hungary: Publishing House.

Krasztev, P., & Van Til, J. (Ed.). (2013). *Tarka ellenállás. Napvilág kiadó*. Budapest, Hungary: Publishing House.

Lévai, K. (Ed.). (1999). *Progress through partnership*. Budapest, Hungary: Social Innovation Foundation (SZIA).

Pratt, J. (September 21, 2006). Financial independence: Six steps. *Non-profit Quarterly*. Retrieved from http://www.nonprofitquarterly.org/management/46-financial-independence-six-approaches.html

Schumpeter, J. A. (1934). *The theory of economic development: An inquiry into profits, capital, credit, interest and the business cycle*. London, United Kingdom: Oxford University Press.

Sheppele, K. (2011, December 19). *Hungary's constitutional revolution*. Retrieved from http://krugman.blogs.nytimes.com/2011/12/19/hungarys-constitutional-revolution/

Tavares, R. (2013, June 25). *Report on the situation of fundamental rights: Standards and practices in Hungary*. Retrieved from http://www.europarl.europa.eu/sides/getDoc.do?pubRef = -//EP//TEXT + REPORT + A7-2013-0229 + 0 + DOC + XML + V0//en

Van Til, J. (2008). *Growing civil society*. Bloomington, IN: Indiana University Press.

Van Til, J., & Krasztev, P. (Eds.). (in press). *The Hungarian patient*. Budapest, Hungary: Central European University Press.

Weisbrod, B. A. (1975). Toward a theory of the voluntary non-profit sector in a three-sector economy. In E. S. Phelps (Ed.), *Altruism, morality and economic theory* (pp. 171–195). New York, NY: Russell Sage Foundation.

Westley, F., & Antadze, N. (2010). Making a difference: Strategies for scaling social innovation for greater impact. *Innovation Journal, 1*(2), 1–20.

ADDITIONAL RESOURCES

Social Innovation Foundation (Hungary) website: http://www.szia.org
Social Innovation Foundation (Hungary) e-mail: szia.org

CHAPTER 9

Resto VanHarte

A Dutch Restaurant Assisting Others to Overcome Social Isolation

Lucas Meijs[1]

Department of Business-Society Management

Erasmus Centre for Strategic Philanthropy

Rotterdam School of Management

Erasmus University Rotterdam

The Netherlands

After having worked a long term abroad for UNICEF and Médecins Sans Frontières (Doctors Without Borders), I returned to the Netherlands in the year 2000. I started volunteering in several cities when I suddenly realized how much the Dutch society had changed while I was abroad. I discovered a diversity of cultures, colors, nationalities, religions, and backgrounds of people. At the same time I noticed aging, secularization, individualism, and a range of new technical developments. I wondered whether people could keep up with all these social changes. Most of all, I was totally shocked and touched by the isolation, lack of perspective, and future opportunities for people, mainly in the multicultural city areas. I felt frustrated with this situation, which I could not accept, and strongly felt I had to do something.

—Fred Beekers, founder and CEO of Resto VanHarte[2]

---

[1] The research for this chapter and the writing of the chapter has been done in close cooperation with Fred Beekers. The author himself has been a member of the supervisory board of Resto VanHarte since 2008. The author also wants to thank Eva van Baren, junior researcher at the Rotterdam School of Management, for assisting with the research.

[2] Source: http://www.restovanharte.nl

THE PROBLEM: LONELINESS IN A WELL-ORGANIZED WELFARE STATE

According to several international research projects, the Netherlands has a nonprofit sector of considerable size and importance (Burger & Dekker, 1998; De Nieuwe Dialoog/CIVICUS, 2006), scoring very high on the Civil Society Index (Salamon & Sokolowski, 2004, p. 78). The Netherlands is clearly an example of a corporatist regime (Salamon & Anheier, 1998) in which the government (partly) subsidizes nonprofit organizations to deliver services, to organize mutual activities such as playing soccer, and to campaign, even against government policy. Several authors have described how this development has led to a nonprofit sector of large service delivery organizations that slowly has been taken over by government, and that lost its connection with the (active) citizens in the civil society (Meijs, 2007; Raad voor Maatschappelijke Ontwikkeling, 2010, 2011). In welfare, this subsidization led to the 2007 Social Support Act (Wet Maatschappelijke Ondersteuning, WMO), which basically is set up to recreate more civil society and more citizen involvement in welfare: "The aim of the Social Support Act is to make sure that all citizens in all facets of the society, receive the services, help and support they need so that everyone is able to participate in society" (http://www.rijksoverheid.nl/onderwerpen/wet-maatschappelijke-ondersteuning-wmo).

Against the background of this naïve view of an all-arranging, all-caring, and all-financing government, in particular, loneliness was a little-recognized issue. Although unimaginable and unrecognized by most Dutch, in reality about 30% of people in the Netherlands seem to be lonely, including 10% who suffer from severe loneliness (van Tilburg, 2007). Whereas local traditions for informal contacts used to be preserved by religion and family within local Dutch communities, modern society is now characterized by a variety of people, cultures, and beliefs. In this day and age, family members live farther away from one another than ever before, and the pursuit of their own personal happiness and success calls for a different set of priorities. At the same time they calculate their behavior in the public domain to maximize government support and benefits, against the firm believe that government takes care of all from the "cradle to the grave." Generally speaking, internationalization, the rapid increase in the use and development of technology, and further individualization cause many people to feel ever more unsafe and misunderstood, to think that they are detached and excluded from our modern society. As a consequence, they more frequently find themselves in isolation. Because few like to admit to loneliness, the problem surrounding this topic remains taboo. Even though this seems to be particularly true for the elderly in a country with an aging population, loneliness and the need for social interaction affects all ages (see, e.g., Hortulanus, Machielse, & Meeuwesen, 2003; Machielse, 2003).

In the Netherlands, voluntary organizations have long made use of meaningful social involvement, including formal volunteering, to fight loneliness. Among others, the Netherlands Red Cross, Humanitas, and De Zonnebloem (the Sunflower; http://www.zonnebloem.nl/) have successfully set up large yet simple voluntary programs that revolve around traditional volunteer involvement. For example, De Zonnebloem has been fighting social isolation among the sick, elderly, and handicapped since 1945 simply by having their volunteers visit or take out their clients. Today the organization has 72,500 guests who enjoy the attention and friendship of more than 40,000 friendly visiting volunteers supported by about 570,000 regular donors. Although very traditional in approach, the organization is still appealing to volunteers, since, in 1997, the amount of volunteers was about 6,000 lower (Meijs, 1997).

More recently, De Zonnebloem, Resto VanHarte, and several other Dutch nonprofit organizations involved in the problem of loneliness have joined forces in an attempt to prevent and alleviate loneliness through the national coalition against loneliness called Erbij. For Dutch society, this is a breach with the recent traditions of first starting with government policy instead of a more civil society initiative. By raising public awareness, among other things, the members of this Dutch national coalition have put themselves in a good position to guarantee that their actions will both address a broader audience, including policy makers at both local as well as national levels, and make an impact when it comes to tackling loneliness, especially among the older population. The seven core members of the Dutch national coalition Erbij are De Zonnebloem (the Sunflower), Resto VanHarte (a community restaurant discussed further), Leger des Heils (Salvation Army), Humanitas (http://www.humanitas.nl/), MOgroep (MOgroup, http://www.mogroep.nl/), Nationaal Ouderenfonds (the national elderly fund, http://www.ouderenfonds.nl/), and Sensoor (a telephone hotline, http://www.sensoor.nl/). The number of organizations, and their underlying volunteer base, seems impressive; but while many of these activation programs are readily in place, social isolation among the Dutch has doubled within the last few years (Sociaal en Cultureel Planbureau, 2011).

To better understand the Dutch situation, Machielse (2003) made a typology that is frequently used in Dutch practice:

SIX TYPES OF LONELINESS

—*The self-reliant*: Those who have no difficulty with social interaction in their everyday life but who are unable to build social contacts in their personal life.

—*The hopefuls*: Elderly who have become alienated from the world but who hope for more.

—*The dependable*: Those who share a very close relationship with their sibling(s), parents, or partner but who live very isolated otherwise.

—*The lonely*: Those without a job but with many superficial contacts who live with the idea that no one can help them.

—*The outsiders*: The true loners who don't have any need for contact.

—*The survivors*: The ones who never had a social network to begin with, who often suffer from psychological problems, and who are so insecure that they do not dare participate in society. (pp. 153–175)

This chapter centers on the example of Resto VanHarte, a dynamic nonprofit organization whose guiding principle is bringing people—from different ethnic communities, generations, economic classes, and religions—in contact with one another through affordable community restaurants (having a primary focus on the neighborhood in which they are located), where they can meet and greet. Today, there are over 30 Resto VanHartes throughout the Netherlands that offer over 100,000 meals a year. Resto VanHarte has about 500 national regular volunteers and 15 regular volunteers per restaurant, and there were about 2,500 episodic volunteers in the restaurants in 2012. Some of the regular restaurant volunteers have moved on from being a client to a volunteer. Not only is Resto VanHarte innovative in the service it delivers (mostly the so-called Plus Program), but in the Dutch context it certainly is also innovative in the extent that it allows for private civil society to support a national organization. It would have been traditional to develop a set of local independent organizations with very close links to local, subsidizing governments with very limited control from a national office. Although not officially stated, Resto VanHarte seems to focus on the self-reliant, the hopefuls, and the survivors. The impression is that people with a very close relationship (the dependable) do use the Resto VanHarte less. It is also important to understand that as a part of the Resto VanHarte approach regular (non-lonely) guests will join the diners.

THE INNOVATION

In 2004, Fred Beekers founded Resto VanHarte. Being concerned with social isolation in the Netherlands, Beekers particularly targeted the prevention of social exclusion and the enhancement of social cohesion among people. His idea of *Restos* where people can eat an inexpensive, three-course, healthy dinner while meeting other people was a practical solution to reintegrating lonely people into society. "The goal is to have an eat-meet-and-talk-between-'strangers' restaurant" (Beekers, personal interview, October 9, 2013).

In almost every country, having dinner is a social experience. Resto VanHarte uses the dinner table as an eat-and-meet concept. Resto VanHarte believes in people's own power, and with that, it fights people's social isolation. Within their community restaurants, both paid staff (one professional cook and one professional manager) and volunteers prepare healthy three-course meals that are served to everyone at the same time. Resto VanHarte does not provide cheap, healthy food to poor people who walk in, but rather runs a limited seating restaurant with a reservation system. In an ideal situation, there are several long tables where people from different backgrounds, lonely and regular, engage in conversation. At the same time, there is always something going on, such as entertainment or a presentation by a professional working in the area as part of the Plus Program. In this way, Resto VanHarte tries to use the dining table as a means to bring together people, in their respective neighborhoods. It does this in close cooperation with national and local district partners.

Working closely together with other organizations such as municipal health and social care organizations, social welfare organizations, religious functionaries, local police, cultural institutions, libraries, educational institutions, and labor reintegration organizations is a means to achieve Resto's main goal. According to Beekers, some for-profit companies, such as insurance companies and banks, are also part of this group in such a way that during dinner at the Restos their local representatives tell the guests about their activities.

By doing so, Beekers explains that "Resto VanHarte focuses on encouraging people to re-enter social structures by creating contacts between the visitors of its restaurants and the above-mentioned local organizations."

The following is an example of a typical evening at one of the local Restos in Utrecht:

> The Resto VanHarte in Utrecht is located in one of the most deprived areas of the city (Kanaleneiland). VanHarte has a restaurant for two evenings a week in the neighborhood's local community center. On a typical evening some 50 guests come together for dinner. About 35 of them are clients, about 15 are "regular" and volunteers. The restaurant manager welcomed everybody, the professional cook explained the menu and the volunteers were recognized. On this particular evening, an artist, together with the guests, made two paintings representing the VanHarte feeling. This initially proved to be a difficult exercise and request for some of the "survivors," but together with the restaurant manager the "regular" visitors at the end got them all to participate. Meanwhile, a volunteer DJ played old vinyl records that (lonely) guests have donated. Just before the dessert a student from Utrecht University gave a presentation on her initiative to set up local food gardens for the poor. (Personal observation by author; see http://www.restovanharte.nl)

The Plus Program forms one of the two innovative parts of Resto VanHarte. The Plus Program is what makes Resto VanHarte more than just a restaurant for deprived or poor people. The Plus Program is aimed at strengthening the social, mental, and physical resilience of the Resto guests and neighborhood volunteers, which, in turn, encourages them to become more self-directed and to participate more in Dutch society. Basically, the Plus Program is a social activation program in the Restos. In June 2012, the Plus Program was renamed Participation Program to better fit the current priorities of the Dutch government. The Plus Program is organized together with the district partners and consists of the following components:

- **Contact with others** is the first step toward social activation, which takes place in all Restos. Therefore, activities and meetings are at the heart of all Plus Programs. Important in this concept of meetings is the idea of connecting the less affluent communities where the Restos are located with people who come from more affluent parts of the local community.

- **Future work, training, and volunteering** perspectives are being initiated by Restos through reintegration opportunities, gaining of work experience, and social work placements within the kitchens and other areas of the Restos, which are open to people of all ages. This calls for close collaboration with institutions such as Centres for Work and Income (CWI), volunteer centers, rehabilitation centers, and training organizations. The Restos' role is ultimately to make sure that each working placement/internship is tailored in such a way that there will be a good fit with (the individual's needs and) the trajectory that is to be followed.

- A **healthy lifestyle** is realized by preparing fresh and healthy three-course meals at a low price (€6 per meal, €3 for the elderly and those living on minimum wage, and half price for children) while at the same time informing visitors about the importance of eating healthy. This is done in close collaboration with both national and local partners, including health centers. In addition, tips and inspiration are given that should encourage more diverse and healthier eating habits.

- **Physical exercise** is equally as important and makes the Plus Program even more complete. Currently throughout the Restos, diners are linked to other programs and local sports clubs, and also to more recreational activities such as dancing.

- **Fostering of financial independence** is also one of the aims in which, in connection with the healthy lifestyle component, special attention is paid to the possibilities of buying groceries more economically and sustainably. Another part of this concept is when professionals from insurance companies and local welfare organizations help people fill out forms to get the support available to them.

- Improving systems of **mutual support and reliance** is also emphasized. Through social infrastructure and within neighborhoods, Resto VanHarte promotes reliance on one another. People need each other, and Resto VanHarte encourages people to be meaningful to others and help each other.

The second innovation in the Resto VanHarte concept is encouraging the lonely diners to participate in civil society. These efforts involve many private actors: individuals, companies, and foundations. Individuals can volunteer, but even more important are the links to the corporate world by bringing in many employees as volunteers. Through such arrangements, the concept of "seeing is believing, acting is understanding" is put into practice, and more people become aware of the problems regarding loneliness. As a result, a dynamic Resto VanHarte is one in which guests and volunteers from all walks of life are actively involved in organizing an evening at one of the restaurants. They are, for example, asked to help set the tables, host, and help organize the Plus Program as well as the local additional fundraising, next to the fees that are paid, surrounding the dinner that evening. Resto VanHarte is widely accepted by all in the neighborhoods and cities where they are located, and many are seeking to create a strong local community around the Restos. That is, the local communities are supporting, co-organizing, and financing the Restos. Also innovative in the Dutch context is the broad support of foundations as funders. Some of these foundations support the national organization, while others will mainly support some restaurants. Once in a while, this innovation clashes with the traditional financing and organizing models used by the government.

THE ORGANIZATION'S DEVELOPMENT: THE EARLY STAGES OF THE NPO

When Fred Beekers started Resto VanHarte in 2004, many things were happening in Dutch society that aided his success. First, national welfare policy was starting to focus on neighborhoods instead of on running national programs (Dutch Scientific Council for Government Policy, 2005). Second, formal local Dutch welfare organizations seemed to be trapped in a never-ending cycle of stopping old and starting new projects (the so-called project carousel). Third, the idea was becoming popular for more private citizens to take initiative in social welfare. Fourth, Fred Beekers himself is charismatic and insistent in a good way! Fifth, loneliness was a real, but not yet recognized, issue that needed attention.

The Resto VanHarte foundation was established in 2004 and became operational in 2005 when the first (pilot) Resto VanHarte opened its doors in The Hague. Based on its good experience in The Hague, the organization's committee decided to operate nationwide by opening restaurants throughout the Netherlands. From the start, Resto VanHarte had created broad support within society while at the same time establishing contacts with governments, charitable foundations, companies, and individuals. Right from the start, these third parties, especially some large national funding foundations, were willing to help finance Resto VanHarte; later, a particular financing model was created to ensure that financing is not dependent on just one source. The general idea was that a new restaurant would get funding from a mixture of national funding foundations, local foundations and volunteers, fees from guests, donations in kind from local companies, and subsidies from the local government. All official financial parties would commit to at least 3 years to give the restaurants a good start. During the first few years, the Resto VanHarte handbook was developed, which covered all the necessary steps and procedures for setting up, managing, and maintaining the quality of the Restos throughout the country. A national headquarters structure was developed.

Looking at the development of the organization, three important stages can be found:

Stage 1: When creating the first movement and the first restaurants, the most important issues were to find out how local restaurants would be set up both legally and financially. After an ill-fated experiment with a local legal entity, it was decided to have a national foundation with executive directors and a supervisory board. Financially, systems were set up to control the local Restos and to safeguard the 3-year financial horizon. Most important was to establish a kind of VanHarte formula and culture.

Stage 2: After the first Resto VanHartes were established, the real expansion toward becoming a national organization occurred as multiple Restos were set up throughout the country. This stage accelerated in 2008 when Resto Van Harte was selected to participate in the first edition of the *OranjeFonds Groeiprogramma* (Orange Foundation), a program funded by a national foundation and developed in cooperation with McKinsey Consulting, aimed specifically at helping new social initiatives expand. Financially supported by national arrangements with national foundations and flying on the wings of success, this was a relatively easy stage. With many national foundations' concrete commitments and contracts established for growing the organizations, new restaurants in other cities were opened.

Stage 3: This period started by finalizing the establishment of the first round of Restos throughout the country. Unfortunately, at the time that many Restos needed an extension after the financially safe 3 years, the national financial crisis arose, making the donor-seeking process more difficult. This stage also consisted of evaluating the innovation of the initial successful formula and method. Important but difficult questions that arose were: What were the original goals and have these been accomplished? Should the formula be adjusted?

CONCLUSIONS

As participation in the *Groeiprogamma* has shown, Resto VanHarte is scalable and replicable. But there is a set of warning signs that influence its effectiveness and need to be addressed during expansion:

- Resto VanHarte is about lonely people meeting other people, not about providing inexpensive food to poor people. Of course these two categories overlap, but how can Resto VanHarte prevent that eating becomes more important than meeting?
- The people who visit a Resto VanHarte must be a good mixture of lonely and nonlonely people, and also of returning and new guests (especially lonely people). How can Resto VanHarte make certain that enough new lonely people will come for some visits instead of having the same (former lonely) people showing up every night?
- The Plus Program fulfills a large part of the participation goal that is stated in the Social Support Act (WMO) of Dutch municipalities, but Resto VanHarte must be prevented from becoming part of the subsidized municipality welfare organization. How can Resto VanHarte include the still rather large government subsidies while staying independent from the government's influence?
- As part of proving its efficiency and effectiveness, Resto VanHarte has undertaken several initiatives. Most important are the frequent customer satisfaction surveys and annual national surveys conducted at each Resto to determine the impact the Resto's unique formula has on its guests. The annual survey shows some results that are ambiguous to interpret. For example, the 2012 national survey showed that on average about 40% of the guests come for the meal, while about 50% come to meet others. Only 10% seem to come especially for the activities. On average about 60% of the guests live in the neighborhood the Resto is located in. But maybe the most debatable result is about the recurring nature of many guests. For example, more than 50% of the guests have come more than 10 times to their Resto in the last year. Even more ambiguous, looking at effectiveness, is that 30% of the guests are eating two evenings a week at their Resto, while another 40% eat there once a week. Given the fact that most Resto are only open for two evenings a week, the difficulty is about the balance between recurring visitors and regular guests who occupy valuable spaces that could impact other people's lives, too.
- Second, research commissioned by the Ministry of Economic Affairs, Agriculture, and Innovation, and conducted by the Wageningen University, shows that a joint and healthy Resto meal is an excellent vehicle to keep people healthy. It contributes not only to the physical health of those participating, but also to their mental health as well as their social state of mind.
- The University of Utrecht (Geutjes, 2010) conducted research on the collaboration between Resto VanHarte and its social partners. More specifically, it researched the different roles these partners play within communities regarding activating socially vulnerable citizens. It also sought to understand the way these partners experience their collaboration with Resto VanHarte. The research showed four reasons for traditional welfare organizations to cooperate with Resto VanHarte. First, they really like the concept of eat-meet-and-talk.

Second, they have the feeling that they share client groups with Resto VanHarte. Third, the official and traditional organizations see Resto VanHarte as another way of understanding the social fabric of the neighborhood. The fourth reason is that these organizations see possibilities of placing their own clients as volunteers within the Resto VanHarte, and by that action, achieving their own goals of supporting participation of certain groups.

- In 2014 Resto Van Harte was awarded the "Tom Sebastiaan Gans" award, a Dutch award for successful organizations in social welfare. (http://www.oranjefonds.nl/tom-sebastiaan-gans-fonds)

The research seems to indicate that Resto VanHarte has found an interesting new, easy to understand intervention that has some positive effects. At the same time, the research also shows that there are serious implication issues at the local levels of the restaurants. Although the formula is simple and can be copied elsewhere, including other cultures, too, it is not easy to stay true to the goal of fighting loneliness by offering the extra activities instead of just providing good, healthy, cheap meals to the poor.

Resto VanHarte makes use of the dinner table as a means to bring people together. Although the focus is on those who are socially isolated from society, everyone is welcome to join. The message is simple: "Eat, meet, and activate." People like to eat together. Resto VanHarte creates a friendly environment that makes this possible.

Take a look at this short Resto VanHarte video that takes you into their kitchens, acquaints you with their volunteers and partners, and shows you a variety of Resto activities that are organized throughout The Netherlands, and throughout the year. The following is a nice impression of what Resto VanHarte is all about: https://www.youtube.com/user/RestovanHarte

DISCUSSION QUESTIONS

1. What is the impact of the Resto VanHarte formula on guests, visitors, and participants, as well as on the quality of life in the local neighborhoods?
2. What is the financing structure? Are there other possibilities to finance the organization?
3. To what extent can the political and public advocacy role be carried out?
4. Is there local support for Resto VanHarte throughout the country?
5. Is there a need for a Resto program in your country? Why or why not?

REFERENCES

Burger, A., & Dekker, P. (1998). De grootste nonprofit sector ter wereld. *ESB* (economisch statistische berichten), *83*(4181), 944–946.

De Nieuwe Dialoog/CIVICUS. (2006). *CIVICUS Civil Society Index Report for the Netherlands*. Amsterdam, The Netherlands: Author.

Dutch Scientific Council for Government Policy. (2005). *Vertrouwen in de buurt, rapport 72*. The Hague, The Netherlands: Author.

Geutjes, K. (2010). *Resto VanHarte op de kaart*. Een ASW Bachelor onderzoek naar de maatschappelijke samenwerkingspartners van Resto VanHarte. Retrieved from http://igitur-archive.library.uu.nl/student-theses/2011-0201-200403/Bachelorscriptie%20Geutjes.pdf

Hortulanus, R., Machielse, A., & Meeuwesen, L. (2003). *Sociaal isolement: Een studie over sociale contacten en sociaal isolement in Nederland*. Amsterdam, The Netherlands: Elsevier.

Machielse, A. (2003). *Niets doen, niemand kennen. De leefwereld van sociaal geïsoleerde mensen*. Amsterdam, The Netherlands: Elsevier.

Meijs, L. C. P. M. (1997). *Management van vrijwilligersorganisaties*. NOV Publikaties: Utrecht, the Netherlands..

Meijs, L. C. P. M. (2007). When the state sneezes, the nonprofit sector catches a cold: Reinventing nonprofit in the Netherlands. In G. Donnelly-Cox & C. Breathnach (Eds.), *Differing images: The Irish nonprofit sector and comparative perspectives* (pp. 39–50). Dublin, Ireland: Liffey Press.

Raad voor Maatschappelijke Ontwikkeling. (2010). *Naar een open samenleving? Recente ontwikkelingen in sociale stijging en daling in Nederland*. The Hague, The Netherlands: Author.

Raad voor Maatschappelijke Ontwikkeling. (2011). *Nieuwe ronde, nieuwe kansen: Sociale stijging en daling in perspectief en de resultaten*. The Hague, The Netherlands: Author.

Salamon, L. M., & Anheier, H. K. (1998). Social origins of civil society: Exploring the nonprofit sector cross-nationally. *Voluntas: International Journal of Voluntary and Nonprofit Organizations, 9*(3), 213–248.

Salamon, L. M., & Sokolowski, W. (2004). Measuring civil society: The Johns Hopkins Global Civil Society Index. In L. M. Salamon, W. Sokolowski, & Associates, *Global civil society: Dimensions of the nonprofit sector*. Bloomfield, CT: Kumarian Press.

Sociaal en Cultureel Planbureau. (2011). *Kwetsbare ouderen in de praktijk*. The Hague, The Netherlands: Author.

van Tilburg, T. (2007). Prevalentie. In T. van Tilburg & J. de Jong Gierveld (Eds.), *Zicht op eenzaamheid: Achtergronden, oorzaken en aanpak* (pp. 24–30). Assen, The Netherlands: Van Gorcum.

ADDITIONAL RESOURCES

Andersson, L. (2010). Loneliness research and interventions: A review of the literature. *Aging & Mental Health, 2*(4), 264–274.

Bofill, S. (2004). Aging and loneliness in Catalonia: The social dimension of food behavior. *Ageing International, 29*(4), 385–398.

Killeen, C. (1998). Loneliness: An epidemic in modern society. *Journal of Advanced Nursing, 28*(4), 762–770.

Routasalo, P., & Pitkala, K. H. (2003). Loneliness among older people. *Reviews in Clinical Gerontology, 13*, 303–311.

Seymour, D. (1983). The social functions of the meal. *International Journal of Hospitality Management, 2*(1), 3–7.

CHAPTER 10

Seacology

A Win-Win Collaboration to Protect Island Environments and Peoples

Bruce Sievers

Visiting Scholar and Lecturer, Stanford University

Henry Jones

Former Communications Assistant, Seacology

THE PROBLEM

Biologist Storrs Olson (1989) has called the stunning rate of animal and plant extinctions on islands "one of the swiftest and most profound biological catastrophes in the history of the earth" (p. 52). It's easy to see why: most of the planet's extinctions in the past 400 years have happened to island species, including 88% of extinct birds, 86% of extinct reptiles, and 66% of extinct mammals (Baillie, Hilton-Taylor, & Stuart, 2004, p. 42).

Due to their isolation, islands are hotbeds for endemic plants and animals—species that exist nowhere else in the world. But with limited area, even minor disruptions to an island ecosystem can have devastating consequences. Losing a species is tragic in its own right, but the consequences don't end there. Mere reductions in species populations can further upset the delicate balance of an interdependent ecosystem, harming other species in profound and often unexpected ways. When grey wolves were extirpated from Yellowstone National Park in the 1920s, to name one famous example, booming elk populations led to severe overgrazing of the park's vegetation, compelling the park to reintroduce the wolves in the 1990s.

But connections are not always so neat or obvious. In the 1960s, the ecologist Robert T. Paine found that removing a species of starfish from a tidal plain led to sweeping changes to the ecosystem, a surprising outcome given the starfish's relatively modest share of the ecosystem's biomass. (This came to be known as a *keystone species*.) Paine's discovery inspired a new way of thinking about how ecosystems worked: organisms can have an influence on the ecosystem around them irrespective of their ostensible importance, and in ways not readily obvious.

There can also be a loss to society at large: endemic plants may have medicinal applications yet to be discovered. (One estimate finds that there may be as many as 15,000 plant types with medicinal properties threatened with extinction.) As famed biologist E. O. Wilson (1984) put it, "The loss of genetic and species diversity by the destruction of natural habitats [is] the one folly our descendants are least likely to forgive us" (p. 121).

Unfortunately, these vulnerable island ecosystems throughout the world are not receiving the protection they need. The unique plight facing island environments is not widely known or understood, and conservationists may overlook islands simply because they are often small, sparsely populated, and extremely remote. But even the smallest islands have a huge influence on the health of the ocean, given the vast expanse of sea they may control. For instance, the Federated States of Micronesia, whose total landmass amounts to 181 km^2, enjoys an Exclusive Economic Zone (EEZ) in its surrounding waters of over 2.9 million km^2.

Moreover, conservation efforts on islands (and elsewhere) often overlook the needs of local people who live in or near areas that need protection, undermining indigenous support for conservation efforts. By protecting island environments while helping local people, the nonprofit Seacology can use resources efficiently to target vulnerable habitats and prevent species extinctions while ensuring that local people both honor and benefit from the establishment of habitat reserves.

The Loss of Island Species

Habitat loss imperils the 100 pygmy sloths on an island in Panama. Deforestation and poaching threaten the 65 Cat Ba langurs on an island in Vietnam. Strong storm surges destroy the vegetation eaten by the San Salvador iguanas, which live only on a few small cays in the Bahamas. These are just a few of the endangered endemic species that Seacology projects are protecting, and these examples illustrate the broader dynamic of islands and the fragility of their ecosystems: when a species relies on an island habitat, small changes can be catastrophic (see Figure 10.1).

In the face of the more than 20,000 species throughout the world considered *threatened* by the International Union for Conservation of Nature (IUCN), it can be challenging for one nonprofit organization (NPO) to make a large impact. Traditional conservation efforts tend to

FIGURE 10.1 Share of Island Species Among Total Extinctions

Mammals	62%
Birds	88%
Amphibians	54%
Reptiles	86%
Mollusks	68%

use one of a few basic approaches. Some organizations focus on protecting specific species by conserving relevant habitats, facilitating breeding programs, or lobbying governments for greater protection. Other organizations concentrate on a geographical region—like the Amazon or the Serengeti—and still others specialize in a particular type of habitat—like coral reefs or rainforests. No other organization, however, to the authors' knowledge has focused exclusively on conserving the vulnerable ecosystems of islands throughout the world.

The Need for Local Involvement

One might imagine forest or marine reserves as impregnable havens, but in practice, reserve boundaries can be porous. Reserves can be too big, and government resources too small, to enforce them effectively. This has given rise to the term *paper parks*, used to describe nature reserves that exist in an official sense, but not in reality. On the island of Madagascar, for instance, political instability and economic problems in the past decade have left its parks department virtually unable to protect its many forest reserves. Now a country whose tree cover has declined 90% since human arrival is seeing its natural parks, full of endemic species, exploited by hunters and loggers.

This is not merely a problem of inadequate enforcement. It is important to note that many places in the world cherished for their natural beauty are also inhabited by small, often indigenous, communities who, for generations, have relied on their surroundings for their livelihoods. These people are often overlooked in traditional efforts to establish nature reserves. Many may not even be aware that they live in or near a reserve at all. Even in cases where they do know, they may not have much interest in it: creating a park does not eliminate the incentive for local people to use the area to farm, hunt, or fish.

Seen from this perspective, creating a successful habitat reserve is as much about creating positive, personal incentives for locals and satisfying local needs as it is about enforcement. If locals don't see an advantage to complying with the terms of a habitat reserve, they are unlikely to cooperate. Ensuring that locals benefit from a habitat reserve is not only critical for success, it represents a commitment to fairness in the treatment of the locals.

Other conservation efforts undertaken with good intentions often have unintended consequences, especially in terms of social justice. For example, when a conservation organization buys land it seeks to protect (as opposed to a government agency declaring an area to be a reserve), it can mean taking traditional lands away from local control. Some large conservation NPOs have traditionally treated local indigenous communities as an impediment to conservation, rather than as an ally. Aside from being unjust, this approach is misguided; it ignores what is often hundreds—and sometimes thousands—of years of history of indigenous people living in harmony with nature.

THE INNOVATION

Seacology's success in creating nature reserves around the world works not by attempting to coerce local people to protect those reserves, but by giving them an incentive to do so. In this way, Seacology is able to help protect island environments while improving the quality of life of islanders at the same time.

In a typical Seacology project, villagers agree to protect a certain area of forest or coastal waters in exchange for Seacology's providing funds to build something needed in the village. This quid pro quo creates a win-win outcome for villagers, as well as the threatened animal and plant species that live nearby.

Most of these villages are rural, and some are not listed on maps. To find these communities, Seacology relies on its network of field representatives to use their local contacts to identify cases in which a village needs help protecting its natural resources. (As islanders have become more familiar with Seacology's work over the years, it has become common for villages to seek out Seacology, rather than the other way around.) These field representatives meet with village leaders to formulate a project outline identifying the area of land or sea they wish to protect and the need of their village necessary to make that happen. A plan is eventually submitted to Seacology staff in Berkeley, California, where it is scrutinized to ensure that the exchange is fair, the conservation plan is realistic, and that the project would benefit the whole community. Finalized projects are sent to the Board of Directors for approval.

The agreements are designed to ensure that the villagers are invested in the success of the project. What is built is up to the villagers to decide—typically it might be a new schoolhouse, a health clinic, or community hall. Importantly, the land continues to belong to the villagers—Seacology claims no ownership rights.

Furthermore, the vast majority of villages provide much of the labor themselves on a volunteer basis. This not only saves money, but it cultivates a sense of ownership among the villagers, making it more likely that the building will be maintained over time.

Additionally, working directly with villages means Seacology can usually avoid the delays and complexities of working through local and national governments. While many governments are open to conservation efforts, they don't always make it easy: high administrative turnover can mean having to secure necessary permits and permissions multiple times over, and vague delineations between agencies can leave project proposals in limbo.

However, Seacology has had success working with village chiefs and councils who hold great authority in many island nations. In fact, penalties for violating the terms of a marine or forest reserve imposed under indigenous laws are often more swift and severe than those imposed by a governmental judicial system. A good example can be found in the South Pacific on Vanuatu's Emau Island, where Seacology worked with the Marou community to build a kindergarten in exchange for both a forest and a marine reserve. When some men were caught fishing for *trochus* (a kind of sea snail) in the marine reserve, Marou's chief ordered them to return the *trochus* and pay a penalty of 1 pig, 15 mats, some kava roots, and 10,000 VUV (about $100).

Seacology has found this model to be a versatile and simple vehicle that works on islands around the world. Other examples include:

On Mexico's Guadalupe Island, a small fishing community created a 1,235-acre marine reserve in exchange for funding for a sea water desalination system.

In the South Pacific's Cook Islands, villagers on Atiu Island agreed to create a 297-acre wildlife sanctuary in exchange for an elder care facility.

On Namdrik Atoll, in the Marshall Islands, villagers created an 86-acre marine reserve in exchange for an education center and equipment for pearl farming.

Although this model incorporates a strategic approach to both incentive structures and social justice concerns, it was not developed as a theoretical framework before being applied to cases in the field. Rather, it was invented by Dr. Paul Cox, an ethnobotanist and current chairman of Seacology, in response to a concrete situation confronting a Samoan village in the early 1990s. Dr. Cox came to know the village of Falealupo and its surrounding forests while doing field studies on plant life and of the Samoan flying fox. In 1991, he was shocked to learn that the village had sold logging rights to their 30,000-acre rainforest. When he asked village leaders why they would agree to let the rainforest they cherished be chopped down, he was told that they had no choice: the Samoan government was threatening to remove the village's teachers unless a new schoolhouse was built. Selling the logging rights was the only way they could pay back a loan they had taken out in order to build the school.

Deeply concerned for the people of Falealupo and their natural resources, Dr. Cox offered to assume the entirety of the loan if the village would put a stop to the logging. It was in many ways a hasty offer: though he was prepared to give much of his own money, he knew he would have to raise at least some of the funds from friends and colleagues in the United States.

On its face, this offer was a terrifically good deal for Falealupo. But village leaders were skeptical. Many recalled stories of westerners "tricking" villages into signing over great tracts of their land. Dr. Cox went to great lengths to convince them that he truly had no interest in owning or controlling the land in any way beyond seeing that it was not cut down. Ultimately they agreed—the school was built, the teachers stayed, and the rainforest was saved.

Organization's Development

The Falealupo project was the starting point for what would become Seacology. Initially, Dr. Cox created an NPO simply to facilitate the fundraising he had to undertake for Falealupo. But the success of that project emboldened Dr. Cox and a handful of other donors to experiment with this model in other island villages.

They soon realized that they needed an organizational structure and professional staff to replicate and expand the model. In 1999, they hired Duane Silverstein, a former private foundation CEO with extensive experience in environmental grant making and an unusual combination of organizational and policy skills. Silverstein hired other staff to come up with new win-win island projects and to develop a solid platform of funding from individuals, corporations, and foundations. Meanwhile, the board was expanded from its original four to 20, bringing stability to the organization. During this time, Seacology also received critical donations from two foundations and a venture capitalist.

To help court new, high-wealth donors and board members, Seacology began hosting trips to visit project sites around the world, leveraging the fact that many of Seacology's projects are conducted in exotic locations. These trips enable guests to enjoy a memorable travel experience and also visit one or more Seacology project sites in the area, getting a firsthand look at Seacology's impact on a village. Whether joining a kava ceremony on

Ovalau in Fiji, playing traditional drums with locals on Nanumea Atoll in Tuvalu, or drinking "bush beer" in the woods of Atiu in the Cook Islands, visitors gain a rare insight into local island culture and increase their personal understanding and commitment to the work of Seacology.

An important operational innovation was the hiring of part-time field representatives around the world to find opportunities for new projects and monitor existing ones. Seacology's model emphasizes local competence, and the organization has placed strong emphasis on finding people who live in the region where projects are sponsored, speak English and at least one local language, and are familiar with local customs and culture. Finding good field representatives has been a challenging and at times lengthy process, but doing so has allowed Seacology to maintain a small staff (currently seven) in Berkeley, California, while relying on a network of part-time field representatives working in countries around the world.

Seacology has also succeeded by placing great emphasis on avoiding bureaucratic obstacles. Projects are negotiated directly with villages concerning land or marine resources that belong to them, thereby bypassing governmental bureaucracy and keeping the transactions exclusively within the realm of civil society.

This decentralized approach leads to the greatest challenge Seacology faces in working at the local level: gaining the trust of skeptical villagers. Some simply don't know what to make of Seacology representatives or supporters, and understandably question their motives. In Fiji, for example, one village was perplexed by the Seacology visitors whom they noticed used their free time to snorkel in the bay. Villager leaders suspected a trick. After all, why would these people come all this way just to *look* at the fish, not to catch them? It can take time for villages and Seacology representatives to come to a clear understanding.

This problem has been greatly ameliorated by Seacology's ever-growing network of successful projects on islands around the world and its expanding reputation as a fair and honest player—it is now widely understood that Seacology will not only help villages preserve their natural resources, but also will improve their quality of life while doing so. As of July 2014, Seacology had sponsored more than 150 projects on 152 islands in 54 nations throughout the world.

Seacology has also proved to be an adaptable organization, learning from its mistakes. For example, prior to hiring its field representatives, Seacology had formed an "Island Council" with representatives from islands around the world, but the group, all volunteers, failed to become the outreach institution Seacology had hoped. Sporadic communication between Seacology staff and a disparate group of islanders throughout the world was not enough to motivate these individuals to advocate on behalf of Seacology. It became clear that the help of part-time paid contractors was needed, and so Seacology began hiring field representatives in countries where it wanted to pursue projects. In the beginning, there were few such representatives, and they were expected to cover their own countries plus nearby countries as well. But the cultural boundaries proved to be too problematic. In light of Seacology's aim of maximizing local knowledge and decentralizing control, field representatives now represent only their home countries, with one exception: neighboring nations in Central America, each of which has few islands.

Sustainability

Seacology faces a fundamental question about the long-term efficacy of its conservation efforts: How is the commitment to protection of endangered resources to be sustained over time? In thinking about this challenge, Seacology developed the idea of offering village improvements instead of simply sending cash. Indeed, many organizations use cash as incentives for these purposes, paying locals in exchange for not fishing in certain areas, or not hunting certain species. On an international scale, some developing nations have taken advantage of debt-for-nature swaps where some of their foreign debt is canceled in exchange for achieving certain conservation goals.

While many such arrangements have had near-term success, it remains unclear how the environmental protection will be sustained once the financial payments or debt relief have become distant history. Seacology's unique approach leverages villagers' desire to conserve while, at the same time, promoting cooperation from all members of a community by offering improvements to villages from which they themselves will benefit over the long term. Simply giving money to a council or village leader does not generate the same kind of commitment over time.

That's not to say there are no incentives built into the Seacology model. Many of Seacology's projects call for certain conservation restrictions of a set period of time (typically between 10 to 30 years), and Seacology is just beginning to reach a point where the time limits on their earliest projects are beginning to expire. In these cases, Seacology has begun developing *new* projects with the communities to extend the conservation timeframe and bring even more improvements to the village.

A successful project can lead to other projects in the area as well, because neighboring villages see what can be gained by working with Seacology. If the villages are near each other, this can have the added benefit of having their respective conservation areas combined into one zone, giving the wildlife and flora a larger area of safe places in which to thrive.

Replicability

In theory, Seacology's model could be applied to any situation in which a community confronts a "collective action" problem, that is, a situation in which people are obliged (for economic or other reasons) to pursue short-term interests that undermine pursuit of their long-term communal best interests. This dilemma is especially clear in cases of long-term environmental degradation (often described in terms of Garrett Hardin's classic phrase, "the tragedy of the commons"). But this problem is not limited to the realm of conservation. Many kinds of public goods, such as education, disease prevention, clean water, and the provision of healthy food, are subject to the same dilemmas of individual short-term versus communal long-term interests. Thus, the model of providing external support to offset economic pressures and develop local incentives to secure the long-term public goods could, in principle, be applied to many kinds of problems.

However, there is at least one important element of a Seacology project that might not make sense for other kinds of change endeavors. Seacology leverages the power of a village—often governed by traditional laws—to achieve a consensus among many individuals about how to use its surrounding natural resources. Working in small, close-knit communities seems to be essential to develop these sorts of agreements. This arrangement can be the most practical way to ensure a forest or marine reserve is protected when formal enforcement (from official park rangers, for instance) is just not viable. Such projects might be less successful in larger communities or urban areas: in small communities where everyone knows everyone else, it is difficult to violate the terms of an agreement without others finding out (the classic peer pressure requirement described by Mancur Olsen [1977], Elinor Ostrom [1990], and others in the solution of collective action problems). Therefore, these types of projects may be less successful in larger communities or urban areas.

An operational lesson that could be adopted from Seacology by international NPOs of similar size is Seacology's relentless focus on the things it does most efficiently, and avoiding the temptation (often described as "mission creep") to extend itself into things that other parties could do better. In this regard, Seacology has taken to heart Benjamin Disraeli's dictum, "The secret of success is constancy to purpose." Seacology only works on islands.

CONCLUSIONS

The founding and development of Seacology provides important lessons about the creation of an innovative nonprofit organization. This chapter highlights key factors responsible for Seacology's early success in innovation, including clarity of its overall guiding aims, understanding of its unique role as a civil-society organization, highly strategic organizational choices, and attention to long-term sustainability.

1. Seacology's twin goals of environmental protection and social justice provide a balanced focus.

Most nonprofit organizations that work in this space tend to focus either on environmental preservation or community development. By focusing simultaneously on both these goals, Seacology places an unusual equal emphasis on a social justice aim of concern for the well-being of local populations and an environmental aim of preserving natural island habitats. This dual focus creates a synergy that strengthens its prospects for success in both areas.

2. Leadership that combines the skills of a visionary founder with the talents of an experienced executive director solves a typical "founder's syndrome."

Start-up social enterprise activities typically confront the challenge of blending an inspiring vision with practical expertise of implementation. Seacology is fortunate to have had both dimensions present in its founding leadership.

3. Commitment to working locally with indigenous staff and avoiding government bureaucracies eliminates bureaucratic complexities that often plague start-up organizations.

Seacology prefers to work directly with villages, bypassing regional and national governments. This allows Seacology to avoid the costly red tape impediments and jurisdictional issues involved in working with government bureaucracies.

4. Working through small communities and creating local incentives provides a solution to the classic problem of collective action.

As Nobel Laureate Elinor Ostrom (1990) has documented, the solution to collective action problems in making social change often requires local communities that are small enough to exert sufficient peer pressure to obtain compliance but that have access to sufficient resources (sometimes externally provided) to sustain the communal efforts. Seacology demonstrates this principle at work, emphasizing the importance of having tangible incentives that are chosen by the local island villagers rather than by office workers in the United States.

5. The challenge of sustainability is addressed through developing ongoing philanthropic support by combining stimulating travel experiences with a donor program.

It is possible for an organization to find creative ways to increase interest in its work and cultivate donors. Seacology leverages the fact that many of its projects are in exotic locations by hosting trips to many otherwise inaccessible locations around the world that include visits to Seacology projects.

6. Seacology has maintained a strong single-minded focus on mission.

Having a single focus can help an organization use its resources efficiently. Seacology has successfully avoided "mission creep" by resisting the temptation to work on preservation projects in larger, non-island areas or buying reserves outright.

7. Seacology is beginning to address the long-term challenge of future monitoring and enforcement.

Once the immediate benefit of a local project is a decade or more old, an important question arises about how the preserve will be safeguarded over time. Thus far, the local-based representatives have been able to monitor the projects, but the long-term consequences will only be understood over time.

DISCUSSION QUESTIONS

1. How can one best balance external organizational guidelines with local control? Given Seacology's strong commitment to local control *and* its simultaneous obligation to use funds entrusted to it in pursuit of larger environmental goals, how is the balance between these two aims best struck? If Seacology were to simply buy land from villages, it could pursue its conservation aims but at the expense of local control. What are the advantages or disadvantages of its approach?

2. What are the implications of avoiding most government involvement? Bypassing governments has the advantage of eliminating the often debilitating bureaucratic obstacles of extended approval processes and in-fighting of officialdom. At the same time, this avoidance has the potential downside of lacking the legitimacy and resources of government support. This emphasis on action at the level of civil society might raise questions of regulation and enforcement over time. What are the pros and cons of public versus private action in such conservation projects?

3. What is the limit on the size of communities that can be involved in Seacology-type projects? Seacology focuses on working with smaller communities to develop a consensus for proper use of natural resources. Why is it critical for the community to be small? At what point does a community become too big for this model to work?

4. How might Seacology have developed differently if it had originated as a theoretical model (and then applied to practice) rather than as a practical response to real problems faced in the field? Seacology's program developed as an expansion of a successful experiment tried in one island environment and later expanded to others. What are the pros and cons of each approach?

5. How does such an organization solve the long-term problems of monitoring and enforcement? In what ways could an organization like Seacology promote the long-term success of its projects? How can Seacology ensure that villagers continue to respect habitat reserves and maintain the new buildings or other communal resources it has helped establish?

6. Seacology's model relies on a quid pro quo agreement with a village to conserve an area of land or sea in exchange for Seacology providing funds for something the village needs. In what ways other than conservation could this model be used? Could it work in the fields of education or health?

REFERENCES

Baillie, J., Hilton-Taylor, C., & Stuart, S. N. (Eds.). (2004). *2004 IUCN Red List of threatened species: A global species assessment*. Gland, Switzerland: IUCN—The World Conservation Union. Retrieved from http://data.iucn.org/dbtwpd/html/red%20list%202004/completed/Section3.html

Olsen, M. (1977). *The logic of collective action: Public goods and the theory of groups*. Cambridge, MA: Harvard University Press.

Olson, S. (1989). Extinction on islands: Man as a catastrophe. In M. C. Pearl & D. Western (Eds.), *Conservation biology for the next century* (pp. 50–53). New York, NY: Oxford University Press.

Ostrom, E. (1990). *Governing the commons: The evolution of institutions for collective action*. Cambridge, United Kingdom: Cambridge University Press.

Wilson, E. O. (1984). *Biophilia*. Cambridge, MA: Harvard University Press.

ADDITIONAL RESOURCES

Ascher, W. (1999). *Why governments waste natural resources: Policy failures in developing countries*. Baltimore, MD: The Johns Hopkins University Press.

Brower, V. (2008). Back to nature: Extinction of medicinal plants threatens drug discovery. *Journal of the National Cancer Institute, 100*, 839–839.

Cohen, J., & Easterly, W. (Eds.). (2009). *What works in development? Thinking big and thinking small*. Washington, DC: Brookings Institution Press.

Cox, P. A. (1997). *Nafanua: Saving the Samoan rain forest*. New York, NY: W. H. Freeman.

Exclusive Economic Zones. (2013, April 22). *Sea around us*. Retrieved from http://www.seaaroundus.org/eez/

Estes, J. A., Terborgh, J., Brashares, J., Power, M. E., Berger, J., Bond, W. . . . Wardle, D. A. (2011). Trophic downgrading of planet Earth. *Science, 333*(6040), 301–306.

Farhan-Ferrari, M. (2012, February 1). *Indigenous communities help prevent deforestation Better than conservation. Women's News Network*. Retrieved from http://womennewsnetwork.net/2012/03/16/indigenous-communities-stop-deforestation/

Hardin, G. (1968). The tragedy of the commons. *Science, 162*(3859), 1243–1248.

Isaacson, A. (2012, December 1). Swimming with giants. *Islands.com*. Retrieved from http://www.islands.com/articles/swim-giants-tonga

Kay, J. (2002, August 4). ECOLOGY / Saving species of world's islands / Berkeley group preserves island treasures / Native peoples get benefits for protecting environment. SFGate. *San Francisco Chronicle*. Retrieved from http://www.sfgate.com/bayarea/article/ECOLOGY-Saving-Species-of-World-s-Islands-2786693.php

Paine, R. T. (1966). Food web complexity and species diversity. *American Naturalist, 100*(910), 66–75.

Tsui, B. (2006, December 17). Ecotourism: Traveling the world to help save it. *New York Times*. Retrieved from http://www.nytimes.com/2006/12/17/travel/17journeys.html?pagewanted=all&_r=0

CHAPTER 11

Dialogue in the Dark

Mainstreaming Blind People in Germany

Andreas Schröer

Evangelische Hochschule Darmstadt

The only way to learn is through encounter.

—Martin Buber

How would you react when your boss informs you that you get a blind colleague? When the journalist Andreas Heinecke was teamed up with a blind trainee at his radio station, he soon realized two things. His blind colleague had amazing skills and competencies, which Andreas didn't expect. And second, his colleague was one of the few blind people he knew who were working in a regular, professional job. Those two issues, the social perception of blind people and their integration in the job market, became the driving force behind his passion, and became the reasons for creating a very successful social enterprise.

But before we continue with Heinecke's story, let's look at the facts. The German job market in the 1980s was far from inclusive for visually impaired adults. Estimates suggest a total of 500,000 visually impaired people in Germany, among them 155,000 are blind (Nicolai, 1996). Research in the 1990s suggests that only 30% of visually impaired or blind adults in the employable age range actually have a job compared to 75% in the general public (Schröder, 1997); another third get state pensions (including early retirement), which is twice as high as for the general public. Twelve percent of employed blind people in the 1990s did have a job in sheltered workshops for the blind; another 50% were working in public service.

One reason for such low job market integration is the stereotypical social perception of blindness in German society. Societal perceptions of persons with disabilities are certainly neither homogeneous nor static. After the horrific persecution of disabled people in Nazi Germany (Evans, 2004), and the postwar eras of denial and guilt, the societal perception has shifted toward a deficit-oriented view. Physically impaired people are perceived as being in need of help and support, and they are defined by a deficit.

In this chapter, the author focuses on how one organization, Dialogue in the Dark, tried to mainstream blind people in Germany. Its founder, Andreas Heinecke, was committed to change the social perception of "otherness" toward a competence-oriented view by demonstrating that blind people have strengths and competencies that allow them to do things that even seeing people cannot do.

INTRODUCTION: THE PREVIOUS ATTEMPTS TO SOLVE THE PROBLEM

An example of a traditional approach to support visually impaired people in Germany is the Institution for the Blind Foundation in Frankfurt, a nonprofit organization with a focus on advocacy, housing, and job creation programs for the blind. The organization was founded in 1837. It ran a special school for blind children, a residential home, sheltered workshops, job-training programs, and sociocultural projects, as well as rehabilitation programs. Products (household goods and cleaning supplies such as brooms, brushes, etc.) of the sheltered workshop were high quality and sold all over Germany. However, its well-organized programs remained within deficit-oriented approaches and focused on compensating competency deficits. The foundation's geographical focus remained on Germany. The integration of its clients in the regular job market was limited.

Heinecke, who started working for the foundation, was content with its general purpose but did not feel at ease with the restricted approach the foundation was taking. He was looking for ways to highlight the abilities and competencies of the blind in a way that had the potential to change the societal perception of blindness globally.

THE INNOVATION: AN EXHIBITION IN THE DARK

In 1988, Heinecke found the solution. Together with his wife Orna Cohen (an expert in interactive exhibition design), he invented an exhibition entirely in the dark, using blind people as guides. It was organized at his employer's headquarters in Frankfurt and turned out to be a big success. In fact, it became the cornerstone of his innovative nonprofit organization Dialogue in the Dark (DITD). Its mission is "to facilitate social inclusion of marginalized people on a global basis. Our goal is to raise awareness and create tolerance for Otherness in the general public, thereby overcoming barriers between 'us' and 'them.' We create jobs for disadvantaged people by turning deficits into potentials and thereby strengthen the self-esteem of individuals who are typically under-valued" (http://www.dialogue-in-the-dark.com/about/mission).

Visitors experience an exhibition space, which is pitch-dark, based on a patented technique. After a short introduction and turning off their mobile phones, visitors enter the dark room(s) and experience different "scenes," for example crossing a river over a little wooden bridge, crossing a street with a traffic light in regular traffic, or ordering and paying for drinks at a bar. Within minutes in the dark, visitors realize that they need help to find their way through the exhibition. They certainly turn to other group members, but most important, they rely on the support of their blind guides. The guides seem to be the only people in the room who do not lose the capacity to navigate; they provide support and orientation and stay calm in a situation that makes some visitors uncomfortable or nervous. One visitor gave the following feedback to a guide: "Thank you very much, Jürgen [name of guide]. I was afraid when I went in, and then found I could relax in a dark world." After this experience in the dark, which lasts between 60 and 90 minutes, visitors have learned to interpret the sound signals of traffic lights, they realized how difficult it is to pay a bartender, without seeing coins or bills, and they have learned to trust the competencies of their blind guides. Subsequent to the visit of the dark space, there is an opportunity to exchange experiences among group members and guides. Those conversations take place in daylight and are facilitated by the guides.

DITD has an intangible (change social perception of otherness) and a very tangible goal (mainstreaming the blind for the first job market). The organization can be described as innovative for its process or method, that is, the application of the already existing concept of interactive exhibitions to a new social issue (blindness), as well as for its business model. DITD is an early mover in the field of social franchising and has applied this approach to a new industry (interactive exhibitions).

The Entrepreneur

Heinecke is a trained high school teacher with a PhD in history, a film maker, and journalist. While working at a radio station, he was asked to design a rehabilitation program for a 28-year-old blind colleague who recently lost his eyesight in a car crash. He learned to perceive the world from the perspective of his blind friend, which spoke to some of his own early childhood experiences of being different and excluded. Most important, he saw a connection to his family's history in Nazi-Germany. "He was born to a Jewish mother, whose family was murdered in Nazi camps, and a German father, whose relatives were Nazi loyalists. Why, he wondered, did the Germans fail to transcend their stereotypes and hatreds?" (Rothstein, 2011). Heinecke observed that being different in Germany still leads to social exclusion. The theme of contributing to a positive social attitude toward people who are discriminated against because they are different was at the core of this business idea.

The Organization's Development

Between 1988 and 1996, Heinecke ran his exhibitions as part-time projects, while working full-time at the Stiftung Blindenanstalt. But their number increased steadily from two in 1988 to 17 in 1995. This obvious success, the positive feedback from visitors and colleagues, and his own dedication to the cause finally convinced him in 1996 to quit his job and to create a nonprofit organization: Dialogue in the Dark (DITD). Already 2 years later in 1998, Heinecke received the first of many prestigious awards, the "Stevie Wonder Vision Award"; in 2005, he was awarded the first Ashoka Fellowship in Western Europe (Ashoka, 2005).

DITD used different strategies in the various phases of its organizational development to accrue support and resources. The organization needed a mix of fees, private and corporate contributions, and government support. The basic business model of organizing exhibitions is fee based. But in the early phase and during the creation of the two German permanent exhibitions in Hamburg and Frankfurt, public subsidies played an important role in sustaining the organization. The following paragraphs describe DITD's different strategic approaches to accrue support and resources.

Internationalization

Just 3 years after the first German exhibition, the first international exhibitions were organized in Austria and France. "In Frankfurt for example we met a dancer, who told a friend in Paris about his great experience in the DITD exhibition. This friend calls us up and tells us, that he is organizing a cultural festival in Paris and that he'd like to invite us. So this is how this started, totally unintended, unexpected and beyond our control" (Heinecke, personal communication, August 21, 2008). Later this accidental internationalization became the central growth engine for DITD. Already in 1995, 14 out of the 17 exhibitions were organized abroad; in 2007, 17 out of 19 exhibitions.

Permanent Exhibitions

The exhibition in Hamburg was originally intended as a 2-year project. "It was not planned as a permanent installation" (Heinecke, personal communication, August 21, 2008). But since the venue proved to be beneficial, and the local government approved funding to support job creation for impaired individuals, Hamburg gradually developed into a permanent exhibition. In 2000, the linguist and cultural manager Klara Kletzka, a senior executive of the Hamburg exhibition, started planning with Heinecke the launch of a Dialogmuseum in Frankfurt, which opened its doors in 2005. Kletzka recalls: "In Hamburg we started small and had to add more and more space to the exhibition. In Frankfurt we choose a different path and avoided this adding-on approach, we were self-confident and used by far more space from the very beginning" (personal communication, August 21, 2008). Heinecke and Kletzka, who both invested private money, had to work with external financial investors to realize the project, such as BonVenture limited (a social investment group), the Landeswohlfahrtsverband (social welfare association), and the Blinden- und Sehbehindertenverband (a self-help advocacy association).

Social Franchising

Early on Heinecke realized the potential of the exhibition concept as a brand: "it is a straightforward, good product, which has the potential to be transferred" (Heinecke, personal communication, August 21, 2008). However, there were at least two alternatives to actually tap this potential to lay the groundwork for a sustainable social business. One alternative was to become a traveling circus and tour the world with a certain number of exhibitions per year. The value added to the company would be to do international marketing and to handle demanding logistics for a stable product. The other alternative was a "de-materialization of the product" and to invest in brain ware by developing a franchise model, and sell the concept of the exhibition to franchisees within a global network of partners who facilitate exhibitions and business workshops and share the common goal to promote social inclusion. As Heinecke thought about the two options with a business consultant in the 1990s, he envisioned the traveling-circus concept to be rather cumbersome; in fact, he felt no desire whatsoever to spend his life handling complicated logistical problems. He rather saw himself reinventing the idea and adapting it to different societal and cultural circumstances and market needs. He also had fun talking to people abroad and traveling, and he preferred leaving the actual administration and daily operation of a new exhibition to somebody else. To make a living from exporting his concept to other countries, it was necessary to develop a franchise model.

Social Franchising (Hackl, 2009) became the core business model of Dialogue Social Enterprise (DSE):

> Licensee partners are responsible for initiating and managing the exhibitions and workshops in their location. In return for a license fee to Dialogue Social Enterprise, they are given know-how for creating and managing the service (exhibition, workshop or both); support in recruitment and training of the blind or deaf high-potential candidates who will become world-class guides and trainers; access to Dialogue Social Enterprise's global network; and use of the brand and trademark services. Some of our licensee partners are social entrepreneurs themselves, blind unions, museums, or science centers, professional exhibition companies or corporate companies (www.dialogue-se.com/how/business-model).

The licensing fees depend on the realized revenues of the partner exhibitions; they also account for a starting up phase of 3 years.

Variability and Miniaturization

Due to the German federal state system, different local and state governments funded job creation and job market reintegration programs, which varied in their terms and conditions, for handicapped people. Therefore it was necessary to vary exhibition projects accordingly, mostly regarding duration and size (number of people funded). Adjustments in product design occurred within a wide range of exhibition spaces from 50 to 5,000 square meters, be it a museum, office space, or an old factory.

Another strategy was to vary the duration from very short engagements up to long-term exhibitions. The team had the knowledge and organizational capacity to realize different formats "without a loss of identity or loss of content . . . this gives the whole matter a huge flexibility" (Heinecke, personal communication, August 21, 2008). However, some common standards were necessary: exhibitions had to take place in complete darkness and blind people had to be the guides.

The variability was attractive to corporate sponsors, who supported DITD within their Corporate Social Responsibility programs either by partnering with local exhibition organizers or by inviting Dialogue exhibitions in their office space. Other partners offered pro bono strategic or legal consulting services. The list of DITD corporate partners includes: Bain & Co., Beiersdorf, Bertelsmann, BMW Foundation, BNP Paribas, Daimler Chrysler, Deutsche Bank, SAP, and others.

Diversification

The fifth strategy was to diversify the product line. Based on the original concept of darkness, the idea of "dining in the dark" emerged. The concept was first presented at a festival in Avignon in 1993 by Michel Reilhac, and in 1997, became a successful business, based on the initiative of two former blind guides of a DITD project in Zurich/Switzerland (Blinde Kuh). DITD integrated "Dinner in the Dark" in some exhibition venues, offering surprise multiple-course meals in the dark, which are marketed as a "surprise for palate and culinary culture" and served by blind waiters. In 2012, Dinner in the Dark was served in Hong Kong, Shanghai, Hyderabad, Singapore, Tokyo, Vienna, Frankfurt, Hamburg, and Milano.

DITD also used exhibition space for trainings with different groups, including business managers. Business workshops are booked by international companies like Unilever, Airbus, and Beiersdorf. Other workshop concepts include team development, communication, conflict resolution, and leadership development. Especially for top executives, the experience of total darkness works very well to develop trust and soft skills like emotional intelligence and social competence. In 2011, DITD held 686 business workshop sessions in 13 different venues with 13,560 participants (Meyer, 2012).

Since the interactive exhibition concept worked well for the perception of blindness, it was adapted to different forms of perception by creating an exhibition on nonverbal communication (Dialogue in Silence), in which all guides are deaf or hearing-impaired. The latest brain child of the Dialogue team is an exhibition about the art of aging (Dialogue with Time), which opened in August 2012 at the Israeli Children's Museum in Holon. The guides in this exhibition are all at least 70 years old.

Crucial Stages of Development in the Organization's Growth

In 2008, the organization underwent a thorough consulting process, which helped consolidate the organizational structure, clarify leadership roles, and set clear financial goals.

Financially DITD has managed to break ever since 2003 (except for 2006, due to high startup costs in Frankfurt). With more than 140 exhibitions worldwide and 11 existing permanent exhibitions (Atlanta, Georgia, United States; Campinas, Brazil; Copenhagen, Denmark; Frankfurt, Germany; Hamburg, Germany; Holon, Israel; Milan, Italy; Monterrey, Mexico; Vienna, Austria), the international business is the major profit driver. More than 40% of the international business revenues stem from licensing fees, 30% are consulting contracts, and 20% are generated by workshops. However, an analysis of all DSE's activities in 2007 reveals that the two major revenue sources are entrance fees (40%) and public funds (20%). The most important cost factor is personnel, which accounts for more than 55% of the overall costs.

From a strategic perspective, the international business has three core advantages compared to the other operations of Dialogue Social Enterprise: (1) It has a huge growth potential; (2) it generates increasing revenue and more so increasing profits; (3) it is less cost intensive than running permanent exhibitions, because it generates less personnel costs.

Most of the international business operates as a franchise model. Yet each exhibition has set-up costs, new social entrepreneurs need training to get to know the idea and some best practices. At the moment, DSE calculates 200,000 euro set up costs per new exhibition. The growth of the international business therefore depends on two major factors: (1) finding, recruiting, and training new social entrepreneurs; (2) finding investors to cover the set-up costs. As an alternative, the other businesses would need to generate sufficient money to cover those costs, but given the current situation, this would slow down the growth process enormously. The second best option for further financial growth of DSE would be the development of a new "own" profitable permanent exhibition.

Creating Hybrid Structures—A Path for Further Growth Strategy?

After years of actively searching for private and institutional financial investors to fund DITD's global growth strategy, Heinecke created a "strategy of hybridization." Although the cooperation with venture philanthropists and foundations was successful for DITD, it never provided the kind of money that was needed to expand the business on a global scale. Heinecke started to use his contacts with leaders of global companies whom he met at the World Economic Forum.

His idea to develop a strategy of hybridization was inspired by the model of Grameen Danone Foods Ltd, which was founded in 2006, to reduce poverty by bringing health through food to children using a community-based business model. The joint venture started with a food factory in Bangladesh that produces yoghurt enriched with crucial nutrients at a price of 0.06 euro, which even the poorest can afford. DITD's strategy of hybridization consists of different forms of partnerships with for-profit companies: (a) Licensing contract with U.S. exhibition provider Premier Exhibitions Inc.; (b) Strategic global partnership with employment services industry leader Manpower Inc.; and (c) Collaboration with Allianz Group on innovative training centers.

Premier Exhibitions Inc.

Premier Exhibitions Inc. is a NASDAQ listed major provider of "museum quality touring exhibitions throughout the world" (http://www.prxi.com/prxi.html). The Atlanta based company started its success story with the travelling exhibition "Titanic: The Artifact Exhibition," and among its global bestsellers are "Bodies: The Exhibition" and "Bodies: Revealed," with over 15 million visitors worldwide. The company has built a strong track record in producing, managing, and marketing successful exhibitions.

In 2008, former CEO of PRXI, Arnie Geller, and Andreas Heinecke signed a long-term licensing agreement for the U.S. market. For the U.S. tour, PRXI also partners with Manpower Inc. to advance the training and employment opportunities for DITD's mostly visually impaired employees. In addition to a touring exhibition, Premier Inc. opened a permanent exhibition in Atlanta on August 30, 2008, which closed in March 2012. The goal of this partnership is to create 12 exhibitions in the United States, at least 4 out of the 12 are planned to become permanent exhibitions. Premier manages, produces, and markets the exhibitions; DITD delivers the content and the conception and receives licensing fees in return. The current DITD exhibition in the United States runs in the South Bronx in New York City; it opened its doors in August 2011. The U.S. partnership also created some challenges to DITD's corporate culture, since the intended profit margin for PRXI is 16%, which requires running exhibitions with at least 1,600 visitors a day.

Manpower Inc.

Manpower is a very big international workforce solutions company that offers employers permanent, temporary, and contract recruitment; employee assessment and selection; training; outplacement; outsourcing; and consulting. Its staff in 82 countries serves 400,000 clients per year. According to its social responsibility report, Manpower's (2006) corporate strategy includes investments in placing and training impaired individuals and declares workforce development as the number one goal on its social responsibility agenda. A global partner was needed to help the company get in touch with this target group and the existing job market. DITD had established access to this particular share of the market, had the experience, credibility, and international operations. Manpower offers training opportunities for DITD employees in different countries and helps promote the exhibitions. On May 8, 2009, Manpower announced its cooperation with DITD

> by providing direct temporary jobs to blind candidates as guides at DiTD exhibits. . . . Manpower will invite clients to the show and build awareness in the local business community, with a view to securing permanent jobs for the guides at the conclusion of each exhibition, Manpower will also make available a number of training and skill development programs to the guides in each country and will assist them in their job search (Manpower.com).

As a result, Manpower has recruited and trained the 110 visually impaired guides for the exhibition in Atlanta and has reported this engagement in the corporate social responsibility update in 2009. Both partners hope that their cooperation increases public interest in the employment and training for impaired individuals.

Allianz Global Investors Dialogue Training Center (DTC)

In 2009, the Dialogue Training Center (DTC), which houses Allianz Global Investor's Dialogue in the Dark and Dialogue in Silence training facilities, was officially launched in Munich. DTC operates as a business unit within AllianzGI and "aims to attract German and international businesses which want to capitalize on the innovative employee and management training on offer" (dialogue.allianzgi.com). Allianz Group Diversity Council Marna Whittington explains: "When we first learned about this concept, we realized the potential training in the dark and in silence could have for leadership development. We now have a dedicated, professional human resource training facility which embodies the best of AllianzGI and evokes the qualities that makes AllianzGI a preeminent financial advisor: trust, leadership and diversity" (dialogue.allianzgi.com). Most trainings cover team building, communication, collaboration, and leadership. Moreover, DITD became an integral part of many leadership programs of the Allianz Management Institute.

The Dialogue Training Center is run by Allianz Global Investors in cooperation with Dialogue Social Enterprise. AllianzGI is a big global asset management firm that manages 1.6 trillion USD in assets, has 4,800 employed staff, and serves approximately 75 million clients in Europe, North America, and Asia. AllianzGI provides location, staff, internal clients, and marketing; DITD provides the content and concept of executive trainings in the dark or in silence. The location is Munich, at the headquarters of the Allianz Group, but other venues are planned. Allianz recently hosted 32 DITD workshops at its Corporate Offices in Mexico City in the fall of 2010.

Challenges in the Formation of DITD

Before 2008, the organizational structure was a weak point of DITD. Dialogue Social Enterprise was a loosely coupled system of individual organizations with different ownership structures. There was not one Dialogue company, but many. The link between the different organizations was the founder and inventor of the concept, who held stakes in all the different organizations.

Heinecke created Consens Limited in 1995 as his first company. The permanent exhibition in Hamburg is currently seen as the head office of the different Dialogue organizations; DITD was founded in 2000 as a charitable nonprofit organization. One of the reasons to start out with Dialogue as a charitable nonprofit organization was the subsidies that a charitable organization would get from state and local government as an employer of visually impaired individuals. Heinecke described the process of dealing with the bureaucratic requirements to actually receive these funds as torturous and limiting to his entrepreneurial freedom. Therefore he was looking for ways to contain the influence of government bureaucracy by dividing his operation into for-profit and nonprofit organizations. In 2008, the founder owned shares in the following companies: Consens Ausstellungs GmbH, a limited company that runs the exhibition in Hamburg; Dialogmuseum GmbH, a limited that runs the permanent exhibition in Frankfurt; and Schattensprache GmbH, a limited that runs the permanent exhibition in Rendsburg. Revenues from workshops, trainings, consulting contracts, and licensing fees from international franchisees were bundled in the Consens Andreas Heinecke GmbH, which was a one-person company. The purely charitable aspects of the Dialogue family are run through the still existing nonprofit: "Dialog im Dunkeln [Dialogue in the Dark]—Verein zur Förderung zur sozialen Kreativität." After establishing Consens Exhibitions Ltd., Dialogmuseum Ltd., and Chattensprache Ltd., Heinecke found the shell of the company had become too narrow and asked his closest associates to join a new company: Dialogue Social Enterprise (DSE). Orna Cohen, Laura Gorni, Klara Kletzka, and Thomas Richter agreed, and in 2008, started this new venture with Andreas Heinecke. In the meantime, the exhibition venue in Rendsburg was terminated and integrated into the Dialogmuseum in July 2010 (see Figure 11.1).

More recently, the lasting economic crisis also turned out to be a problem for the organization. The permanent exhibition in Atlanta had to close down, and in April 2013, the Dialogue Museum in Frankfurt had to reduce its services to the core elements: exhibition and trainings. Due to higher personnel costs, Frankfurt had to close the Casino in the Dark, a Kiosk, and the Dinner space (Michels, 2013).

The Solution's Efficiency, Effectiveness, and Replicability

According to Ashoka (2005),

> Dialogue in the Dark, has empowered more than 4,000 blind people in 19 countries and more than 130 cities from disadvantaged backgrounds by giving them for the first time in their life the opportunity to showcase their talents and skills. They manage

FIGURE 11.1 Organizational Structure of Dialogue Social Enterprise

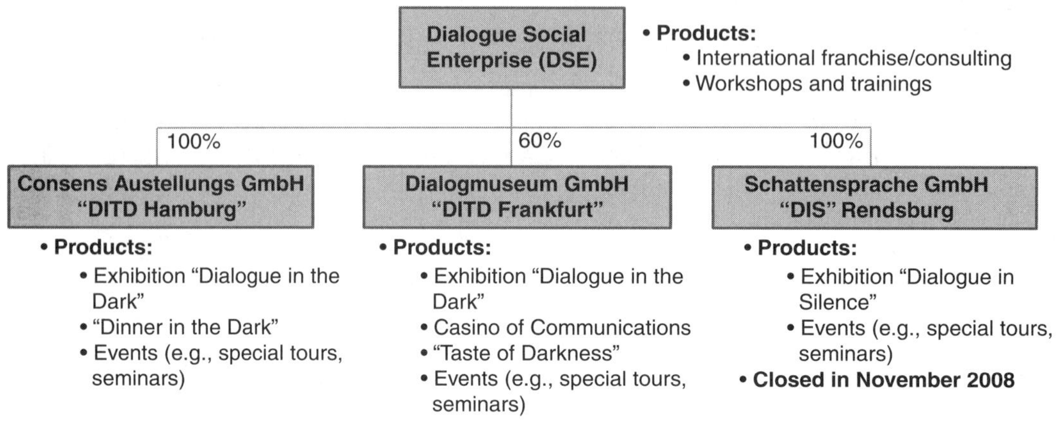

the platform and teach visitors (including senior executives from companies) how to see without eyes, thereby acquiring leadership, communication, and management skills (in traditional rehab programs, disabled people seldom have direct interaction with the public and rarely exercise leadership with the public). The vast majority of the "Dialogue in the Dark" employees have never held a formal job before, and 40 percent of them successfully gain a job placement with a "normal" company in the private or public sector between a week and a year and a half with Dialogue.

According to DITD's 2012 annual report, DITD franchisees hosted exhibitions at 21 sites across the world, serving a total of 699,000 visitors and workshop participants, employed 392 visually impaired people, and trained 97 new guides and trainers in 2011. Of DITD's worldwide employees, 63.4% are blind or visually impaired (Meyer, 2012). By 2012, DITD had employed and empowered over 7,000 blind people.

SHM, a strategy and innovation consulting firm based in London produced a positive impact study on DITD guides in 2007. Over 40 past and present guides in six different sites were interviewed. The interviews explored positive and negative impacts on guides of participation in DITD and sought to establish the aspects of DITD that are effective. The study found impacts on the guides' mindset (psychological); the impact on relations and community integration (social), as well as impacts on skills, employability, and the wider economy (economic).

Empowerment, improved quality of life, the opportunity to mobilize skills and prior experiences, enhanced sense of individuality, security, and stability, as well as enhanced communication and interaction were identified as psychological impacts for the guides. Social impacts were altered feelings about their blindness, enhanced relationships, as well as enhanced peer support. Finally, SHM found the following economic impacts: Enhanced self-belief, improved communication skills, as well as the guides' ability to put their blindness to use and to develop a "sense that blindness can be considered a skill" (SHM, 2007).

The study's critical findings were mostly about the transferability of the guides' skills into other forms of employment. Although DITD helps their guides develop transferable mainstream skills, the organization could do more to prepare their employees for conventional employment (skill accreditation, skill development, workplace familiarization, and hiring more blind employees in management jobs).

Another study, by Orna & Co., analyzed the impact of DITD on its visitors: schoolchildren, individual visitors and families, and companies and their members. Over 1,000 visitor comments, chosen at random from the last four guest books, were analyzed, in addition to a random sample of 50 phone interviews with visitors who visited the exhibition in 2000. Five years after the visit researchers found that visiting DITD is a positive emotional experience, including a common feeling of gratitude and respect toward the guides. About 37% of all comments mentioned growing self-awareness as a result of the visit. DITD was also perceived as a physical and intellectual discovery of blind people and their world. While 100% of the visitors interviewed by phone still remember their visit after 5 years, 98% still talk about it, 76% talk about the encounter with a blind person, and 80% felt they have more knowledge about blindness than before. Fifty-eight percent think that their attitude toward visual impairment has changed since visiting the exhibition, while 48% still confirm the concept's immediate impact (Orna & Co., 2006). Since 1988, DITD has been experienced by over 7 million people in over 130 cities in more than 30 countries around the world.

CONCLUSIONS

Here are some themes in the nonprofit discourse that can be discussed, based on this case:

- *Social entrepreneurship*: Social entrepreneurs are considered to combine revenue generation and social innovation (Nicholls, 2010). DITD generates income by selling a service, that intends to solve a social problem. But part of the decision to change the nonprofit status into a limited company was the level of dependency on local government authorities and bureaucratic regulations, which in Heinecke's view compromised sound management decisions.

- *Innovation*: Social innovation often occurs at the intersection of sectors (civil society/market) or at the intersection of organizational fields (art exhibition/social work) (Howaldt & Schwarz, 2010). DITD's process (interactive exhibition on blindness) and business model (social franchise) innovation occurred at such intersections.

- *Social investment market*: The hope of many social entrepreneurs is the creation of a new social investment market (Nicholls, 2008). However, for DITD, it was still difficult to find social investors for its global growth strategy; Ashoka, Schwab, other foundations, and new venture philanthropists didn't provide sufficient resources.

- *Cross-sectoral partnerships* become increasingly important: DITD partners with different kinds of organizations. Of particular importance are organizations that are capable of providing DITD with vital resources, especially financial capital. Therefore, DITD cooperates with Social Venture Investors, a for-profit employment service company; the for-profit insurer, Alliance Group; and Premier Exhibitions Inc., a for-profit museum content provider. Questions occur about the shared value base among partners and external pressures to cooperate based on a scarcity of available resources.

- *Learning organization*: the management team is constantly improving their business model, changing their organizational structure, and cooperating with consultants and scientists to keep the operations up to date. DITD has never stopped developing new product lines, like diners, management trainings, and so on.

- *Intermediary or bridge building functions*: DITD acts as a mediator, primarily, between blind and seeing people and helps both groups increase their mutual understanding. Furthermore, DITD mediates between different rationalities or languages. The first and second generation of social entrepreneurs in the company is not only open-minded about the use of business management language, but they are also seeking to adapt this language to their particular social enterprise. The key leaders in the company, like Andreas Heinecke, Klara Kletzka, and Orna Cohen, have a background in education, cultural management, or the arts and are not originally trained as business managers.

DISCUSSION QUESTIONS

1. Creating social innovation is among the key criteria for social entrepreneurship. What makes Andreas Heinecke a social entrepreneur?
2. Which problem is Dialogue in the Dark trying to solve? How would you describe the societal role of this organization? (social service, vanguard, advocacy, value preservation)
3. Do you see a conflict between the organization's need for financial resources and its original social mission?
4. Would you consider Dialogue in the Dark to be a successful nonprofit?
5. Would you consider Dialogue in the Dark to be an innovative nonprofit? How so?

REFERENCES

Ashoka. (2005). Andreas Heinecke. *Ashoka innovators for the public*. Retrieved from https://www.ashoka.org/node/3661

Evans, S. E. (2004). *Forgotten crimes: The Holocaust and people with diabilities*. Chicago, IL: Ivan R Dee.

Hackl, V. (2009). *Social franchising* (p. 197). St. Gallen, Switzerland: Universität Sankt Gallen.

Howaldt, J., & Schwarz, M. (2010). *Social innovation: Concepts, research fields and international trends* (p. 88). Dortmund, Germany: Sozialforschungsstelle Dortmund.

Manpower. (2006). *2006 annual responsibility report: Take alook around*. Retrieved from http://www.manpowergroup.com/wps/wcm/connect/b80a8abb-2a19-498c-9dd5-4d6dc2910789/SR_Report.pdf?MOD = AJPERES

Meyer, A. (2012). *2011 Annual results summary* (pp. 1–10). Hamburg, Germany: Dialogue Social Entreprise. Retrieved from http://www.dialogue-in-the-dark.com/files-dse-did/DID_RESULT_2011_Short-Version.pdf

Michels, C. (2013, January 15). Dialog-Museum ringt um Zukunft. *Frankfurter Rundschau*. Frankfurt/M.

Nicholls, A. (2008). *The landscape of social investment: A holistic typology of opportunities and challenges* (p. 231). Oxford, United Kingdom: Skoll Centre for Social Entrepreneurship, Saïd Business School.

Nicholls, A. (2010). The legitimacy of social entrepreneurship: Reflexive isomorphism in a pre-paradigmatic field. *Entrepreneurship Theory & Practice*, *44*, 611–633.

Nicolai, T. (Ed.). (1996). *You see? A bridge to the visually handicapped and the blind*. Bonn, Germany: German Federation of the Blind.

Orna & Co. (2006). *Dialogue in the Dark. What are its consequences and how can they be proved?* (p. 22). Hamburg, Germany: Author.

Rothstein, E. (2011, August 19). Darkness visible, and palpable. *New York Times*, p. C21. Retrieved from http://www.nytimes.com/2011/08/19/arts/design/dialog-in-the-dark-at-south-street-seaport-exhibition-review.html?_r = 2&

Schröder, H. (1997). Die Beschäftigungssituation von Blinden. Ausgewählte Ergebnisse einer Befragung von Blinden und Unternehmen. *Mitteilungen aus der Arbeitsmarkt- und Berufsforschung*, *30*(2), 502–513.

SHM. (2007). *Keeping the dialogue going. An evaluation of the impact and outcomes for guides employed by Dialogue in the Dark* (p. 29). London, England: Author.

ADDITIONAL RESOURCES

Dialogue Social Enterprise: http://www.dialogue-se.com

DITD (international website): http://www.dialogue-in-the-dark.com

Video on Experience in DITD: http://www.youtube.com/watch?v = 33b_CWNAu-A

TED Talk with Andreas Heinecke (2008): http://www.youtube.com/watch?v = cSAkJ4VyPxo

Siegried Saerberg on Dining in the Dark: http://dsq-sds.org/article/view/24/24

Dialogue in Silence: http://www.dialogue-in-silence.com

Dialogue with Time: http://www.dialogue-with-time.com

This case study is based on several interviews with Andreas Heinecke and Klara Kletzka; one interview with Marna Whittington (Allianz); a visit to the Dialogue exhibitions in Hamburg and Frankfurt; and conversations with visitors, guides, and consultants, as well as extensive document analysis, including financial data.

CHAPTER 12

Krembo Wings

A Youth Organization for Children With Disabilities in Israel

Michal Almog-Bar[1]

Paul Baerwald School of Social Work and Social Welfare, Hebrew University of Jerusalem, Israel

INTRODUCTION

Almost 10% of Israeli children (210,000) have a severe disability that affects their daily functioning (Weissblay, 2011). Most of them live in the community and receive services there. To find meaning and purpose, all people, and especially people with disabilities, need to participate in the social and recreational life of the community. To form a strong self and social identity, people need to develop skills and competencies, form friendships and relationships, achieve mental and physical health, and express creativity (Brown & Gordon, 1987; King et al., 2004; Schleien, Green, & Heyne, 1993). Nonetheless, in many communities, children with disabilities have limited inclusive opportunities for social and recreational activities (King et al., 2003; Law et al., 2007). Sadly, such opportunities for children with disabilities are conducted in segregated settings in which there is no interaction with children without disabilities. These opportunities may also be limited in their range and variety as compared to social opportunities for children without disabilities. Moreover, many social activities and recreational opportunities may be provided in locations that are physically inaccessible to children with disabilities (King et al., 2004). All these factors contribute to limited inclusive social and recreational activities.

In Israel, the treatment of children with severe disabilities in the community is entrusted to different systems of health, education, and welfare, which supply them education,

[1] Data for this chapter were collected through six semi-structured in-depth interviews conducted with board members, parents, and senior staff members of the organization. The author also analyzed a variety of documented materials about the organization and its activities, including minutes of meetings, reports published by the organization, and relevant media coverage.

rehabilitation, and health services. However, there are significant gaps in the volumes of both supply and consumption of services among populations residing in different areas of the country (Weissblay, 2011). Children with disabilities in the peripheral areas and among lower socioeconomic populations face a considerably lower range of services in their communities. There is a significant shortage of social after-school services for these children. Afternoon leisure services for children with disabilities are offered in only a small number of local authorities, where they usually take the form of volunteer mentors who come to the children's homes (Sagiv, Milshtein, & Ben, 2011).

In many local authorities, the social services departments suffer from ongoing shortages of budget and human resources. The development of community services for children with disabilities is not their top priority, and they find it difficult to allocate the required resources. The number of afterschool services for these children is also inhibited by low awareness in the community of the needs of children with disabilities and their families' difficulties in meeting the payments for services.

This chapter presents an innovative attempt to deal with the social isolation of children with disabilities and to increase their social participation in the community, as well as to foster social change in the perceptions of youth regarding these children. Krembo Wings is the first and only youth organization in Israel that integrates children and youth with disabilities with youth without disabilities. Krembo is a popular Israeli sweet, chocolate-covered marshmallow on a cookie, each one individually wrapped. Similarly, each child in Krembo Wings is "wrapped" personally with love, care, and the belief that he or she can spread his or her wings and fly.

THE PROBLEM: THE LONELINESS AND SOCIAL ALIENATION EXPERIENCED BY CHILDREN WITH DISABILITIES IN ISRAEL

The beginning of the social solution that would later become a youth organization starts with the story of a friendship formed between two children, Kfir and Adi. Kfir Kobi was born in Jerusalem, Israel, in 1996, and was diagnosed with severe cerebral palsy (CP). While his parents, Claudia and Raffi, acknowledged the hardship of raising a child with a disability, they decided not to relate to Kfir as having a disability and limitations and would make every effort necessary to provide him with the conditions for leading an active life.

When Kfir was 3 years old, his mother gave birth to her second child. The new situation created new family dynamics—a newborn child and a child with a severe disability who was highly dependent on his parents' care—that led Kfir's mother to seek outside assistance. She approached one of the well-established Israeli nonprofit organizations serving people with disabilities operating in her town and asked for a volunteer to help her one afternoon a week. Due to Kfir's physical impairments and lack of speech capabilities, her plan was that the volunteer would be with the baby, allowing her to be with Kfir.

A few months later, she was approached by a 12-year-old girl who the organization had sent to help her. Adi Altschuler started to visit the house once a week as a volunteer. Interestingly, Adi insisted on playing with Kfir rather than being with the baby. They quickly learned to understand each other and established a strong connection. She started to spend more time at Kfir's home, participating in different indoor and outdoor activities with the boy and his family. In her 4 years of meeting with Kfir and his family and with their friends—other children with disabilities and their families—she learned, not surprisingly, that children with disabilities have as strong a need for social activity and interaction as nondisabled children; they need company and want to have friends with whom to socialize. She also learned that the hardworking, exhausted parents of disabled children needed both time on their own to relax and rest and time to spend with their other children.

In Adi's view and experience, she had met with a child with severe cerebral palsy who could not speak, but had many ways to communicate with her; who could not walk, but was physically very active; who was happy and friendly, despite his physical limitations; who had exceptional social capabilities; and who was proud of himself and wanted to be part of what was going on around him. In her words, she felt that "through his self-confidence and Kfir's belief in himself, I managed to develop a sense of capability and faith in myself . . . Kfir created a place and a sense for me and I created the same for him."

While Adi clearly recognized and valued the reciprocal nature of the relationship, she did not feel that people in the community understood how much she was getting out of it. People around her chose to define the relationship in the traditional frame of the healthy teenager who had come to the assistance of the "needy, helpless" child; she realized that she was respected for being compassionate and helpful. However, she felt that this picture was wrong. The true picture was of a teenager with problems making and maintaining friendships with peers and experiencing a tough situation at home because her parents were going through the process of divorce. Adi's relationship with Kfir and his family gave her comfort, support, and a sense of a real home, as well as someone to talk to. She realized therefore that young people without disabilities can get as much out of such a relationship as the children with disabilities. She also realized that attitudes toward children with disabilities among youth and adults are based on ignorance, prejudices, and stigmas. Based on her personal experience, Adi understood that these biases could and should be overturned through contact with people with disabilities.

While the other organizations serving children with disabilities in Israel focused their activities on daycare and school services, as well as individual treatments, they did not invest many resources in afterschool activities and the children's social needs. Some of the organizations operated programs that had teenage volunteers coming to the homes of children with disabilities. However, these visits occurred only within the home of each child and did not allow them to socialize with other children.

A hierarchical, uneven relationship of a helper and a needy person was created and did not allow for the formation of a more equal relationship among children. Youth organizations and youth movements, which are very popular among Israeli children and youth, were not accessible to children with disabilities in general and to children with severe disabilities in particular. As a result, children with disabilities did not have many opportunities to meet with peers without disabilities and were largely socially isolated.

Children with disabilities who wanted to socialize after school were dependent on their parents for providing the arrangements for transportation and meetings with other children with disabilities. This was done on an informal and irregular basis. Making such arrangements was difficult for many parents, because children with disabilities who go to the same school live in different cities; they needed to drive long distances to get the children together and also deal with the difficulties of setting up meetings with parents who have other children, obligations, and engagements.

THE INNOVATIVE SOLUTION: A YOUTH ORGANIZATION FOR CHILDREN AND YOUTH WITH DISABILITIES

When Adi was 16, she joined LEAD, a project designed to develop and train young people in leadership skills. As part of the 2-year training, she was asked to create, plan, and implement a social project in her local community. The first thing she thought of was creating a project that would deal with the social isolation and low social participation of children with disabilities after school.

Adi developed the initial idea together with Kfir's parents and other friends of hers from the LEAD project. They aimed to create a group of children with disabilities who would meet on a regular basis outside their homes for social activities, with the supervision and mediation of youth without disabilities. They formed the first group in 2002 in the town where Kfir and Adi lived. It consisted of a group of children with disabilities who knew each other from past activities. While the children were socializing in the group, their parents socialized in a café or at one of their homes. The children's activities were mostly games suited to children with physical disabilities. They were directed by youth without disabilities who had been recruited by word of mouth. Children with disabilities were referred to the group by the local welfare department.

After a short while, another group opened in a different city. Within a few years, these meetings had become institutionalized into Krembo Wings, a youth organization of more than 1,600 members; it is a social framework for social, educational, and cultural activities for children and youth with disabilities that integrates them into social and educational activities with youth without disabilities.

The organization was established to meet the social-educational needs of children with severe disabilities who cannot be accepted into the other national youth organizations and movements operating in Israel. In most cases, these children remain in isolation and, unlike other children their age, lack social opportunities suited to their unique needs. The members of the new organization comprise two main groups: the first is members who are children and youth aged 7 to 21, with different kinds of disabilities—physical, cognitive, spatial, visual, aural, psychiatric, and those relating to speech and language. Due to the social isolation that is forced on them as a result of their disabilities, for many of them this organization is the only social setting that they experience outside of school, as well as the only opportunity for social relations with children and youth without disabilities. The second group comprises members who are youth without disabilities and who act as mentors. They are aged 14 to 18, and come from the mainstream education system. For many of them, this is their first encounter with peers with disabilities.

The organization operates 21 branches around the country. In each branch, there is a members' meeting at least once a week for 3 hours in the afternoon. The organization provides transportation for every member to and from the activity, in an accessible vehicle. An adult volunteer always escorts the children with disabilities home.

All branches of the organization employ a professional caregiver, who provides technical assistance to the children with disabilities during the activities. All the activities are adapted to the needs of the children with disabilities. The regular weekly activities are held around issues that are of interest and importance to children and youth—such as art, theater, cooperation and conflict, countries and cultures, and Jewish and Muslim holidays.

The professional staff members of the organization plan the gatherings, with a detailed outline guiding each of the meetings and activities. Peak events are held throughout the year alongside these regular activities. These include the annual opening activity, distribution of Krembo Wings uniforms and neckties, heritage activities, holidays and graduation events, and the "wings parade," at which the Krembo Wings badge is awarded to the members. During the summer holidays there is an annual summer camp for all members, their families, and their mentors. The activities, values, and procedures were established as the organization grew. The participants themselves created the value-based activities, the moral songs, the uniforms, the training needed for newcomers with and without disabilities, and the communication with the parents.

The weekly activities in the branches are accompanied by training and team-building activities for branch managers, leading teams, and mentors. Much effort and many resources are dedicated to the long, complex training process of the nondisabled mentors designed to turn 14-year-old youth into creative, sensitive, knowledgeable, and experienced mentors to children with disabilities. The training process includes familiarization with different kinds of disabilities, the environment in which children with disabilities live and operate, different forms of communication, the development of creative thinking, learning the language of ability (as opposed to disability), and the development of different modes of interacting with children with disabilities.

Each of the organization's branches is administrated by youth, usually veteran and experienced mentors. The executive leading team of each branch goes through a long, continual training process for the different executive roles. The team is guided and supervised by professional staff in the organization, including an organizational and educational training specialist, a social worker, and students of helping professions who are former mentors.

Given the absence of a youth organization in Israel that strives for the inclusion and integration of children and youth with disabilities, this new organization needed to develop a unique approach as a model for the integration of children with disabilities into mainstream youth organizations. This model would guide all the operating procedures of the organization, its teaching materials, and the training and instruction of youth serving as mentors of children with disabilities.

The model is based on three main premises. The first is a universal model of relationships between people with disabilities and those without disabilities that is based on the view that both parties benefit from such mutual interaction. The organization's motto therefore became: "Creating together a place and meaning for every person." This means that in the social activities of the organization everyone has a place and the right to a social life where skills and capabilities are expressed rather than disabilities.

This model makes the organization a meeting place for different populations and a reflection of the human fabric that makes up Israeli society. The members who are mentors come from all parts of Israeli society: religious and secular; veteran youth organizations and those who have never experienced them; Jews, Muslims, and Christians. These young mentors seek to be empowered through their activity in the organization, to find a place and meaning, as well as to find a second home for themselves. They are expected to become youth leaders who will lead toward a social change in relation to people with disabilities in their local communities, among their peers, and in general society. There is also an expectation that, when they later become adults, they will contribute to the community and work toward a more just and less stigmatizing society. The training and professional guidance given to the mentors is therefore based on the understanding that real integration and a connection between youth with and without disabilities will be possible only when the relationship is based on a more egalitarian approach and not out of compassion and pity.

The second premise of the organization's model is that people with disabilities have many abilities. The difference between a person with a disability and one without a disability is the level of outside support that this disabled person needs. Thus, every child with a disability has the right to an active social life, and the organization has a responsibility to make this possible, regardless of the support he or she needs as a result of his or her disability. The name that the founders chose for the organization—Krembo Wings—attests to this premise. Furthermore, all the organization's activities are designed to meet the needs of every participant.

The third premise rests on the view that the mentoring and mediation carried out by the nondisabled members is not based on a therapeutic relationship between a supporting therapist and a needy patient. Rather, it aims to create an equal opportunity for the member-trainees with disabilities to participate actively in the various activities, making full use of their individual capabilities.

The mentor is an active member in the organization, as well as a mediator for the trainee (a child with a disability). Again, he or she is not a therapist. He or she is expected to mediate the activities for the trainees, according to their capabilities and ways of communicating. He or she is expected to act as an enabler, who will provide the necessary support for the trainee to participate actively in the activity, but not act instead of the trainee. Mentoring the child with a disability is personal, but it is done as part of a group activity: the mentor helps the trainee participate in the activity according to his or her wishes and abilities.

At the same time, however, the mentor experiences the activities and the values of the model embedded in them. It is assumed that the perceptions of the youth acting as mentors will change as a result of their ongoing participation in the organization's activities. For example, a mentor from one of the branches explained that "I forget that I have a trainee who is mentally challenged . . . for me she is a partner in the activity and a member of the organization."

THE DEVELOPMENT OF THE ORGANIZATION

In its 12 years of existence, Krembo Wings has gone through three crucial stages of development. The first—its establishment and formation—took place from 2002 to 2006. Adi Altschuler, the founder—together with Kfir Kobi's parents and some of her friends in the

LEAD project—created the first group of children with disabilities, who met with youth without disabilities in the town where they both lived. During these 4 years, another three branches were opened in different cities, some of them by other participants in the LEAD project and some by parents who had heard about the initiative and wanted to establish groups in their own communities. The operations of the founders, who constituted the organization at this point, were mostly informal and lacked central planning and management capabilities. Local authorities granted spaces for meeting places for the different branches, and children with disabilities and youth were recruited through the local welfare departments or on a word-of-mouth basis. Activities were supported by small donations from the various communities and the parents of the children involved.

In 2004, the organizations started to arrange a transportation system for children with disabilities from their homes to the branches in the different locations. This required more resources. This formation stage was generally characterized by highly intensive work on the part of the founders, who initiated, promoted, and established the organization's activities and worked tirelessly to obtain support from the community for them (see Hasenfeld & Schmid, 1989).

It is important to note that, in this case, the founder was a 16-year-old girl, lacking any formal entrepreneurial or managerial experience. While the literature on social entrepreneurs asserts the importance of life experience in general and former entrepreneurial experience in particular for successful entrepreneurs (Light, 2008), in this case both her young age and her inexperience may actually have helped the organization in its early stages of development, especially for establishing its legitimacy and obtaining support.

First, because of her young age, Adi was able to do things that an adult would probably have considered childish and embarrassing; but the community perceived her actions as courageous, if a bit audacious. For example, when the organization needed a space for the its meetings, and after leaders had tried continually to approach the mayor's office without any response, Adi decided to ambush the mayor and his entourage at a café while he was drinking coffee with his friends. She went there with her friends a couple of times, until she found the mayor there and judged the right time to approach him. When she asked him to give her a space for the afternoon meetings, she did so in front of other people in the café, knowing that the mayor would be embarrassed to refuse her in public. She was right, and he immediately took care of the matter. Given her age, her action was perceived as acceptable, legitimate behavior.

Second, Adi and the organization enjoyed for some time the appeal of being the "young and the bold" entrepreneur who managed to create and fulfill her dream and run an organization at the age of 16. She became a symbol of the productive and sensitive Israeli youth who are the future of the country. During these years, using this public appeal together with high motivation, tenacity, and charm, Adi managed to form many good, strong relationships with important public figures, such as people in government, journalists, artists, and leaders of businesses, who helped the organization in its attempts to raise funds and support.

In 2006, there were already four operating branches and requests to open others in different places. There also appeared to be a growing need to raise donations to support the transportation arrangements and the growing activities of the organization.

The founders also realized that they wanted to develop the initiative into a national project. As a result, the organization decided to register as an official nonprofit organization, entering the second stage of its development, which can be seen as both formalization and survival. On the one hand, registration as a legal nonprofit organization required the formation of entities and institutions such as the board of directors, a general manager, and monetary supervision, leading to greater formalization of the organization. On the other hand, the massive growth in activities and the growing demand to open more branches required the attainment of more financial, as well as human, resources. The organization was dealing with survival, trying to get donations from different sources and, in a few instances, facing the threat of closure, due to a lack of resources. The founders were still putting in a lot of hard work and effort.

In 2008, Adi completed her term as director and a new director was recruited, bringing the organization into its third stage of development. The new director started to formalize the managerial processes, initiated formal training, and arranged insurance coverage of the organization's activities. In 2009, the organization brought in a new deputy director of training and development and a new general manager with a background in human resources management.

Since then, the number of branches has doubled, as well as the budget of the organization. In 2011, the financial turnover of the NPO was five million shekels (US $1.25 million). Most of the income came from private donations, although the government (mostly local) granted some (about 10%). Another deputy director of resource development has joined the staff, as well as a social worker who is in charge of the connections with the members' parents.

The managerial process has become much more strategic. Strategic planning is evident in the proactive search for new funding opportunities that would allow the opening of new branches in different locations and for different populations. For example, they have approached philanthropic foundations that support Arab-Jewish coexistence to obtain funding for branches in communities with Jews and Arabs. They have also contacted foundations supporting specific populations such as Beduins, who live in the southern desert area, to open a branch for Beduin children with disabilities. Furthermore, the organization has formed many new partnerships with businesses and government, expanding its activities to include a summer camp and trips abroad.

The organization has gained respect and legitimacy from the surrounding communities and is now considered to be among the leading youth organizations in the country. In 2009, it won the most prestigious award for a nonprofit in Israel, awarded by the country's president for the leading volunteer organization.

The most significant process that the organization launched in this period is the professionalization of all activities in the organization, including work procedures, training processes, and the writing and elaboration of the operating work model that guides every activity in each branch.

However, the human resource management has continued to delegate and remained participative. Despite the great expansion in the number of branches and the budget, the staff still operates without formal offices, and the organization is still struggling to secure funding that will allow both the functioning of the 21 operating branches and the opening of new ones.

In addition, at the initiative of member Tommy Brtz'nko, a child with a disability, the organization established a youth advisory board in 2012. This organ consists of members who are mentors and trainees, who meet to discuss issues arising from the various activities in the branches. After debating these matters, the youth advisory board members then present their views and arguments to the board of the organization for further discussion. Participation in the young board reflects the significant place of children and youth with disabilities in the organization, and strengthens their involvement and commitment for both themselves and for others, regardless of their limitations. For example, Tommy does not speak; he is the chairman of the young advisory board and communicates through a communication device.

CONCLUSIONS

The evolution of Krembo Wings is an example of a social innovation created by a social entrepreneurs "who realized where there is an opportunity to satisfy some unmet need that the state welfare will not or cannot meet, and who gather together the necessary resources and use these to 'make a difference' . . . and create sea-change movements and a major impact" (Thompson, Alvy, & Lees, 2000, pp. 328, 336).

Looking back at its first decade, the organization has achieved many of its initial aims, remaining true to its core ideology and vision of fostering social change through integrative activities for children with and without disabilities. Although there are no academic studies of the organization's interventional efficiency and effectiveness, in the last 4 years the organization has administered surveys for assessing the views and experiences of the members and their parents of the organization's activities. Overall, the results of these surveys show that the training, the participation in the activities, and the connections formed between the mentors and the children with disabilities have a significant, broad, deep, and positive effect on the maturation processes of the mentors. These experiences are contributing to making them leaders who initiate changes in their communities.

In 2012, 574 mentor-members were surveyed, indicating the following: 95% felt they know well the capabilities and limitations of their trainee; 84% felt that participation in the organization's activities increases their social involvement; and 90% said that the mentoring experience developed their sensitivity toward people in general and toward people with disabilities in particular, as well as the discovery of their own new capabilities and willingness to volunteer and contribute to their community.

One of the mentors explained:

> Krembo Wings makes such a significant social change and I am lucky to take part in this social change in the community. In our world jealousy and hatred blind us from seeing that we are not so different. We all have the same moon and sun and we stand on the same land and all dream about the future. The organization proves to me time and again how one person can create a change in the environment, and how one person can change the world. I never thought that something would affect me as the organization has. I learned a lot about my community, that there are many young people, that it's important for them to take an active part in society.

Another mentor explained:

> Shira, the member I mentor, is my best friend in the world. She is an amazing girl who has taught me a lot about life, about how I should not give up, and about true friendship. Shira and I are part of something much bigger; we are part of friendship and real love. Krembo Wings is a youth organization that I am proud to be a part of. It's a place where I feel at home. If a child cannot speak, it does not mean that he has nothing to say. That does not mean he cannot choose and decide for himself. In his special need he needs help, but it does not mean that he is not a human being with wants and rights of his own. Children with physical or cognitive disabilities can do many things, make decisions and choose everything in their special ways.

Another mentor asserted that:

> In Krembo Wings, we create a new world together; while we appreciate and grant a space and a meaning to every person; we make the members see themselves as independent. I hope that Krembo Wings will become a youth movement all around the world, to protect the human rights of children with disabilities.

Parents of children with disabilities, who participate in the organization activities that were surveyed, reported that their children were empowered by it, that participation in the organization raised their self-confidence and contributed to better functioning at home and school. One of the mothers of a teenager with a disability said:

> Every Sunday my daughter's eyes sparkle and she is proud to belong, to be equal, to be loved and significant. We see her anticipation of the activity and her ability to contribute to others and not only to receive from them . . . These are the two hours that allow her to leave the house once a week and meet with her friends without the need to make special accommodations.

To date there have not been any significant, long-lasting attempts made to replicate the Krembo Wings model of youth organization for children with disabilities outside of Israel. However, it seems reasonable that with similar vision and devotion and with the appropriate resources and inspiring leadership, this model could be replicated to the benefit of other children with disabilities, their families, and youth without disabilities in other places around the world.

Krembo Wings grew out of the strong bond that was formed between Kfir, a child with a severe disability, and Adi, a nondisabled teenager. The short, but full, life of Kfir Kobi—the first member of Krembo Wings—sadly ended in 2008, when he was only 11.5 years old. However, his joy of life and his wish to be socially, actively engaged and surrounded by friends is being realized on a daily basis in the activities of the 21 branches and the 1,600 children of this unique and pioneering youth organization. This has been the inspiring force behind a massive and successful social change, which is giving children with disabilities, their families, and youth without disabilities a lot of joy, fulfillment, and hope.

DISCUSSION QUESTIONS

1. What are the main factors that hinder social participation by children with disabilities in youth organizations?
2. What are the advantages and disadvantages of being a youth social entrepreneur?
3. What do you think are the major factors that led to the success of this social initiative?
4. What are the advantages and what are the limitations of operating a special youth organization for children with disabilities?

REFERENCES

Brown, M., & Gordon, W. A. (1987). Impact of impairment on activity patterns of children. *Archives of Physical Medicine and Rehabilitation, 68*(12), 828–832.

Hasenfeld, Y., & Schmid, H. (1989). The life cycle stages of human services organizations. *Administration in Social Work, 13*(3/4), 243–269.

King, G., Law, M., King, S., Hurley, P., Hanna, S., Kertoy, M., . . . Young, N. (2004). *Children's assessment of participation and enjoyment* (CAPE) *and preferences for activities of children* (PAC). San Antonio, TX: Harcourt Assessment.

King, G., Law, M., King, S., Rosenbaum, P., Kertoy, M., & Young, N. (2003). A conceptual model of the factors affecting the recreation and leisure participation of children with disabilities. *Physical & Occupational Therapy in Pediatrics*, 23, 63–90.

Law, M., King, J., King, S., Kertoy, M., Hurty, P., Rosenbaum, P., . . . Hanna, S. (2007). Patterns of participation in recreational and leisure activities among children with complex physical disabilities. *Developmental Medicine & Child Neurology, 48*(5), 337–342.

Light, P. C. (2008). *The search for social entrepreneurship.* Washington, DC: Brookings Institute.

Sagiv, N., Milshtein, E., & Ben, E. (2011). *Centers for families of children with special needs in Israel.* Jerusalem, Israel: Brookdale. (Hebrew).

Schleien, S. J., Green, F. P., & Heyne, L. A. (1993). Integrated community recreation. In M. E. Snell (Ed.), *Instruction of students with severe disabilities* (pp. 526–555). Columbus, OH: Merrill.

Thompson, J., Alvy, G., & Lees, A. (2000). Social entrepreneurship—A new look at the people and potential. *Management Decision, 38*(5), 328–338.

Weissblay, E. (2011). *Community services for children with special needs.* Jerusalem, Israel: The Research and Information Center of the Knesset. (Hebrew).

ADDITIONAL RESOURCES

http://www.krembo.org.il/default.asp

A mother story—Noa and Ya'ara:

http://www.youtube.com/watch?v = XTvhffVs2mI

Dolev Toledano: A mentor story:

http://www.youtube.com/user/KremboWings

A young girl story—May Ofir:

http://www.youtube.com/watch?v = Qb223xgsw4k

The story of Krembo Wings—A youth organization for children with disabilities:

http://www.youtube.com/watch?v = tA6EsWnYqYU&feature = youtube_gdata_player

CHAPTER 13

The Center for Rural Development in Appalachia

Linking 45 Counties for Better Service Delivery

Margaret F. Sloan

School of Strategic Leadership Studies, James Madison University

INTRODUCTION

The Appalachian region of the United States has historically been an impoverished and negatively stereotyped section of the country, bringing forth images of feuding, moonshining, and illiteracy. The Appalachian region, as defined by the Appalachian Regional Commission, covers parts of 13 eastern U.S. states and runs through the central and southern portion of the Appalachian Mountain chain from southern New York to northern Mississippi, encompassing roughly 205,000 square miles and more than 23 million people. Forty-two percent of population is rural, compared with 20% of the national population.

In the 1930s, U.S. President Franklin D. Roosevelt brought the New Deal to parts of Appalachia, damming up rivers to bring electricity for the first time to many sections, and advocating better farming practices among other strategies in an effort to help alleviate the widespread poverty of the region. Despite the New Deal, economic and living conditions for many remained traditional and familiar; in 1964, U.S. President Lyndon B. Johnson famously declared a War on Poverty, and the still economically troubled Appalachian region was squarely focused in his sights as evidenced by the creation in 1965 of the Appalachian Regional Commission (ARC), a federal-state partnership.

The region's economy, once highly dependent on mining, forestry, agriculture, chemical industries, and heavy industry, has become more diversified in recent times and now includes a variety of manufacturing and service industries. These gains have transformed the Appalachian region from one of widespread poverty to one of economic contrasts: some communities have successfully diversified their economies, while others still require basic infrastructure such as roads and water and sewer systems.

The ARC counts 420 counties in 13 states as being in the Appalachian region. Although all of West Virginia is included in the region, the state with the most counties, and certainly one of the most rural and poverty stricken areas, is Kentucky, where 52 Appalachian counties are found. Forty-five of those Appalachian counties in eastern and south-central Kentucky reside in the state's 5th Congressional District. Although rich in natural resources such as coal and timber, and a people with fierce, independent spirits and strong work ethics, the area has historically been plagued by poor infrastructure, high poverty, high unemployment rates, low educational attainment, high outmigration, and a lack of political or economic collaboration across county lines. Amazingly homogeneous in both problems and ethnic makeup, each county viewed itself as very distinct from its neighbors, a vestige of earlier history, prejudices, and geographic barriers.

THE PROBLEM

While other portions of Appalachia have transitioned toward, or even attained, various degrees of educational and economic success, Eastern Kentucky counties have been less successful in ameliorating poverty than other Appalachian counties with similar characteristics (Appalachian Regional Commission, 2007). Each year the ARC analyzes each county in its service area and provides a label about its economic well-being, either distressed, at-risk, transitional, competitive, or attainment (see Map 13.1). The designation is a comparative index created by compiling a 3-year average for unemployment, poverty rate, and a market share indicator. A distressed designation indicates that a county is among the worst 10% of counties in the nation. The following map demonstrates the differences in economic stability for counties across the Appalachian region in 2011, where Eastern Kentucky is notably concentrated as a high distress area.

As a result of this persistent regional distress, many young people seeking a higher quality of life leave their homeplace in search of economic opportunity. This outmigration may benefit the individual, but the net effects damage the region further by exacerbating educational deficits and discouraging homegrown industry for those remaining behind.

THE INNOVATION

Along with federal initiatives, numerous nonprofit agencies have tried addressing some aspect of this region's problems. The Mountain Association for Community Economic Development was created in 1976 to try to help influence policy decisions for the region, particularly those decisions impacting the environment. In addition, the Southern Kentucky Tourism Development Association, the Southern Kentucky Economic Development Corporation, Southern and Eastern Kentucky Agricultural Development Association, and Forward in the Fifth with an educational development mission, all sprang up in the 1980s and early 1990s to address part of the problem from a regional perspective.

MAP 13.1 Economic Levels Of Appalachian Regional Commission Counties

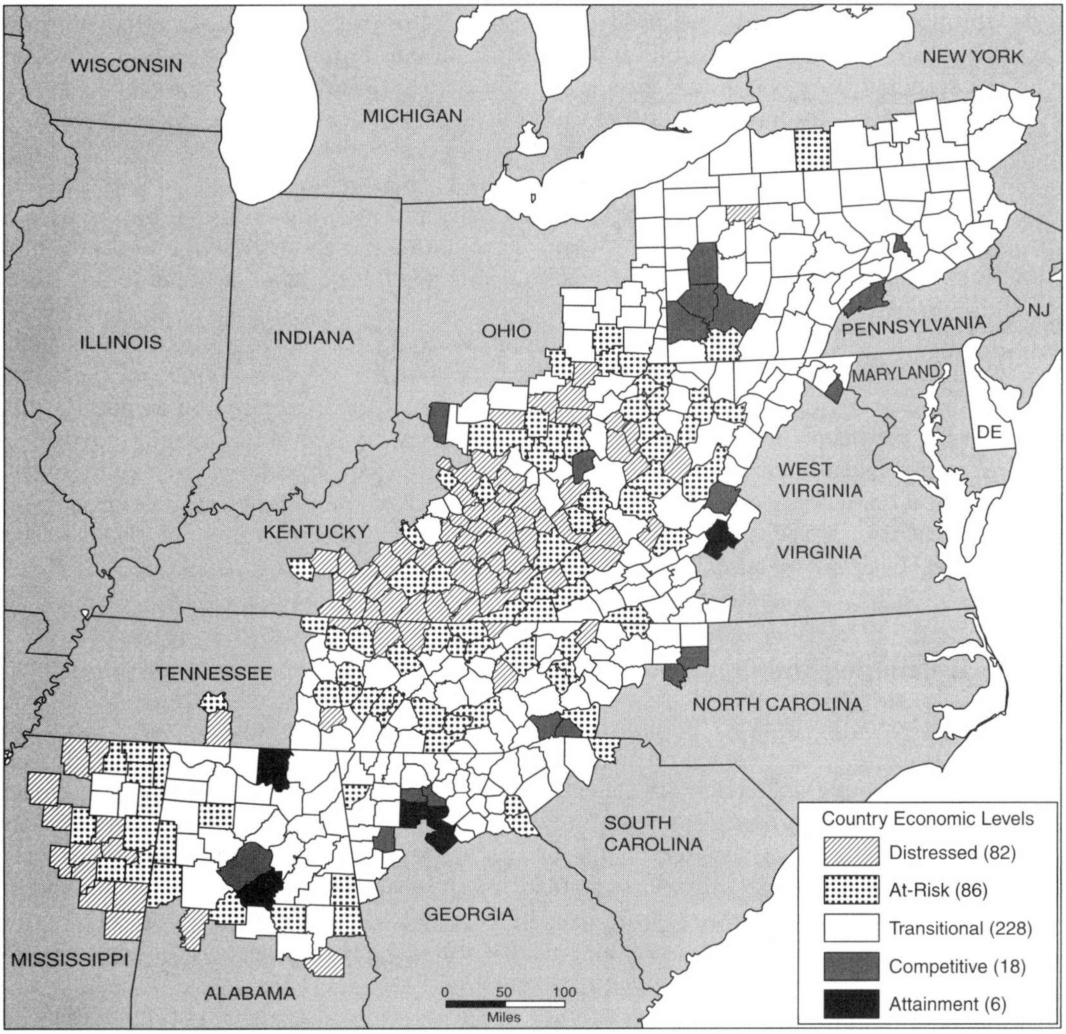

Map by: Appalachian Regional Commission, March 2010.
Data Sources: U.S. Bureau of Labor Statistics, LAUS, 2006-2008;
U.S. Bureau of Economic Analysis, REIS, 2007;
U.S. Census Bureau, 2000 Census, SF3.

Effective October 1, 2010 through September 30, 2011.

Source: http://www.arc.gov/research/MapsofAppalachia.asp?MAP_ID = 54

The innovative solution that emerged from these forerunners to deal with the economic and educational deficiencies faced by Kentucky's 5th Congressional District took physical form in The Center for Rural Development (CRD), a nonprofit entity focusing on economic development strategies for rural Southern and Eastern Kentucky. The Center is designed not only to work more collaboratively and on a larger scale than the single-issue nonprofits, but also serves as a national pilot project for addressing rural development problems through its holistic and synergistic programming. The CRD supports a variety of outreach programs including leadership and entrepreneurship training, telecommunication services, public safety programs, artistic and cultural opportunities, and other ventures.

In addition to outreach and programming, the physical structure is composed of a 26,000 square foot facility including a convention center, theater, video wing, and office space housing various other development nonprofits for the region. Through partnering with other nonprofits serving a similar area and focusing on numerous aspects of economic development such as tourism, agriculture, and commerce, the CRD strives to fulfill its mission statement "that no young person will have to leave home to find his or her future."

"If a state agency or another institution is not doing it, then we try to provide it," said Lonnie Lawson, CEO and executive director of the CRD since 2001. While not every program they design is unique and other organizations support the shared location of like service providers, the Center's strength of innovation lies in its ability to reframe the conversations about individual problems by bringing everyone together so that county lines, political boundaries, historic entrenchment, and lack of community resources dissolve in a discussion of productive regional solutions. The mission is broad and inclusive, allowing for creativity, partnership, and innovation to flourish.

Phase I: Bringing the Players Together

With the intent of trying to improve economic opportunities for his constituents and encourage growth in the region, in the early 1980s, U.S. Congressman Harold "Hal" Rogers began gathering stakeholders to collectively address the region's problems. Three outreach organizations were created, including the Southern Kentucky Economic Development Association, the Southern Kentucky Tourism Development Association, and the Southern Kentucky Agricultural Development Association. These organizations had independent boards with representation from various counties in the 5th Congressional District. They served both as incubators of ideas to address needs in the region and as a way for the congressman to keep his constituents informed.

While these groups experienced limited success in addressing their particular issues, it was apparent that the problems of the region required a more comprehensive approach. The CRD, while a highly collaborative venture, was spearheaded by Congressman Rogers who operated as the social entrepreneur. Rogers's innovation enabled a historic problem to be addressed through novel partnerships and a holistic design. The idea began to germinate that the Center would provide a synergy of purpose if all of the organizations seeking to improve the economic development of the region in various ways were to be housed in the same facility, providing a "one-stop shop" for economic development services for the region.

The congressman, the local mayor, city councilmen, and prominent businesspeople in the community began to discuss this idea, its feasibility, and how to take the idea from paper to reality. While considering how to house all the organizations in one place and how to provide a performing arts center for the community college, the group also began to brainstorm other facilities that might provide economic stimulus to the community and region. As the community leaders' plans for the CRD solidified, more partnerships developed to extend the service reach of the organization to include local arts organizations, regional businesses, local nonprofit groups, and political networks. These partnerships continue to evolve so that newer partnerships have also been created with several state higher education institutions, Kentucky state police, and environmental groups.

By virtue of his long-standing public service in the House of Representatives since 1981, and the wide-spanning network he had amassed, Rogers was able to bring together various community stakeholders over a period of years with a joint goal to improve the economic opportunities of the Southern and Eastern Kentucky region. Rogers also brought political clout to the proposal as a member, and later chair, of the House Appropriations Committee.

Agencies and organizations at all levels of government, including the Appalachian Regional Commission, the state Rural Telecommunications Network, and city and county governments, as well as numerous nonprofit partners, including Kentucky Educational Television (KET), Southern Kentucky Tourism Development Association (SKTDA), the Southern Kentucky Economic Development Corporation (SKEDC), Southern and Eastern Kentucky Agricultural Development Association (SKADA), began working together to provide technical expertise, communication networks, research, and funding that would not only help the CRD become a reality, but also help in its operation.

Funding for the facility was provided by a number of sources. The ARC provided financial support for a feasibility study in the late 1980s to assess whether the idea of a convention center and one-stop economic development shop had merit. After the ARC study affirmed the achievability of the idea, the ad hoc planning committee moved forward with the facility. The group formed a partnership with the University of Kentucky, which provided leadership for the agricultural economic development group, and whose community college affiliate sought a performing arts center. As articulated by a memorandum of understanding, the University would build the facility and the emerging organization would be charged with managing the facility. Funding for the facility came from various local and federal sources in the form of grants from the federal Small Business Administration along with those from city and county governments.

The University of Kentucky provided architects to plan the facility and manage its construction. As the architects began planning the facility, its purposes and scope expanded. Originally designed to house the economic development organizations, an exhibit hall, and a theater for the college, the building grew to include some federal offices (a Department of Commerce Import-Export Center and Small Business Administration branch), University of Kentucky Extension Agent offices, art exhibition space, and a technology suite including a distance learning classroom, a broadcasting area, and video production room.

The first architectural plans did not include plans for the technology suite. However, members of the planning committee sought a mechanism for supplying greater access to educational programming and courses for residents located in disparate counties where mountainous roads often made travel difficult and no public transit system was available. The planning committee sought the expertise of the executive director of the state's public broadcasting station, Kentucky Educational Television (KET), in connecting the region through its satellite technology, particularly the three other community college campuses located in the service area. Once KET agreed to partner, architects began adding the technology wing and making plans for installation of a satellite dish to transmit between the community college campuses. After several years of bringing together local, state, and federal agencies and groups, the CRD was ready to move off the planning board and become a brick and mortar reality.

But where would it be located? The city of Somerset, the largest city in the service region as well as the headquarters for the congressman, was chosen as the physical site for the Center. Land located adjacent to the community college and the community's main thoroughfare was selected, although some residents were unwilling to sell. In the end the city acquired the land through the use of eminent domain, which resulted in some negative press for the emerging facility. Most publicity for the proposed entity, however, was positive. In the earliest stages the planning committee and affiliate organizations managed the project, but as it increased in complexity and required more attention to detail, the group began seeking an executive director to head the fledgling organization.

Phase II: Bringing the Region Together

In 1994, while the facility was still under construction, the first executive director for the CRD, Hilda Gay Legg, was hired. A dynamic woman with roots in the region, political savvy, and experience in administration as federal cochair of the Appalachian Regional Commission, Ms. Legg was able to keep the partners involved and excited about the emerging entity. During the first year, the Southern Kentucky Economic Development Corporation paid the salary for Ms. Legg and shared space in its facility with the CRD staff.

Ms. Legg's first hire, after her administrative assistant, was a marketing director to begin gathering clients for the event space and managing its use. Shortly afterward, a director of planning and policy was added to the management team to keep focus and bring expertise in addressing the organization's larger mission of improving the region's economic development. The final director hired before occupying the facility was a telecommunications director whose expertise aided the development of the technology suite and its subsequent programming. As the vision for the organization progressed, more staff were added, including a director of training to help facilitate educational opportunities for students and professionals in the region[1].

The first tasks for the Center's CEO were to formulate the organizational bylaws and create the more permanent board of directors that would supplant the planning committee and interim executive committee. The University of Kentucky and each of the economic development organizations held permanent positions on the CRD board's executive committee. In addition to these permanent positions the board was to have representation from

[1]The author worked as an employee of The Center for Rural Development from 1995 to 2000 and served on the Board of Directors from 2005 to 2012. Information for the case study was obtained through personal interactions while working with the organization, interviews with the current and prior CEOs, and archival documents including board minutes, annual reports, and evaluation documents provided by the organization.

each of the 42 counties in its service area (expanding to 45 representatives later when the service area added three more counties).

In 1994, the articles of incorporation were approved by the Internal Revenue Service and adopted by the executive committee, giving the organization official 501(c)(3) nonprofit status. When final construction of the facility was completed in 1996, various groups and agencies that served the region were finally located under one roof, ostensibly making it easier for those seeking these services to obtain them and creating a synergistic environment for innovation.

Long-standing partners like Lake Cumberland Performing Arts, a local arts group instrumental in the early management of the arts programming, as well as new affiliates like Eastern Kentucky PRIDE (Personal Responsibility in a Desirable Environment), a regional nonprofit launched in 1997 and dedicated to cleaning up the region's illegal dumps and straight pipe sewage systems, also helped shape the character of the fledgling organization. As all the components of the organization and its partner groups came together, each with its own programming goals but with a collective target area, questions that had been subdued about how to make the organization relevant to the region and fulfill the directive of serving as a national model for development became acute. With the Center's promotion of all the partner groups and their diversified missions, maintaining its own identity while bringing these disparate groups together was tricky, but necessary. Legg insisted that promotional materials and press releases call the organization "The Center" as a means of reinforcing the one-stop nature of services and programming for the community needs and forging the regional identity.

Along with the challenge of bringing together diverse organizational partners, one of the earliest challenges was also bringing together community partners. In keeping with the historic isolation and independent nature of the political institutions at the local level, county residents and officials often felt they had to manage problems alone. One of the Center's goals was that counties would finally stop thinking about problems from an individual perspective (my problem) and begin thinking about problems from a regional perspective (our problem). It was a difficult mindset to overcome, but critical, and success would allow the CRD to come up with regional solutions rather than 42 separate solutions. The board composition was a key component in this task since it gave the group a forum to begin forging a regional identity in addition to their county affiliation.

One strategy during the early phase of the CRD's opening was a series of community meetings in each of the service area counties. Staff held open forums in each county and asked about its needs, problems, and vision for the future. Time and again county participants would voice concerns and desires similar to other counties in the region, and one voice began to emerge.

These meetings served several important functions for the new entity. First, they conveyed that each county was important to the Center's mission and that its identity and needs would not be lost or swallowed in the composition of the whole; they also served to announce the CRD was open for business and to put a face on the entity; and they also provided a platform to educate the service area about the services provided by the CRD, particularly the potential benefits of the technology network. "Technology is not the silver bullet," said Legg in many of these meetings, "but it is a tool that we can use to get above the mountains that separate us and move the region forward."

A mission statement had been articulated, but it did not offer a prescription for how opportunities were to be created or how the partner groups would work together. This flexibility actually helped the organization achieve its goals by fostering innovation and creative partnerships, resulting in a wide variety of pilot programs and projects to address educational, economic, and business development.

Phase III: Innovation Beyond the Region

In 2001, Ms. Legg left the CRD for an appointment in the Bush administration, and Lonnie Lawson, the director of business and finance for the organization, stepped up to take the Chief Executive Officer post. Under Lawson's leadership The Center for Rural Development's energy and creativity, spawned during its start-up process, has continued to the present day. Its primary service area has expanded to 45 counties, with some programs taking on a state or national focus. Actors within the organization created markets for several different programs related to the Center's overall goal; however, those programs were not prescribed a priori. Rather, opportunity and resource acquisition factored into these decisions. "The biggest reason we did some of these things was out of necessity," said Lawson. "We went out of 42 counties, moving out of the service region to a national model, expanding service to the Kentucky Community and Technical College System (KCTCS) statewide and then nationwide programs, as a means of survival."

For example, the Center expanded nationally to include a public safety program, which was not conceived by the original planning committee but rather grew out of a need for greater access to crime databases and information for rural law enforcement officials. "Law enforcement became something we were good at," Lawson noted of the national initiative. "After receiving an equipment grant for rural programs, we saw the need for greater support for rural law enforcement nationwide." This program is now one of four core programming areas, with the CRD serving as a host agency for the National Law Enforcement and Corrections Technology Center's (NLECTC) Small, Rural, Tribal and Border Regional Center (SRTB-RC) as well as the Rural Domestic Preparedness Consortium and Institute for Preventive Strategies.

Another service that arose under Legg's tenure was one to help address the lack of educational and entrepreneurial opportunities for youth in the region. Later becoming known as the Rogers Scholars Program, the goal was to provide training in community leadership, technology, and entrepreneurship to rising high school juniors. Some of the region's top students were suddenly talking via the CRD's new telecommunications network to scientists, writers, and business leaders, receiving training in telecommunications, leadership, and entrepreneurship, and being responsible for creating and implementing a project for their home counties that would help address a community need.

The program has proved so successful that it has doubled the number of students it accepts every year; its success has also led to the creation of two additional youth programs that more intentionally encourage entrepreneurship and technological skill building. These programs have given practical skills training to over 1,300 high school students and provided them with scholarship money at several colleges within the state, including all Kentucky's public institutions. There is also some evidence that these efforts are proving fruitful. A phone survey of Rogers Scholars participants in 2008, almost 10 years after the program's founding, indicated that 98% of these young people attended college, and ongoing social media contact indicates that 80% of these students still live in the region or plan to come back after graduating from college.

As in the youth programs, technology provides the backbone of many of the Center's outreach efforts and services including web-based education and support services (19,200 Kentucky Community and Technical College System courses are managed by the Center) and videoconferencing through the CenterNET2 network at 162 sites across the state. Gaining national recognition, CenterNET2 received a 2006 Innovation and Technology Award from the National Association of Development Organizations for excellence in "Technology in Education" and a 2009 "Best Practices" Award for Distance Learning Programming from the U.S. Distance Learning Association for groundbreaking videoconferencing programs delivered to secondary and postsecondary students and other network users. These programs have brought international Nobel laureates and Holocaust survivors face-to-face with youth program participants and linked Southern and Eastern Kentucky organizations with NASA and The Library of Congress, among others.

As a central component of programming since the organization's inception, the CRD's arts programs have encouraged the growth of regional artists through its exhibition opportunities, introduced thousands of rural school children to theater through its School Time Theatre, and created a venue for classical performers as well as popular musicians and entertainers. Nearly 8,000 events and performances have been held at the CRD since its opening, including 369 theater performances with over 166,000 attendees.

The Center's entrepreneurial training resources are available to all individuals or groups, and leadership training opportunities have encouraged the growth of small business and civic participation throughout the region. Partnerships between the organizational actors, both formal and informal, their immediate networks, and those organizations and citizens within the proximate geographic area provide the ideas for programming and training modules.

Finding resources to support all the CRD initiatives has always been a challenge. At one point about 80% of the organization's service revenue came from federal grants, contracts, or other government procurements, but that figure has dropped over the years so that in 2012 it was down to just under 50%. This decreased reliance on federal funds was the result of a deliberate management strategy to diversify revenue. Additional resource streams have been bolstered and are now more productive through fees for service with the conference center, theater, training programs, and technology services. Realizing the need to increase private support not only for itself but for all nonprofits in rural Kentucky, the CRD recently has developed the Appalachian Philanthropy Project to encourage those within the region, as well as the region's expatriates, to give back. This consortium works with communities to plan and create community foundations and to help create a culture of philanthropic giving in the region.

Hal Rogers still holds the Congressional office, lives in the community, and can often be seen visiting with constituents during Center events. His retired chief of staff, a long-time supporter of the CRD's efforts, now serves as an at-large member of the organization's executive committee. Although many changes have been made to the board over the years, a few founding individuals have served since the beginning, providing some continuity along with the infusion of new ideas. The University of Kentucky and the key affiliate groups continue to hold positions on the executive committee, and the full board of county representatives meets once or twice a year so that each community maintains a voice in the Center's direction. These individuals, all with disparate perspectives, priorities, and local affiliations, share a passion for the region and its people, and they are committed to seeking joint solutions to improve the quality of life in the 5th District.

CONCLUSIONS

Most assessments of the CRD's efficiency and effectiveness have been internal evaluations of its programs; however, in 2001, the University of Kentucky Gatton College of Business and Economics Center for Business and Economic Research conducted an economic impact study of the organization. This study assessed the cumulative economic impact of the Center on its regional service area from 1997 to 2001 to be $24,895,000 in output, $8,728,000 in worker earnings, and 338 jobs (or 68 jobs each year). Arts events held at the Center were estimated to make an additional contribution to area quality of life worth approximately $808,000 per year. No outside assessment has taken place since that time.

While much has been accomplished regarding creating a regional identity and working toward broad-based solutions to common problems, building strength at the local level is still a priority. Two targeted efforts to strengthen local capacity are the Center's philanthropy initiative that encourages the development of local community foundations, and a mini-grant program that helps counties carry out unfunded projects within their strategic plans.

The CRD experienced a unique founding, and through the tremendous influence of Congressman Rogers, it was able to leverage funding and partnerships that were extremely advantageous for the organization's inception and that continue to have a positive, though mitigated, influence into the present time. These circumstances may not be replicable for other start-up organizations. However, some aspects of the CRD are easily replicated by other communities and regions; these include the holistic approach to problem solving, broad partnerships that complement and do not compete with existing services, the use of technology to link disadvantaged populations to resources, and a combining of long-term goals with short-term returns.

What began as an innovative pilot project in regional rural development, bringing together disparate resources and widespread communities for the accomplishment of common goals and a common identity, has become ensconced as a source of help and entertainment for individuals, communities, and the region. It has also taken a leadership role in rural development on a national scale. The CRD's holistic and comprehensive approach to development is efficient in terms of economies of scale. For rural communities where resources and expertise are often in limited quantities, this approach may prove a critical component for the long-term sustainability and improvement of these and similar areas.

The Center's service area still faces formidable odds, and large-scale economic transformation has been elusive; however, opportunities may be more prevalent because the region's population seems to be stabilizing rather than declining further, according to recent U.S. Census counts. Somerset, Kentucky, the community where the Center is headquartered, has been noted as one of the fastest growing cities in the state. How much of this is attributable to the CRD is uncertain, but organizational accounts demonstrate that numerous lives have been positively impacted by some aspect of this organization's work. Where will the future take the Center? It's anyone's guess. "We're still a unique model. There are none like us that we know of anywhere in the country," said Lawson. "There's no road map."

DISCUSSION QUESTIONS

1. To what extent was the CRD's growth dependent on Congressman Rogers's political power? Could the organization have been created without him? Could it have grown without him?
2. A large initial investment for infrastructure, both physical and technological, was in place in the organization's start-up phase. How dependent is the organization's success on this shared infrastructure? If an organization did not have this infrastructure, could it replicate the successes of the CRD?
3. The Appalachian region, like many other identified problem areas, has received much attention from government, including federal funding. Do you think this labeling and attention helps or hurts a region's own initiative for improvement. Why? Or why not?
4. What are some of the main problems faced by early stakeholders of the CRD? How did the organizational entrepreneur and founders overcome these obstacles?
5. The Appalachian region is a very homogenous section of the country. Do you think this homogeneity has helped or hurt the region in addressing its issues and problems? Why?

REFERENCE

Appalachian Regional Commission. (2007). *Sources of regional growth in Non-Metro Appalachia*. Economic Development Research Group, Inc., Regional Technology Strategies, Inc., MIT Dept. of Urban Studies and Planning. Retrieved from http://www.arc.gov

ADDITIONAL RESOURCES

http://www.centertech.com: the organization's main webpage offers information about services and programs

http://www.kyean.org: the Kentucky Entrepreneur Accelerator Network (KyEAN) website, which provides information about the Center's entrepreneurial training programs

http://www.rogersscholars.com: this website offers information about one of the organization's youth programs, Rogers Scholars, including the application process and scholarship opportunities

http://www.centerNET2.com: this website is a specialized videoconferencing portal for those wanting more technical information, departmental contacts, and updates on the latest technical advances

http://www.centertech.com/arts: this sister website to centertech.com is designed to be a clearinghouse for arts-related information in the Center's primary service area of Southern and Eastern Kentucky

CHAPTER 14

Living Cities

Reinventing Philanthropy to Serve Poor Communities

Avis C. Vidal

Wayne State University

Living Cities is an innovative philanthropic collaborative of 22 of the world's largest foundations and financial institutions with a broad, ambitious mission: to improve the lives of low-income people and the cities where they live.[1] It began as a quite different organization in 1991 as the National Community Development Initiative (NCDI)—a uniquely lean, distinctively governed effort to accomplish a tightly targeted goal and then "go out of business." It is a remarkable example of organizational innovation and adaptation. This chapter examines the three phases in the evolution of this original enterprise, whose name changes track its development.[2]

THE PROBLEM

The Presidential campaign of 1980 focused renewed attention on distressed urban neighborhoods: both President Jimmy Carter and candidate Ronald Reagan made much-photographed visits to the vast swath of abandonment in the South Bronx. National attention bolstered on going efforts to respond to the crisis, including the creation of three national community development intermediaries between 1979 and 1981: Local Initiatives Support Corporation (LISC), The Enterprise Foundation (now Enterprise

[1] See http://www.livingcities.org/who-we-are/

[2] The National Community Development Initiative operated from 1991 to 2001. It became Living Cities: The National Community Development Initiative in 2001 and incorporated as a 501(c)(3) the following year. A strategic assessment led to an expanded mission, major supportive organizational changes, and the simplified name Living Cities in 2007.

Community Partners), and the Neighborhood Reinvestment Corporation (now NeighborWorks). These organizations tap capital at the national level to provide financial and technical support to community development corporations (CDCs) to strengthen poor neighborhoods across the country.

The intermediaries are a distinctive innovation in the community development field, and are widely viewed as major contributors to the dramatic growth of the community development industry. During the 1980s they devised strategies to increase the effectiveness of small, widely dispersed CDCs, ensure project and program quality, and both reduce and spread funders' risk (Vidal, 2012; Vidal, Howitt, & Foster, 1985; Walker, 1993). During the 1980s, the number of CDCs, dedicated principally to affordable housing and community economic development, grew from a few hundred to more than 2000, and they chalked up some impressive accomplishments (National Congress for Community Economic Development, 1991; Vidal, 1992).

Despite this progress, the community development field faced continuing challenges. The typical CDC, with a staff of seven and an annual operating budget of less than $250,000, remained too small to undertake significant neighborhood improvements. CDCs' housing production was growing, but only a dozen cities in the country had at least five CDCs able to produce ten housing units a year. Most CDCs worked in localities that did not provide strong, consistent support for their work, that is, well-functioning local housing and community development programs, private lenders who understood community lending, predictable access to housing production subsidies, and a workable regulatory environment. As a result, the field remained "below the radar."

THE INNOVATIVE SOLUTION

Peter Goldmark set out to change this situation when he became president of the Rockefeller Foundation in 1988. As a founding member of LISC's Board of Directors, Goldmark was impressed by the CDCs' accomplishments and frustrated that the potential of this approach was not more widely known and supported. He resolved to "take the CDC movement to scale."

He set two priorities for community development programming at Rockefeller. First and foremost was to "ratchet up" CDCs' housing production, their primary development activity. Goldmark viewed housing as "a step toward a larger objective: the reintroduction of social standards in communities that no longer had them, and whose residents no longer enforced them. That's what successful community development is really all about" (Goldmark as cited in Kohler [2007], p. 218).[3] The overarching problem was distressed urban neighborhoods, but the immediate challenge was, from his perspective, actualizing an unrealized opportunity.

Goldmark knew that achieving the objective would require a substantial infusion of new resources—more than Rockefeller could provide—so attracting new "deep-pockets"

[3] Goldmark's Keynote Address at LISC's 30th Anniversary Gala in 2011 clarified his understanding of "social standards." He underlined the fact that bricks and mortar are not the main outcome of community development, but the vehicle for "human cooperation, an ethic of responsibility and self-help, neighborhood values and mutual obligations."

funding partners was essential. Partners would be attracted by a compelling framework for accomplishing the goal, with enough flexibility to allow participants to work out the programmatic details.

In 1989, after convening a series of meetings to elicit ideas about how best to move forward, Goldmark asked Mitchell "Mike" Sviridoff, former Vice President for National Affairs at the Ford Foundation and founding President of LISC, and James Pickman, a lawyer and long-time associate with a deep understanding of community development, to flesh out an initiative to address the goal. He wanted a simple design that relied on existing community development intermediaries, worked mainly with CDCs, and had the potential to raise $250 million over 10 years (Pickman, 2011).

The program structure, elaborated over many months in collaboration with national philanthropic and corporate partners, and with LISC and Enterprise, was ingenious yet simple. Launched in 1991, NCDI was a "virtual" entity, overseen and coordinated by Pickman (acting under the unassuming title of Secretary) and implemented by LISC and Enterprise, each in a strong position to channel significant new resources to a highly dispersed network of community groups. In a significant departure from standard philanthropic practice, senior officers (usually presidents) of the eight original funders (seven foundations and an insurance company) served as NCDI's unofficial board.[4] This enabled the funders to monitor the initiative's progress, make sure that it stayed on target, and deepen their knowledge about the field. Initial financial commitments—$62.5 million in grants and loans (Teltsch, 1991), the largest sum of private funds ever deployed for neighborhood renewal—were for 3 years (Round I). However, in another major departure from standard practice, the initial members shared an understanding that if the program model lived up to its promise, they would stay with it for a decade to ensure significant progress toward the goal. Since they intended NCDI to be a finite effort, not creating a new formal organization that would itself have growing pains and require extended support seemed both sensible and economical.

This structure—the virtual organization, multiyear commitments to collaborative decision making by presidents and senior officers from both philanthropic and corporate funders, and implementation by established intermediaries—was the core innovation. It was unique at the time and has served as a direct model only once since, although collaboration among foundations and philanthropic engagement with the private sector have both become much more common.

LISC and Enterprise each identified cities where they had experience and believed that targeted investments had strong potential to produce demonstrable impacts. They identified places where seasoned or promising CDCs were numerous enough to support a local program and where local foundations and financial institutions seemed receptive to the proposed approach. The Board chose 20 cities in which to begin.[5] Some had numerous

---

[4] The original funders were the William and Flora Hewlett Foundation, the John S. and James L. Knight Foundation, Lilly Endowment, the John D. and Catherine T. MacArthur Foundation, Pew Charitable Trusts, Prudential Insurance Company of America, the Rockefeller Foundation, and the Surdna Foundation.

[5] The initial cities were Atlanta, Baltimore, Boston, Chicago, Cleveland, Columbus, Denver, Indianapolis (in addition to a statewide program), Kansas City (MO), Los Angeles, New York, Newark, Philadelphia, Portland, San Antonio, San Francisco Bay Area, Seattle, St. Paul, and Washington, DC. Dallas, Detroit, and Phoenix were added in Round II.

CDCs with strong track records. Others were relative newcomers to the field, with fewer and newer CDCs and funders who had less experience with community development programming.

THE NATIONAL COMMUNITY DEVELOPMENT INITIATIVE

NCDI's development over the decade is best understood by examining the four key strategies it devised to take the CDC movement to scale and their results. The strategies were increasing the field's access to capital by attracting new partners, refining the program's scope, building CDC capacity, and building systems of support for CDCs at the local level. All required creative work; the first and last required genuine innovation.

Attracting New Partners From All Sectors

The strength of the program design, including the high profile of the early funders, and the strong track record of the intermediaries, which led to visible results fairly quickly, enabled NCDI to attract significant new funding. This was essential if CDCs were simultaneously to increase in number and become stronger.

A major advance came in 1993 when conversations between Pickman, Sviridoff, and senior staff at the U.S. Department of Housing and Urban Development (HUD) came to fruition with the passage of Section 4 of the HUD Demonstration Act of 1993. It made NCDI eligible for noncompetitive grants to develop the capacity of CDCs to undertake community development and affordable housing projects and programs. These grants had to be matched on a three-to-one basis with private funds. The grants were very flexible and came with few strings attached; HUD agreed to participate as an equal partner—a second major innovation.

HUD's participation was a boon. It helped leverage additional private dollars. Symbolically, it legitimized NCDI as the best vehicle to build CDC capacity. Financially, it provided an incentive for private funders to join by adding credibility—a "good housekeeping seal" of good financial controls and reduced risk (General Accounting Office, 2003). It also substantially increased the proportion of NCDI funds that could be used for capacity-building. Increases in CDC capacity in turn reduced the risk of projects supported by loans from the private sector. Tapping federal funds also provided a strong incentive for the intermediaries to strengthen their ability to account for them, and provided an impetus to build financial management capacity at the CDC level (Walker, Gustafson, & Snow, 2002). This financial management capacity, in turn, made it more feasible for CDCs to access federal funds from other sources, such as the Community Development Block Grant (CDBG) program.

The benefits of HUD's role have been a strong NCDI legacy. Amendments to Section 4 have allowed funds to be used for a wider range of activities, and for activities outside the NCDI cities, including rural areas. All awards are now competitive, but LISC, Enterprise, and Habitat for Humanity International are the only eligible grantees.[6] By 2003, Section 4 had

---

[6] See http://portal.hud.gov/hudportal/HUD?src=/program_offices/administration/grants/fundsavail/nofa14/cbcdah-sec4, retrieved August 10, 2013.

become the intermediaries' largest single source of federal funds to support CDC capacity-building (General Accounting Office, 2003).

New national foundations and financial institutions, including some new to community development, joined NCDI in each of the two following rounds of fundraising. Over the initiative's life, 11 foundations and six major financial institutions participated. Participation by financial institutions was key, since they could make below-market-rate loans critical to the affordable housing production process. They also brought financial expertise and discipline, and their participation advanced the broader strategy of increasing the flow of private capital into disinvested neighborhoods. NCDI commitments, including HUD's, rose to $87.9 million in Round 2 (1994–1997), enabling the initiative to add three new cities, and to $103.0 million in Round 3 (1997–2001) (Walker et al., 2002).[7] Of the three-round total commitment of $253.7 million, 60% was in the form of loans, both loans from financial institutions and program-related investments (PRIs) from foundations. Since NCDI typically provided only a modest fraction of the total cost of developing CDC real estate projects, these funds supported over $2.23 billion of real estate development in the 23 cities over 10 years.

New foundations and corporations also began to support community development at the local level. Over the course of the decade, the proportion of intermediary funding for CDC development projects that came from NCDI fell steadily, especially after 1996, because the intermediaries were increasingly able to attract capital from new players (Walker et al., 2002). Mirroring the national program, local funders acted as a board, working with the local office of the intermediary to decide which CDC projects and programs to support.

Refining and Broadening the Program's Scope

Affordable housing was the core of the NCDI agenda. It was the common activity that large numbers of CDCs had demonstrated they could do successfully. It was also considered the key to providing poor households with economic security, stabilizing neighborhoods, and improving neighborhood quality, that is, the core agenda was rooted in broad goals of neighborhood revitalization. This enabled NCDI programming to be flexible, a critical program attribute because the participating cities differed markedly. For example, housing was not always the cutting edge priority in cities where the CDC industry was already well-developed, so early NCDI funding supported the development of single room occupancy units in Boston and child-care centers and community centers in New York City (Teltsch, 1991).

To attract new funders, especially in cities where community development was new, NCDI focused its project funds mainly on the stages of projects that were riskiest and hardest to finance locally: property acquisition, predevelopment activities (e.g., feasibility studies), and construction. NCDI also packaged its resources with funds from the federal HOME Investment Partnership Program to broaden the housing agenda, helping many CDCs to develop affordable, for-sale housing for the first time. NCDI funds constituted a

[7] Two of the initial funders did not provide new funding in both subsequent funding rounds, and consolidation in the financial services industry led to name changes for some participating banks and mergers for others. See Walker et al., 2002, for details.

larger portion of project support than on rental projects to ease local funders and lenders into this new type of activity (Walker et al., 2002).[8]

Over the decade, NCDI gradually enabled more CDCs to move beyond housing. Under NCDI, CDC development of commercial and industrial real estate, in which seasoned groups had at track record, became more widespread, and new activities, such as the development of community centers and charter schools, became part of the repertoire. The strategy was consistent: for each new activity, NCDI supported the riskier phases of development and its funds constituted a larger total share of project support to reduce the perceived risk for local funders and lenders until they gained experience with the new activity (Walker et al., 2002).

Building CDC Capacity

The intermediaries had always understood the importance of building CDCs' organizational capacity, but in the absence of dedicated funding for it they had pursued this objective mainly via a learn-by-doing approach: they gave CDCs small grants and technical assistance to help them undertake progressively larger and more complex projects (Vidal et al., 1985). NCDI's capacity-building funds enabled them to become much more proactive. Local stakeholders used NCDI funds to develop four new capacity-building strategies (Walker & Weinheimer, 1998):

- *Core operating support programs*. These combined NCDI and local funds from multiple sources to give selected CDCs multiyear commitments to cover part of their core operating costs, reducing their fundraising burden. These programs multiplied over the decade as their effectiveness became clear.
- *Formal capacity-building programs*. Many NCDI cities developed variations on a 1986 demonstration program in Boston that combined core operating support, funding for targeted organizational improvements (e.g., financial management), and performance standards.
- *Training programs*. These ranged from comprehensive, multiyear trainings for CDC staff and boards to shorter trainings on specific topics, such as fundraising.
- *Greater use of, or expanded roles for, local or state CDC associations*. These associations enable executive directors to share information, identify common problems, and develop collective public policy advocacy agendas. In some cases, they influenced the local NCDI-supported agenda.

Building Systems of Support

A key structural problem facing the community development industry at the start of NCDI was the complexity of using the federal subsidy dollars needed to make housing

[8] The HOME Investment Partnership Program is a federal block grant devoted exclusively to housing for low- and moderate-income households. Created in 1990, it doubled the funds available to localities for affordable housing (U.S. Department of Housing and Urban Development, 1997). Many localities chose to devote at least a part of their HOME funds to homebuyer assistance and to subsidies for the development of housing for owner occupancy. At least 15% of the funds had to go to nonprofit developers. Localities had to provide a match of at least 25% of total project costs (Schwartz, 2010); funds from NCDI and the intermediaries "counted" as matching funds.

affordable to low- and moderate-income households. The major housing production mechanism, the low-income housing tax credit (LIHTC), was new and legally complex. It provided a shallow subsidy, so many different sources of subsidy (sometimes as many as six or eight) were commonly needed to make a project feasible. Easing and regularizing access to public and private development capital was thus a major priority in all but a few NCDI cities.

Bringing local funders together created a framework around which to build what came to be known as *systems of support*—relationships among funders, including state and local government, that provided different types of capital to housing developments in a timely, predictable fashion (Keyes, Schwartz, Vidal, & Bratt, 1996; Walker & Weinheimer, 1998). Local financial supporters of LISC and Enterprise approved all projects, including those that moved CDCs into activities that were new locally. Local funders worked with intermediary staff to develop capacity-building programs and made key decisions about whether performance benchmarks were being met. Over time, the funders deepened their understanding of the field and one another, developed mutual trust, and became more comfortable undertaking new things together. Simply put, they built social capital.

The move from funder collaboratives to broader systems of support was uneven, and sometimes slow. Some cities had stronger histories of local collaboration than others. More important, local governments differed considerably in the importance they assigned to neighborhood improvement, and in their ability to deliver programs and administer regulations effectively. Government's role in the development of affordable housing is critical, so a city government that performed key functions poorly presented ongoing challenges. Nevertheless, support systems for affordable housing production did improve in most cities. Those systems were adapted over time to support new CDC activities, either by building CDC in-house expertise or through structured partnerships (Vidal & Keyes, 2005). Some adaptations entailed notable innovations, such as specialized industrial retention staff shared by several CDCs, sometimes paid by the city, or a newly created provider of a specialized service (e.g., business development) governed by a board comprised of CDC executive directors.

Social capital grew among the national funders, as well. Foundation presidents and senior corporate officers from very different organizational cultures, accustomed to acting independently, committed to shared decision making when they joined the funder group; this commitment was formalized in a multiyear master agreement. They received briefings from the intermediaries and from field experts, and approved semiannual work plans prepared by the intermediaries under Pickman's direction—often after vigorous discussion.[9] The Chair rotated annually, so many members had the opportunity to work with Pickman between meetings and gained a deeper understanding of the program and its challenges. As the funder group grew, the members established working committees on key issues that enabled more people from both the funders and the intermediaries to become involved. In short, participation in NCDI gave funders a unique opportunity to engage with peers around important, meaty problems and to develop smart strategies to address them.

[9] Pickman, retained as a consultant, remained Secretary for the entire NCDI decade. Early in the program, it became clear that periodic site visits could be valuable as part of program oversight and development; Reese Fayde, another seasoned community development consultant, became his Deputy to take on this role.

Results

The Urban Institute's 10-year evaluation confirmed what the funders had already concluded: NCDI had fostered substantial improvements in the community development field (Walker & Weinheimer, 1998; Walker et al., 2002). CDC capacity had increased. Housing production had risen sharply. The number of CDCs in NCDI cities that could consistently produce more than 10 housing units a year had more than doubled, and all cities registered gains, although in varying degree. Many CDCs had broadened the scope of their work, with about a quarter of them pursuing *five* or more types of neighborhood revitalization work. The quality of community development practice improved as strong models helped localities move closer to national standards. In most cities, the reputation of CDCs as effective agents to address neighborhood problems improved in the eyes of local stakeholders, and in two thirds of the cities observers credited at least one neighborhood "turnaround" to the community's CDC.

Improved support systems made this possible. The combination of joint problem solving by local supporters and the strategic use of NCDI funds to fill gaps in the production system led to stronger relationships and new programs. Access to private capital increased noticeably in two thirds of the cities (it had already been readily available in all but one of the others when NCDI began). Housing production systems were streamlined in almost half the cities, and those systems broadened to enable multiple CDCs to move into several new activities in a third of the cities.[10]

From the perspective of the members, NCDI provided clear evidence that CDCs, properly supported, effectively promoted healthier neighborhoods, and the intermediaries were key to their operating strength: they both supported capacity building and held CDCs accountable. Together, they laid the foundation for a more comprehensive approach at the community level, which could be sustained by strengthening and aligning local systems of support.

More broadly, NCDI's results confirmed the benefits of collaboration among funders: significant capital, drawn from a combination of philanthropic, private, and public sources and deployed strategically over time, could make a bigger impact than individual members could do singly. Funder meetings in 1999 to do strategic planning for the final, close-out year and consider the possibility of extending the work for an additional round led the group to conclude that collaboration provided a platform from which to launch a broader agenda, both at the neighborhood level and nationally. They made the unexpected decision to commit to a second decade, dubbed D2. Planning for D2, including the decision to incorporate legally, began early in 2000.

LIVING CITIES: THE NATIONAL COMMUNITY DEVELOPMENT INITIATIVE

Living Cities: The National Community Development Initiative embarked in 2001 on an agenda that built squarely on the successes of NCDI with CDCs and the intermediaries,

[10] The evaluation acknowledged that the entire community development industry grew dramatically during the 1990s, and that CDC housing production did, as well, because federal funding for housing increased sharply. Nevertheless, it argued that NCDI made clear contributions to increased industry strength in the cities it targeted. The deep experience of the intermediaries, strategic use of NCDI funds to fill gaps in support systems, major investments in capacity building, dissemination across cities of new programs and organizational models, and consistent emphasis on demonstrating that funds were being wisely spent all paid off. Progress was clearly uneven, but NCDI made a difference, particularly at the system-building level in cities where community development was relatively new.

but framed its goals more broadly: to combine the resources, knowledge, and experience of leading foundations, financial institutions, and the federal government to improve the lives of people in distressed neighborhoods. It also embedded the agenda in a wider context: connecting urban neighborhoods to the regional economy, making better use of information technology, and shaping public policy.

It retained many organizational features that served NCDI well, but *formalizing* those relationships and arrangements was another innovation: senior funder representatives now comprise the Board of the organization in which their foundation or corporation invests. Funding commitments continue to be made in 3-year cycles, but the Chair is now elected for a 3-year term. The funders committed to making the new organization more member-driven and created a committee structure in which members assumed leadership roles (including fundraising responsibilities) on issues important to them. Reese Fayde, Pickman's Deputy, became the first CEO and created a working organization that remained quite lean throughout her 6 years in office.

The existing structure for working with LISC and Enterprise in 23 cities, renamed The Cities Program, carried forward as the organization's core activity, and its momentum continued to build. Financial support to the intermediaries, both grants and loans, increased in each of the next two funding rounds (2001–2004 and 2004–2007), although loans to support CDC real estate projects increased much more dramatically than grants because new financial institutions became members. This support enabled the intermediaries to leverage a steadily expanding pool of private capital over time, greatly increasing the program's impact, and intermediary-assisted investments in housing and other real estate developments rose steadily. With Living Cities' support, the intermediaries continued to broaden the range of projects undertaken, and reach a growing number of CDCs (Metis Associates, 2006; Metis Associates, 2008).

The Board's interest in working in new ways at the neighborhood level took hold more slowly. The Pilot Cities Initiative selected four cities—Baltimore, Chicago, Miami, and the Twin Cities—in which local foundations could design programs to test new ways to align local and national resources across sectors into a single, coordinated neighborhood revitalization investment strategy (Willis, 2004). One of the Pilot City programs—the New Communities Program, launched in 2003 by the MacArthur Foundation and Chicago LISC—gained national recognition, but developing a set of crosscutting themes that could serve as the basis for comparative learning across the cities proved difficult.[11]

The desire to raise the national profile of the urban policy agenda moved forward on two fronts. One sought to improve the quality of information about cities and neighborhoods that shapes public and private investment decisions. Living Cities: NCDI supported the Brookings Institution's Urban Markets Initiative (2004), designed to close "the urban information gap" by making both federal and local data on assets in cities and urban neighborhoods more accessible, with the goal of stimulating the flow of investments into urban areas and making urban markets more efficient. This included an important emphasis on

[11] The New Communities Program designated a lead agency (sometimes a CDC, sometimes not) in each of 16 targeted neighborhoods. That agency was responsible for convening a broad-based quality of life planning process, and with help from LISC, was then responsible for helping organizations throughout the neighborhood connect with resources to implement the comprehensive plan. This holistic approach, adapted to the distinct circumstances in the cities where LISC works, became the defining element of its Building Sustainable Communities program, launched in 2007.

making data available to CDCs and others at the local level using Geographic Information Systems (Willis, 2004).

Working through Living Cities: NCDI, Board members were also able to work on issues and engage directly with Congress in ways they could not as presidents of their respective foundations. Living Cities engaged a policy advisor to keep members informed and help the organization cultivate relationships on Capitol Hill. This work led to the creation in 2006 of the bipartisan Congressional Former Mayors Caucus, which continues to be active.

Nevertheless, Board members were increasingly unsatisfied with the organization's progress. This may have reflected, in part, some efforts that did not come to fruition.[12] But the more fundamental concern was that the platform the collaboration had created to support bold new work was not living up to its potential. The letter from the Co-Chairs of the Board that introduced the 13-year assessment of The Cities Program surfaced this key issue. It pointed to the clear record of accomplishment. It acknowledged that many challenges remained. But it concluded "the community development model now has a proven record; it has long since moved out of the realm of wishful thinking and into the toolbox of a modern economy" (Metis Associates, 2005). Differently stated, with 20/20 hindsight, the opportunities for testing fresh approaches to changing systems that constrain access to opportunity for poor urban residents, and learning from the results, lay elsewhere.

The Board undertook a strategic assessment in 2006. The Strategic Planning Committee recommended that the organization build on its track record of substantial accomplishment, and "expressly broaden, reconstitute, and strengthen Living Cities' purposes, structures, and staffing in order to demonstrate—over the next 3 years—the possibility of generating a far larger, more pivotal, and lasting impact on the rapidly changing environment for community development practice and urban policy in the United States" (Living Cities, 2006). The Board accepted this recommendation, and the result is Living Cities as we know it now.

LIVING CITIES TODAY

Living Cities retains the initial NCDI goal of improving the lives of poor people in cities, but it now seeks to pursue a much wider range of approaches to advancing that goal. It continues to recognize the importance of strengthening neighborhoods, but asserts that doing so requires strengthening the cities that surround them and changing the broader systems, both public and private, that have created and sustained concentrated poverty. It remains committed to data-driven decision making and learning from experience but has raised its aspirations to include knowledge building, leadership development, research, and program development.

[12] The Human Capital Development Initiative (HCDI), an $8 million, multiyear effort to address human capital issues in the CDC industry, was partially funded by NCDI and managed by the National Congress for Community Economic Development. Launched during Round 3 and concluded in Round 4, it registered some clear accomplishments, but was generally regarded as disappointing. Round 4 included the Office of Community Services at the U.S. Department of Health and Human Services as a Living Cities member, reflecting grants awarded to activities supported by Living Cities in some of the 23 cities; but unlike the relationship with HUD, it could not be sustained. An effort to take national the New York City Acquisition Fund, which provides predevelopment loans to developers of affordable housing, was not successful because the risk management issues involved in scaling up proved too complex.

The current organizational structure differs from the one established when Living Cities incorporated in three important ways. The first, and most obvious, is the expanded staff—now more than 20, housed in offices in New York and Washington, DC—to support the broader agenda. It is led by President and CEO Ben Hecht, a lawyer and CPA whose experience includes expanding poor households' access to technology as well as community development. The second, and less obvious, is the fact that senior officers other than CEOs more commonly serve on the Board. Many CEOs are still active, but the mix has changed, and sending alternate representatives has become more common. Finally, and a major innovation, is the fact that all Board committees except the Executive Committee now include senior staff from member organizations in addition to Board members. In addition, shorter-lived Working Groups charged with program development in specific areas of interest (e.g., green economy, transit-oriented development) are comprised entirely of staff from member organizations. This enables Living Cities to quickly "staff up" to respond to issues, to draw on the expertise embedded in its member organizations, and to be more member-driven.

In its strategic assessment, the Board affirmed its belief that the intermediaries remained very attractive, high-capacity prospective partners and its desire to continue to work with high-capacity partners. However, it noted that Living Cities' work with the intermediaries as structured under NCDI and The Cities Program followed a program development agenda framed principally by LISC and Enterprise rather than the Board and was no longer testing new approaches. Accordingly, in Round 6 (2007–2010) the intermediaries received a final package of loans roughly comparable to Round 5, but only modest grant support. The grants were not for operating support or capacity building, but rather to create an opportunity for the intermediaries to identify fresh ways to engage with Living Cities in the future.

Since it seeks to test alternative approaches to leveraging change, Living Cities emphasizes core values rather than strategies or programs and sees those values as central to the organization's ability to realize its mission. They are:

- Collaboration—across sectors, with a respectful, open exchange of ideas;
- Innovation—take risks and test new approaches to changing broken systems;
- Leadership—ask difficult questions, enable others to do the same, and seek strategic opportunities to move innovation into the mainstream; and
- Impact—make material improvements, evaluate our own effectiveness, and reflect on the results.[13]

Two initiatives illustrate the range of approaches this value-driven perspective can foster: the Foreclosure Mitigation Initiative, which (like the original NCDI) was very tightly focused, and The Integration Initiative, which is quite broad.

[13] See http://www.livingcities.org/about/values

The Foreclosure Mitigation Initiative (FMI) exemplifies the strategy of getting "out in front" of an emerging problem or opportunity and developing models or practices that can be scaled up through public policy.[14] The Board focused on the emerging foreclosure crisis, especially its concentrated effects in low- and moderate-income neighborhoods, in mid-2007. A Working Group on home mortgage foreclosure designed FMI, which Living Cities launched late in 2007. In 2008, it made awards totaling $5.25 million to 10 strong organizations on the cutting edge of developing programs to acquire and resell foreclosed homes to stabilize neighborhoods. The goal was to invest in organizations that would quickly implement programs that could serve as models when widely anticipated federal funding for acquisition of foreclosed homes became available.

The suddenness of the financial and real estate crisis meant that even seasoned, high-capacity organizations were new to this type of work. All found forging the new institutional arrangements, including financial relationships needed to acquire properties, more difficult and time-consuming than expected. Living Cities extended the grant period; adapted the program to support program development costs, including core staff, in some places; and made loans to establish risk-reduction reserves for investors in others.[15] Program delays limited its ability to influence the design of the federal response, but some of the pilots did become program models when Neighborhood Stabilization Program funds became available.

In contrast with many foundation-funded evaluations that are made public, the interim evaluation report was remarkably frank. Predictably, it highlighted important systemic obstacles. Less predictably, and consistent with the Impact value articulated above, it included candid discussions of what worked and what did not, and of the Initiative's cautionary lessons for philanthropy about the challenges of trying to respond to crises (Mayer & Temkin, 2009).

The Integration Initiative (TII) tackles the broad systems-change agenda and has clear roots in the comprehensive community initiatives that have received significant philanthropic support over the past 25 years. Launched in 2010, this 10-year effort initially targeted five competitively chosen cities (Baltimore, Cleveland, Detroit, Newark, and the Twin Cities) in which local stakeholders already had a track record of working together on a broad, shared agenda and seeks to ratchet up the level and impact of that work. Each site was required both to identify at least one target neighborhood and to incorporate the following high-impact strategies to drive systems transformation and achieve impact at scale:

- Move beyond delivering programs to transforming systems, for example, transportation, jobs.
- Build a resilient civic infrastructure, operationalized as "one table" that brings together decision makers from all sectors to define and address complex social

[14] Another example of this approach is Living Cities' work on the green economy, especially retrofitting buildings to improve their energy efficiency. The American Reinvestment and Recovery Act of 2009 (the Stimulus) included substantial federal funds to improve energy efficiency. Living Cities convened a Green Boot Camp in 2009 to help 16 cities begin to scale their work under the Stimulus, and this group of cities, working with others, both implemented local programs with Living Cities support and developed guidelines that became part of the President's Better Buildings Initiative in 2011, implemented by the U.S. Department of Energy.

[15] This brought the total cost of the initiative to $7 million.

problems. "The stakeholders themselves must create and implement the solution because the problem itself lies in their attitudes, priorities or behavior, and only a change within and between them will produce a solution."

- Bring disruptive innovations into the mainstream and redirect funds away from obsolete approaches toward what works.
- Supplement traditional government and philanthropic funding streams to drive the private market to work on behalf of low-income people.[16]

The importance of changing the way the private market works is embedded in the funding package: of the initial 3-year investment of $85 million, only $13.75 million was in the form of grants. In 2011, each site received $2.75 million in grants, $3–4 million in below-market-rate debt from the Living Cities Catalyst Fund, and $9–14 million in commercial debt. The Catalyst Fund consists of program related investments. Commercial debt is provided by member financial institutions and is the largest component of a broader effort by Living Cities to improve the flow of capital into disinvested areas.

An ambitious evaluation with both site-specific and cross-site components reported early results that were mixed (Mount Auburn Associates, 2012), but encouraging enough that all five sites were invited to renew (at different funding levels) for Phase 2; all accepted except Cleveland. Living Cities is also making 1-year planning grants to five additional sites in the South and West, where the challenges differ considerably from those in the Phase 1 cities and are therefore expected to lead to new types of learning. Based on the Phase 1 experience, the four high-impact strategies to drive systems transformation and achieve impact at scale have been reframed for Phase 2 to focus on: (1) Results, (2) Collective Impact, (3) Capital Innovation and (4) Public Sector Innovation.

The contrasts between Living Cities today and the original NCDI, both organizationally and programmatically, are striking, but the threads connecting them are quite clear. The innovative funder-driven approach that integrates the strengths of philanthropy and corporate investments evolved over time in response to experience and changing conditions, but it remains intelligent and results driven. The ultimate impact of the new strategic thrust adopted in 2007, especially the overarching systems-change goal, remains to be seen, and assessing that impact will be much more challenging than assessing NCDI because the programming is now so diverse—but the organization's innovative history clearly suggests that the future bears watching.

DISCUSSION QUESTIONS

1. What were the pros and cons of the "virtual" organizational form of NCDI?
2. At the end of the first decade, the members of NCDI decided to continue their work together, but became dissatisfied with the result. How might you account for the

[16] See http://www.livingcities.org/integration/principles/

"disconnect" between what they said they wanted, what they did, and their lack of satisfaction with the results? What factors worked against the organization making more changes after Living Cities incorporated?

3. What are the major opportunities and challenges presented by the broader mission and more diverse agenda adopted by Living Cities in 2007?
4. What are the pros and cons of having greater participation of staff from member organizations on the Board, Board Committees, and Working Groups?
5. Given the apparent advantages of collaboration among the funders of Living Cities, why do you think collaborations of this sort have not become more common?
6. When compared with more service-oriented strategies for assisting low-income households, what advantages did the focus on the development of real estate, a mortgageable asset, give the intermediaries and Living Cities in raising funds? In demonstrating impact?

REFERENCES

Brookings Institution. (2004). *Urban Markets Initiative: Using information to drive change—General program background*. Washington, DC: Metropolitan Policy Program.

General Accounting Office. (2003, September 15). *Capacity building: Section 4 program has expanded and evolved*. (Report GAO-03-975). Retrieved from http://www.gao.gov/assets/240/239708.pdf

Goldmark, P. (2011, April 15). LISC 30th Anniversary Gala: Keynote address. Local Initiative Support Corporation. Retrieved from https://www.google.com/search?q=goldmark+LISC+30th+gala&ie=utf-8&oe=utf-8&aq=t&rls=org.mozilla:en-US:official&client=firefox-a

Keyes, L. C., Schwartz, A., Vidal, A. C., & Bratt, R. G. (1996). Networks and nonprofits: Opportunities and challenges in an era of federal devolution. *Housing Policy Debate, 7*(2), 202–229.

Kohler, J. S. (2007). Living Cities: The National Community Development Initiative, 1991. In J. L. Fleishman, J. S. Kohler, & S. Schlinder (Eds.), *Casebook for the foundation: A great American secret* (pp. 217–219). New York, NY: Public Affairs.

Living Cities. (2006, November 20). *Strategic planning committee final report: Executive summary* (unpublished document). New York, NY: Living Cities.

Mayer, N., & Temkin, K. (2009). *Evaluation of the Living Cities Foreclosure Mitigation Initiative: Final interim report*. Washington, DC: The Urban Institute.

Metis Associates. (2005). *Improving the vitality of urban neighborhoods in 23 American cities*. New York, NY: Living Cities: The National Community Development Initiative.

Metis Associates. (2006). *The Cities Program follow-the-money report: Analyzing how funds are used for real estate investment and production*. New York, NY: Living Cities: The National Community Development Initiative.

Metis Associates. (2008). *The Cities Program follow-the-money report: Analyzing how funds are used for real estate investment and production* (July 1, 1991–June 30, 2007). New York, NY: Living Cities: The National Community Development Initiative.

Mt. Auburn Associates. (2012, October). *The Integration Initiative interim outcome report*. Cambridge, MA: Retrieved from http://www.livingcities.org/knowledge/media/?action=view&id=91

National Congress for Community Economic Development. (1991). *Changing the odds: The achievements of community-based development corporations*. Washington, DC: Author.

Pickman, J. (2011). *Dynamic collaboration: Reflections on Living Cities at 20* (p. 29). New York, NY: Living Cities.

Schwartz, A. F. (2010). *Housing policy in the United States* (2nd ed.). New York, NY: Routledge.

Teltsch, K. (1991, March 1). New alliance plans housing in 20 cities. *The New York Times*. Retrieved from http://www.nytimes.com/1991/03/01/us/new-alliance-plans-housing-in-20-cities.html?src=pm

U.S. Department of Housing and Urban Development. (1997). *Expanding the supply of affordable rental housing*. Washington, DC: Department of Housing and Urban Development, Office of Policy Development and Research.

Vidal, A. C. (1992). *Rebuilding communities: A national study of community development corporations*. New York, NY: Community Development Research Center.

Vidal, A. C. (2012). Housing and community development. In L. Salamon (Ed.), *The state of the nonprofit sector* (2nd ed.). Washington, DC: Brookings Institution.

Vidal, A. C., Howitt, A. M., & Foster, K. P. (1985). *An evaluation of the Local Initiatives Support Corporation: Findings from phase II* (Discussion Paper D86-1, December). Cambridge, MA: State, Local, and Intergovernmental Center, Kennedy School of Government, Harvard University.

Vidal, A. C., & Keyes, L. C. (2005). *Beyond housing: Growing community development support systems*. Washington, DC: Urban Institute.

Walker, C. (1993). Nonprofit housing development: Status, trends, and prospects. *Housing Policy Debate, 4*(3), 369–414.

Walker, C., Gustafson, J., & Snow, C. (2002). *National support for local systems change: The effect of the National Community Development Initiative on community development systems*. Washington, DC: Urban Institute.

Walker, C., & Weinheimer, M. (1998). *Community development in the 1990s*. Washington, DC: Urban Institute.

Willis, M. A. (2004). Living Cities: Collaborative investing for healthy neighborhoods. *Journal of Urban Affairs, 26*(2), 139–149.

CHAPTER 15

Overcoming Constraints in the U.S. Human Services System

How New York City Uses Collaboration to Encourage Innovation

Lauren A. Miltenberger

Villanova University

INTRODUCTION

Under the framework of devolution, privatization, and contracting out, the work of nonprofit and government administrators has become more and more deeply intertwined in recent years. The trend of government contracting out public services to nonprofits has risen alongside the rising recognition of the potent value of nonprofits' familiarity with local knowledge. This has prompted massive expansion in the use of contracting, vouchers, and other collaborative service arrangements that reach across into the nonprofit realm. This is especially the case in the social services, where these trends have effectively transformed parts of the nonprofit sector into routine, core front-line agents of delivery for a whole array of critical government services for those in need.

One of the major advantages claimed by government to having nonprofits deliver services is their innovative and flexible nature that allows them to adapt to the needs of their communities in useful ways. Countless papers emphasize the assumed comparative advantages of nonprofits—they are innovative, nimble, and flexible; adjust quickly to change and to local differences; and operate close to those they wish to benefit (Alexander, 2000; Dichter, 1999; Reisch & Sommerfeld, 2003). The innovative and flexible nature of the nonprofit sector is seen as a huge advantage and one that the government can capitalize on by using their contracted services.

However, a paradox between innovation and constraint is created by the human service delivery system. The genesis of this paradox comes from the public sector's belief that human services are best delivered by nonprofit organizations due to their ability to be flexible and create services that are specific to the needs of clients. Although devolution promised that states and localities can and should innovate and adapt programs to their communities, the individuals who deliver these services to clients, the street-level nonprofit workers, are often constrained in their discretion when applying program policies to individual needs (Abramovitz, 2002; Campbell, 2002; Dias & Maynard-Moody, 2007). Also, proponents of privatization commonly cite the innovativeness and flexible approach of nonprofits as a major asset to social service program delivery, especially in contrast to the bureaucratic nature of the government (Salamon, 1995; Smith & Lipsky, 1993; Young, 2000). Nonprofits are unable to be innovative and flexible because they are forced to follow the rules that were created without their input (Curtis & Copeland, 2003). These changes also can create a situation where nonprofits may have a loss of autonomy and a loss of the ability to respond quickly and flexibly to changing social needs (Evans & Shields, 1998).

The purpose of this chapter is to describe a paradox that exists in the ideological design of human service policies and the actual practice of these programs by nonprofit organizations. Nonprofits are inherently innovative in nature, having a long history of creating new solutions to community problems. However, the current human service delivery system puts constraints on nonprofits through (a) block grant provisions and specific contracting requirements that do not foster and develop communication between government and nonprofits, and (b) the human services system that is fragmented and complex and takes up too much administrative time and leaves little time for flexibility and innovation. Over time, this service-delivery "system" has evolved through a complicated process, and left nonprofit human service providers on the front lines dealing with the challenges associated with a complicated system of contracting. The current complex and fragmented system of contracting has created an environment where it is difficult for nonprofit innovation to occur.

THE PROBLEM: A COMPLEX, FRAGMENTED HUMAN SERVICE DELIVERY SYSTEM

The system of contracting for human services carries with it certain challenges and obstacles that nonprofits must face. Boris, de Leon, Roeger, and Nikolova's (2010) study on this phenomenon, the first-ever national study on this topic, has produced comprehensive data on the structure, results, and scope of this relationship. A major finding from their survey is the intricate nature of this system and the obstacles that nonprofits must face. They found that nationally 76% of the nonprofit respondents indicated that the complexity and time required for reporting on contracts and grants was a problem (Boris et al., 2010). They also found that 75% indicated that the application process was too complicated and time consuming. This "system" of nonprofit-government contracting has inherent challenges associated with it, but it is the system that ultimately guides social policy in the United States. The rationale for the devolution and contracting out of social services rests on the assumption that nonprofit social service agencies are in a better position than state agencies to assess problems, coordinate resources, and customize services to meet families' needs. In other words, the innovative nature of the nonprofit sector is a huge asset that the government can use to provide better services than through bureaucratic institutions.

Therefore, nonprofit social service agencies operate in a multifaceted environment where they are on the receiving end of state, county, and city contracts. These contracts are the products of a complicated federal block grant system where different social services are funded by the federal government. The federal government then provides the funds to the states and turns over the responsibility of service delivery to the states to allow them to have some local decision making and flexibility. The federal block grants that affect the human service delivery system are the Temporary Assistance for Needy Families (TANF) block grant, the Social Services Block Grant (SSBG), the Community Services Block Grant (CSBG), the Mental Health Services Block Grant (MHSBG), the Substance Abuse Prevention Block Grant (SAPBG), the Nutrition Programs of the Older Americans Act, and the Ryan White Care Act providing funding for HIV/AIDS services. These block grants are the starting points for analysis on the human service system as they represent the current federal public policies dealing with these interconnected issues. These block grants then trickle down to the states to be disbursed, most of which turn into contracts. The human services contracting system has been created piecemeal via vertical lines of block grants trickling down to state government agencies, which then create service contracts that are provided by nonprofit organizations.

This results in a fragmented system with little coordinated communication, strategy, or planning between the government and its nonprofit social service contractors. But once it goes to the nonprofits, how does the government effectively address the entire problem, how does it create a system or network of services where providers and funders have a dialogue about the changes in population, changes in services needed, and ultimately changes in policies that correctly address the effective delivery of social services?

From the research that has been done on the effects of privatization on nonprofits, there has been evidence that the innovativeness of the nonprofit sector is being stifled by government contracts that do not include nonprofits in the decision-making process. With private social services now predominantly financed by government, benefits accrue in part because public policy is more likely than private charity to ensure well-financed, equitable, efficiently administered, and uniformly available social services. But voluntary social service agencies may find that sustaining the distinctive normative climates that ensure uniqueness and innovation is increasingly difficult (Abramovitz, 2002; Curtis & Copeland, 2003; Hasenfeld & Powell, 2004; Lynn, 2002). The contracting culture has been fraught with hazards of funding uncertainty, goal deflection, and organizational instability. It invokes crisis management, thwarts long-term planning, and stifles innovation expected of the nonprofit sector (Bischoff & Reisch, 2000; Mulroy, 2003; Rosenthal, 2000).

Hasenfeld and Powell (2004) discuss the particular advantages nonprofits are presumed to possess that include (a) the ability to provide individualized services, (b) the capacity to access and mobilize resources on behalf of clients, and (c) the capacity to create innovative practices that become models of service delivery. However, they argue that these benefits are only realized when the environment they are operating in cultivates these strengths. Their research found that this was not the case. Instead, the nonprofits from their study were working in an unsupportive environment that set "explicit constraints on who they can serve, what services they can offer, and what service outcomes they are expected to attain" (Hasenfeld & Powell, 2004, p. 106).

The purpose of illuminating the above paradox between theory and practice is to stimulate debate on how to improve the design of human service policies to encourage nonprofit innovation. Fortunately, there are some examples of innovative human service systems that have been designed to overcome constraints to innovation. Specifically, a collaborative and coordinated governance approach can stimulate nonprofit innovation within the human services system.

THE SOLUTION: COLLABORATION BETWEEN NONPROFITS AND GOVERNMENT AND A MORE COORDINATED SYSTEM

Even within the constraints of the contracting system, a hopeful sign for the future is in a stream of research demonstrating that obstacles seemingly inherent to the contracting system can and should be overcome (Van Slyke, 2003). In fact, a key conclusion in the research on the nonprofit-government relationship is the move toward a collaborative approach to governance (Austin, 2003; Brown & Troutt, 2004; Denhardt, 2003; Milward & Provan, 2000; Poole, 2003). Due to fragmentation in the structure and funding of human services, these studies argue that a collaborative governance structure is needed. A collaborative governance model can also influence the way nonprofit innovation is cultivated and created.

Empirical studies on this topic provide evidence that contracts for human services are best implemented when focused on creating partnerships and collaborations between nonprofits and government. Current issues related to contracting for social services, like TANF programs, job assistance, and childcare, reflect less of the old principal-agent dimensions of privatization and more of the community-building and networking dynamics of partnership development (Austin, 2003). Another study finds that rather than assume the traditional arm's-length role of service delivery, state agencies overseeing human service contracts can accomplish more by adopting a partnering role with local nonprofit organizations (Poole, 2003). Milward and Provan (2000) state that evidence shows that stability and collaboration are key elements of effective relationships between government and nonprofits. And last, researchers in Canada found that high levels of trust, respect, and collaboration produced positive outcomes. It was discovered that a participatory process with significant input from nonprofits into the design of standards, structure, and design diminished problems and contributed to a trusting and collaborative relationship in which both parties worked together smoothly to fulfill the common mission of providing services (Brown & Troutt, 2004).

The complexities of the current human service system combine to inhibit collaboration. Nonprofits and government must work together to overcome the structural obstacles to collaboration and design new systems built on reciprocity, trust, mutual commitment, and a strong sense of joint ownership of positive outcomes. Creating collaborative structures will improve the human service delivery system and reduce the obstacles facing the nonprofit and government sectors (Bryson, Crosby, & Stone, 2006). Collaborative structures will also encourage the development of nonprofit innovation in two ways: (1) by reducing complexities in reporting and application requirements that combine to generate administrative burdens and make it difficult for nonprofits to have time to be innovative, and (2) when a collaborative system is created, a two-way exchange of ideas is formed that allows an innovative nonprofit idea to trickle up to the government agency.

The advantages of collaboration are being recognized in practice, because cities and states are moving closer toward creating collaborative contracting relationships with their nonprofit partners. New York, New Jersey, and Connecticut are a few examples of states that are currently designing new systems to guide a collaborative relationship. Making these systems work demands enormous investments, informal adjustments, and the building of trust among diverse state agencies, different levels of government, service providers, and community organizations (Austin, 2003). Another benefit of a collaborative system is the increase of nonprofit innovation. New York City is an interesting case study in its developments of a collaborative system, which demonstrates how a collaborative system can foster and encourage nonprofit innovation.

THE DEVELOPMENT OF A COLLABORATIVE SYSTEM—PROFILE OF NEW YORK CITY

At a public forum at the Robert F. Wagner Graduate School of Public Service in April 2009, New York City Mayor Michael Bloomberg announced a new collaborative initiative aimed at enhancing the contracting process between the city and its nonprofit vendors. The Mayor's Nonprofit Initiative was designed to help reduce nonprofit organizations' fixed costs, improve the city's contracting procedures to help nonprofits work with city agencies, and provide dedicated support to strengthen nonprofit management. The Nonprofit Initiative would be governed by the Mayor's Office of Contract Services (MOCS) and supported by the creation of a number of key new roles, task forces, and offices to carry out the daily operations and planning. The Strengthening Nonprofits Task Force, chaired by Deputy Mayor for Health and Human Services Linda I. Gibbs and United Way of New York City President and CEO Gordon Campbell, advises the city on the development and implementation of nonprofit initiatives. The office of Capacity Building and Oversight (CBO) acts as both an oversight and support function for MOCS. And the Nonprofit Contract Facilitator—a unique and innovative position, one of the first of its kind—is the head liaison between the city and local nonprofits.

According to 2009 statistics, there are 42,428 nonprofits registered in New York City, employing over 470,000 individuals (http://www.nyc.gov/html/mocs/html/vendors/NYCNonprofitContracting.shtml; accessed July 11, 2014). In 2011 alone, New York City facilitated nearly 55,000 contracts worth close to $15 billion, of which 2,200 were contracts with nonprofit agencies. While the number of nonprofit contracts seems rather small when compared to the whole, the total amount of contracts that go to nonprofits is huge. Each year, the nonprofits receive roughly $4 billion in contracted services from New York City government. Thus, just over 2,000 contracts are responsible for almost one third of the city's entire total procurement budget.

In addition to the fact that nonprofits provide a large amount of contracted services for New York City, there is one other large influence that created and maintained this collaborative initiative—the two leaders involved. The first is Marla Gibson, who came to MOCS with a background in the nonprofit sector and understood the sector's frustrations. Prior to Gibson's hire, MOCS would not speak directly with nonprofits, or *vendors* as they called them, and the relationship was unmistakably one-sided. The second is Deputy Mayor for Health and Human Services Linda I. Gibbs, who took the initiative to Mayor Bloomberg and asked for his support. Gibbs believed that the new emphasis on collaboration would make working with the city a less complicated endeavor for nonprofits. Together, these two women, one with government experience and the other with nonprofit experience, saw the struggles of the human service system and ushered New York City's nonprofit-government relationship into its new collaborative phase.

MOCS, CBO, and the Strengthening Nonprofits Task Force rallied around the belief that a vibrant and robust nonprofit sector will help keep New York City strong. They also appear to appreciate the considerable challenges that nonprofits encounter when they enter into a contract with the city and the unnecessary strain that this places on some of the city's most critical partners. These challenges included first and foremost different contracting procedures for each of the 13 city agencies. This resulted in long and complicated Request for Proposals processes, complicated funding patterns, and diverse reporting requirements. But Gibson and Gibbs realized that without nonprofits the city would neither be able to fulfill its state-mandated requirements nor its mission. It is the city's acknowledgment of this key component that creates the beginnings of a successful partnership, one built on mutual benefit and cooperation. Although MOCS and CBO have legal and necessary oversight roles to perform, their missions incorporate a dual component of support and collaboration.

COLLABORATION ENCOURAGES NONPROFIT INNOVATION

New York City's Collaborative nonprofit-government system encourages innovation in two ways: (1) It reduces administrative constraints and therefore enables nonprofits to be more innovative, and (2) it also embeds a two-way communication process into the system, which allows the innovative nonprofit voice to be heard. Below are four specific ways that nonprofit innovation is cultivated in New York City.

1. HHS Accelerator

The HHS Accelerator is another initiative designed to streamline the contracting process and provide visibility for health and human services nonprofits. This tool will allow a nonprofit to maintain its core organizational information in a secure electronic database that it can then leverage to complete and submit its response to an RFP. Rather than entering the same information into a template or proposal every time, the nonprofit can primarily focus on developing project scope and budget. Currently, there are two main components. The first is the document vault, housed on an online portal, that nonprofits can use to store nonconfidential documents. Nonprofits can, of course, push this information to city agencies, but they can also use it to contact private foundations in the grant-making process. The second phase is an enhanced RFP and solicitation process. The information that nonprofits publicly maintain in the vault will be used to send advance notice about RFPs that might be of interest to the organization. The HHS Accelerator thus encourages innovation through the reduction of administrative constraints.

2. Standard Human Services Contract

One of the most remarkable outcomes of this collaboration is the new standard human services contract. It is a streamlined contract that every city agency in New York City now uses to contract with nonprofits. Prior to this development, each of the 11 city agencies had its own rules and procedures guiding the contracting process. This translated into a complex web of contracting arrangements that nonprofits were expected to navigate on their own. The development of the standard human services contract took over 4 years to develop and demanded Gibbs and Gibson to coordinate with both government agency personnel and staff from nonprofit organizations. This standard contract increased organizational efficiencies for nonprofits, because they now avoid the complexity of a different contract for each service provided for each city agency. The single contract also benefits MOCS because it streamlines the system internally. Again, the standard human services contract encourages innovation through the reduction of administrative constraints.

3. Collaborative Structures Foster Communication and Innovation

The collaborative arrangement between New York City's government agencies and its nonprofits was designed to develop and provide structure for communication between the two partners. This collaborative arrangement realizes the importance of verbal coordination, communication, and planning between these groups of public and private actors. A collaborative approach that emphasizes a shared vision and a clear communication strategy, one that regularly allows both partners to discuss programmatic decisions, is the ideal format for the delivery of human services. Through regularly scheduled meetings, nonprofit service contractors have the ability to discuss new innovative ideas with their government colleagues, and from these discussions new innovations in service delivery can take shape. Collaboration enables more effective formal communication with government agencies—in so doing, nonprofit innovation can be recognized, ideas can be shared, and new policies can be developed.

4. Concept Paper

One of the most concrete examples of the encouragement of innovation in the New York City case is the use of concept papers. Prior to the city creating an RFP for a new contract, the agency first asks for nonprofit service providers to respond to a concept paper. This process allows nonprofits to suggest ideas and innovations to be used in the RFP. The government agency then uses the ideas generated from all the concept papers submitted to shape the RFP.

EFFICIENCY, EFFECTIVENESS, AND REPLICABILITY

There is an inherent paradox in the human service system that results from contracting, whereby (a) the fragmented system constrains the creation of nonprofit innovation, and (b) nonprofits are responding to "state-level" policies in the form of contracted services, yet they are not necessarily included in the development of these contracts. This complex, fragmented procurement system constrains nonprofit innovation. One outcome of this service delivery system is a paradox whereby the rhetoric of wanting nonprofits to deliver innovative services to communities, exists at the same time as a contracting system that produces constraints on innovation. One way to make the system more effective and efficient is to create collaborative structures that can have positive impacts on innovation by nonprofit organizations.

Regarding replicability, industrialized countries around the world have been moving toward more collaborative forms of government-nonprofit relations and an institutionalization of the types of interactions between the sectors (Salamon, 2005). Symptomatic of this shift in the social contract between governments and nonprofits is the emergence of new structures and processes that seek to overcome the tensions between the sectors and give explicit recognition to the unique role of the nonprofits in service delivery and policy consultation.

The United Kingdom provides an example of how a public-private partnership may be utilized in practice to achieve this lofty goal of "collaborative advantage." The public sector in the United Kingdom has been promoting the use of partnerships with private agencies for public service delivery for approximately 10 years. Many organizations in the United Kingdom not only endorse the partnership idea but also actively employ it as a programmatic tool for adapting to what they perceive as changing needs and circumstances (Linder, 1999). Innovation in the United Kingdom has come in the form of strategies to develop interrelationships, trust, and collaborations in an environment of resource scarcity where organizations would typically be oriented to protect and defend themselves behind their walls of bureaucracy (Lowndes & Skelcher, 1998).

Nine states in the United States have currently developed state government and nonprofit task forces to realize the advantages of collaboration. The National Council of Nonprofits is working with these nine states to understand how these relationships are forming on the ground. One of the states leading the collaborative movement is Connecticut, with the creation of a Human Services Cabinet and a Nonprofit Liaison to the Governor. It is one of the first states to establish these positions and structures to guide the human services system and move it toward collaboration. The creation of joint, collaborative government-nonprofit contracting reform task forces offers a promising first step to fix broken contracting systems that harm governments and nonprofits as well as those they serve. These collaborative task forces create an environment in which pragmatic reform efforts can be proposed, evaluated, developed, and then successfully implemented to improve the human services system overall and encourage innovation.

CONCLUSIONS

The fragmentation of public sector organizations over recent decades has been widely discussed (Bovaird, 2006; Dias & Maynard-Moody, 2007; Skelcher, 2005). Devolution, privatization, and contracting out have had broad systematic consequences on programmatic human service delivery (Hasenfeld & Garrow, 2012). Indeed, the rationale for utilizing devolution, privatization, and contracting out is based on a logical argument—put the states, local agencies, and innovative nonprofits in control of deciding what is best to support the needs of their particular constituencies (Fording, Soss, & Schram, 2007). However, when the nonprofit agencies on the street-level are not involved in the development of state-level contracts, an outcome is a fragmented and dysfunctional social service delivery system.

The innovation-constraint paradox can ultimately be viewed as an outcome of the fragmented system of human services. The call for collaboration and the use of collaborative partnerships between nonprofits and the government can reduce the amount of constraints in the system and encourage innovative nonprofit practice. By describing how the contracting system can limit innovation, government administrators can better understand and resolve these issues and attempt to alleviate some of the stresses facing nonprofits and help them practice innovative strategies that benefit communities. The case study of New York City sheds light on how a collaborative system can encourage nonprofit innovation. Within a collaborative framework, nonprofits can spend less time on administrative reports and RFPs and more time on innovative solutions to society's most pressing problems. Partnership between government and nonprofits can be reformed to promote innovation, collective models of impact, and streamlined processes, which all serve the long-term interests of taxpayers and communities.

DISCUSSION QUESTIONS

1. A paradox between innovation and constraint is created by the human service delivery system. Human services are best delivered by nonprofit organizations due to their ability to be innovative, flexible, and create services that are specific to the needs of clients. However, the contracting system is fragmented and inflexible in ways that create obstacles for nonprofit innovation to occur. How did NYC's collaborative and coordinated governance approach stimulate nonprofit innovation and reduce constraints within the human services system?

2. New York City's collaborative nonprofit-government system encourages innovation in two ways: (1) It reduces administrative constraints, and therefore enables nonprofits to be more innovative and (2) also embeds a two-way communication process into the system that allows the innovative nonprofit voice to be heard. Can you think of other ways that innovation can be encouraged?

3. What are the leadership implications from the case study of New York?
4. How can nonprofits and government specifically design a collaborative human services system? What factors must be identified and accomplished? What lessons can be applied to other cross-sectoral relationships?

REFERENCES

Abramovitz, M. (2002). *In jeopardy: The impact of welfare reform on nonprofit human service agencies in New York City*. New York, NY: Task Force on Welfare Reform, New York City Chapter, National Association of Social Workers, United Way of New York City.

Alexander, J. (2000). Adaptive strategies of nonprofit human service organizations in an era of devolution and new public management. *Nonprofit Management and Leadership, 10*(3), 287–303.

Austin, M. J. (2003). The changing relationship between nonprofit organizations and public social service agencies in the era of welfare reform. *Nonprofit and Voluntary Sector Quarterly, 32*(1), 97–114.

Bischoff, U., & Reisch, M. (2000). Welfare reform and community-based organizations: Implications for policy, practice, and education. *Journal of Community Practice, 8*(4), 69–91.

Boris, E. T., de Leon, E., Roeger, K. L., & Nikolova, M. (2010). *Human service nonprofits and government collaboration: Findings from the 2010 National Survey of Nonprofit Government Contracting and Grants*. Washington, DC: The Urban Institute Center on Nonprofits and Philanthropy.

Bovaird, T. (2006). Developing new forms of partnership with the "market" in the procurement of public services. *Public Administration, 84*(1), 81–102.

Brown, L. K., & Troutt, E. (2004). Funding relationships between nonprofits and government: A positive example. *Nonprofit and Voluntary Sector Quarterly, 33*(2), 5–27.

Bryson, J. M., Crosby, B. C., & Stone, M. M. (2006). The design and implementation of cross-sector collaborations: Propositions from the literature. *Public Administration Review, 66*, 44–55.

Campbell, D. (2002). Beyond charitable choice: The diverse service delivery approaches of local faith-based organizations. *Nonprofit and Voluntary Sector Quarterly, 31*(2), 207–230.

Curtis, K. A., & Copeland, I. (2003). *The impact of welfare reform on nonprofits and the people they serve in Delaware*. Washington, DC: Nonprofit Sector Research Fund, Aspen Institute.

Denhardt, K. (2003). The procurement partnership model: Moving to a team-based approach. *IBM Center for the Business of Government Paper Series.*

Dias, J. J., & Maynard-Moody, S. (2007). For-profit welfare: Contracts, conflicts, and the performance paradox. *Journal of Public Administration Research and Theory, 17*(2), 189–211.

Dichter, T. W. (1999). Globalization and its effect on NGOs: Efflorescence or a blurring of roles and relevance? *Nonprofit and Voluntary Sector Quarterly, 28*(4), 38–58.

Evans, B., & Shields, J. (1998). *"Reinventing" the third sector: Alternative service delivery, partnerships and the new public administration of the Canadian post-welfare state* (Working Paper No. 9). Toronto: Centre for Voluntary Sector Studies, Ryerson University.

Fording, R., Soss, J., & Schram, S. (2007). Devolution, discretion, and the effect of local political values on TANF sanctioning. *Social Service Review, 81*, 285–316.

Hasenfeld, Y., & Garrow, E. (2012). Nonprofit human-service organizations, social rights, and advocacy in a neoliberal welfare state. *Social Service Review, 86*(2), 295–322.

Hasenfeld, Y., & Powell, L. E. (2004). The role of nonprofit agencies in the provision of welfare-to-work services. In H. Schmid (Ed.), *Organizational and structural dilemmas in nonprofit human service organizations*. Binghamton, NY: Haworth Press.

Linder, S. H. (1999). Coming to terms with the public-private partnership. *American Behavioral Scientist, 43*(1), 35–51.

Lowndes, V., & Skelcher, C. (1998). The dynamics of multi-organizational partnerships: An analysis of changing modes of governance. *Public Administration, 76*(2), 313–333.

Lynn, L. E. (2002). Social services and the state: The public appropriation of private charity. *Social Service Review,76*(1), 58–82.

Milward, H., & Provan, K. (2000). Governing the hollow state. *Journal of Public Administration Research and Theory, 10*(2), 359–379.

Mulroy, E. (2003). Review of the book *Settlement houses under siege: The struggle to sustain community organizations in New York City*. *Social Service Review, 77*(2), 315–317.

Poole, D. L. (2003). Scaling up CBO's for second-order devolution in welfare reform. *Nonprofit Management and Leadership, 13*(4), 325–341.

Reisch, M., & Sommerfeld, D. (2003). Interorganizational relationships among nonprofits in the aftermath of welfare reform. *Social Work, 48*(3), 307–319.

Rosenthal, M. (2000). Public or private children's services? Privatization in retrospect. *Social Service Review, 74*(2), 281–305.

Salamon, L. M. (1995). *Partners in public service: Government-nonprofit relations in the modern welfare state.* Baltimore, MD: Johns Hopkins University Press.

Salamon, L. M. (2005). Globalization and the civil society sector. In S. Hewa & D. H. Stapleton (Eds.), *Globalization, philanthropy, and civil society*. New York, NY: Springer.

Smith, S. R., & Lipsky, M. (1993). *Nonprofits for hire: The welfare state in the age of contracting*. Cambridge, MA: Harvard University Press.

Van Slyke, D. M. (2003). The mythology of privatization in contracting for social services. *Public Administration Review, 63*(3), 296–314.

Young, D. R. (2000). Alternative models of government-nonprofit sector relations: Theoretical and international perspectives. *Nonprofit and Voluntary Sector Quarterly, 29*(1), 149–172.

CHAPTER 16

The YMCA

A Pioneer of Organizational Innovations

Martti Muukkonen[1]

Doctor of Theology, Chaplain of Lutheran parish of Nurmijarvi, Finland

INTRODUCTION

Once upon a time there were no summer camps for youth, no gyms, no basketball, and no volleyball. There were no international youth conferences, no military canteens, no refugee aid, and no international development cooperation. There was neither ecumenism nor interfaith dialogue. Why? Because the Young Men's Christian Association (YMCA) had not yet been born.

The YMCA has been a pioneer in many social activities, organizations, and practices that we regard as self-evident today. The YMCA is perhaps the oldest (founded in 1844) and largest (45 million members today) of contemporary youth organizations, and it has been a laboratory of youth work methods, like youth clubs, youth centers, gang work, youth camps, and international youth assemblies—as well as basketball and volleyball, interconfessional and interfaith dialogue, and work for victims of war.

The organization has been either a mother or a midwife to many large nongovernmental organizations, such as Boy Scouts, American United Service Organization (Muukkonen, 2002, pp. 340–344; USO, 2012), World Council of Churches (Rouse, 1993b, p. 327), and the United Nations High Commissioner for Refugees (Holborn 1975, p. 124f). As these organizations emerged, they got their leadership, as well as their working methods and practices, from the YMCA.

In this chapter, the author focuses on the interplay between the ideology of the YMCA and the new challenges that led to new organizational and programmatic innovations

[1] This article is based on the author's dissertation, *Ecumenism of the Laity—Continuity and Change in the Mission View of the World's Alliance of Young Men's Christian Associations, 1855–1955,* which was written mostly on archive materials found in the archives of the World Alliance of YMCAs in Geneva, Switzerland.

during the first hundred years of the YMCA. The author first gives an overview of the birth and the ideology of the YMCA and then focuses on four aspects of YMCA innovations: organizational models, physical education, youth work, and services for the victims of war.

THE YMCA IDEOLOGY

Human beings do not see events or things "as they are" but always filter their observations through their previous experiences and beliefs. Ulric Neisser (1976) uses the concept of schema to describe this. According to him, schema directs our observation and, thus, we see what we want to see. Ralph H. Turner and Lewis M. Killian (1959, pp. 58–79), while arguing on emergent norms, emphasized the impact of past experiences and beliefs on new situations. Therefore, in the same time when the challenge is described, it is important to describe the basics of the belief system that directs the interpretation of the identified problem.[2] Thus, below these two themes are intertwined.

The Birth of the YMCA

The first YMCA emerged in London in 1844. Although there had been older associations in Germany, it was the London YMCA that gave a name to the movement and was the *primus motor* in its spreading.

In the beginning of the 19th century, the emergence of youth as a recognized age group (Ariès, 1962; Gillis, 1974) brought forth the special needs of this age group. London was crowded with young people: 80% of migrants from English villages to London were 15 to 25 years of age (Gillis, 1974, p. 55). The problem of this vast in-migration was solved like social problems were traditionally solved in British society: by local parishes, private philanthropy, and voluntary associations rather than by state action (Thane, 1996, p. 5ff). At its beginnings, the London YMCA was just one peer group of young shop assistants who aimed to better the lives of its members. Their connection to the business world gave the London YMCA an important resource that saved it from being just another shooting star like many other previous similar organizations. These young businessmen knew the importance of fundraising, and therefore many YMCA activities (like libraries, reading rooms, and various courses) required either an entrance or annual fee. When they matured and had more influential positions in their companies, they found wealthy sponsors and spread the idea of the YMCA through their business networks (WConf, 1855, p. 67f; Shedd, 1955b, pp. 30ff, 42, 68; The YMCAs of the World, 1958, pp. 28, 39, 138, 197.).

[2] Other scholars that have emphasized the influence of past practices and way of thinking, are Paul David (1985) and Brian Arthur (1989) who argued on "path dependency" and Peter L. Berger and Thomas Luckmann (1972, pp. 55–58, 113–122) who speak of "routinization of thinking."

The YMCA Mission

The major factor that directed the path of the YMCA and its innovations may be found in the ideology expressed in the Paris Basis statement and in the North American YMCAs' Triangle Principle. Therefore it is necessary to understand *what* YMCA leaders aimed toward before trying to understand *what* and *how* it happened.

When the YMCA leaders met in Paris during the World Exhibition in 1855, they established the World Alliance of YMCAs and accepted a statement that was a manifestation of their faith that defined the identity, ideology, and the mission of the movement. It is known as the Paris Basis, and it stated:

> The delegates of various Young Men's Christian Associations of Europe and America, assembled in Conference at Paris, the 22nd August, 1855, feeling that they are one in principle and in operation, recommend to their respective Societies to recognize with them the unity existing among their Associations, and whilst **preserving a complete independence as to their particular organization and modes of action**, to form a Confederation on the following fundamental principle, such **principle to be regarded as the basis of admission of other Societies in future**:
>
> The Young Men's Christian Associations seek to unite those young men who, regarding Jesus Christ as their God and saviour according to the Holy Scriptures, desire to be His disciples in their faith and in their life, and to associate their efforts for the extension of His Kingdom amongst young men.
>
> This fundamental principle being admitted, the Conference further proposes:
>
> That **any differences of opinion on other subjects**, however important in themselves, but not embraced by the specific designs of the Associations, **shall not interfere with the harmonious relations of the confederated Societies**. (Muukkonen, 2002, pp. 93–106)

The Paris Basis laid the rails for the further organizational development of the YMCA in several ways. First, the "independence clause" in the Preamble (presented in bold), was probably due to American, German, and Swiss hesitancy to adopt the British and French "mother association model" in which local associations were just branches of the one in the capital and without decision-making power (Shedd, 1955b, pp. 56, 77, 94–97; WConf, 1855, 52, 77). The accepted structure of independent local associations was originally based on the Lutheran *Augsburg Confession* (1530) and its article VII, where local variety in ceremonies is approved. Thus, the federal structure that emerged was a manifestation of the movement's basic beliefs. This independence clause had a significant impact on the future plurality of the movement.

A second influence was the requirement that future associations adopt the Paris Basis. In this way, the Basis, which, following anthropologist Clifford Geertz's (1973, p. 93) terminology, was a *model of* the YMCAs in 1855 and became a *model for* the future associations. Although the interpretation of what is "according to the Paris Basis" was left to the local level, this expressed unity in diversity enabled both the flow of innovations in the YMCA and mutual help in the times of troubles. Moreover, the basic YMCA model gave institutional respect to new YMCAs when they started to work.

A third factor arose from the Basis' Fundamental Principle, from which the movement developed its "open membership—Christian leadership"—principle, that enabled the YMCA to serve people of other faiths and thus promote interfaith dialogue. The fourth influence stemming from the first proposal (which later was adopted as the Second Fundamental Principle) promoted neutrality on issues not mentioned in the Fundamental Principle. This guideline gave the YMCA the possibility to serve, for example, prisoners of war and refugees across frontiers as a neutral agency.

Some associations used the Paris Basis as a personal statement that an individual member had to sign, and others used it as a basis for the association. However, some national movements, like the North American YMCA, developed their own bases and saw the Paris Basis as a bond between national YMCA movements. Accordingly, North American associations have been free to make their own definitions of their purpose (Muukkonen, 2002, p. 179f).

While the Paris Basis presented the ideology of the YMCA, the anthropology of the YMCA was crystalized in the symbol of the Red Triangle, which Luther H. Gulick (1918) proposed in 1889. It states that a human being is a totality of body, mind, and spirit. During World War I, this triangle with the YMCA initials became the best-known YMCA symbol throughout the world. Sometimes the triangle is surrounded by a circle and then it is equivalent to the Four-fold Programme (= triangle – principle + society). There are hundreds of modifications of the Red Triangle because different activities have developed their own logos to symbolize both their attachment to the YMCA and their special activity (see Figure 16.1).

FIGURE 16.1 Examples Of YMCA Logos

First row: (1) Triangle with explanations; (2) Standard triangle; (3) Four-fold Programme; (4) YMCA scouts; (5) YMCA choir/orchestra.

Second row: (6) YMCA refugee work (modified along the lines of UNHCR logo); (7) Partnership; (8) Development cooperation; (9) Mainly Anglo-Saxon Y-logo.

THE INNOVATIONS

Organizational Innovations of the YMCA

In the middle of the 19th century, the World Alliance of YMCAs emerged from the correspondence between local associations. As noted above, a federal model was a matter of faith for the World Alliance. Contrary to many other organizations, the YMCA never created a strong central office. The emphasis is, as the Paris Basis declares, on the local level.

However, there were practical hindrances in applying this ideal in the middle of the 19th century: railways were still in their infancy; sending messages across the Atlantic meant letters, and crossing the ocean was done mainly with sails. These slow means of communication explain the development of numerous "International Committees" (Red Cross, Olympic committee, YMCA) that emerged in the 19th century—they were the only way to organize effective work since attending executive meetings was not possible for those who lived far away from the headquarters.

After the First World Conference in 1855, the London YMCA acted as a center of correspondence, but it did not have any power over other national YMCA movements. The board of the next host of the next World's Conference served as the planning committee of the conference (Muukkonen, 2002, p. 237f).

Later, when the world "grew smaller," the development of the World YMCA structure followed on with the new developments in communications. When the main railway network in Europe was ready, the YMCA established its Central International Committee (CIC) in 1878; a headquarters was located in Geneva, and the first World's Secretary was appointed. This advance in transportation changed the YMCA from a network of loosely attached associations to an international organization. However, because of the fear of centralization, the CIC was never given enough resources to enable it to take leadership in the movement. Moreover, when most members of CIC resided outside Switzerland, one can only imagine how difficult the decision making was via correspondence, even when the YMCA eagerly utilized the new innovation: the telegram (Muukkonen, 2002, p. 238f).

Without previous models, and in a rapidly changing world, the CIC developed and tested new organizational models that could best implement the YMCA idea of global unity and local independence. Because of the distances, especially between North America and Geneva, there was continuous tension between efficiency needs and democracy needs. As a resolution to this tension, the YMCA created a yearly plenary system of CIC (Muukkonen 2002, p. 239).

In 1955, with the emergence of relatively fast airplane connections, the system was restructured again. World Conferences were replaced with the World Council, which meets every 4 years, and the Executive Committee whose members meet each year (http://www.ymca.int/who-we-are/structure/).

The expansion of the movement led to the founding of several Area Alliances (http://www.ymca.int/who-we-are/structure/ymca-area-alliances/). Their purpose has been to facilitate such international activities in various continents for which the global body is too distant.

Innovations in Physical Education

Howard C. Hopkins (1951, p. 12f) notes that rapid urbanization of the 19th and 20th centuries increased crime in industrialized countries and argues that the Temperance Movement, reform movements, Tract and Bible societies, and other similar organizations were reactions to this negative development. In addition, urbanization brought the fear that "middle-class boys were growing weak and effeminate," as David I. Macleod (1983, p. 44) put it. Along with the later uniform-dressed religious organizations (like the Boys' Brigades and Scouts), YMCA physical education answered the need of strengthening growing boys' masculinity.

Because the negative attitude toward amusements was based on theological doctrines of Calvinism, Pietism, and Methodism, this positive attitude toward physical education had to be based on theological arguments as well. This support was given in 1858, at the Second World's Conference of YMCAs in Geneva by John H. Gladstone from London. He argued that associations should offer good recreational programs to young men and defended his thesis mainly with historical examples and some biblical quotations (Shedd, 1955b, p. 157; WConfPrep, 1858).

When the recreational activities got religious legitimacy, Americans developed the philosophy of the triangle principle mentioned above. It had its biblical roots in Luke 2:52 (KJV): "And Jesus increased in wisdom [mind] and stature [body], and in favour with God [spirit] and man [society]." Another frequently cited verse that legitimated physical education was 1 Cor 6:19 (KJV): "Know ye not that your body is the temple of the Holy Ghost."

In the 1860s, the Triangle Principle gave rise to the Four-Fold or Character-Building Programme, which saw man as a physical, social, spiritual, and intellectual unity. Physical activities were seen as an extension of the social work of the YMCA and as one method in the "post evangelization" work (i.e., offering good activities to those who have converted during the revival meetings) of the association. This program became the flagship of the North American YMCA (Johnson, 1979, pp. 27–42; Macleod, 1983, p. 73).

Along with religious justifications, the character-building program developed was legitimated by popular psychological beliefs that the mind is "composed of several major faculties: intellect, emotion, will, and sometimes conscience" (Macleod, 1983, p. 30). These elements could be trained, like muscles, through exercise. This idea of a link between muscles, brains, and even soul legitimated the YMCA emphasis on physical education as a method of Christian youth work. When the gymnasium had gained legitimacy within the North American YMCA, the idea spread rapidly (Macleod, 1983, p. 30).

The positive economic consequences of providing gymnasiums for associations helped the diffusion of the idea, as well. Mayer N. Zald (1970) argues that traditional collections and donations "did not provide much financial stability" (p. 43ff) and that both residences and gymnasiums stabilized the economic status of YMCAs.

Along with the physical education emerged boys' clubs, camps, student conventions, international youth meetings, and the like. As L. Wilbur Messer noted in his report to 1898 Basle World's Conference, the aim of the Four-fold Programme was "to spiritualise the secular" (WConfPrep, 1898, p. 8). However, as Kenneth Latourette (1957) mentions, the coaches and teachers of secular subjects "tended to leave the 'religious work' to secretaries who began to be appointed as specialists in that field" (p. 28). Thus, unfortunately, the means became ends in themselves and often this led to situations where people wondered where is the "C" in the associations' activities.

Youth Work

The growth of youth work—or Boy's Work, as it was then called—after the Geneva Conference in 1858 was both spontaneous and rapid. Gladstone's presentation gave legitimization to "amusements," and this provided the possibility for the YMCA to develop various recreational activities where physical education played a major role.

The boys' work is nothing without stories, and therefore it would be proper to include here a short story on how U.S. Hi-Y (High School YMCA) clubs began:

> It was a tough life for a schoolboy back in the horse and buggy days of the last century in the American West. Still feeling the wounds of a bitter civil war, the young nation was in full spate of pioneer development, and the comforts of daily living were few in the mushrooming communities along the frontier.
>
> These were thoughts that must have passed through the mind of science teacher D. F. Shirk as he sat in his empty classroom in Chapman, Kansas, one day in 1889. His class had just left after the day's lessons, yet many of the 137 boys in school could not go home—they lived over a scattered area in Dickinson County, and lack of transportation prevented some of them from getting home even at weekends. In their behaviour, Shirk noticed the effects which the absence of the helps, restraints and disciplines of settled home life was having.
>
> So he decided to form a club for his schoolboys. Soon after he got it going he asked the YMCA for assistance. The YMCA responded—and thus was born the first YMCA schoolboys' club with a continuous existence until the present day. (*World Communique,* May–June, 1964, p. 4)

The idea spread and became a model for U.S. YMCA work in schools. The purpose was "to create, maintain and extend throughout home, school and community, high standards of Christian character" (*World Communique,* May–June, 1964, p. 5).

In Britain, the leaders of the Junior Department of the English National Council took an active part of starting their own model for Boys' Work: scouting. The first experimental camp was held in 1907, and R. S. S. Baden-Powell gave his first presentation on scouting at the Birkenhead YMCA in January 1908. Although the Scout Movement was formed as an independent movement, the YMCA gave Baden-Powell a channel to distribute his ideas. In many countries YMCAs started Scout groups and formed their own National Scout Associations for YMCA Scouts for cooperation. At the international level there were International YMCA Scout Camps and meetings of Scout leaders (Macleod, 1983, pp. 97, 140, 146; Strong, 1955b, p. 623; Warren, 1986, p. 388).

When the Boy's Work in Europe spread, French-speaking leaders of work among boys gathered in 1893 in Geneva. They founded the Central Commission of French-speaking Boys' Associations which became a powerful actor in propagating Boys' Work in Belgium,

France, and Switzerland. Paul Des Gouttes, the president of the World Alliance (and the secretary of the International Red Cross), referred to it later as the first international body for Boys' Work. A year later the total membership of this body was 1,720 with 165 voluntary directors (Shedd, 1955a, p. 323f).

In 1913, the First General Assembly of Association Workers with Boys of North America met at Culver, Indiana, Besides the delegates from North America, there were also participants from 12 countries from all other continents save Africa. The next year, the First World's Conference of YMCA Workers with Boys took place in Oxford, England. In that conference there was an agreement that Boys' Work should be an integral part of every Association (Strong, 1955a, 616f).

After that, the model was locked in and the idea spread rapidly. The contribution of the World Alliance of YMCAs was to bring youth workers together in international conferences. This, in turn, enabled locally developed new methods to spread rapidly when activists and professionals shared their experiences.

The YMCA youth work has given its contribution to science as well. Perhaps the first international survey of the life of youth was first presented to the Helsingfors [Swedish name for Finland's capital, Helsinki] World's Conference in 1926. In the same conference, there was also another novelty: the use of group work as a conference method (WConf, 1926, 2f).

The methodology of the work both reflected and modified the YMCA's mission among boys. The study outline for the Third World Assembly of YMCA Workers with Boys (Toronto 1931), *The Technique and Methods of YMCA Work with Boys*, states that the starting point is the Paris Basis, and from it arises more detailed principles: message principle, curriculum principle, personality development principle, and crusade for a cause principle (WConfPrep, 1931, p. 5f). In other words, there was a message to be delivered to youth; this message was to be delivered systematically; this delivery is best done with "learning by doing"; and finally, youth should be given a purpose for their lives.

These principles were then carried out on three levels: work dealing with individual boys, work with small groups, and work with large masses. This endeavor was, again, legitimated with theological argumentation. Ralph G. Cole, in his presentation to the Toronto Boys' Workers Assembly in 1931, recalled Jesus as an example:

> Surely in Him and in His way of working with people we can find a useful technique for modern YMCA work. We find Him repeatedly using the individual or personal work method. No finer illustration of group work is given us in history than that of Jesus and His disciples. His faith in mass or larger group work is illustrated by his frequent meetings and experiences with the crowds. (BWConf, 1931, p. 22)

The methodology in these levels differed from each other and it was mainly the task of the large movements and the World's Alliance to collect, develop, and distribute adequate methodology for each level. Cole made a distinction in methodology among different ages as well.

> A further study into the methods of our Lord shows a different technique with different ages. He called the little children to His arms and blessed them. He asked the boy with the fishes to help Him by the gift of them. He challenged the young man to "go and sell all and give it to the poor." He commissioned His disciples to "go into all the world and preach the Gospel." (BWConf, 1931, p. 22)

Although the focus was on methodology in different ages, the general task of the YMCA can be seen in this presentation. On every level, the YMCA aimed to teach boys and young men to take such responsibility as they can. Boys learn responsibility when they are asked to help. Young men can be challenged to take their faith seriously, and trained laymen can be given responsibility for the work.

By the end of WW II, the Four-fold Programme had been accepted worldwide, and the challenges of political movements (especially Nazism and Communism) had forced the YMCA to deal with ethical and political issues as well. This can be seen in the decisions of the 1950 World Consultation on Boys' Work at Green Lake, Wisconsin. Although the ultimate goal, to "bring the boy closer to God" (BWConf, 1950, p. 16), remained, the focus had changed from the association's goals to the boy's needs. Instead of knowing what would be good for the boy, the movement now asked, like Jesus, "What do you want Me to do for you?" (Luke 18:41). When compared to the old approach, where the preacher knew both the problems and the cure without asking the boy, this was a fundamental change. This new attitude led, according to the YMCA Work with Boys, "to a great development of work amongst handicapped and anti-social boys" (BWConf, 1950, p. 17). In the conference resolutions we can see that the idea of the general welfare of boys has replaced the task of evangelizing them. This does not mean that the "C" was dropped from the message. On the contrary, the fundamental task was "to reach out a hand to the boy, accept him as he is with all his needs and problems" and to "lead him to a full understanding of and loyalty to God and the Christian way of life" (BWConf, 1950, p. 20).

The pioneer stage of the YMCA boys' work ended during the 1950s. Although the YMCA continued its boys' work, after that the work and methods diffused to churches and to other youth organizations and became standard work methods.

Serving the Victims of War

Already during the First World's Conference in 1855, the tensions felt in North America led the American delegate Abel Stevens to deliver the First Additional Proposal (see above) of the Paris Basis (WConf, 1855, p. 19f). When the Civil War broke out, it had direct consequences for the YMCA's work. An American representative, Stephen H. Tyng, talked to the London YMCA in 1862 about the beginning of the work with armed forces as follows:

> As soon as it broke out, our Young Men, in all parts of the country, flocked to the army; they were removed from our influence and the influence of the Church, and we were obliged to follow them . . . As the army has spread the work has gone on, and last winter a conference of all the associations was held at New York, for the

> purpose of uniting the different efforts and of forming a Christian mission, the object of which is to evangelize the army. (Quoted in Shedd, 1955a, p. 164; see also Morse, 1913, pp. 60–65; Hopkins, 1951, pp. 84–98)

Besides spiritual guidance, the work of the YMCA in the Civil War also included nursing and carrying messages home. However, at this stage the work could be described merely as a temporary project. The work among soldiers obtained its permanent place in the U.S. YMCA during the Spanish-American War in 1898 (WConfPrep, 1902, pp. 7–10), in Britain in 1902, in India in 1907 (David, 1992, p. 132), and in Germany in 1914 (Hjelt, 1918, pp. 4–6). The earliest records from Switzerland are from 1856 (AFCons, 1960, p. 11). Before the First World War, young men in armies were served by the national YMCAs in all major wars on both sides of frontiers (Strong, 1955a, p. 546n).

The Franco-Prussian War in 1870–1871 also had a direct effect on the YMCA. The war was the first real test of the YMCA's unity. Christian unity was, unfortunately, suppressed under nationalistic emotions, and the relationships between German and French YMCAs were as bad as the relationships between these two peoples in general. After the war, relations between these two movements were chilly. When emotions were calmed, the Amsterdam World's Conference in 1872 unanimously resolved that the first proposal of the Paris Basis be added as a Second Fundamental Principle along with the original Fundamental Principle (Shedd, 1955b, p. 190; WComPle, 1953, p. 4; Willis, 1972, p. 4).

The two World Wars affected the YMCA as well, although not as directly on the Paris Basis as the Franco-Prussian War. On one hand, the World Wars reduced normal activities, but on the other hand, they created needs for new ones. Governments needed the services that the YMCA gave to armed forces (on literature, see Muukkonen, 2002, p. 17n. 2–4). These included canteens and other recreational services that helped keep up the morale of the troops. The YMCA practically took care of the whole canteen service for soldiers in the United States and Britain.

The World Wars directed the YMCA's mission to develop other activities as well. The work for Prisoners of War (POWs) was a natural continuation of the work with armed forces (because POWs were also part of armed forces). During the First World War, the Prisoners Aid of the World Alliance YMCAs ran recreational and educational projects in POW camps on both sides of the frontier. In these countries, the YMCA POW work secretaries were from neutral countries. In nonbelligerent countries such as Denmark, Holland, Japan, Sweden, and Switzerland, similar services were given to internees (Strong, 1955a, pp. 546–559).

Most of the work was on a reciprocal basis—all prisoners were helped in the same way on both sides of the frontier. Exceptions to this rule were the Soviet Union and Italy, which did not give the YMCA permission to work in their territory, and thus, Russian and Italian prisoners were excluded from receiving help. At last, as Hugo Cedergren (1969, p. 73f), GS of the Swedish YMCA tells in his memoirs, out of sheer pity many of the camp commandants in Germany urged the YMCA to send supplies to the Russian POWs as well. Although War Prisoners' Aid was not allowed to work in Italy, it served Italian POWs in Allied countries (Strong, 1955a, pp. 562, 573).

There was a mutual understanding regarding cooperation between the YMCA and the International Committee of the Red Cross. The burden was shared in a way that the YMCA took care of educational, recreational, cultural, and spiritual activities of prisoners, and the Red Cross concentrated on holding camp inspections, organizing a central information agency with mail facilities, handling of all shipments, and distributing all materials sent by the national Red Cross Societies (Cedergren, 1969, 70; Strong, 1955a, p. 557f)

After both World Wars there was a huge refugee problem, and the YMCA found its new niche among them. The former POWs became refugees and YMCA work among POWs turned to work among refugees and displaced persons—in the same camps with the same people (Strong, 1955a, pp. 572–578). After WW I YMCA worked with the Russian emigrants (Anderson, 1963 pp. 27–78; Latourette, 1957, pp. 374–382; Rouse, 1993a, p. 605; Zernov, 1993, p. 661f) and after WW II with European and Palestinian refugees and displaced persons (DPs) (Kilpatrick, 1955).

Refugee work grew to be the widest activity of the World Alliance of YMCAs for decades. It was done mainly in Europe but also in Palestine (Palestinians), in India (DPs of the separation of Pakistan from India), and in South Eastern Asia (Vietnamese boat refugees). In its refugee work, the YMCA has maintained close working relationships with most intergovernmental agencies, churches, YWCA, Red Cross, and other voluntary movements (Kilpatrick, 1955, p. 608f). When the United Nations High Commissioner for Refugees (UNHCR) started its work after World War II, the first and largest agencies that gave assistance were five denominational agencies and the YMCA (Holborn, 1975, p. 124f).

CONCLUSIONS

The YMCA has been a successful organization during its history. It has been able to carry its mission and even diffuse its ideas and working methods to other organizations, such as churches, youth and sports organizations, and so on. Actually, the whole concept of youth work is a YMCA invention. It was the YMCA that first appointed youth workers, first created professional training for them, first raised youth centers and camp centers, soldiers homes, and so forth. Today these programs are self-evident for us.

The impact of the YMCA youth work has been in two main areas. First, it developed and tested new working methods that other youth organizations—as well as older institutions like churches and schools—adopted. In this sense, the YMCA has been a laboratory of both religious and general education.

Second, the YMCA has been a field of "practical training" for many leaders of the ecumenical movement and INGOs. Even today, when one visits Geneva and talks with staff of various international organizations, he or she may be surprised by how many of them have YMCA background.

Thus, the first lesson for any organization is: cooperate. Don't compete with such organizations that might do part of your work and may serve you as a test field of new ideas.

The second lesson is that all nonprofit organizations must make sure that they have credibility. An organization with a good reputation always has better access to resources than a marginal one, and governments are willing to delegate some tasks (as well as resources) to it. In the case of the YMCA, the whole work for the victims of war would not have been possible without credibility. This reputation can be achieved by getting support of the leading members of the community, as did the founders of the YMCA, and/or being part of a larger and respected network. Organizational mortality is extremely high in cases where a project is kept only local and without leaders of the community on its board.

Third, an association leader must always remember the difference between membership and clientele. Without committed members' "flame of the spirit," the intensity of the work remains low and the organization becomes just one more bureaucracy among others. Thus, as St. Paul advised:

> Do not quench the Spirit, do not despise prophesying, but test everything; hold fast what is good, abstain from every form of evil. May the God of peace himself sanctify you wholly; and may your spirit and soul and body be kept sound and blameless. (1 Thess 5:19–23 RSV)

DISCUSSION QUESTIONS

1. What we can learn from the interplay of ideology and context from YMCA history?
2. What can we learn from the effects of networking in YMCA history?
3. What can we learn from applying the existing models from YMCA history to new situations?

REFERENCES

AFCons (Armed Forces Work Consultation). (1960). YMCA work with armed forces. Report of a consultation 4th to 13th April 1960. In archives of the World Alliance of YMCAs, Geneva, Switzerland, T3, Box 386.

Anderson, P. B. (1963). *A study of orthodoxy and the YMCA*. Geneva, Switzerland: World Alliance of YMCAs.

Ariés, P. (1962). *Centuries of childhood. A social history of family life*. New York, NY: Vintage books.

Arthur, B. (1989). Competing technologies, increasing returns, and lock-in by historical events. *Economic Journal, 99*(394), 116–131.

Augsburg Confession. (1530). Project Wittenberg. Retrieved from http://www.projectwittenberg.org/pub/resources/text/wittenberg/wittenberg-boc.html#ac

Berger, P. L., & Luckmann, T. (1972). *The social construction of reality*. London, United Kingdom: Cox & Wyman Ltd.

BWConf (Boys' Work Conference). (1931). The world task of the YMCA with boys. Being the official account and report of the Third World Assembly of YMCA Workers with Boys. Toronto, Canada, July 27–Aug. 2, 1931. In archives of the World Alliance of YMCAs, Geneva, Switzerland, T1, Box 43.

BWConf (Boys' Work Conference). (1950). YMCA work with boys. World Consultation on Boys' Work. Green Lake, Wisconsin, USA. May 14–21, 1950. Geneva: World's Committee of YMCAs. In archives of the World Alliance of YMCAs, Geneva, Switzerland, T1, Box 44.

Cedergren, H. (1969). *Mitt liv med KFUM* [My Life with the YMCA]. Västerås, Sweden: KFUM i Västerås.

David, M. D. (1992). *The YMCA and the making of modern India*. New Delhi, India: National Council of YMCAs of India.

David, P. (1985). Clio and the economics of QWERTY. *American Economic Review, 75*(2), 332–337.
Geertz, C. (1973). *The interpretation of cultures: Selected essays.* New York, NY: Basic Books.
Gillis, J. R. (1974). *Youth and history: Tradition and change in European age relations 1770–present.* New York, NY: Academic Press.
Gulick, L. H. (1918). What the red triangle stands for. *Association Man, 43*(10), 774–775, 809. Retrieved from http://cdm15370.contentdm.oclc.org/cdm/ref/collection/p15370coll2/id/553
Hjelt, A. (1918). *NMKY:n sotilastyö muualla ja meillä.* [YMCA work among soldiers in our country and elsewhere]. Porvoo, Finland: WSOY.
Holborn, L. W. (1975). *Refugees: A problem of our time. The work of the United Nations High Commissioner for Refugees 1951–1972* (Vol. 1–2). Metuchen, NJ: Scarecrow Press.
Hopkins, C. H. (1951). *History of the YMCA in North America.* New York, NY: Association Press.
Johnson, E. L. (1979). *The History of YMCA physical education.* Chicago, IL: Association Press.
Kilpatrick, W. S. (1955). Ministry to displaced persons and refugees. In C. P. Shedd et al., *History of the World's Alliance of Young Men's Christian Associations.* London, United Kingdom: SPCK.
Latourette, K. S. (1957). *World service: A history of the foreign work and world service of the Young Men's Christian Associations of the United States and Canada.* New York, NY: Association Press.
Macleod, D. I. (1983). *Building character in the American boy: The Boy Scouts, YMCA, and their forerunners, 1870–1920.* Madison: University of Wisconsin Press.
Morse, R. C. (1913). *History of the North American Young Men's Christian Associations.* New York, NY: Association Press.
Muukkonen, M. (2002). *Ecumenism of the Laity—Continuity and change in the mission view of the World's Alliance of Young Men's Christian Associations, 1855–1955.* Joensun, Finland: University of Joensuu. Retrieved from http://epublications.uef.fi/pub/urn_isbn_952-458-207-4
Neisser, U. (1976). *Cognition and reality.* San Francisco, CA: W. H. Freeman.
Rouse, R. (1993a). Other aspects of the ecumenical movement 1910–1948. In R. Rouse, S. C. Neill, & H. E. Fey (Eds.), *A history of the ecumenical movement 1517–1968* (4th ed., Vol. I, 1517–1948). Geneva, Switzerland: WCC.
Rouse, R. (1993b). Voluntary movements and the changing ecumenical climate. In R. Rouse, S. C. Neill, & H. E. Fey (Eds.), *A history of the ecumenical movement 1517–1968* (4th ed., Vol. I, 1517–1948). Geneva, Switzerland: WCC.
Shedd, C. P. (1955a). Expanding vision, 1878–1913. In C. P. Shedd et al., *History of the World's Alliance of Young Men's Christian Associations* (pp. 199–429). London, United Kingdom: SPCK.
Shedd, C. P. (1955b). Formative years, 1844–1878. In C. P. Shedd et al., *History of the World's Alliance of Young Men's Christian Associations* (pp. 15–198). London, United Kingdom: SPCK.
Strong, T. (1955a). Service with prisoners of war. In C. P. Shedd et al., *History of the World's Alliance of Young Men's Christian Associations.* London, United Kingdom: SPCK.
Strong, T. (1955b). The World's Alliance in a changing world. In C. P. Shedd et al., *History of the World's Alliance of Young Men's Christian Associations.* London, United Kingdom: SPCK.
Thane, P. (1996). Government and society in England and Wales, 1750–1914. In F. M. L. Thompson (Ed.), *The Cambridge social history of Britain 1750–1950* (Vol. 3). Cambridge, United Kingdom: Cambridge University Press.
Turner, R. H., & Killian L. M. (1959). *Collective behavior.* Englewood Cliffs, NJ: Prentice Hall.
USO. (2012). *History.* Retrieved from http://www.uso.org/history.aspx
Warren, A. (1986). Sir Robert Baden-Powell, the Scout movement and citizen training in Great Britain, 1900–1902. *English Historical Review, 101*(399), 376–398.
WComPle (World's Committee Plenary Documents). (1953). Senaud Auguste: Historical statement about the Paris Basis. PleG No.12/ Com.II/B. World's Committee of YMCA Plenary Meeting Geneva July 23–31, 1953. In archives of the World Alliance of YMCAs. Geneva, Switzerland, T2, Box 180.

WConf (World's Conference Report). (1855). Report of the General Conference held in Paris, August, 1855. Occasional Paper No. III. 1956. London, United Kingdom: Young Men's Christian Association. In archives of the World Alliance of YMCAs, Geneva, Switzerland, T3, Box 319.

WConf (World's Conference Report). (1926). Youth faces life. Being the report of the XIXth World Conference of YMCAs at Helsingfors August 1–6, 1926. Geneva, Switzerland: World Alliance of YMCAs. In archives of the World Alliance of YMCAs, Geneva, Switzerland, T3, Box 336.

WConfPrep (World's Conference Preparatory Material). (1858). Gladstone John H.: Du besoin de délassement chez les jeunes gens. Rapport lu à la seconde Conférence universelle des Unions chrétiennes de jeunes gens, réunie à Genève en Août 1858 par Mr le Dr J. Gladstone. Genève, Switzerland: Pfeffer & Puky. In archives of the World Alliance of YMCAs, Geneva, Switzerland, T3, Box 319.

WConfPrep (World's Conference Preparatory Material). (1898). Messer Wilbur L.: The present standing of the American Young Men's Christian Associations: The privileges which they enjoy. A paper Prepared by L. Wilbur Messer, General Secretary, Chicago, for the Fourteenth Conference of the Young Men's Christian Associations in All Lands, held at Basle, Switzerland, July 6–10, 1898. New York, NY: The International Committee of Young Men's Christian Associations. In archives of the World Alliance of YMCAs, Geneva, Switzerland, T2, Box 322.

WConfPrep (World's Conference Preparatory Material). (1902). Canfield James H.: The North American Young Men's Christian Associations in the twentieth century. Presentation to the 15th World's Conference of Young Men's Christian Associations. Christiania (Oslo), Norway, August 19–24, 1902. New York, NY: The International Committee of YMCAs. In Archives of the World Alliance of YMCAs, Geneva, Switzerland, T3, Box 323.

WConfPrep (World's Conference Preparatory Material). (1931). The aim of YMCA Boys' Work. Series C—Number XV. 1931—World Conferences Study Outlines. Geneva, Switzerland: World's Committee of Young Men's Christian Association. In Archives of the World Alliance of YMCAs, Geneva, Switzerland, T3, Box 339.

Willis, F. (1972). *The Paris Basis—The second principle*. Unpublished manuscript. In Archives of the World Alliance of YMCAs, Geneva, Switzerland, T2, Box 179.

World Communique May–June, 1964.

The YMCAs of the World. (1958). Geneva, Switzerland: World Alliance of Young Men's Christian Associations.

Zald, M. N. (1970). *Organizational change. The political economy of the YMCA*. Chicago, IL: Chicago University Press.

Zernov, N. (1993). The eastern churches and the ecumenical movement in the twentieth century. In R. Rouse, S. C. Neill, & H. E. Fey (Eds.), *A history of the ecumenical movement 1517–1968* (4th ed.).

ADDITIONAL RESOURCES

World Alliance of YMCAs: http://www.ymca.int

YMCA of the USA: http://www.ymca.net

Wikipedia article on YMCA: http://www.en.wikipedia.org/wiki/YMCA

Martti Muukkonen's Dissertation *Ecumenism of the Laity:* http://www.epublications.uef.fi/pub/urn_isbn_952-458-207-4/urn_isbn_952-458-207-4.pdf

CHAPTER 17

Helping Social Change Bloom

Two Capacity-Building Innovations at Third Sector New England

Diane Vinokur-Kaplan

School of Social Work

University of Michigan

Jonathan Spack

Executive Director

Third Sector New England

Chair, Steering Committee—National Network of Fiscal Sponsors

INTRODUCTION

In the United States, the charitable nonprofit sector reflects efforts to serve those with the fewest resources and to advocate for social change, social justice, and civic participation. The organizations that especially focus on these goals range in size from large, established institutions and think tanks to much smaller nonprofits with limited staff and strong reliance on volunteers. It is these smaller organizations that face particular challenges to meet their goals. They themselves have limited resources, are often located in large cities with high rents and volatile real estate markets, and lack access to modern technology for their work. This case presents the story of the evolution of a large institute that moves from supporting public and community health projects to becoming a modern haven for these social justice and advocacy organizations in Boston.

THE PROBLEM

Social justice and social change organizations work hard to bring inspiration, public mobilization, and needed improvements to society; yet one of the major problems they face in these pursuits (at least in the United States) is the management of labor-intensive, "back-office" functions. These functions include securing, managing, and complying with grants and contracts, formally hiring personnel, correctly allocating fringe benefits, and producing accurate financial reports.

In addition, social justice organizations must manage their office environments, including having a decent, productive place to do their work. Rent or occupancy costs are often the largest line item in their budgets following personnel. Thus, with the unstable real estate markets of recent years, they can frequently be forced to move, thereby disrupting their important work. Moreover, the offices they can afford often lack access to the quick technologies that contemporary advocates require (cf. Boris & Maronick, 2012, p. 395).

Furthermore, these time-consuming "business" activities take executives and staff away from more mission-driven activities, such as developing and providing advocacy and maintaining important relationships with other organizations and individuals in their environments. While developers of social change nonprofits are driven by their passion to improve the world, they may not have adequate management resources—such as knowledge, skills, time, or motivation—to develop their idea into a well-functioning organization. If so, such initiatives fail to become vibrant, sustainable organizations. When such breakdowns occur, these initiatives' contributions to their communities and society are lost and civil society is diminished. How then can passionate, committed individuals and groups find ways for their ideas to become well-managed realities?

THE INNOVATIONS

One solution to growing and promoting such progressive social initiatives is to provide them with the administrative infrastructure and management capacities they need so that their staff can continue to work on more mission-related activities. Third Sector New England, in Boston, Massachusetts, is a 501(c)(3) nonprofit that has developed such a center, one where social justice and social change organizations can further develop and maintain their causes as successful, sustainable enterprises. There, an array of capacity-building services is offered for social entrepreneurs and their organizations, with specialization in two critical management fields: (1) fiscal sponsorship, to ease their administrative burdens, and (2) colocation, to provide them with modern office space among like-minded organizations.

Fiscal Sponsorship

Third Sector New England emerged from a prior Boston organization called the Massachusetts Health Research Institute that started in 1959. This institute was founded by a widely respected public health pioneer, who together with leaders from the medical, public health, and business communities, sought to provide more efficient financial and administrative services to community-based public health projects and research laboratories. They were dissatisfied with the amount of time it took to get projects up and running and by the challenge of laying off staff once the projects were completed. Thus, the nonprofit institute became the fiscal sponsor of such projects, administering them under its wings. Their revenues eventually amounted to US $30 million, with the majority coming from partnerships with the state's Department of Public Health.

Since fiscal sponsorship is an often misunderstood process to develop social change organizations, (and admittedly, it has been misused on occasion [Cohen, 2012a, 2012b]), we pause here and summarize it below:

> Fiscal sponsorship has evolved as an effective and efficient mechanism for starting new nonprofits, seeding social movements and delivering public services. Fiscal sponsorship means a nonprofit organization (the "fiscal sponsor") agrees to provide administrative services and oversight to, and assume legal and financial responsibility for, the activities of groups or individuals engaged in work that furthers the fiscal sponsor's mission (National Network of Fiscal Sponsors, n.d., p. 1)

Thus, instead of social entrepreneurs worrying about the correct amount of payroll taxes to withhold from their small staff, they became projects of the fiscal sponsor; thus, that entire process is managed by another larger and more experienced organization—a like-minded partner, or parent organization—with business knowledge and skills. In this way, social innovators can concentrate on further developing their programs and gaining public support instead of worrying about the tax authorities sanctioning them for incorrect calculations.

An additional benefit of fiscal sponsorship is that it allows individuals to conduct charitable activities and receive tax-exempt grants and donations without building a full organizational infrastructure or (necessarily) receiving a formal 501(c)(3) (charitable nonprofit) status from the U.S. Internal Revenue Service (the American tax authorities) (Tides Center, 2006).

"Fiscal sponsors are 501(c)3 charitable corporations that give unincorporated groups whose missions are aligned with their own a tax-exempt home" (Spack, 2005, p. 23). Although sponsored programs are not completely independent—they are legally part of the sponsoring organization—they nevertheless retain programmatic autonomy and often have separate advisory boards making their strategic decisions. They are responsible for their own fundraising, and they absorb any shortfall and retain any surplus.

Typically, the sponsor provides accounting, human resources, and other back-office services, with its cost covered by an administrative charge applied to the revenues or expenses of the sponsored program (Spack, 2005, p. 23).

Thus, a social change initiative or organization may choose to become a project of a fiscal sponsor because

> it is more efficient than operating as a stand-alone nonprofit organization. Other times, a group chooses to be a project because their work is short-term (such as a film project). In still other cases, the group wishes to be a project of a fiscal sponsor until such a time that they can incorporate as an independent nonprofit organization. (LaFrance Associates, 2006)

Additionally, there is relative ease of entry and exit from a fiscal sponsorship relationship as compared to being an independent incorporation; in the case of organizational failure, the leaders do not have to unwind a corporation and dispose of its assets (see Spack, 2005, p. 23).

This easy arrangement can be an incentive for social entrepreneurs to take a chance on riskier ventures. Moreover, at the front end, groups do not have to go through the major aggravation—and long wait—to receive federal tax exempt status. At present, that is a very big barrier to startups that fiscal sponsorship enables them to avoid (see Sattely, n.d., pp. 8–9).

Another common form of fiscal sponsorship is the re-grant relationship, used most commonly with arts projects. In that arrangement, the fiscal sponsor receives funds from a foundation or private donor pursuant to an agreement that it is for a particular project that does not have tax-exempt status. The sponsor re-grants the funds to the recipient group or artist but retains oversight to the extent necessary to ensure that the funds are spent for their intended purpose; that is, the recipient reports back on how the funds were spent.

Back to the case. The Massachusetts Health Research Institute continued until the 1990s. At that time, an intentional internal process of strategic planning encouraged this health organization to serve more of a broader social justice mission. External factors hurried this process along. In 1996 and 1997, the Commonwealth of Massachusetts publicly—and wrongly—accused the institute of keeping royalties from a patent that allegedly belonged to the state. This legal complaint was made despite explicit contracts to the contrary. Ultimately, the institute won a decisive victory in court; but the hubbub resulted in the end of its partnership with the Massachusetts Department of Public Health, reducing its revenue by 85%.

Under these circumstances, the institute needed to decide its direction in these reduced circumstances. It increasingly called itself Third Sector New England (TSNE) to reflect its new, broader social justice mission. This evolution was midwifed by lawyer Jonathan Spack, the Executive Director of TSNE, who had also served as Executive Director of the institute for more than a decade. His legal skills helped not only with the court case, but he also came with a strong dedication to social justice, as reflected in his prior work in public legal services and progressive nonprofits. He was the right man in the right place with the right skills and commitment. Moreover, most of the institute's board were supportive of the new direction, which reflected their basic social values.

Today, TSNE's mission is as follows:

> Third Sector New England builds the leadership and effectiveness of individuals and groups to create a more just and democratic society. We act also to promote wider recognition of community-based organizations as the primary stewards of our core societal values. The ultimate intention of our work is to shift power and influence in our society by actively engaging with our constituents in order to hold responsible the systems that affect our lives. (http://www.tsne.org/our-mission-values)

TSNE is further inspired by its vision statement, which envisions "a society grounded in and guided by principles of social and economic justice and mutual respect, where community-based organizations take the leadership role in shaping the country's future" (http://www.tsne.org/our-mission-values). It further believes that "to realize this future, people must be actively engaged in building and holding responsible the systems that affect their lives" (http://www.tsne.org/our-mission-values).

Now, within this structure social entrepreneurs and their staff can further develop their program's mission, plan and manage program activities, secure tax-exempt program funds, recruit and interact with top-notch advisory board members, support staff development and create high-performing teams, and monitor and approve program expenses.

Today TSNE's fiscally sponsored projects work for social change in the Boston community and in communities across the country. All focus on generating systematic solutions to pressing social problems, among them education reform, economic inequality, and health equity. Other important areas on which their partners concentrate include immigrant organizing, jobs creation programs, and the protection of the rights of the elderly and other vulnerable populations. As of December 2012, TSNE was home to 42 fiscally sponsored projects with more than 290 program staff in 24 states (Third Sector New England, 2013, p. 6). TSNE's 2012 financial statement reported that the combined revenue of the program funds it manages for its fiscally sponsored projects totaled $17.5 million (Third Sector New England, 2013, p. 15).

Together, TSNE and its fiscally sponsored projects monitor the financial health of the program; communicate with funders; prepare project budgets; and ensure that human resource practices, from hiring to disciplinary actions, are aligned with the programs' and TSNE's social justice values, while complying with constantly evolving labor law and practice.

In addition, TSNE provides ways for the project to connect with other nonprofits through its other training services and its role of convener of community groups. It provides the projects with free or reduced trainings and knowledge-sharing events at TSNE's NonProfit Center located in downtown Boston; free organizational assessments; a limited amount of free organizational development consultation; and access to knowledge and information from peers among TSNE's family of fiscal sponsorship projects, or from staff at TSNE with experience in strategic communications, community organizing, federal contracts management, and more.

In recent years, fiscal sponsorship is only one of the services that TSNE offers to build nonprofit capacity; it represents about one third of TSNE's overall operational revenues. While still using the expertise gained from the earlier health institute, TSNE also developed further capacities to give social change organizations a modern, supportive physical home and to sharpen their leadership.

The NonProfit Center Colocation

TSNE took another innovative step to nurture progressive nonprofits in 2004 by purchasing a building that would exclusively house charitable nonprofit organizations that embodied its social change mission in one modern space. It took a 10-year vision to develop this first mission-based NonProfit Center in Massachusetts for progressive social change nonprofits, now located in the heart of Boston's political and financial hub. This colocated center brings together in a shared space organizations committed to pursuing social and economic change.

The NonProfit Center is housed in an architecturally distinctive property, listed on the National Register of Historic Places, and is an easy walk to the Massachusetts State House and Boston City Hall, convenient for those doing legislative research and advocacy. It gives a home both to organizations that need an office suite and to social entrepreneurs who for now only need a desk, a computer, and a fast connection to the Internet.

This building has eight floors totaling over 110,000 rentable square feet. Each floor has high-tech meeting space available to the center's nonprofit tenants at no additional cost. It provides a certified healthy environment of "green design," featuring indoor bike racks, showers, and a recycling area—with more improvements already planned.

The NonProfit Center has been awarded certification from the Leadership in Energy and Environmental Design (LEED) Commercial Interiors Program. This voluntary standard is granted by the U.S. Green Building Council to recognize buildings that incorporate innovative environmental design and construction practices. Building maintenance and security is also provided (see www.nonprofitcenterboston.org/office-meeting-space; www.nonprofitcenterboston.org/our-green-building).

Four major factors provide tenants of the NonProfit Center with significant planning, productivity, and fundraising advantages: (1) *Stability:* tenants enjoy long-term affordable rents with secure leases so their rent is stable and predictable; (2) *Resources:* shared infrastructure provides cost-effective access to office resources and trainings normally beyond the means of social change organizations; (3) *Synergy:* an environment that fosters collaboration and joint action with like-minded groups; and (4) *Greater community visibility for tenant organizations' social change work*. Furthermore, access to a high quality conference center in the NonProfit Center enables tenant organizations to host seminars and meetings that carry their message even further.

Being in the shared space that helps build their capacity is a financially smart move for these nonprofits. They pay only for office space they use and share the costs of a T1 line Internet connection, fax, and copier. Thus, more of their funds can go into programs, instead of rent, equipment, and meeting space. The NonProfit Center also helps nonprofits recruit top-notch interns to work in these offices because of its central location and collaborative working environment. Examples of social change organizations there include: Amnesty International, Green Restaurant Association, Campaign for Commercial Free Childhood, Nonprofit Voter Engagement Network, and the Disability Rights Fund.

CONCLUSIONS

Administrative costs are of great concern to nonprofits' budgets. It is estimated that "a well-run nonprofit can expect to spend between 20–30% of its annual revenue on administrative and overhead expenses" (Tides Center, n.d.). In comparison, at TSNE, a fiscally sponsored organization allocates only 10% to 14% of its annual expenses in return for being a fiscally sponsored project. Thus, fiscal sponsorship cannot only provide a back-office infrastructure for nonprofit projects, but also a cost-effective one as well.

TSNE's effectiveness is shown by its successful fiscal management of many projects over the years, the high retention of the NonProfit Center's clients, and the high quality of the leadership seminars. Tenant turnover is low, and there is a waiting list for shared space. Still, TSNE constantly looks for new ways to improve the practice of fiscal sponsorship and promote its value to society.

In this spirit, TSNE and seven other organizations initiated the National Network of Fiscal Sponsors. This organization is a community of fiscal sponsors from across the country, devoted to building best practices for fiscal sponsorship, enhancing the nonprofit sector, and increasing capacity to advance public benefit (www.fiscalsponsors.org). In 2003, as a part of a strategic planning initiative, the Tides Foundation in San Francisco conducted a benchmarking study that led to the first gathering of fiscal sponsors to discuss the issues and challenges of using fiscal sponsorship as a mechanism to support innovation in the nonprofit sector. By early 2004, the leaders of these organizations decided to meet regularly to collaboratively define and build the relatively unknown, and greatly misunderstood, field of fiscal sponsorship within the nonprofit sector.

Today, the National Network of Fiscal Sponsors is led by a Steering Committee comprised of organizations that are broadly representative of the models and missions that make up the practice of fiscal sponsorship across the country (www.nonprofitsponsors.org). It includes: Community Initiatives (San Francisco), Community Partners (Los Angeles), Colorado Nonprofit Development Center (Denver), Earth Island Institute (Berkeley, California), Fractured Atlas (New York City), Fusion Partnership (Baltimore), Third Sector New England (Boston), Tides Center (San Francisco), and Urban Affairs Coalition (Philadelphia); Jonathan Spack serves as the chair of this Steering Committee.

A recent study of nonprofit fiscal sponsors (Sattely, n.d.) found that fiscal sponsorship has been growing in the sector, especially among community foundations and arts organizations. It seems reasonable that new organizations with a similar vision, commitment, and resources could replicate the model of Third Sector New England in other cities. They would benefit society by supporting worthy projects that otherwise would not be relieved from many administrative burdens. As noted by Sattely (n.d.),

> Comprehensive Fiscal Sponsorship furnishes projects with comprehensive personnel policies, liability insurance, and financial and administrative expertise. It also keeps projects abreast of and trained on new government regulations as they arise. Having these reliable operational mechanisms in place affords project leaders peace of mind, eliminating many of the stresses that can derail an operation. This intangible quality cannot be underestimated. (p. 2)

A project leader's time and thoughts will not be sidetracked by the plethora of issues inherent in managing the back-office operations of any organization. Project staff works toward mission fulfillment knowing that administrative tasks and compliance matters are being efficiently addressed. Comprehensive Fiscal Sponsorship (CFS) keeps the engines of their projects humming, allowing passionate mission-driven project leaders and staff to focus on the activities that are core to the project's existence.

The vision of TSNE to provide a shared-space building to enhance the capacities of progressive nonprofits was inspired by a conference organized by the Tides Foundation in San Francisco in 2001. There, dozens of individuals from around the country gathered to discuss the general feasibility of multi-tenant nonprofit centers providing healthy, efficient, quality, mission-enhancing workspace. Many groups that attended, as well as others, have gone on to develop such buildings successfully, so this innovative nonprofit center model is already a reality that can be further replicated to house and support social change organizations (see http://www.nonprofitcenters.org/centers).

In addition to the Fiscal Sponsorship Program and the NonProfit Center, TSNE provides still additional services to build the capacities of nonprofits. They include: consulting, executive transition and search, coaching for leadership and teams, a capacity-building fund, an inclusion initiative, meeting space, organizational transitions, nonprofit management and leadership training, and sharing of best practices and creative solutions. Thus, it provides a strong firmament that nurtures the capacity of progressive social change organizations and helps them bloom.

DISCUSSION QUESTIONS

1. What are the advantages and disadvantages of becoming a sponsored project for an individual or group nonprofit enterprise?
2. What are the advantages and disadvantages of becoming a fiscal sponsor?
3. What do you think each party to the partnership should check out about the other?
4. What are the advantages and disadvantages of colocation for emerging and established nonprofits?

REFERENCES

Boris, E. T., & Maronick, M. (2012). Civic participation and advocacy. In L. M. Salamon (Ed.), *The state of nonprofit America* (2nd ed., pp. 394–422). Washington, DC: Brookings Institution.

Cohen, R. (2012a). Another nonprofit fiscal sponsor collapses—with client's cash. *The Nonprofit Quarterly,* April 9. Retrieved from http://www.nonprofitquarterly.org/management/20115-another-nonprofit

Cohen, R. (2012b). A global nonprofit Ponzi scheme? Lessons learned from a fiscal sponsor's collapse. *The Nonprofit Quarterly,* January 14. Retrieved from http://www.nonprofitquarterly.org/management/19812-a-global-nonprofit

LaFrance Associates. (2006, July). *Fiscal sponsorship field scan: Understanding current needs and practices* (A Tides Center White Paper). San Francisco, CA: Tides Center. Retrieved from http://www.tides.org/fileadmin/user/pdf/WP_FiscalSponsorFieldScan.pdf

National Network of Fiscal Sponsors. (n.d.). *Guidelines for comprehensive fiscal sponsorship.* Retrieved from http://www.tidescenter.org/nnfs

Sattely, J. (n.d.). *A White Paper on comprehensive fiscal sponsorship.* Boston, MA: Third Sector New England.

Spack, J. (2005, Fall). How fiscal sponsorship nurtures nonprofits. *Communities & Banks,* 22–24.

Third Sector New England. (2013). *Annual report 2012.* Boston, MA: Author.

Tides Center. (2014). *Costs.* Retrieved from http://www.tides.org/i-want-to/turn-my-vision-ideas-into-a-nonprofit-project/fiscal-sponsorship-at-tides/service-overview/costs/

Tides Center. (2006). *Fiscal sponsorship field scan: Understanding current needs and practices.* San Francisco, CA: Tides Center White Paper. Retrieved from http://www.tides.org/fileadmin/user/pdf/WP_FiscalSponsorFieldScan.pdf

ADDITIONAL RESOURCES

The NonProfit Center in Boston, Masachusetts' website: http://www.nonprofitcenterboston.org

Third Sector New England's website: http://www.tsne.org

National Network of Fiscal Sponsors website: http://www.fiscalsponsors.org

Nonprofit Centers Network's website: http://www.nonprofitcenters.org

CHAPTER 18

Metro TeenAIDS

Serve and Advocate

Alan J. Abramson

Center for Nonprofit Management, Philanthropy, and Policy, George Mason University

Lehn M. Benjamin

Lilly Family School of Philanthropy, Indiana University

Stefan Toepler

Center for Nonprofit Management, Philanthropy, and Policy, George Mason University; and National Research University Higher School of Economics, Moscow

INTRODUCTION

Many nonprofit organizations in the United States focus almost exclusively on either providing services or engaging in policy advocacy; that is, relatively few nonprofits devote significant resources to both activities. Unfortunately, this narrow focus of nonprofits persists despite expert advice that committing to both service and advocacy is a key to high performance by nonprofits (Bass, Abramson, & Dewey, 2014; Crutchfield & Grant, 2008; Grant & Crutchfield, 2007; Light, 2002, 2010). For example, in their book, *Forces for Good,* authors Leslie Crutchfield and Heather McLeod Grant (2008) highlight "advocate *and* serve" as the first of six recommended high-impact practices (pp. 30–54). In a related article, the authors report that "[h]igh-impact organizations . . . eventually realize that they cannot achieve large-scale social change through service delivery alone. . . . Ultimately, all high-impact organizations bridge the divide between service and advocacy" (Grant & Crutchfield, 2007, p. 35).

The most common approach to innovation in both the nonprofit and social enterprise literatures is to focus on innovation related to service provision. Often, social innovation is about changing the existing approach to service provision, adapting and introducing services in different contexts (replication and diffusion), or taking new service methods to scale (scaling up).

While all these approaches to innovation are clearly still in great need of further analysis, this case study suggests that the concept of social innovation could be usefully enlarged by exploring the role that nonprofits and social enterprises play in pursuing advocacy. Thus, social innovation could involve service organizations engaging in advocacy for the first time or in developing new approaches to advocacy. This perspective shifts the focus somewhat from service provision to advocacy as the strategic orientation of an innovative organization.

This case study, in particular, tells the story of how one service-oriented nonprofit organization, Metro TeenAIDS (MTA) in Washington, DC, generated a significant impact by starting to engage in advocacy activities, and thereby greatly improved its reputation, sustainability, and impact.[1] Cnaan and Vinokur (this volume) define *innovation* generally as "a radically new solution to an existing problem." In this case, MTA's introduction of advocacy efforts to supplement service provision and protect the organization's ability to pursue its mission goals proved to be just such a radically new solution. Faced with a protracted problem (HIV/AIDS crisis), an ineffective government response, and budget cuts that further undermined MTA's ability to provide services and even threatened its very existence, MTA's development of an advocacy-focused response was an unusual and creative reaction that successfully tackled the existing problem in a more effective fashion than could have been achieved by continued service provision alone. Given the success that this organization experienced by leaving its service provision comfort zone, other service-focused nonprofits may be well advised to think more creatively of mixing service provision and advocacy for the benefit of their clients, communities, and missions.

Metro TeenAIDS, the subject of our case study, was founded in Washington, DC, in 1988 by Lawrence D'Angelo, a doctor at Children's National Medical Center Hospital (previously Children's Hospital) in Washington, DC, who had begun treating young people with AIDS shortly after the disease first appeared in the early 1980s. The organization was originally founded as the Washington Area Consortium on HIV Infection in Youth but quickly changed its name to Metro TeenAIDS.

In its early years, MTA focused on providing supportive services for youth with AIDS, educational activities to help youth avoid infection, and related outreach, counseling, and testing. In its first 15 years, MTA engaged in little advocacy. This all changed in the mid-2000s when the organization faced a funding crisis that undercut its programs and its ability to serve the young people of Washington, DC.

THE PROBLEM

Before discussing these funding cuts and MTA's response in more detail, this section first describes the severe youth HIV/AIDS problem in the nation's capital that MTA was established to address.

[1] To tell the story of MTA's embrace of advocacy, this case study draws on a series of interviews the chapter's authors conducted with key informants in the spring and summer of 2013 as well as a review of relevant historical and current documents. Interviewees were promised anonymity to encourage candor.

Background on HIV/AIDS

The Human Immunodeficiency Virus (HIV) destroys an infected individual's immune cells, thereby making the individual susceptible to a broad range of opportunistic infections, many of which are life threatening. When an infected individual's immune cell count falls to a low level or the individual develops one of about 20 specific clinical conditions, the HIV-infected individual meets the definition for the Acquired Immunodeficiency Syndrome (AIDS) (DC Appleseed Center and Hogan & Hartson LLP, 2005, p. 16–21; U.S. Centers for Disease Control and Prevention, 2013b). HIV affects specific cells of the immune system, called CD4 cells or T cells. Over time, HIV can destroy so many of these cells that the body can't fight off infections and disease. When this happens, HIV infection leads to AIDS (U.S. Centers for Disease Control and Prevention, 2013b).

HIV/AIDS first appeared in the United States in the early 1980s, infecting and then taking the lives of many gay men, drug users, recipients of blood transfusions, and others who had acquired the virus through the exchange of bodily fluids with infected individuals. Fortunately, however, new drugs were developed in the mid-1990s that have been of great help to infected individuals, and those taking antiretroviral therapy are now living much longer and, according to new research, are less likely to transmit HIV.[2]

High Rates of HIV/AIDS in Washington, DC

While new treatments have now changed the face of the disease, in the early to mid-2000s—the time period on which our case study focuses—the epidemic was still at its heights. Washington, DC, was one of the areas in the United States hardest hit by HIV/AIDS and had, at that time, the unfortunate distinction of having HIV/AIDS rates that were among the highest in the country. In August 2005, the DC Appleseed Center, a respected local think tank, released an important report describing the troubling reality of HIV/AIDS incidence in the nation's capital. An estimated one out of every 20 District residents was infected with the HIV virus, and nearly one out of every 50 people in the District was living with AIDS. Rates for minorities were especially high. The District's annual rate of new AIDS cases was over ten times the national average and was believed to be the highest of any major U.S. city (DC Appleseed Center and Hogan & Hartson LLP, 2005, p. 2). In fact, the incidence of HIV/AIDS in the District was at the same level as was found in some developing countries like Nigeria and the Congo (Greenberg et al., 2009, p. 1677).

This case study focuses, in particular, on the HIV/AIDS problem among youth in Washington, DC. In the mid-2000s, it was clear that many of the District's young people had already become infected with HIV—an estimated 2,242 in the Washington area in 2004 (DC Appleseed Center and Hogan & Hartson LLP, 2005, p. 80)—with many more facing a serious

[2] As far as current statistics on HIV/AIDS, in a February 2013 fact sheet the CDC (2013a) reports that approximately 636,000 people in the United States with an AIDS diagnosis have died since the epidemic began, and that more than 1.1 million persons aged 13 years and older are currently infected. In recent years, new HIV infections have stabilized at about 50,000 per year. An estimated 15,529 people with an AIDS diagnosis died in 2010.

risk of infection. Nationally, more than a quarter of Americans living with HIV/AIDS at the time had become infected during their teen years, and more than half of new HIV infections were occurring in individuals under the age of 25 (DC Appleseed Center and Hogan & Hartson LLP, 2005, p. 80).

In the case of Washington, DC, what was perhaps especially troubling was that youth reported engaging in sexual and other high-risk behavior during that period at much higher rates than the national average. In a 2003 survey, 64% of District students reported having sexual intercourse at least once, compared to 47% in the United States overall. Moreover, 45% of District students reported having sexual intercourse with one or more people during the past 3 months, compared to 34% nationally (DC Appleseed Center and Hogan & Hartson LLP, 2005, p. 80). Specifically with regard to HIV, DC Department of Health data indicated that infection rates among DC youth 13 to 24 were increasing at an alarming rate, with the infection rate tripling in the period 2000 to 2005 compared to what it had been in the previous 5 years (Ogusky & Tenner, 2010, p. 358).

Ineffective Response by Local Government

Compounding the tragic health impacts of the disease in Washington, DC, was the lack of an effective response by the District of Columbia government. The DC Appleseed Center report identified a range of serious shortcomings in the local government's handling of the HIV/AIDS epidemic in the city: frequent changes in leadership of the government's HIV/AIDS agency, weak coordination of the many public and private agencies providing HIV/AIDS services, lack of adequate data about the disease; insufficient testing and limited condom distribution, inadequate HIV education in schools, and weak needle exchange and substance abuse treatment programs (DC Appleseed Center and Hogan & Hartson LLP, 2005, p. 2; Greenberg et al., 2009, p. 1678).

Specifically, with regard to the significant HIV/AIDS problem among youth in Washington, DC, the District and its public school system were doing much too little. In September 2007, a recent DC high school graduate and HIV peer educator named Monica passed away as a result of AIDS. Before her death, she had testified to the local school board that "ten minutes [of HIV education] in tenth grade wasn't enough" (Ogusky & Tenner, 2010, p. 34S). As one local activist put it, for too many DC youth, the first person who educated them about HIV was the person who gave them a diagnosis that they were positive for the HIV virus.

The DC Appleseed Center report (2005) identified a broad range of problems with the way the District of Columbia Public Schools system (DCPS) was handling the challenges of youth HIV/AIDS:

- Absence of system-wide, DCPS standards for HIV/AIDS education at particular grade levels;
- No tracking of HIV/AIDS education received by students;
- No standards for the quality of HIV/AIDS education delivered to students;
- Few principals and teachers receiving training for HIV/AIDS education;

- Limited collaboration and coordination between the District government and community-based organizations working with youth; and
- Lack of sufficient evaluative data about DCPS HIV education programs and their impact on students. (pp. 82–84)

LIMITED REACH OF METRO TEENAIDS AND OTHER COMMUNITY-BASED ORGANIZATIONS

MTA and other community organizations could not offset the weak response of the DC public school system and other local government agencies. MTA was only reaching 10% of Washington youth with HIV/AIDS prevention information, and other nonprofits did not have sufficient resources to close the information and service gap (Ogusky & Tenner, 2010, p. 35 S).

Federal Funding Cuts

Unfortunately, in 2004 funding shifts by the federal Centers for Disease Control (CDC) would reduce the HIV/AIDS services provided by youth-serving organizations even further. The CDC was a major indirect source of funding for community-based HIV/AIDS organizations serving youth, with federal CDC funds flowing through state governments, as well as directly, to local nonprofit agencies. In 2003 and 2004, when the CDC began focusing more of its funding on people who already had HIV—mostly adults—rather than on prevention—which also included youth—funding for youth-serving agencies was significantly reduced. Robert Janssen, director of the CDC's HIV-prevention programs, indicated the shift was mostly a matter of targeting limited resources. "'The reality is that the disease is far more prevalent among older Americans, and that's where the money should go,' he said. 'This is very much a disease of people in their twenties, thirties, and forties,' Janssen said. 'It always has been'" (Becker, 2004, p. B1). However, others suggested that the funding shifts may have also stemmed from the Bush administration's discomfort with health and sex education programs for teenagers that were teaching safe sex rather than abstinence. The change also represented an implicit paradigm shift from prevention efforts to a focus on medical issues related to HIV/AIDS.

Regardless of the reasons for it, the CDC shift resulted in almost $1 million in funding cuts for four nonprofits serving DC youth in the DC metropolitan area. In particular, Metro TeenAIDS, our case study agency, lost $250,000 in federal funding or about one third of its budget. As a result, MTA laid off three of four outreach and education specialists out of a total staff of 12, with the prospect of more program cuts to follow (Becker, 2004, p. B1). MTA's board and staff faced critical questions about the agency's future.

THE INNOVATION

In the face of these challenges—the high rate of HIV/AIDS incidence in Washington; the ineffective local government response to the public health challenge; the limited reach of youth-serving HIV/AIDS organizations; and federal funding shifts that were reducing the service capacity of youth HIV/AIDS agencies even further—MTA's board and staff considered what to do next.

One option for MTA was to engage in advocacy to try to raise the priority of youth HIV/AIDS for the local and federal governments, including the local school system. However, the reality is that many service-oriented nonprofits, which MTA was at the time, do not do much policy advocacy.

The reasons for this are multifaceted but are commonly associated with a deep-seated fear of many nonprofits that by engaging in advocacy they may violate tax code restrictions on lobbying activities and thus risk closer examination and potential penalties by the Internal Revenue Service (IRS). In part, this fear results from not-too-well understood distinctions between lobbying and general advocacy, with the former subject to restrictions and the latter being permissible without limitation. But it also results from a lack of clear standards regarding how much and what kind of lobbying activities are permitted. The ambiguity in the law and regulations leaves significant discretion to the IRS in making a determination about allowable policy activity, and many nonprofits fear the IRS may rule against them. The well-publicized story of how the IRS revoked the Sierra Club's charitable status in the 1960s, after the Club succeeded in blocking the federal government's attempts to dam the Colorado River and flood the Grand Canyon, was perceived as a clear warning shot, whose echoes still reverberate within the nonprofit sector (Berry, 2005).

In addition to the concern that advocacy may not be an allowable activity for charitable nonprofits, there are a number of other, significant obstacles to greater advocacy by human service agencies, including

- Lack of board and staff experience with advocacy;
- Desire of agencies to focus maximum resources on programs rather than advocacy;
- Fear of retribution from government funders;
- Lack of private donor support for advocacy;
- Concern that advocacy will not generate sufficient benefits; and
- Difficulties in evaluating the success of advocacy. (Bass et al., 2014)

For MTA, in particular, a major obstacle was the lack of organizational and staff experience with advocacy. MTA Executive Director Adam Tenner had never thought of himself as an advocate. Tenner had been politically involved in college, but he had contributed toward transportation for others to get on the bus to advocate in Washington rather than make the trip himself. In his previous job in Seattle, Tenner had relied on other, more fearless advocates who were better at "baring their teeth" and making demands. Tenner preferred to play the more diplomatic, conciliatory role.

However, when the CDC funding cuts hit MTA in 2004, Tenner was encouraged by key board members and funders to become an advocate. MTA Board Chair Mark Del Monte, himself a Washington lobbyist for the American Academy of Pediatrics, accompanied Tenner to a summer 2004 meeting with MTA's young staff and clients where the CDC cuts and their impact on MTA were discussed. Del Monte's reaction was to turn to Tenner after the meeting and ask why Tenner, his colleagues at MTA, and the youth affected by the cuts weren't getting mad and fighting the CDC changes. At the same time, key MTA funders, including the Moriah Fund and the Washington AIDS Partnership, were also encouraging MTA to take up advocacy. In fact, the crisis situation caused by the federal funding cuts seemed to give MTA few options—either fight the cuts or shrink the organization. There just didn't seem to be that much else to do.

Despite his previous lack of experience leading an advocacy effort, MTA Executive Director Adam Tenner was persuaded that the organization should give advocacy a chance. As board chair Del Monte had advised, Tenner in fact decided to "get mad." Feeling that a small, local organization like MTA could probably not succeed in taking on the CDC, he reached out to national organizations that MTA was a member of and that, he hoped, would be natural advocates around the CDC cuts. However, the national organizations seemed very cautious about taking on the federal government, perhaps fearing reductions in their own federal funding. Tenner and MTA "realized there was no cavalry coming to save" them and that "the CDC couldn't hurt them more," and so began their own advocacy effort. They began by calling the influential major newspaper in the nation's capital, the *Washington Post*, to report on how bad the situation was becoming for at-risk youth in the Washington area, and the *Post* chose to run the story (Becker, 2004).

MTA's success in generating news coverage by a major newspaper that is read carefully throughout the federal government constituted a major breakthrough and turning point for MTA. Previously, only a small local service provider, MTA quickly gained notoriety among key national players in the HIV/AIDS field, and even the CDC was forced to respond after the media highlighted the CDC's policy shift. Although the CDC did not restore MTA's funding, MTA's embrace of advocacy proved crucial in at least two respects:

1. Externally, its reputation and influence increased considerably beyond the boundaries of its prior service work—MTA felt that it was now being "treated differently"; and

2. Internally, the quick success validated the shift toward a greater advocacy focus—with Tenner beginning to feel more comfortable in his new role and the board so pleased that it added advocacy to MTA's mission statement in 2005.

In addition to the more aggressive outreach to media, MTA Executive Director Adam Tenner organized several events to protest the funding cuts. In mid-2004, Tenner led two dozen people to deliver petitions at the U.S. Department of Health and Human Services headquarters building in Washington, DC. The protesters were met by federal building guards but were able to deliver their petitions anyway. A short time later, MTA organized a vigil to pressure the CDC to restore the funding cuts for prevention programs.

While these efforts targeted the federal government, MTA also directed its advocacy efforts at the local District of Columbia government. MTA began to track government spending on youth HIV/AIDS, which was not easy given the relatively opaque city budget, and then began to engage in budget-related advocacy. Tenner and other MTA staff and clients visited city council member offices, showed up at budget hearings, and testified. Youth were trained to tell their own stories, which proved to be very powerful. In a short time, MTA's efforts had helped double the dollars that were flowing (from national and local sources) for HIV prevention services for DC youth. MTA also worked with DC Department of Health officials to use best practice research to prioritize how dollars were spent on youth HIV/AIDS programs. Finally, MTA competed for grant funding, often successfully, once the District's HIV/AIDS dollars became available.

As MTA's staff increased its experience and skills with advocacy, the organization turned its focus toward those systems that could have the greatest impact on reducing HIV. However, to move forward, additional funds were needed. These ultimately came from the Summit Fund of Washington. The Summit Fund had traditionally focused on pregnancy reduction but made an exception in supporting MTA's work on HIV/AIDS.

In the mid-2000s, MTA found an ally in a School Board member and together they launched a sustained effort to bring much-needed systemic change to HIV/AIDS programs in the District's public school system. In 2004, MTA asked the DC Board of Education to update its HIV/AIDS policies, which had last been revised in the early 1990s, and to improve HIV/AIDS education and services in DC schools. MTA's strategy for advocacy related to the public school system eventually had three components:

1. *Mobilize grassroots support:* MTA persuaded 30 local community organizations to join together to form the DC Healthy Youth Coalition. As part of the coalition effort, individual organizations received training to increase their advocacy capacity.

2. *Engage parents*: MTA and its allies reviewed similar change efforts in other locales. In some local areas, small numbers of vocal parents had been able to capture significant media attention with their opposition to any HIV/AIDS educational activities that went beyond abstinence. To guard against this possibility, the Coalition sponsored a poll of DC parents that found widespread support for the Coalition's reform efforts. While some parents in DC were opposed to more progressive HIV/AIDS education, a large majority were supportive of comprehensive sexuality education that would teach about both abstinence and various forms of contraception. The Coalition used the poll results to educate city leaders about the true dimensions of support and opposition to such reform efforts.

3. *Educate city leaders*: The MTA-led Coalition undertook a series of one-on-one meetings, expert briefings, and public testimony to reinforce for the mayor, city council members, city government staff, and others the need for the public schools to adopt new standards for comprehensive sexuality and HIV/AIDS education.

The advocacy work that MTA began in 2004 continues today and has been generally a very positive experience for the organization. Internally, MTA has suffered relatively few organizational stresses and strains because of its advocacy work. And externally, MTA's advocacy activities have helped the organization win increased standing and funding. Two notable achievements have been the 2007 adoption of new Health Education Standards by the District of Columbia State School Board and the 2010 passage of the Healthy Schools Act, which increased the amount of health and sex education in DC schools. The next section provides more background on MTA's organizational development, and then the following section discusses in more detail the impact of MTA's advocacy work on youth-focused HIV/AIDS efforts.

ORGANIZATIONAL DEVELOPMENT

Following its founding in the late 1980s, MTA was relatively stable organizationally until 1999 and 2000 when it experienced two quick leadership transitions as the executive director and then the first interim executive director left the organization. In 2001, Adam Tenner was recruited as the second interim director. Tenner had become interested in AIDS after a favorite college teacher died of the disease. He was especially passionate about educating youth about AIDS and how to avoid the disease. Tenner grew up in New Jersey, attended college in New York, and then moved west to begin his professional career in Seattle in 1992 as an outreach worker in a homeless youth organization. Because of his leadership skills, he was director of the program 5 years later. From 1997 to 2000, Tenner served as the HIV Prevention Planner for the Seattle-King County Health Department (Eugene and Agnes E. Meyer Foundation, 2010). He moved to Washington in 2000 to become interim director of a national youth organization and then transitioned to MTA as its interim executive director in 2001.

MTA was in poor financial shape when Tenner became interim executive director, running a deficit of about $150,000 out of a $600,000 budget. Tenner's first objective was to stabilize the organization's finances, since the alternative was to shut the organization down. Tenner's initial meetings with the MTA board involved deciding which board member would pay the electric bill and which the postage. Tenner's strategy was to cut expenses in half, close unfunded programs, and say no a lot. By 2004, he had stabilized MTA and gained great respect from MTA's board, funders, and other stakeholders for the turnaround he had achieved.

In 2004, the newly stabilized MTA was hit with the CDC funding cuts described previously. Once again, MTA's board and staff had a significant challenge to address. And once again MTA's leadership quickly steadied the agency, and the organization has continued to grow since 2004. In 2013, MTA was a $4 million organization with three core programmatic goals:

1. Enable DC youth who are already HIV positive or are living with AIDS to enjoy as healthy lives as possible;
2. Achieve attitude and behavior shifts among DC youth that help them avoid HIV/AIDS; and
3. Promote DC public and charter schools providing high-quality HIV and sexual education. (Metro TeenAIDS, n.d.[a])

To achieve these goals, MTA's services now include:

- Free counseling, testing, and referrals;
- Outreach and education, including through public and charter schools;
- Support for young people living with HIV/AIDS and their families;
- Public policy activities;

- Capacity-building assistance to other youth-serving organizations in Washington, DC; and
- Evaluation of the services MTA is delivering. (Metro TeenAIDS, n.d.[b])

Because MTA's target population is youth, it employs outreach tactics appropriate for this audience. Finding that youth are often most responsive to their peers, MTA trains young people to become peer educators. MTA reaches youth on the street, in their neighborhoods, in schools, through social media, and on the Internet. During its 25 years in operation, Metro TeenAIDS has reached more than 200,000 young people and family members. However, the organization envisions a day when its services are no longer needed.

SOLUTION'S EFFICIENCY, EFFECTIVENESS, AND REPLICABILITY

While MTA's services may someday no longer be needed, that day is surely some years in the future. However, even with much work yet to be done, MTA has had some notable successes. In particular, MTA's advocacy work, which is the focus of this case study, has contributed to several important achievements. In the first place, MTA's advocacy work has helped raise the organization's visibility, reputation, and funding. MTA's staff, board, and funders all noted how MTA's advocacy work had been a smart investment that had benefited the organization in many ways.

Additionally, MTA's advocacy work helped raise youth HIV/AIDS as a priority for Washington, DC's, local government. In 2007, then DC Mayor Adrian Fenty named HIV/AIDS as the city's number one public health priority (Ogusky & Tenner, 2010, p. 37 S). Reflecting the Mayor's interest in the issue, in June 2007, the DC Department of Health (with input from Metro TeenAIDS and other community-based organizations) released an ambitious 3-year "Youth and HIV Prevention Initiative Plan: 2007–2010" that proposed to use social media and other tools to raise awareness among youth of risks and available services relating to HIV/AIDS; ensure high-quality, HIV education for all DC youth; and strengthen government-community partnerships to coordinate HIV prevention efforts (District of Columbia Department of Health, HIV/AIDS Administration, 2007, p. 5).

Finally, with prodding from MTA and others, DC Public Schools has significantly increased its efforts related to HIV/AIDS education. In December 2007, the DC State Board of Education approved new standards for comprehensive health education, including provisions related to HIV education, and implementation of the plans followed in succeeding years (Ogusky & Tenner, 2010, p. 40 S). And in 2010, MTA worked with other advocates to create the Healthy Schools Act 2010, which (a) clarified that all schools (public and charter) needed to meet the Health Learning Standards, (b) mandated minimal instruction time for health education, and (c) clarified the role of the Office of the State Superintendent for Education (OSSE) in measuring student progress in health education. The school system's progress has been reflected in the annual report cards issued by the DC Appleseed Center as a follow up to its 2005 report. For example, the school system earned a D grade in 2007, but moved up to a B+ in 2012.

As part of MTA's strategy, it became clear that in the post No Child Left Behind world of education, what gets measured gets done and health had been relegated to "elective" status. So the organization began, as Tenner says, "to change the incentive structure for schools" so that schools would want to succeed at teaching health. Once the Healthy Schools Act was passed, MTA began working closely with OSSE to create a mechanism for assessing students' progress on health education like it measures reading and math. Finally, after being criticized for failing to evaluate its HIV education efforts in successive DC Appleseed Report Cards, in 2012 OSSE included questions on sexual education in the standardized tests it administers to students, a first for any jurisdiction in the country. While some poked fun at exam questions focused on sexual education, advocates argued that this was a legitimate and necessary approach to assessing the impact of the city's HIV and sex education initiatives (Brown, 2012).

To be sure, although MTA's advocacy efforts to date have contributed to some significant achievements, important problems remain that additional advocacy can help address:

- *HIV/AIDS education in charter schools*: One of the more significant challenges for social (and other types of) innovation is the issue of diffusion; how can an innovation be replicated in different locales, cultures, and contexts. In this case, a remaining challenge is to find ways to adapt the advocacy strategy that worked well with the public school system to the somewhat different context of charter schools. Charter schools now educate 43% of DC's public school students (Editorial Board, 2013), but, according to the DC Appleseed Center, sexual education programs in charter schools are uneven and poorly monitored. The challenge for advocates like MTA is that these schools, in contrast to the public school system, are difficult to impact as a group.

- *Federal health care reform*: It is still unclear what impact health care reform will have on HIV/AIDS services for youth. However, it is clear that organizations like MTA need to be engaged in analyzing the new law and being advocates for youth, whose interests may otherwise be ignored when important implementing decisions are made. MTA is also exploring strengthening its links to insurance companies that may benefit from the preventive work that MTA does.

- *Monitoring implementation*: While MTA and its allies have had some success in prodding DC government and DC Public Schools to enact positive legislation and develop impressive plans, tracking the implementation of these laws and plans presents new challenges. Obviously, good plans that go unfulfilled are of little help to DC youth. Unfortunately, the ongoing monitoring work that is necessary can be time-consuming, unglamorous, and hard to fund. However, ways must be found to sustain the important monitoring work.

CONCLUSIONS

In this case, we discussed the adoption of an explicit advocacy approach by a traditional service provider as a distinct social innovation approach. MTA's advocacy work has not replaced its service provision but has provided a new strategy for addressing a protracted problem that mere service provision could not resolve. While MTA still has work to do in adapting its innovative approach to other contexts and changing policy landscapes, we hope that others working in and with nonprofits will benefit from learning about and reflecting on MTA's experience. While there are significant barriers to nonprofits engaging in advocacy, there can also be significant gains, as demonstrated in the MTA case. It will be helpful for scholars and nonprofit practitioners to explore additional cases and develop more systematic analyses as well on this important issue.

DISCUSSION QUESTIONS

1. What is needed for a service organization to take on advocacy successfully? How can an organization's leaders instill a "culture of advocacy" in an organization?
2. As noted at the start of this case study, service and advocacy can be a powerful combination for nonprofits, but the reality is that many organizations stick largely to one type of activity or the other. Why was MTA able to join advocacy to service delivery? Our analysis suggests the following were some of the important factors that contributed to MTA's success in taking up advocacy:

- Board, staff, and funder support for advocacy;
- A strong, smart executive director;
- A crisis situation, with few other appealing alternatives for the organization;
- Learning from the experience of others (e.g., MTA's polling parents because of antireform advocacy elsewhere);
- Engaging clients—MTA's youth—in advocacy; and
- The development of a virtuous cycle, in which initial success was rewarded with increased access to funding and other positive reinforcement, such as an enhanced profile and stronger reputation.

REFERENCES

Bass, G. D., Abramson, A. J., & Dewey, E. (2014). Effective advocacy: Lessons for nonprofit leaders from research and practice. In R. J. Pekkanen, S. R. Smith, & Y. Tsujinaka (Eds.), *Nonprofits and advocacy: Engaging community and government in an era of retrenchment* (pp. 254–293). Baltimore, MD: Johns Hopkins University Press.

Becker, A. L. (2004, July 19). Lost grants hurt AIDS prevention efforts for teens. *Washington Post*, p. B1.

Berry, J. (with Arons, D.). (2005). *A voice for nonprofits*. Washington, DC: Brookings Institution.

Brown, E. (2012, December 12). D.C. releases results of nation's first-ever standardized test on health and sex ed. *Washington Post: Post Local: D.C. Schools Insider*. Retrieved from http://www.washingtonpost.com/blogs/dc-schools-insider/post/dc-releases-results-of-nations-first-ever-standardized-test-on-health-and-sex-ed/2012/12/12/c52da276-4494-11e2-8061-253bccfc7532_blog.html

Crutchfield, L. R., & Grant, H. M. (2008). *Forces for good: The six practices of high-impact nonprofits*. San Francisco, CA: Jossey-Bass.

DC Appleseed Center and Hogan & Hartson LLP. (2005). *HIV/AIDS in the nation's capital: Improving the District of Columbia's response to a public crisis*. Washington, DC: DC Appleseed Center.

District of Columbia Department of Health, HIV/AIDS Administration. (2007). *Youth and HIV Prevention Initiative Plan: 2007–2010*. Retrieved from http://doh.dc.gov/sites/default/files/dc/sites/doh/publication/attachments/hiv_youth_prevention_initiative_4.pdf

Editorial Board. (2013, July 6). D.C.'s charter schools get a gold star. *Washington Post*. Retrieved from http://articles.washingtonpost.com/2013-07-06/opinions/40404884_1_charter-schools-conventional-schools-twenty-seven-schools

Eugene and Agnes E. Meyer Foundation. (2010). *2010 Meyer Foundation Exponent Awards: About Adam Tenner*. Retrieved from http://meyerfoundation.org/exponent2010/tenner

Grant, H. M., & Crutchfield, L. R. (2007). Creating high-impact nonprofits. *Stanford Social Innovation Review, 5*(4), 32–41.

Greenberg, A. E., Hader, S. L., Masur, H., Young, A. T., Skillcorn, J., & Dieffenbach, C. W. (2009). Fighting HIV/AIDS in Washington, D.C. *Health Affairs, 28*, 1677–1687.

Light, P. C. (2002). *Pathways to nonprofit excellence*. Washington, DC: Brookings Institution Press.

Light, P. C. (2010). *Driving social change: How to solve the world's toughest problems*. Hoboken, NJ: John Wiley.

Metro TeenAIDS. (n.d.[a]). *Welcome: About us*. Retrieved from http://metroteenaids.org/site/

Metro TeenAIDS. (n.d.[b]). *What we do: MTA's departments*. Retrieved from http://metroteenaids.org/site/

Ogusky, J., & Tenner, A. (2010). Advocating for schools to provide effective HIV and sexuality education: A case study in how social service organizations working in coalition can (and should) affect sustained policy change. *Health Promotion Practice, 11*(Suppl. 1), 34S–41 S.

U.S. Centers for Disease Control and Prevention. (2013a). *HIV in the United States: At a glance*. Retrieved from http://www.cdc.gov/hiv/statistics/basics/ataglance.html

U.S. Centers for Disease Control and Prevention. (2013b). *What is HIV?* Retrieved from http://www.cdc.gov/hiv/basics/whatishiv.html

ADDITIONAL RESOURCES

Resources on advocacy for nonprofit organizations:

Avner, M. (2002). *The lobbying and advocacy handbook for nonprofit organizations: Shaping public policy at the state and local level*. Saint Paul, MN: Fieldstone Alliance.

Bass, G. D., Arons, D. F., Guinane, K., & Carter, M. F. (with Rees, S.). (2007). *Seen but not heard: Strengthening nonprofit advocacy*. Washington, DC: Aspen Institute.

Bobo, K., Kendall, J., & Max, S. (2001). *Organizing for social change: Midwest Academy manual for activists*. Santa Ana, CA: Forum Press.

Bolder Advocacy, An Initiative of Alliance for Justice: http://bolderadvocacy.org/

Cohen, D., de la Vega, R., & Watson, G. (2001). *Advocacy for social justice: A global action and reflection guide*. Bloomfield, CT: Kumarian Press.

Independent Sector. (2012). *Beyond the cause: The art and science of advocacy*. Washington, DC: Independent Sector.

Shaw, R. (2001). *The activist's handbook: A primer*. Berkeley: University of California Press.

CHAPTER 19

Empowering Social Workers in Social Service Organizations in South Korea

Chulhee Kang

Yonsei University

Sangchul Lee

Dong Seoul College

THE PROBLEM

Have you ever felt that your best efforts are taken for granted and expectations of your work are unrealistic? This is the daily reality for social workers in South Korea.[1] Those working in nonprofit social service organizations, as well as governmental social service divisions, have to face a variety of challenging issues in their practices. Because their sacrifice on behalf of community and society has been taken for granted by the public and funders, their responsibilities are burdensome and overwhelming. Thus, Korean social workers frequently feel frustrated, disappointed, disempowered, and even guilty (Korea Association of Social Workers, 2012).

Furthermore, these feelings easily lead to their mental and physical exhaustion (Kim & Yang, 2002) and even cause suicide attempts. In 2013, four public social workers consecutively committed suicide due to extremely high job stress, and it has become a social issue in South Korea.

---

[1] In South Korea, the average annual working hours (2,351 hours in 2005 to 2,090 hours in 2012) are substantially longer than in European countries and elsewhere in the world's advanced economies (OECD averages: 1,804 hours in 2005 to 1,765 hours in 2011) (OECD, 2013). One important reason is that Koreans display hard work based on the Korean work ethic (Aidos, Gulmira, Gulnar, Mansya, & Gulnapis, 2013). The other important reasons are that workers in South Korea are less likely to receive paid annual leave than their counterparts in advanced economies, and those Korean workers who do receive paid time off generally cannot use paid annual leave and holidays due to their workloads and the organizational culture that is very restrictive regarding their paid time off (Expedia, 2012; James & Raphael, 2012).

Social workers in South Korea are particularly overwhelmed with heavy workloads, taking on more cases per worker compared to their counterparts in advanced economies while also dealing with administrative work at the same time (Korea Association of Social Workers, 2012). Currently, there are about 13,000 public social workers who have to assist around 4,000 economically dependent citizens per public social worker (Ministry of Health & Welfare, 2012). Social workers in nonprofit human service organizations are in almost the same situation. Their job loads are somewhat lower than public social workers' job loads, but generally compensation and fringe benefits for them are lower than for public social workers.

Even in this nonprofit situation, Korean social workers are required to satisfy high social and organizational expectations, adapting to new knowledge and regulations, and pointing out newly emerging social problems. Eventually, they can easily fall into despair; they can feel lethargic and be prone to exhibiting negative attitudes toward their job and themselves (Korea Association of Social Workers, 2012; Lee, 2004).

In South Korea, social workers' devotion without adequate rewards has been taken for granted because they were regarded as charitable volunteers with good souls (Kang & Choi, 2007; Lee, 2004). With the many changes in socio-politico-economic situations in South Korea, helping professionals including social workers have experienced some favorable development regarding their social recognition and working conditions; particularly, the government has recognized the legal status of social workers with modifications of the Korean Social Service Act. However, with relatively low compensation and low social status, strong expectations still exist that social workers will make sacrifices for society without being fairly recognized and compensated (Korea Association of Social Workers, 2012).

Given this situation, organizational or social support for South Korean social workers is essential for those who perform such intensive emotional labor with diverse populations with unmet needs (Kang & Lee, 2011). However, the possibilities for employers to further support them have been very limited. Their employers do not have adequate levels of funding to fairly compensate their employee or provide them with adequate fringe benefits (Kang, Lee, & Jong, 2009). They also cannot fund support programs such as regular time off, which could refresh them and provide them with the opportunity to broaden and strengthen their insights about their career, interactions with clients, and self-efficacy. Although such issues are important to social workers in South Korea, adequate opportunities to support them have not been provided for them. In summary, social workers in South Korea also need to be cared for by their organizations and society, but they have not received such consideration. Although they also have to be empowered to adequately assist and empower their clients, they have not had such treatment and care in their own organizations and society.

The problem described above has been addressed in part only by relevant professional associations such as the Korea Association of Social Workers, the Korea Association of Community Welfare Centers, and the Korea Association of Residential Welfare Facilities because of pragmatic reasons. The approach throughout such associations' unified efforts has emphasized increases in governmental support. This is because the funding for most human service organizations in South Korea comes from governmental subsidies and contracts. However, such an associational approach to solve social workers' work difficulties has only been partially effective because governmental responses are basically bound by laws and very restrictive regulations. Also, such advocacy is often regarded as a kind of interest maximization behavior by one of many interest groups in society.

In South Korea, most of the nonprofit human service organizations are similar to operating foundations in Western countries. Their programs for poor citizens and disadvantaged people have been funded mostly by foundations and public charity organizations (Beautiful Foundation, 2009; Community Chest of Korea, 2012). In particular, corporate foundations, such as the Samsung Welfare Foundation, and independent foundations such as the Asan Welfare Foundation, have been very active in providing funds for such service programs. But again, there have been no support programs for helping professionals such as social workers who are very valuable and essential mediators between society and poor citizens and disadvantaged people. Despite the fact that it is urgent and vital to protect helping professionals from being burned out and to promote their quality of life throughout diverse intervention programs, foundations as well as nonprofit human service organizations have not engaged in dealing with these workers' difficulties because these agencies have had very limited funds for this issue, and foundations have treated social workers' overload and under-treatment as a very minor issue.

THE INNOVATION

All innovation begins with creative ideas that are novel and useful (Amabile, Conti, Coon, & Herron, 1996). While creativity is related to the production of novel and useful ideas, innovation is related to the successful implementation of creative ideas within organizations, communities, and societies (Amabile et al., 1996; Oldham & Cumming, 1996). In innovation, there can also be diverse typologies using different standards. Osborne (1998) and Walker, Jeanes, and Rowlands (2002) use two dimensions (new output vs. old output in service type, and new customers vs. existing customers in customers' type) to create a typology of innovation in the public and voluntary sectors.

The Jungbu Foundation is a recently founded foundation in Korea that was looking for social innovations to support. Using this typology, its approach can be evaluated as seeking total innovation (new services for new customers). Thus rather than developmental (incremental) innovation (existing services for existing customers), expansionary innovation (existing services for new customers), or evolutionary innovation (new services for existing customers), the Jungbu Foundation has discovered new problems (social workers' stressful and unfairly undervalued lives in organizations and society) and an underserved population (see Figure 19.1) through its own executive committee's regular search efforts for appropriate intervention areas.

DIFFUSION OF INNOVATION PROCESS

Such innovative solutions by the Jungbu Foundation have been implemented by a systematic process in which three different actors have played key roles in a balanced manner.

FIGURE 19.1 Innovation Type of the Jungbu Foundation

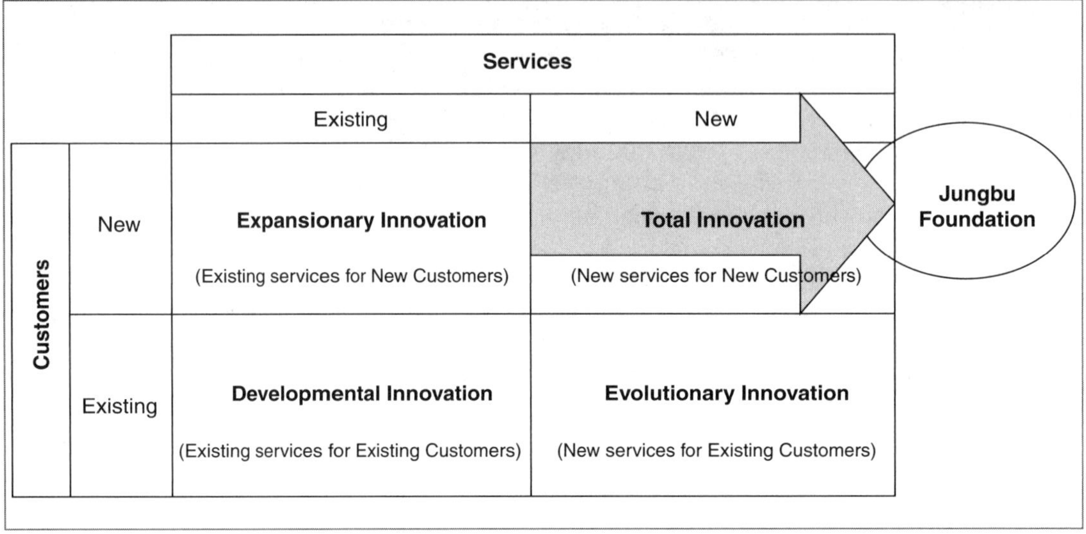

Source: Drawn from Osborne, 1998

The first and most important contributor is the chairperson who established the Jungbu Foundation based on a calling to become a stewardess of God. She has always pursued higher and more meaningful impact in her philanthropic work. The chairperson's aspiration to support novel and useful programs as her mission was the major source of the innovative business of the foundation.

The second contributor is an advisor who has consistently assisted and guided the chairperson in discovering new customers and new services that fit the chairperson's mission during and after the establishment period of the foundation. The advisor's professional service to connect target populations and issues with the founder's aspirations was an equally important source of the innovative business of the foundation.

The third contributor is the executive committee that consists of the chairperson, the advisor, and two board members (a professor in social welfare and the secretary general of the Korea Association for Social Workers) from the social service sector of South Korea. This committee has contributed to further elaborating the new ideas and new opportunities suggested by the chairperson and the advisor. Thus, the innovative solutions of the Jungbu Foundation have been actualized by the balanced collaboration among these three actors in the foundation: the founder's pursuit of novel and useful endeavors; the advisor's timely response with new ideas and new program options; and the executive committee's elaborative efforts for successful implementation of new programs, along with examination of new ideas (See Figure 19.2).

Specifically the Jungbu Foundation has provided new services that support social workers and their families: namely, a sabbatical month, social workers' graduate study, support

FIGURE 19.2 Innovation Diffusion Process of the Jungbu Foundation

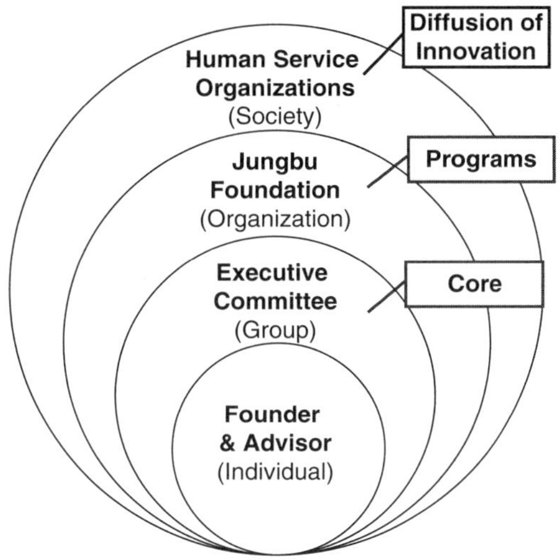

for their children's college study to become social workers, workshops to develop social workers' knowledge and skills, 12-week seminars to strengthen social workers' managerial capacity, support for networks among social workers, and support for building an e-library for social workers, among other things. Discovering new customers and developing new services that are necessary for them, the Jungbu Foundation has truly supported helping professionals in South Korea.

One of the most interesting programs among the Jungbu Foundation's innovative solutions is the Sabbatical Month Program for Social Workers. In today's workplace, professional employees need sabbaticals (an extended leave or personal retreat), which may mean a break of any time period from 1 month to a couple of years (Miller & Kang, 1997). According to Toomey and Connor (1988), sabbaticals historically have been viewed as a way to prevent and deal with stress and job burnout, to broaden professional skills, and to provide an opportunity for personal growth. Indeed, in South Korea, sabbaticals can allow social workers who are oppressed by heavy workloads and unfairly high expectations to have a rest and otherwise alleviate burnout (Kang, Kim, & Lee, 2011). Sabbaticals can function as an ideal device for preventing occupational stress. Moreover, they can give social workers the opportunity to reflect on their work, think about careers, redefine their goals and objectives in life, and reconsider their roles and relationships with families.

Despite the general belief that breaks and rests help people enhance their quality of life and become more productive employees, such programs for supporting rest, growth, and development of helping professionals such as social workers were never institutionalized in the Korean social service context organizationally or socially. In addition, in South Korea, where helping professions such as social work have had recent growth, there was a lack of discussion and intervention regarding their stressful lives, burnouts, and suicides. Organizationally or socially, it was necessary to institutionalize support programs for them since such leaves from work were truly urgent and significant for sustaining social workers' work and mental health.

Starting in 2005, the Jungbu Foundation initiated a financial support program for nonprofit human service agencies that agree to institutionalize their own Sabbatical Month Program for Social Workers for their employees within 4 years after receiving a Jungbu grant. More specifically, the foundation started to provide a 1-month salary for each human service organization whose employee is selected by the Jungbu Foundation as a participant of the program. With the program, each participant was encouraged to use the 1-month sabbatical autonomously and to do whatever he or she plans to do with the leave. The financial support of at least $1,500 could be used with discretion by his or her organization, with up to $1,000 for employing temporary workers or offering incentives for the participant's colleagues to take over his or her responsibilities, and up to $500 for participants to use for activities during their leave.

The program had one goal and three main objectives: the goal was to institutionalize the Sabbatical Month Program in nonprofit human service agencies, and the objectives were to protect social workers from being burned out, promote their quality of life, and improve relationships between social service agencies and social workers. Indeed, the program did not have any requirements for participants during and after their sabbatical leave, so participants engaged in many different activities during the sabbatical leaves such as taking a rest and doing nothing at all, gaining experience-related to work, planning for their future careers, catching up with daily errands, spending time with elderly parents, having intensive medical examinations and treatments, taking a trip to the back country, helping out with family affairs, and examining their life as a professional in a human service organization. Thus, the contents of the program were discretionarily decided and performed based on individual needs.

Since 2005, the Jungbu Foundation has supported 194 helping professionals in 155 nonprofit human service agencies that have decided to institutionalize the Sabbatical Month Program. From 2013, nonprofit human service agencies' adoption of the sabbatical month will be expanded and further promoted through financial collaboration with the Kyobu Life Insurance Company, one of the leading insurance companies in South Korea.

THE ORGANIZATION'S DEVELOPMENT

The Early Stages

In the early stage of the Jungbu Foundation's development, the most important goal was to develop its mission, vision, and core values for the basis of its operation. These properties have guided the innovative work of the Jungbu Foundation from the beginning. For example, the vision of the Jungbu Foundation is specified by three subcategories: (1) be a partner for social workers' happiness, (2) be a guide for the change and development of human service agencies, and (3) be a pioneer to expand human energy for philanthropic activities. Because the Jungbu Foundation had a systematic preparation period for its successful establishment and operation under the collaboration of the founder and the advisor, it could concentrate on programs related to its mission, vision, and core values from its early operational stages. However, at the beginning, like other Korean foundations that pursue a stable operation with general grant making for human service organizations, the Jungbu Foundation gave a higher priority to grant-making programs for social service agencies rather than support programs for helping professionals such as social workers. Because the community impacts that the founder expected were practically invisible with its grant-making programs for social service agencies, the Jungbu Foundation needed new alternatives. Then, the first vision on empowering social workers who empower people with problems provided an opportunity for developing and elaborating new programs that have a more visible impact.

Core Support and Resource Systems

In the process of bringing higher impact through the more focused projects on social workers, the Jungbu Foundation co-opted two professional bodies: the Korea Association for Social Workers and the Korean Academy Association of Social Welfare. For its board composition, the Jungbu Foundation invited three professionals to be board members: the president of the Korean Academy Association of Social Welfare, a professor in social welfare with experience in human service agency management, and the general secretary of the Korea Association for Social Workers. At the same time, to expand new projects more stably, the Jungbu Foundation obtained additional financial support from Jungbu City Gas Corporation, which is owned by the Jungbu Foundation founder's husband. Thus, the strategic preparation in governance made it possible for the Jungbu Foundation to more efficiently develop new projects for social workers, and the financial support from the mother company provided major backing for the foundation to practice and expand diverse experimentations through new programs.

Journey of the Jungbu Foundation Toward Innovative Programs

The Jungbu Foundation was established in 2003 as an independent foundation. In the beginning, the Jungbu Foundation operated two types of support programs; the first one was a support program to upgrade nonprofit social service systems in the founder's business region. This grant-making program was for social service programs that would have high community impacts. The second one was a support program to develop social workers through scholarships for their studies at graduate school. Both programs could be evaluated as simultaneously conventional and innovative. While the funding programs for impactful social services and the scholarship program were very typical among those Korean foundations that had a very high priority on social service programs for needy citizens and human capital development through education, the focus on high community impact and social workers' growth and development was very new and unique among the projects of many foundations in South Korea.

In the beginning, the Jungbu Foundation attempted to operate its programs as a mix between conventional and new approaches. With the pursuit of higher and more meaningful impacts on community and society, however, the foundation began to give more weight to supporting social workers who work under relatively unfavorable circumstances and need special care such as empowerment. Thus, with concern for social workers' low quality of life and their lower level of knowledge and skills that needed further development, the foundation adopted new support programs for social workers in 2005: (1) a financial support program for nonprofit social service agencies, which gives employees (social workers) a sabbatical month; and (2) a workshop program for improving social workers' knowledge and skill development. In 2010, the foundation began to operate a half-day education program for 12 weeks to broaden and strengthen middle-managers' managerial capacity in nonprofit social service agencies. In 2012, the foundation adopted new financial support programs to activate network building among social workers of different agencies and communities and to build an e-library for social workers with the collaboration of the Korea Association of Social Workers. In 2013, the foundation began to expand the financial support program to nonprofit social service agencies for social workers' Sabbatical month through financial collaboration with a leading insurance company (Kyobo Life Insurance Company), which has evaluated the uniqueness and value of the Jungbu foundation's Sabbatical Month Program very highly (See Table 19.1).

EXTERNAL SOURCES OF DIFFUSION OF THE JUNGBU FOUNDATION'S INNOVATIVE PROGRAMS

There are two crucial external sources for the Jungbu Foundation's organizational growth and development: one is social recognition and the other is collaboration with other organizations. Because of the Jungbu Foundation's unique and innovative works, it has been spotlighted by the media and government of South Korea. Major media, particularly leading newspapers, have several times introduced and praised the meaningful programs for social workers and social service agencies carried out by the Jungbu Foundation. In addition, the founder received an award from the minister of the Ministry of Health and Welfare because of the Jungbu Foundations' contributions and achievements for social workers and social service agencies. With the recognition of the foundation's achievements and contributions, the Jungbu Foundation has been evaluated highly in its operational quality and eventually requested to collaborate with other organizations. Currently, the major collaborators of the Jungbu Foundation are the Korea Association for Social Workers for the E-library Project for Social Workers and the Kyobo Life Insurance Company for the Sabbatical Month Program. Such collaborations with major partners have further promoted the visibility and value of Jungbu Foundation's innovative work. Indeed, social recognition and collaborations have been the external sources invigorating further development, implementation, and stabilization of the Jungbu Foundation's innovative projects. Indeed, two such actors have reconfirmed the founder's calling and the foundation's trajectory and strengthened other members' commitment to the foundation and its innovative work.

TABLE 19.1 The Jungbu Foundation's Programs: Outputs and Expenditures

Type of Program	Year Begun	Outputs	Expenditures *(Total Expenditures/ Cost per Unit)*
1. Social workers' sabbatical month	2005	• 194 helping professionals • 155 social service agencies • In 2013, expansion for social workers' respite program with family and global trip program with colleagues on the basis of financial collaboration with Kyobo Life Insurance Company	**$391,600** *($2,019)*
2. Social workers' graduate study	2005	• 85 social workers	**$334,558** *($3,936)*
3. Workshop for social workers' knowledge and skills development	2005	• 1,400 social workers with 10 workshops	**$68,644** *($49)*
4. Support for undergraduate study of social workers' children	2009	• 79 children of social workers who study social welfare or social work	**$95,900** *($1,214)*
5. Vision school (12 weeks education program for middle managers in social service agencies)	2010	• Middle managers of 75 social service agencies to strengthen their managerial capacity	**$53,292** *($711)*
6. Support for social workers' network building	2012	• 42 groups that consist of 402 social workers	**$60,389** *($150)*
7. Construction of e-library for social workers	2012	• 61,355 social workers who are members of the Korea Association of Social Workers	**$60,000** *(98 cents)*

SUMMARY

Efficiency

Like some other Korean grant-making foundations for social services, the Jungbu Foundation has not had any special interest in evaluating its innovative solutions for social workers regarding efficiency. Therefore, it is not possible to rigorously discuss the degree of efficiency of Jungbu's programs. In this situation, only output such as total program expenditures and numbers of program beneficiaries can provide basic information for the discussion of the efficiency of the programs.

Focusing only on the Jungbu Foundation's efforts for social workers in South Korea reveals that the Jungbu Foundation has had expenditures of (all shown in U.S. dollars) $391,600 to support 194 social workers' sabbatical month in 155 social service agencies; $334,558 to support 85 social workers' graduate study; $95,900 to support the undergraduate study of children of 79 social workers who want to be social workers; $53,292 for an intensive education program of 12 weeks to strengthen social workers' managerial capacity in 75 social service agencies; $60,389 to support network building activities of 42 groups, which consist of 402 social workers; $68,644 to support workshops for 1,400 social workers' knowledge and skill development; and $60,000 for the initial construction of an e-library for the 61,355 social workers who are currently employed in South Korea. The cost per unit is shown in Table 19.1 in the last column on the right.

Effectiveness

It is somewhat difficult to precisely evaluate the degree of effectiveness only by considering expenditures of programs and sizes of program beneficiaries. However, the Jungbu Foundation has attempted to evaluate somewhat different aspects of its programs—their achievements, impact, and limitations. Thus, the Jungbu Foundation has quantitatively and qualitatively had a kind of effectiveness evaluation by employing external evaluation experts. On the Sabbatical Month Program, for example, the Jungbu Foundation had an evaluation done by an expert group, and subsequently a seminar on social workers' needs and situation for the sabbatical program was held in collaboration with the Korea Association of Social Workers.

The evaluation showed that from a macro perspective, Jungbu's Sabbatical Month Program has the following effects: (a) it has positive effects on generally promoting the necessity and recognition of institutionalizing a sabbatical leave program for social workers in South Korea, and (b) it actually made significant contributions to institutionalizing sabbatical leave programs in 98 social service agencies in South Korea (Kang et al., 2011). In addition, throughout the evaluation research project, the Jungbu Foundation found that the sabbatical leave program can be a very effective tool in dealing with social workers' burnout, general health, organizational commitment, and sense of well-being (Kang et al., 2011).

More specifically, the results from the evaluation project suggested, at least in South Korea where working circumstances for helping professionals such as social workers have yet to be improved, that the sabbatical program can be a remedy that soothes their mental and physical hardships and provides momentum for them to think about their professional growth and development (Kang et al., 2011).

Thus, it showed, at least in South Korea, that providing social workers with a chance to take a long break can be an invaluable intervention for them to reduce stress, avoid burnout, and return to work refreshed and revitalized with a stronger commitment to their work and agencies. Considering the abovementioned effects at the micro (individual) level, as well as the degree of institutionalization of the sabbatical program at the macro level (Korean social service agency or sector level), the Jungbu Foundation's Sabbatical Month Program is evaluated as very effective.

Replicability

In 2013, in light of the evaluation of the novelty and usefulness of the Sabbatical leave program for social workers, the Kyobo Insurance Company offered a collaborative relationship with the Jungbu Foundation. It provided a grant of U.S. $200,000 allowing the Jungbu Foundation to expand its sabbatical program with two new programs: (1) the social workers' respite program with family (2) and the global trip program with colleagues. In South Korea, even though social workers take joy in their helping profession on the one hand, social workers' families as well as social workers bear the high stress and financial burdens on the other hand. Hence it may also be necessary to strengthen social workers' families with some support for respite. So in 2013, the Jungbu Foundation commenced support for social workers' respite with their families. This program provides a break for social workers and their families that may prove beneficial to family members as well as social workers.

In addition, because social workers in South Korea have very high needs for professional growth and development, despite their difficult situations, the Jungbu Foundation commenced support for social workers' global trips with colleagues. In that program, the Jungbu Foundation pursues broadening and strengthening social workers' capacities through providing opportunities to learn advanced services and practices in diverse service fields abroad. Indeed, such new expansions indicate possibilities for diversely replicating Jungbu's programs. For example, in 2013, the Korea Association of Social Workers benchmarked the Jungbu's programs and started a new program to support social workers' domestic trips with colleagues for 3 days to assist their revitalization. This example indicates that the Jungbu's Sabbatical Month Program has some evidence in the replicability among many organizations that want to support and empower social workers of South Korea.

It is possible to replicate the Jungbu Foundation's innovative approach if organizations such as professional associations or corporate philanthropic foundations have the following properties that Jungbu Foundation has preserved: mission-faithful leadership, a competent advisory group with a high level of expertise or highly competent experts, and stable financial resources. These three properties are sufficient conditions to be innovative nonprofits.

First, the mission-faithful leadership consistently practiced by the founder and chairperson, which pursues authenticity, trust, accountability, and stewardship, is the most salient key factor in explaining how the Jungbu Foundation's innovations succeed. Indeed, the leadership has made it possible for the Jungbu Foundation to modify existing programs whenever necessary, consistently explore new opportunities with diverse experimentation, stabilize new programs more confidently, and pursue constructive collaborations with both the beneficiary market and grant-making market.

Second, the competent advisory group with a high level of expertise is certainly another key factor in explaining the Jungbu Foundation's innovative projects. With a faithful followership, the advisory group has functioned as a dependable and responsible guide for the mission-based leadership; it has successfully complemented and supplemented the leader's own relatively limited expertise.

Third, stable financial resources reflect what is very true in most nonprofits' successful or innovative operation: no money, no mission. With relatively stable financial resources from the endowments and the financial contributions from Jungbu City Gas, the Jungbu Foundation has maintained its own way relatively easily toward innovative projects without having any fluctuations in them.

In summary, based on the Jungbu Foundation case, the authors conclude that to replicate their programs, three properties should be sufficient in balance: mission-based leadership, highly competent experts having insights into the target markets, and stable financial resources.

CONCLUSIONS

Unlike some other professionals, social workers have unique attributes of using themselves as the direct tool of intervention. Therefore, protecting their own well-being is essential for them. In general, however, the reality surrounding social workers in South Korea is very far from their desired professional life: they work under relatively poor working environments without appropriate support programs. Particularly, in South Korea, they currently need to be empowered with carefully designed staff support programs to be able to empower their clients: such empowered social workers will have a positive influence on the quality of client services.

The Jungbu Foundation has proactively taken the role to empower and care for social workers for the first time in South Korea, where their working conditions are still very different from advanced societies. Thus, the foundation has actively developed and successfully implemented new services such as the Sabbatical Month Program, the network building program, managerial capacity-building program, professional capacity development program, and other support programs for the new niche market called social workers. For example, in the Korean social service sector, the financial burden of institutionalizing a sabbatical program exists as a barrier for social service agencies. Jungbu as a private foundation has initiated new efforts to assist social workers and their social service agencies and institutionalized a long break program such as a paid sabbatical leave program. As a result of such efforts in South Korea, the Jungbu Foundation is currently regarded as a true friend and hope of social workers.

As described above, in the development and implementation of the Jungbu Foundation's innovative programs for social workers, three properties of the Jungbu Foundation have been essential: mission-based leadership, a competent advisory group with a high level of expertise, and stable financial resources. More broadly, it is believed that to be successfully innovative, nonprofits need to have three properties in balance: the leader's firm and clear mission and vision, a competent advisory group (experts) who can appropriately guide the mission-based leader, and stable financial resources to develop and sustain new mission-based programs.

DISCUSSION QUESTIONS

1. Consider some social innovations with which you are familiar. What type are they? (Use Figure 19.1).
2. Do you think that there are special characteristics in innovative nonprofits that guide their success?

3. Are there any differences in the major characteristics of innovative nonprofits and those of innovative for-profit organizations?
4. How can nonprofits be innovative nonprofits? What are the necessary conditions to be an innovative nonprofit?
5. Do you think that it is possible for nonprofits to be innovative consistently over time? If yes, what characteristics are required to be innovative consistently?
6. What can be barriers for other nonprofits to bring in innovations like the Jungbu Foundation?

REFERENCES

Aidos, A., Gulmira, A., Gulnar, K., Mansya, S., & Gulnapis, A. (2013). The role of work ethic in the development of Singapore, South Korea, Malaysia, Japan and European countries. *World Academy of Science, Engineering and Technology, 75,* 23–27.

Amabile, T. M., Conti, R., Coon, H., Lazenby, J., & Herron, M. (1996). Assessing the work environment for creativity. *Academy of Management Journal, 39*(5), 1154–1184.

Beautiful Foundation. (2009). *Corporate giving of Korea 2009.* Seoul, Korea: The Center on Philanthropy at the Beautiful Foundation.

Community Chest of Korea. (2012). *Community Chest of Korea annual report 2012.* Retrieved from http://www.chest.or.kr/05_library/annual/2012/PC/2012.html

Expedia. (2012). *Vacation deprivation findings by country.* Retrieved from http://www.expedia.com/p/info-other/vacation_deprivation.htm

James, P., & Raphael, R. (2012, November 30). Koreans receive fewer paid vacation. *The Korea Times.* Retrieved from http://koreatimes.co.kr/www/news/opinon/2012/11/137_125901.html

Kang, C. H., & Choi, M. M. (2007). A comparative study of the public's image on helping professions: Comparison between social welfare professional and other professionals. *Korean Journal of Social Welfare, 59*(1), 171–197.

Kang, C. H., Kim, M. O., & Lee, J. E. (2011). The effect of a month-long sabbatical program on helping professionals of nonprofit human service organizations in South Korea: Burnout, general health, organizational commitment, and the sense of well-being. *Administration in Social Work, 35,* 20–45.

Kang, C. H., Lee, S. C., & Jong, S. W. (2009). A study of social workers' affective commitment: Analysis on moderator effect of work-life benefits. *Journal of Korean Social Welfare Administration, 11*(1), 91–122.

Kang, S. Y., & Lee, C. H. (2011). The effect of emotional labor on burn-out of employees in social welfare organization according to their emotional intelligence. *Journal of Social Science, 37*(2), 53–72.

Kim, Y. I., & Yang, O. K. (2002). *Social work supervision.* Seoul, Korea: Yangseowon.

Korea Association of Social Workers. (2012). *Basic statistical yearbook on Korea social worker.* Seoul, Korea: Korea Association of Social Workers.

Lee, M. S. (2004). Burnout process model of social workers: Analysis of the paths from the job-related stressors, job-stress and professional self-efficacy to burnout. *Korean Journal of Social Welfare, 56*(4), 5–34.

Miller, M. T., & Kang, B. (1997). A case study of post sabbatical assessment measure. *Journal of Staff, Program and Organization Development, 15*(1), 11–16.

Ministry of Health & Welfare. (2012). *The number of public social workers.* Retrieved from http://stat.mw.go.kr/front/statData/majorIdctView.jsp? menuId = 17&guidSeq = 166&ctgr = F00006.

OECD. (2013). Employment and labour markets: Key tables from OECD. Average annual working time: Hours per worker. Retrieved from http://www.oecd-ilibrary.org/employment/average-annual-working-time_20752342-table8

Oldham, G. R., & Cumming, A. (1996). Employee creativity: Personal and contextual factors at work. *Academy of Management Journal, 39*(3), 607–634.

Osborne, S. P. (1998). *Voluntary organizations and innovation in public services.* London, United Kingdom: Routledge.

Toomey, E. L., & Connor, J. M. (1988). Employee sabbaticals: Who benefits and why. *Personnel, 65*(4), 81–84.

Walker, M. R., Jeanes, E., & Rowlands, R. (2002). Measuring innovation: Applying the literature-based innovation output indicator to public services. *Public Administration, 80*(1), 201–214.

ADDITIONAL RESOURCES

Homepage of Jungbu Foundation: http://www.jbfoundation.or.kr

CHAPTER 20

Social Innovations in Mature, Faith-Based, Social Service Nonprofit Organizations

Two German Case Studies

Björn Schmitz

Philiomondo

INTRODUCTION

The German landscape of nonprofit organizations is covered by a considerable number of organizations that were founded in the 19th century. From a lifecycle perspective (Greiner, 1972; Pümpin & Prange, 1991) these organizations can be perceived as being mature organizations. According to this, lifecycle theorists assume that mature organizations lack innovativeness. In addition, research on innovations in nonprofit organizations commonly neglects innovations in such old organizations, but instead focuses on younger organizations (see Schmitz & Scheuerle, 2012, for an exception). Sometimes even the founding act of a social venture is understood as an innovation itself. However, it is worth taking a closer look at mature nonprofit organizations to test the validity of these assumptions.

To understand social innovations within mature nonprofit organizations in Germany, we first need to reveal the context and structure of the German welfare system and how traditional nonprofits are embedded within it. And this context has changed tremendously in recent years due to well-known reasons like shrinking governmental funds (Kerlin & Pollak, 2010; Priller & Zimmer, 2003; Seibel, 2002; Weisbrod, 1998), privatization of goods and services (Ziegler, 2009), managerialism at large (Curtis, 2008; Meyer, 2009), and increased competition for funding (Backhaus-Maul & Olk, 1994; Bogumil & Holtkamp, 2002; Priller et al., 2012). There is also a rising debate about the desirability of new, flexible, entrepreneurial, and problem-focused start-ups that are putting mature organizations under pressure.

Traditionally, a division of labor between public and free welfare organizations, which are traditional nonprofits in Germany, evolved due to specific interests of both parties. The roots of this division of labor go back to the 19th century when social policies in Germany emerged. From the beginning, this system was aimed at maintaining the current political system (Boeßenecker, 2005). Starting with the so-called "Sozialistengesetze" (socialist laws) in 1878, social insurances for sickness, accidents, and retirement emerged. The state needed these interventions to obtain its position and legitimacy, which was threatened by increasing poverty and hardship in wide parts of Germany and throughout counties affected by the industrial revolution. But these interventions remained far behind expectations. Many people still lived in poverty. Thus, social welfare organizations with Protestant and Catholic backgrounds flourished subsequently. From the beginning, the intent of these early initiatives was to be an advocate, a social service provider, and a generator for solidarity in the most efficient way. That being said, it was clear that the intention was to position these organizations as being free in the sense of independence from the state in the belief that they would be more innovative and efficient if they were autonomous from the state.

These self-conceptions still remain today, and the six big umbrella organizations that dominate the German welfare landscape today call themselves free-welfare associations (Boeßenecker, 2005; Zimmer & Toepler, 2000). More precisely, the six umbrella organizations contain: three religious associations, which are the Caritas (Deutscher Caritasverband), the Diakonie (Diakonisches Werk der Evangelischen Kirche in Deutschland), and the Jewish Welfare (Zentralwohlfahrtsstelle der Juden in Deutschland); the more politically motivated (social democratic) Worker´s Welfare Service (Arbeiterwohlfahrt), the Parity Association of Non-affiliated Charities (Deutscher Paritätischer Wohlfahrtsverband), as well as the Red Cross Germany (Vilain, 2002; Zimmer & Toepler, 2000). Taken together, these six organizations alone employ 80% of the entire third-sector workforce, which is almost 4% of Germany´s total workforce.

On average, third-sector organizations in Germany are bigger than their private and public counterparts (Priller et al., 2012). Today we can find huge welfare organizations in the field of health care and social services that often have existed for about 150 years. However, the new situation of shrinking governmental funds, commercialization, and increasing social problems has affected these traditional organizations regarding their partnership with the state. For a long time, the financing of the organizations belonging to the free welfare associations was a privileged one. They were preferred recipients of funds from the governmental side due to social services contracts the state established with them (Priller et al., 2012; Thränhardt, 2003; Zimmer et al., 2004). Nevertheless, this privileged position has been criticized, since these contracts were not based on effectiveness or efficiency measures (Vilain, 2002).

The reason for their dominant status was due to the historic "principle of subsidiarity" (Zimmer et al., 2004), popular especially since the 1960s; it is a specific German societal concept incorporated into German law. The principle of subsidiarity means that superior societal and organizational units (especially the state) should only take over tasks that could not be carried out by subordinated units (especially individuals and families and also organizational units). The state will only intervene in cases where there is no other authority that is able to fulfil a public task appropriately (Boeßenecker, 2005).

THE PROBLEM

In the mid-1990s, this principle and the privileged role of the free welfare organizations were altered due to several reforms. The former autonomy of free welfare organizations was more constrained by the planning and decision-making processes of public authorities. More precisely, there was an increase in competition on the one hand, and the call for more transparency and quality in service delivery on the other hand. Since the implementation of nursery insurance in 1995, the law does not differentiate between private and not-for-profit organizations as was usual in former social legislation. Nursery organizations were defined simply as commercial units. What is more, the governmental maxim of "supporting and requiring" (i.e., giving the best support possible from governmental bodies on the one hand, but demanding a specific amount of effort and encouragement from the party supported) was implemented with new social welfare laws in 2003 and 2005. In cases where Service Provider A offers a service that is equal in terms of content, extent, and quality to the service of another Service Provider, B, the compensation for A's services is not allowed to be higher than the one for Service Provider B. The result of this legislative change was increased competition among agencies, first between service providers regarding financing (subsidies, grants, donations), and second for potential customers, since in Germany there is individual free choice for service provision (Boeßenecker, 2005).

Nevertheless, regarding the financing of third-sector organizations in Germany, the most substantial portion is the financing by governmental funds. However, two thirds of all third-sector organizations report an increase or decline in governmental funds (Priller et al., 2012), which affects the operations of the organizations and forces flexibility in terms of covering operating costs. In case the funding stability of governmental funds erodes on the one hand, and on the other hand more competition is a fact in social service delivery, the situation of social service providers and nonprofit organizations in general is characterized by increased insecurity and higher pressures. What is more, while the public's awareness of increased social problems, such as the effects of demographic change or the exclusion of marginalized groups, has grown, fewer and fewer people are willing or able to pay for the traditional and conventional services that have been offered for decades and instead are requesting new solutions and services.

Related to that situation and parallel to developments in the field of social service delivery and public problem awareness, the call for start-up social entrepreneurs has become louder in the last two decades. New social entrepreneurs combining social missions with commercial means and business models are perceived as the remedy needed in the current situation (Mair & Martí, 2006). What has been neglected in recent years is the social innovation potential of mature social service providers. The next two cases investigate the potential for social innovation among these types of organizations given the situation described so far.

THE INNOVATIONS

Evangelische Stiftung Hephata (Evangelical Foundation Hephata)

In 1859, the Priest Franz Balke founded the Evangelische Stiftung Hephata (Evangelical Foundation Hephata) in Mönchengladbach-Rheydt. At that time, Hephata was the first institution in all of Prussia taking care of people with mental handicaps. Children and teenagers with mental handicaps were perceived as unable to learn. As a reaction of that claim, Hephata was established to educate mentally handicapped youth and to encourage their talents. In the beginning, the organization was supported by several evangelical entrepreneurs and the Order of Saint John. In the 1870s, Karl Barthold developed curricula for the students, and those are still reference points for such work today. Currently, one would say that Hephata was an innovative organization right from the beginning and served as a role model for many other social service organizations.

To understand the initial start of Hephata, it is interesting to give some background about the idea of closed communities or "Anstalten" in Germany. It was in 1889 in Paris at the world exhibition that Germany's exhibition presented the idea of Anstalten. *Anstalten* means that for a specific task and group of people, rules were defined, such as rules how to behave in public swimming pools. As a result of the idea of Anstalten, the institutions for people with mental handicaps were established at separate places, often apart from the normal social life.

Today, Hephata has facilities in 30 different cities or towns across North Rhine-Westphalia (a western state of Germany), with more than 150 different sites to enable people with mental handicaps to pursue a self-determined life. It employs more than 2,600 people today. The main fields of activities, which include education and working opportunities, as well as housing, are now significantly diversified and include an advisory service branch, a gardening shop, and household-related services.

In the mid-1990s, Hephata faced a very critical situation and was close to financial collapse. There were huge overhead costs, and the organization was preoccupied by its own affairs without critical self-reflection. As a reaction, the church completely changed the board of directors and hired a head-hunter to search for new executives.

Parallel to these steps, a professional and ethical discussion started about the services offered at that time and what is suitable for today and what is not. One outcome was that the approach to social care and nursery work in closed, isolated communities (Anstalten) was found to be patronizing to the inhabitants. In contrast, the modern approach to living facilities for people with disabilities is built on the idea of an active neighborhood located close to city centers. This modern approach, in all its facets, seeks to give the mentally handicapped as many possibilities for a self-determined life as possible. Furthermore, today the clients live in smaller accommodations, as compared to the older, larger institutions.

Linked to this discussion, the foundation had to change its strategy in two main aspects. First, its former approach, which presumed that the people would come to the foundation, needed to be replaced by a more active search for potential customers; it needed to open up new sites at those places where the customers already lived.

Second, Hephata's new approach is not only about innovation. The foundation says that actually it is not that innovative in a strict sense. What is more important is that the foundation is a very good imitator. This is made possible due to the comfortable financial position the foundation has had, and that often enough, an imitator develops the approach further in an incremental way. Thus, the main function of the Stiftung Hephata is to detect good ideas and to bring them to scale quickly.

One of the main innovations of Hephata is the supervised parenthood program (Unterstützte Elternschaft). The problem was that there was no support for parents with mental handicaps. The responsible actors like the youth welfare office are often overrun with such cases. Here the solution of Hephata was to have the parents with handicaps live in flats and get support regarding how to live a self-determined life and live as a normal family. This idea was generated internally. One of the employees came up with this idea that is now one of the most attractive offerings of the organization.

The foundation says that it opens up something new every 3 to 4 weeks, which is an indicator of its intensive growth path and inclination for trying out new things. Often new ideas are not covered by conventional financing structures, which is traditionally governmental funding in Germany. In the cause of a new venture, the financing structures of the government sometimes would follow up with funding the service, or otherwise the organization needs to be creative in finding another revenue stream. Within that constant tension between mission and economic pressures, new innovations arise; today, the organization states that it lives from its innovations, because in the first years the margin is comfortable, in comparison to later years when adopters and competitors have entered the market.

When asked for its most important innovations, the foundation answered that these were decentralization in combination with improved work-flow techniques. Decentralization means that the former main site was split up, with 140 different sites following the strategy to go to where people are in need instead of waiting for people to come to the former main site. This decentralization was the basis for further innovations because the new thrust of service delivery was reconsidered over and over again. Furthermore, at different sites, new ideas for services according to the specific needs of the people were addressed. This decentralization process led to the problem that coordination within the agency was not as easy as before. People were working in geographically distinct sites from each other, and agency-wide decisions were harder to negotiate. Informal encounters did not occur randomly as before, and more costs were generated to conduct planned negotiations.

What is more, in the former model, the identification of employees and also the customers took place via the central site, but this was no longer true. As a solution, the foundation implemented work-flow technologies that were automated with individualized software technology. Documentation of a patient is available virtually, and this facilitated cooperation tremendously. Highly important, the work-flow technology saved a lot of money. This money was then spent on group meetings to revitalize employees' identification with the organization, as well as toward efforts to continuously improve the services. As this example shows, a process innovation was most important for the foundation Hephata, because this innovation led to incremental and sometimes radical social innovations due to savings in time and increased money for daily operations.

Hephata has only been able to initiate new programs because of its power position and its size. The central point in its strategy is not only to innovate for itself, but also to copy interesting ideas from others and be good in adapting as well as replicating them. Trying out new ideas with an average budget of 50,000 euros is not risky for such a big organization like Hephata. If a project does prove to be unsuccessful, Hephata finishes it; in case it is successful, it can be transmitted rapidly to the widespread network of different sites. As this example illustrates, it is clear that risk leveraging is different in such huge organizations in comparison to start-ups.

Stiftung Liebenau (Foundation Liebenau)

With the purchase of the castle Liebenau, Chaplain Adolf Aich established the foundation for the Stiftung Liebenau in 1870. At that time people with hardships like mental diseases were excluded from society and were a shame for the families they belonged to. Also elderly people or younger ones with special education needs were in the focus of Aich when he decided to give these people a home, a place to live. The castle became a sanatorium for long-term ill clients, and it served as a refuge for people who were difficult to look after. In the beginning, six nurses worked in the castle, and the Stiftung Liebenau was founded in 1873. Until today the organization has grown continuously and has become a very large social service provider in Germany; it employs about 6,200 people at 100 different locations, generating total revenue of more than 283 million euros in 2011.

Stiftung Liebenau offers a total of 260 different facilities and services. The spectrum of tasks varies widely but is arranged around the pillars of health care, housing, education, and jobs close to the residence of the target groups. Due to the German type of social insurances, which cover a lot of services in the field of health care and nursery, the Stiftung Liebenau became dependent on governmental funding structures, like so many other providers. Even though the Stiftung continuously generated new service and facility ideas, it needed to find ways of optimal financing.

In 1995, after a strong growth phase, the Stiftung Liebenau established a new holding structure. Imagine, the Stiftung Liebenau had become this complex organization offering so many different activities, especially in the relatively rural area where it is located. These activities, among others, include a fishery, hotels, a water power plant, and a diaper incinerator. In the former organizational structure everything was concentrated on one board. Now, with subunits being relatively autonomous, the organization is more flexible and manageable.

Another influencing factor for the holding structure is issues of flexibility due to changes in welfare transfers. In the mid-1990s, nursery insurance was implemented at a time when the state was more oriented toward markets and private competitors. Thus, the Stiftung asked itself where its future would be: in the commercial activities it was now performing or the more traditional nonprofit branches it had that were still an integral part of the organization and important for its identity.

One of the main reasons for splitting up the organization into various subunits, of which some are for-profit legal forms, was due to the limited pay scales for nonprofit legal forms. Another one is because of tax regulations. For some activities the nonprofit status can no longer be upheld. In cases where either a for-profit or a nonprofit status is possible, the main reason for choosing a for-profit status was to avoid criticisms from for-profit competitors in corresponding fields regarding advantages that would result from the nonprofit status. The idea is to have equal preconditions from a legal and tax perspective and also to generate an environment of recognition for the people being employed.

It is hard to list all the foundation's services and facilities here. That is why we need to pick some innovative examples. Asked for its most important innovation of the last two decades, the Stiftung Liebenau pointed out the ongoing project "Lebensräume für Jung und Alt" (living-spaces for young and old) (http://www.st.anna-hilfe.de/einrichtungen/standorte/lebensraeume0/index.html#ende). But for the foundation it was not an easy decision to select one of the innovations, because there were so many very different ones, incomparable and of high importance. The Lebensräume is a new housing concept that is especially designed for elderly people to give them an alternative to living in a retirement home. Lebensräume are located centrally in the city and close to shops, doctors, and other important infrastructure that enable the residents to participate in the social and cultural life of the community.

Most elderly people today would like to live as long as possible, self-determined and in a normal living environment, ideally in their own house or flat. But in cases where they need assistance, family members are often unable to help, and ambulatory care is too expensive. Taking care of that demand, Lebensräume is a house with 15 to 80 flats. Two thirds of the residents are older than 60, and one third is younger. Thus, the Lebensräume is a multigenerational living concept in which the residents take care of and support each other. On a voluntary basis, the residents can also do gardening, work as a house master, or support needy neighbors by doing their shopping or cooking. The Lebensräume can be described as an active neighborhood. Each Lebensräume has a service center as its local heart. Here, the residents find facilities for encounters, offices, and facilities for nursery services, which are available for all. Collective activities can take place here, for example, a group for babies, a gym, collective meals, or performances, which are normally organized by the residents themselves.

The financing of the Lebensräume is set on different pillars. The residents generally pay for the rent, the operating costs, and their living expenses. The specialty of the Lebensräume of the Stiftung Liebenau is the employed community worker who provides consultancy and mediation for nursery services. This community worker is paid by a social fund that is set up by the community and the Stiftung Liebenau. The fund is financed by revenues from selling apartments, donations, and money from the community. Nursery services themselves are normally covered by the German nursery insurance.

Without a doubt the Lebensräume are innovative, efficient, and replicable. Today 25 Lebensräume exist with a total of 800 flats and 1,400 residents. The advantages of this innovation are manifold. On the one hand, these living projects can be seen as schools of responsibility, because residents generally show a high level of support for each other. Furthermore, the dialogue between generations is reinforced, which is lacking in modern societies since the model of having the whole family under one roof has become outdated. What is more, elderly people can live as long as possible in a self-determined way, and the need for nursery services for residents can be delayed or prevented. Social work is performed in a new way. As a result, the costs for nursery services covered by the national insurance can be reduced, which is a very positive side effect in times of empty government coffers. The Stiftung Liebenau itself benefits from new insights and impulses for new services from this housing innovation.

As an example, the shopping facility is a mixture of shopping experience, social networking, and cultural offerings. The main goal is to provide working and training possibilities for handicapped people, yet the people going shopping in that facility will not directly realize that there are people employed with very diverse handicaps. The main intention of the Stiftung for all its activities for handicapped people is not to create artificial spaces but rather real spaces where people with all kinds of abilities can encounter each other. For the handicapped this is important for their feelings of belonging.

The Stiftung Liebenau is often asked to be a partner for various activities, because it can provide competence, organizational size, economic power, and an organizational form that is attractive to others. This is why many initiatives have been realized in partnership. For example, the first hospice for children in southern Germany was created in partnership with a foundation that has been created out of an association. Another example is a castle that had formerly been a boarding school. After the boarding school closed down, the owner of the castle needed a partner to find a new concept for using the building. Today the castle is a nursing hotel. But also partnerships abroad need to be mentioned here.

Another interesting innovation is that retired people sign over their house to the foundation. In return, they get a pension for living and can live as long as possible in their house, which is now owned by the foundation. It could happen that the people need care shortly after the transmission of their home, or they might live there until the end. For the Stiftung Liebenau these homes are an interesting donation, and for the retired it is not only a financial benefit but also a social product, because the home donation is a sign of giving back to society.

Another example of socially innovative solutions are the child-parent stations in which children with a handicap receive psychological treatment, and some or all of their family lives live there too for up to 4 weeks. During that time, the family is integrated into the treatment and gets assistance for how to handle their child. Afterward, these learning processes should be transferred to everyday life at home. Today there is a waiting list for approximately half a year for these facilities. Innovative are also kindergartens where volunteers help realize an integrative vacation offering. Here children both with and without handicaps participate in the program.

To initiate new projects and organizations, the foundation often uses a network or partnership approach. A project is funded and run together with other organizations. Here the sharing of project expenses is an important argument that also leverages the risks for each of the members involved. Furthermore, these networks create some kind of pressure for each partner that helps them strengthen their commitment to the project. In addition, networks with partners are used to opening up the doors to new markets. Often there is no chance for the organization to run a new project or organization—especially abroad—without local partners. The Stiftung Liebenau is active in Bulgaria, Austria, and Italy, exporting its innovative services to other countries.

To gain a climate of innovativeness within the organization, the degree of independence has been emphasized. Also important is the employee selection process and an organizational culture advocating a climate of generating and testing new ideas. Normally people are busy with their day-to-day business, but the foundation reinforces employees' to searches for improvements and to visit other organizations nationally and internationally to get impressions of what others are doing. Unconventional thinking is more than allowed, and new ideas—whether from the governing board or not—are tested on a small scale. The employees—especially managers—are given far-reaching freedom; they are supported by coaching, advanced training, and staff development meetings. The organizational climate was termed as *appreciation culture* and *recognition culture*.

CONCLUSIONS

The two cases presented are interesting cases for social innovation in mature organizations that are commonly subsumed under the term *social intrapreneurship*. These cases were not a specific description of a single innovation; rather they showed the innovation potential these mature organizations possess. Indeed, they are still performing well in an increasingly uncertain and changing environment. What is more, the organizations are actively searching for new ideas and implementing them on a continuous basis. Their success shows that this is a suitable way in these uncertain and challenging times. Furthermore, the innovations presented show a high degree of replicability, regardless of whether they were replicated by the organization itself or by competitors.

Despite the current economic pressures, the social orientation of the organizations still remains; in some instances it is the starting point for a reorientation (see also Priller et al., 2012). Both organizations are focused on their social mission. This becomes evident at least in their executive board structure. At Hephata there is one clerical and one business executive director. At Stiftung Liebenau it is the same plus another executive director with a legal background. And it is the Christian basis that prevents these organizations from losing their way regarding mission drift. Also in other Christian-based organizations, we can find a reorientation toward their Christian values regarding identity work in times of uncertainty and change.

Given that Germany's social welfare system is dominated by mature organizations, one may ask about the pros and cons of this situation regarding innovation and diffusion activities. Do they contribute to a socially innovative climate in Germany's social welfare structure, or are they stubbornly wedded to outdated ways of doing things? On the positive side, since the resource situation is often comfortable for mature organizations, they have the resources to try out new things or to perform some types of cross-subsidization. Once learned, new knowledge and competencies can be relatively easily transferred to other sites. Also, existing and long-grown network structures are a plus for mature organizations. Moreover, their size helps them address their interests in the political arena. Regarding the complex bureaucratic challenges in Germany, it is a plus to be an experienced organization and to have the necessary internal infrastructure to handle these challenges. Furthermore, various actors within the nonprofit sector and its ecosystem are increasingly supporting and encouraging social innovations. Thus, inside and outside factors allow mature nonprofit organizations to leverage risks better in recent years.

But on the negative side, there are often still very long decision-making processes in mature organizations such as those presented, due to their complex organizational structures. This is a barrier when it comes to establishing partnerships with young and very flexible organizations. Also, innovative nonprofit organizations like the two presented herein may irritate and meet resistance from some other big and mature social welfare organizations regarding the innovative and proactive climate they are actualizing.

DISCUSSION QUESTIONS

1. In the beginning, both organizations presented were quite innovative. But after decades, one is less likely to assume them to still be innovative. Why is this the case? For how long should one normally call an organization an innovative one after an initial innovation? What makes them be perceived as a continuous innovator? And does the organization gain back its innovative status in the same sense when it introduces new services or products after a period of stagnation? What does that say about organizational life cycles?
2. There were many different innovations presented. Would you classify them as social innovations? Have these examples enhanced your understanding of social innovation? If so, in what way?
3. Can we distinguish different forms of innovativeness?
4. Which power relations within the field have to be investigated further? Are they supportive or inhibitory in regard to social innovations? Is there any chance for new organizations to enter the market? What kind of barriers might these organizations face?
5. Often we found network approaches in the cases. What might a younger and smaller organization fear regarding a proposed cooperation with such a mature and big organization like the cases described above?
6. Risk is a very rare term used in the field of social innovation. What do you think: Is there a considerable amount of risk to be discussed in the field? What is the role of risk taking for social innovation in general? What types of risk would you differentiate?
7. Both examples above are Christian-based organizations. What is the influence of this Christian basis regarding innovativeness? What is the role of these incorporated religious values when an organization faces strong market forces and uncertainty? Is this value base an advantage or disadvantage in modern, secular times? Do market forces promote or inhibit social innovations?

REFERENCES

Backhaus-Maul, H., & Olk, T. (1994). Von Subsidiarität zu "out-contracting": Zum Wandel der Beziehungen zwischen Staat und Wohlfahrtsverbänden in der Sozialpolitik. In W. Streek (Ed.), *Staat und Verbände, Sonderheft 19 der Politischen Virteljahresschrift* (pp. 99–134). Opladen, Germany: Westdeutscher Verlag.

Boeßenecker, K.-H. (2005). *Spitzenverbände der freien Wohlfahrtspflege*. Weinheim and Munich, Germany: Juventa.

Bogumil, J., & Holtkamp, L. (2002). *Bürgerkommune konkret: Vom Leitbild zur Umsetzung*. Bonn, Germany: FES.

Curtis, T. (2008). Finding that grit makes a pearl: A critical re-reading of research into social enterprise. *International Journal of Entrepreneurial and Behaviour & Research, 14*(5), 276–290.

Greiner, L. E. (1972): Evolution and revolution as organizations grow. *Harvard Business Review, 50*(4), 37–46.

Kerlin, J. A., & Pollak, T. H. (2010). Nonprofit commercial revenue: A replacement for declining government grants and contributions? *American Review of Public Administration, 41*(6), 686–704.

Mair, J., & Martí, I. (2006). Social entrepreneurship research: A source of explanation, prediction, and delight. *Journal of World Business, 41*(1), 36–44.

Meyer, M. (2009). Wie viel Wirtschaft verträgt die Zivilgesellschaft? Über Möglichkeiten und Grenzen wirtschaftlicher Rationalität in NPOs. In I. Bode, A. Evers, & A. Klein (Eds.), *Bürgergesellschaft als Projekt* (pp. 127–144). Wiesbaden, Germany: Verlag für Sozialwissenschaften.

Priller, E., Alscher, M., Droß, P. J., Paul, F., Poldrack, C. J., Schmeißer, C., & Weitkus, N. (2012). *Dritte-Sektor-Organisationen heute: Eigene Ansprüche und ökonomische Herausforderungen: Ergebnisse einer Organisationsbefragung*. Discussion Paper SP IV 2012-402, Berlin, Germany: WZB. Retrieved from www.wzb.eu/org2011

Priller, E., & Zimmer, A. (2003). Dritte-Sektor-Organisationen zwischen "Markt" und "Mission." In D. Gosewinkel, D. Kocke, W. van den Daehle, & J. Rucht (Eds.), *Zivilgesellschaft: National und transnational* (pp. 105–127). Berlin, Germany: Wissenschaftszentrum Berlin für Sozialforschung.

Pümpin, C., & Prange, J. (1991): *Management der Unternehmensentwicklung. Phasengerechte Führung und der Umgang mit Krisen*. New York, NY: Campus Verlag.

Schmitz, B., & Scheuerle, T. (2012). Founding or transforming? Social intrapreneurship in three German Christian-based NPOs. *Journal of Social Entrepreneurship Perspectives, 1*(1), 13–36.

Seibel, W. (2002). Das Spannungsfeld zwischen "Mission" und "Ökonomie" im Nonprofit-Sektor—Eine organisationstheoretische Einordnung. In R. Schauer, R. Purtschert, & D. Witt (Eds.), *Nonprofit-Organisationen und gesellschaftliche Entwicklung: Spannungsfeld zwischen Mission und Ökonomie* (pp. 15–37). Linz, Austria: Trauner.

Thränhardt, D. (2003). Engagement und Effizienz: Wohlfahrtsverbände im Wandel. In W. Lange & U. Hunger (Eds.), *Wohlfahrtsverbände im Wandel: Qualitätsmanagement und Professionalisierung* (pp. 7–19). Münster, Germany: Civil Society Network.

Vilain, M. (2002). *Nonprofit management: Current challenges for personnel management in German welfare organisations*. Retrieved from http://www.stiftungsverbund-westfalen.de/download/Vilain_Nonprofit-Management_-_Current%20Challenges.pdf

Weisbrod, B. A. (Ed.). (1998). *To profit or not to profit: The commercial transformation of the nonprofit sector*. Cambridge, United Kingdom: Cambridge University Press.

Ziegler, R. (2009). Introduction: Voices, preconditions, contexts. In R. Ziegler (Ed.), *An introduction to social entrepreneurship: Voices, preconditions, contexts* (pp. 1–20). Cheltenham, United Kingdom: Edward Elgar.

Zimmer, A., Gärtner, J., Priller, E., Rawert, P., Sachße, C., & Graf Strachwitz, R. (2004). The legacy of subsidiarity: The nonprofit sector in Germany. In A. Zimmer & E. Priller (Eds.), *Future of civil society: Making central European nonprofit organizations work* (pp. 681–711). Wiesbaden, Germany: VS-Verlag.

Zimmer, A., & Toepler, S. (2000). Government policy and future issues: Federal Republic of Germany. In A. Zimmer (Ed.), *The third sector in Germany. Münsteraner Diskussionspapiere zum Nonprofit-Sektor* (pp. 23–79). Retrieved from http://www.aktive-buergerschaft.de/fp_files/Diskussionspapiere/2002wp-sband03.pdf

CHAPTER 21

Lessons Learned

Themes Observed From Successful Nonprofit Social Innovations

Diane Vinokur-Kaplan

School of Social Work University of Michigan

Ram A. Cnaan

University of Pennsylvania

INTRODUCTION

We wish to encourage nonprofit innovation, so in this volume we have presented a wide array of examples of successful innovative nonprofits in the United States and abroad. We have included those that start new organizations, those that innovate internally, and those that innovate through collaboration. In this concluding chapter, we discuss selected themes that have emerged from the various cases and provide the reader with a basic understanding of what it takes to be innovative. We organize our discussion using a systems theory approach and adopting a logic model framework including resources, activities (often called *process*), output, outcome, and impact that is further explained below[1] (cf. W. K. Kellogg Foundation, 2004). We acknowledge that this linear sequence of the logic model does not adequately reflect the complexity, backtracking, and new iterations that often occur in social innovations, but it is used as a heuristic device to organize our findings.

As we discussed in the introductory chapter, for us, nonprofit innovation is a wide field of planned social or organizational change that has an impact on quality of life and the

[1] We acknowledge that other various conceptual frameworks used in the organizational change literature could be applied fruitfully to the topic of social innovation, such as life cycle, teleological, and dialectical (e.g., see Hickman, 2010, Table II.1). We chose a logic model approach (cf. W. K. Kellogg Foundation, 2004), based on systems theory, given its simplicity and widespread use in applied social disciplines. Also, it somewhat parallels the claims-invention-implementation-diffusion model of social innovation earlier discussed by Schmitz in Chapter 2.

public good.[2] Further, we noted that social innovation starts with what Björn Schmitz called a *claim* in Chapter 2, that is, with a great idea about a problem or an issue that is either ignored or underserved (Amabile, Conti, Coon, Lazenby, & Herron, 1996). However, such claims or ideas alone are never enough; they are prerequisites that are insufficient without action and implementation. Many socially good ideas are conceived all the time by many people, but they are soon forgotten or are not brought to fruition. While creativity is strongly reflected in the production of novel and useful ideas, social innovation reflects *the successful implementation* of creative ideas within an organization, a community, or society.

The socially innovative idea needs one or more champions who advocate for it and persuade others of its relevance and contribution to individuals and the public good. The champion (or champions) of this initial idea faces hard work and should expect to spend much time and energy on marketing the innovation and bringing it to fruition. Hence, social innovation is the combination of a creative idea and proponents investing numerous hours, resources, and skills to have the idea become a reality. Such prolonged effort was shown in all the chapters herein.

In addition, for an innovative idea to succeed, it must arise at the right time and place. In many of the cases in this book and elsewhere, success was only possible because it was adequately consonant with current organizational-socio-political-cultural-technological conditions or responsive to relevant changes therein. Even when the innovative idea is consonant at the outset, the first attempt(s) to apply it might not succeed. The proponent(s) can make strategic mistakes that can derail the innovative idea. But often, the proponents fight back and overcome these mistakes as in such cases as HelpHOPELive. When mistakes were not made early on, there are still many subsequent challenges to successful implementation of any innovation—as there are with any complex project—and those advocating for the innovation have to face many decisions along the way.

We also found that no change was implemented independently by a solo social entrepreneur. In all cases, the person(s) behind the innovation had to recruit financial and political support, volunteers, and people who believed in the innovation. Finally, we found that while the innovation may be large-scale and comprehensive, it must also be pointedly focused. Successful nonprofit innovations were those whose missions were explained cogently and communicated easily with others.

The following sections address the themes we identified while reading the various cases in this volume, and they correspond to our understanding of essential components for successful nonprofit innovation. These are not specific *guidelines* as have been found in the world of business (cf. Harvard Business Review, 2011); rather these themes are *guideposts* that represent a conceptual summary of these nonprofit cases and notable issues to think about when contemplating nonprofit innovation. In each section of the framework, we present the relevant themes and illustrate them with a few examples from the cases that compose the majority of the book. We assume that people will read this chapter after having read the cases and will be familiar with them. As such, we only note the cases. The themes are clear even without the examples, but the cases are referenced for a more meaningful reading.

---

[2] For our purposes here, social change is conceived of as an unplanned macro process, while social innovation is characterized by planfulness and follow-through (cf. Schmitz, Ch. 2). They can certainly influence one another. We also realize that certain literatures use such terms as *social change agent* instead of *social innovator* or *social entrepreneur*.

INPUTS

This section notes characteristics of both individuals and the social environment that seem critical to begin the process of social innovation. They include the necessary human, financial, organizational, and community resources directed toward the work (cf. W. K. Kellogg Foundation, 2004, p. 2).

1. Change Agents With Alternative Visions

In almost all instances, social innovation begins with passionate, committed individuals who see something that most others fail to see. Some of them are people with prior experience of social innovation, as in the case of Resto VanHarte. Many, however, are people who observed a problem and decided to invest their time, money, and energy to better solve it. In other words, innovation does not happens on its own; it needs an agent (or agents) who have an alternative vision of how things should be to champion them.

These agents are particular people who, under various circumstances may become innovators. The couple who championed HelpHOPELive was a husband and wife who were a cardiologist and a nurse; the duo who started the Welfare Reform Liaison Project was a professor of social work and a reverend—all people with many other obligations. However, each perceived a need or a solution to a need, or a means to make things significantly more efficient, effective, just, or sustainable, and each set out to actualize their vision.

While many people come up with ideas, fewer carry them through to the next stage. These successful social entrepreneurs are passionate and committed, but most of all they persevere. Where most people would give up, these innovation agents keep pushing and trying. Their commitment to the desired change is serious, and they are willing to invest the work required to bring about a change. We saw this type of dedication in the Dialog in the Dark case. When Andreas Heinecke, a German radio personality, had an accomplished intern who was blind and more than talented in the field, he came to realize that blind people do not get a fair chance in society. This realization propelled him to change people's perspectives about blind people and to start Dialogue in the Dark, an experience where being blind is an advantage. As the author of this case wrote: "Its founder, Andreas Heinecke, was committed to change the social perception of 'otherness' toward a competence-oriented view by demonstrating that blind people have strengths and competencies, which allow them to do things that even seeing people cannot do." In so doing, Andreas Heinecke became a social innovator.

Similarly, in the case of New York City's Nonprofit Initiative, which increased collaboration between government and nonprofit organizations in the human service delivery system, two change agents recognized their mutual frustrations in this field. Marla Gibson's background in the nonprofit sector and Linda I. Gibbs's role in the mayor's office made them an effective duo to combat this problem, and together they spearheaded the effort to make government-nonprofit collaboration more than just a lofty idea. Likewise, in the case of the Social Innovation Foundation (SZIA as it is known in Hungary), the founding members were all social scientists who cared about the quality of social care in post-Communist Hungary.

They joined together to form a nonprofit organization that would serve as a catalyst to promote quality of care standards.

Some social innovators were directly affected by the problem that the nonprofit aims to solve. There were people like Kristin Heying, who moved to Portland, Oregon, and found that single mothers like her had no space to meet. She came up with the idea of Café au Play to solve this problem. There were also people who were not directly affected by welfare reform, like Bob Wineburg and Odell Cleveland, but nevertheless developed a welfare-to-work project for poor, unemployed men and women. Similarly, Adi Altschuler established Krembo Wings for disabled youth. The latter individuals were not solving a problem that plagued them personally but rather tackling a communal problem about which they cared. In both cases, passion and human caring were the foundation of the nonprofit innovation.

As the case studies unfolded, it became clear that in each of them, a person or a small group of people were behind the innovation. We could not find specific characteristics of these change agents. Most innovators had no previous experience in innovation, some were mature and some very young, and some were professionals, while others were novices. Most came from middle class backgrounds, but this is not true for them all. It seems that most of all what made them innovators was their commitment to the change they championed and the people it represented. They are all people who would not take "no" for an answer and exhibited passion coupled with relentlessness. It seems that the phase of taking an idea into action demands such devotion.

2. Single-Minded Focus and Expression of the Social Innovation

A key challenge for any nonprofit organization is to maintain a clear focus on solving a specific problem at hand, while still adopting a holistic approach to the problem. Often the temptation to expand beyond one clear goal or mission is irresistible, and organizations lose both focus and efficacy by taking on too much. By the same token, people who can come up with creative and innovative ideas sometimes produce too many new ideas, often making them complicated and too difficult to follow. However, in successful cases, the basic innovative idea is often quite simple and easy to express, even though its implementation is often a complex process that requires some adaptation. Indeed, at times when other people are introduced to the innovative idea, their first response is: "Why didn't somebody think of it earlier?" If the basic idea is too complicated or cannot be clearly communicated, it makes recruiting supporters, raising funds, and implementing it very difficult, and it increases the chances for failure.

Seacology provides a clear example of adopting a holistic approach to island conservation while remaining committed to their initial goal to orchestrate localized projects. As discussed in Chapter 10, many attempts at preservation take a heavy-handed approach, with governments or organizations buying up large tracts of land and deeming them reserves. While this strategy is swift and might result in higher short-term impact, Seacology resists such a top-down approach. By remaining committed to individualized projects that incorporate local populations, Seacology both ensures greater long-term preservation and avoids the type of mission creep that would render their organization less effective.

In the case of Café au Play, recognizing that single mothers have no place to meet and relax and that an accommodating nonprofit coffee shop could be the solution was again single-focused, elegant, and doable. In the case of Third Sector New England, the simple solution was to provide social justice nonprofit organizations with the modern space and range of technical sponsorship services they need to succeed (human resources, book keeping, insurance, auditing, etc.).

While a single-minded focus might seem limited to small scale organizations, this is not necessarily the case. In the example of the Center for Rural Development in Kentucky, tackling the problem of rural economic and educational deficiency requires a broad-scale, multifaceted approach. This innovation rested not in establishing another stand-alone agency to stimulate rural development in the Appalachia region, but rather in obtaining synergy by merging the existing resources and funds of many small nonprofit agencies to form the Center. By overcoming divisions and pooling resources, the Center has been better able to orchestrate the wide variety of programs and projects required to stimulate economic development on a regional scale. Similarly, in the case of The Mind Trust, the goal was broad and captured the transformation of the educational landscape in Indianapolis through initiating and promoting innovative educational initiatives. But this goal was also direct and singly focused on education.

In sum, what emerged is that the successful cases, both from the United States and from abroad, focused on one problem or one key organizational innovation. The innovation can be broad and implemented in various ways, but it seems that when the message can be explained and delivered simply and in a short time, the chances of success are much higher.

3. Adequately Conducive Ecology/Environment Surrounding the Social Innovation

Many individuals' ideas are ahead of their time and do not succeed to be implemented. For an idea to lead to an innovation, it must be grounded to some extent in its time, context, and social ecology. This understanding comes from the organizational theory literature that suggests that internal operations of organizations are directly impacted by, and respond to, external environmental factors (Drori, Meyer, & Hwang, 2006; Jones, 2006; Mulroy, 2004). This adaptation is especially true when there is change in the external environment (cf. Garrow & Hasenfeld, 2010). Put simply, changing economic, political, cultural, social, and technological landscapes create pressures and demands on all players to evolve, restructure, and change. In some cases, the response is the creation of an innovative nonprofit. As Shier and Handy noted in Chapter 7, the innovative nonprofit capitalizes on its current environment and proactively comes up with innovative solutions.

For example, an organization such as Seacology is unlikely to have existed in earlier times when environmentalism and nature preservation were not a public ideology and priority. Only in an era in which some segments of society are actively and publicly concerned with environmental degradation and the disappearance of many species can such an organization be likely to become successfully established. If it had been proposed and championed some years earlier, it probably would have been viewed as impractical and of low priority.

HelpHOPELive emerged with organ transplant. Only when this medical advancement became prevalent and the cost remained prohibitive was there room for an innovative organization that helped uninsured or underinsured people benefit from such treatments. Again, 20 years earlier, no such treatments existed and the need to ensure expensive medical care for all was less of an issue. This organization and its solution arose at an appropriate time.

In the case of GiveIndia, the rampant corruption, evolving information technology, and the rise in the number of rich people willing to donate to worthy nonprofit organizations created an environment in which GiveIndia emerged, again with an alternative vision. Using a web-based platform and a reliable method of auditing allowed GiveIndia to assure donors that their money would go to nonprofit organizations they want to support, and to have a measure of control over the use of the money. In societies with higher public trust or with a lower technological base, such an innovation would not have been applicable. It is the constellation of ecological forces that gave GiveIndia room to evolve and made it acceptable to many in Indian society.

In the case of the SZIA, it was clear that Hungary's transition from a Communist regime to a capitalist way of life created many challenges to individuals and to policy makers that required innovative solutions. Coupled with the willingness of Western European organizations to help, the support of the British Council provided the fertile ground in which SZIA emerged.

Similarly, as the founder of Resto VanHarte observed, when he returned to the Netherlands in 2000 after many years abroad, there had been a notable cultural and societal shift brought on by continuing modernization and technological innovation. In an aging and increasingly secularized and individualized Netherlands, there was a marked rise in social isolation and loneliness. This unique atmosphere spurred founder Fred Beekers into action, and it is only with this evolution in society that new organization battling loneliness could thrive.

Likewise, after the welfare reform act that passed under the Clinton administration in 1996, there was a new need to form local arrangements to help the poor transition from welfare to work. This was a nationwide challenge, and in many communities coalitions were formed and organizations were designated—yet very little innovation emerged. In Greensboro, North Carolina, a joint effort by one church and a school of social work used the new social environment to form an innovative service for people who wished to join the job market. This innovative Welfare Reform Liaison Project could not have existed before the 1996 legislation. However, this legislation changed the social ecology of welfare, and the people behind this project, using their own expertise, capitalized on this change.

While the respective environment is crucial in establishing a successful nonprofit innovation, it is difficult to predict changing ecologies and their impact on different locations. When circumstances are shifting and needs are changing, ideas about change arise. Times that are ripe with instability are often the best times to conceive an innovative idea and move forward with its implementation.

PROCESS

Once there is a dedicated individual or group with a vision of an alternative way that things could be, motivation to achieve it, and enough of a supportive environment for success, several steps or interventions are typically taken during the social innovation process, as shown in the case examples presented below. As Hartley, Sørensen, and

Torfing (2013) noted: "in order to avoid conflating innovation with creativity, we insist that innovation not only involves the generation but also the practical realization of new, creative ideas" (p. 822; see also, Damanpour, 1991; Van de Ven, 1986).

4. Wrong the First Time, but Resilient

An interesting theme present in many of the cases is that while an idea emerged and a serious attempt to actualize it followed, this first attempt was often futile, and even wrong, and implementation failed. In the case of HelpHOPELive, the founders attempted first to find support from large existing organizations, and when that effort failed, they decided to collaborate with a fundraiser. The fundraiser did not provide them with a fair share of the funds raised and also left them with a sizeable debt. In the case of Metro TeenAIDS (MTA) in Washington, DC, the leaders sought national AIDS organizations to come to their rescue before realizing that these organizations were reluctant to help.

Similarly, in the case of GiveIndia, the original idea was that the online donation platform be part of a bank's social responsibility program. The innovator, Venkat Krishna, initially planned that GiveIndia would be taken over by the ICICI Bank. He perceived it as an e-commerce platform to facilitate and transfer donations to local nongovernmental organizations through the bank. But after two years of fostering this relationship with ICICI Bank, GiveIndia instead became independent (although it still maintains a working relationship with ICICI Bank, particularly with its payroll donor program). Being an independent organization is an important part of the GiveIndia appeal, but it was definitely not the original intention of its leader.

Likewise, in the case of Seacology, adaptation was necessary after an initial model of island outreach failed. Initially, the organization was built around one project in one island nation; however, Seacology eventually found itself growing in size and funding. Thus, it began searching for other additional preservation opportunities. The California-based staff found they needed local representatives to advocate on behalf of Seacology, and they formed an Island Council composed of representatives from islands throughout the world. When this centralized model failed, the organization began hiring paid contractors from each nation to serve as local liaisons. Through trial and error, Seacology overcame issues of communication and cultural boundaries to develop their effective working model.

In the case of the Jungbu Foundation, the chapter's authors reported that when it was founded, the foundation intended to operate in a completely different direction than it eventually did. In their words:

> [A]t the beginning, like other Korean foundations that pursue a stable operation with general grant making for human service organizations, the Jungbu Foundation gave a higher priority to grant-making programs for social service agencies rather than support programs for helping professionals such as social workers. Because the community impacts that the founder expected were practically invisible with its grant-making programs for social service agencies, the Jungbu Foundation needed new alternatives.

Another organization that has evolved from its original model into a more efficient working model is Living Cities. Established as the National Community Development

Initiative (NCDI) in 1991, Living Cities has gone through three distinct phases of evolution in the past 30 years. The founders had to be willing to let their organization evolve from its initial narrow focus and "virtual" status into what it is today—one of the world's largest foundations and financial institutions. If these leaders had not recognized the merits of changing the agenda and expanding collaboration, Living Cities would not be the effective community development organization it is today.

Rarely were there cases in which the solution—how to implement the innovation—was clear from the beginning. Being wrong with the first attempt—or even the first few attempts–was quite common. In many of the cases, the path to a successful new nonprofit organization or a significant change in a nonprofit structure or operations came after a series of trials and errors. Usually, there was no clear linear path from the evolution of the idea to the successful innovation.

5. Hard Work & Perseverance

All the cases reported in this volume document successful nonprofit innovations that were achieved after years of hard work. There is no magic wand to wave in order to bring about immediate change. Once the idea is pronounced, the road to implementation is paved with hard work. For example, in the case of Metro TeenAIDS (MTA) in Washington, DC, once it was agreed that the organization should mix advocacy activities along with serving clients, the executive director and key staff members worked hard to locate reporters to write about the cause, to force their way to deliver messages to the various government offices, to attend community forums, and to keep delivering the message to anyone willing to listen. Similarly, it took 10 years for Third Sector New England to actualize and build its Nonprofit Center.

The leaders of the SZIA in Hungary are another good example of perseverance and hard work. As is detailed in Chapter 15, these volunteer leaders spent numerous hours, made endless calls and appeals, and withstood major political resistance and opposition. While their original idea was cemented in a pub in London, the implementation and sustenance of the organization required more work and commitment than anyone could have imagined.

6. Recruitment of Supporters

An idea for nonprofit innovation may be the product of one person or a small group, but the execution of the idea and bringing it to life takes a large number of people, especially when its scale is large. Each social innovator in these cases was supported by a group of colleagues or people who were recruited to the task. In existing nonprofit organizations that underwent an innovative change, staff and board members were recruited to support the innovation. In such cases, the innovator was not only supported but also both challenged and nurtured by others in the organization.

For example in the case of MTA, the agency director Adam Tenner was encouraged by key board members and funders to become an advocate. It was ultimately his decision, but without a network of advisors and supporters, he could not have added advocacy to the agency's core activities. Tenner also managed to recruit *The Washington Post* to write an article about youth and AIDS that helped champion the agency's cause and bring other supporters. The authors of this case also report that in the mid-2000s, MTA found an ally in a School Board member, and together they launched a sustained effort to bring much-needed, systemic change to HIV/AIDS programs in the District's public school system.

In the cases of the formation of new nonprofit organizations, the founders could not undertake their task alone. They had to recruit supporters, find volunteers or staff, advocate for their idea, and collaborate with others as needed. Seacology again serves as an effective model because their bold idea for international grassroots preservation was not only radical, but also expensive. To fund their local projects, Seacology sought out potential wealthy donors to take trips to the project sites and witness the positive impact of the organization on the local culture and society. These firsthand experiences bred understanding and commitment to the organization, and thus they widened Seacology's net of advocates and financial support.

The more radical and new the idea behind a new nonprofit organization, the more many supporters need to be recruited. In the case of the Welfare Reform Liaison Project, the host agency (Mt. Zion Church) and outside grants helped develop a fiscal foundation, and allowing local churches to join the effort yielded thousands of hours of volunteering. Most important for the Welfare Reform Liaison Project was its collaboration with the local United Way, which opened the door for getting access to contributed in-kind goods and distributing them to other nonprofits for an administrative fee. Without this wide network of supporters, even the best idea could have failed.

In the case of The Mind Trust in Indianapolis, it was clear from the outset that neither this organization nor other local organizations alone could solve the educational problems that city faced. As such, the Mind Trust invested in attracting nationally established educational reform organizations to Indianapolis and providing them with ongoing support. They recruited and collaborated with such organizations as: Teach for America, Indianapolis Teaching Fellows, College Summit, and Stand for Children. Each of these organizations provided a needed expertise, and together they helped support the mission of The Mind Trust.

In the case of Café au Play, the organization secured its location through collaboration with a community association and its president, and it was rescued financially when a local chef helped put together an auction dinner event. As the author of Chapter 7 stated:

> Every successful business, nonprofit or social enterprise knows that their survival depends on their personal and organizational networks that can be mobilized for information and support. We have learned that the embeddedness of an organization in these networks increases with the number of times they are activated and the trust that is built from successful engagement and visible accomplishment (Granovetter, 1985). We have learned that the most powerful relationships are those that evolve over time into multistrand linkages of mutual support.

In the case of Dialogue in the Dark, the founder Andreas Heinecke was first employed by the major German nonprofit organization for the blind, the Stiftung Blindenanstalt. His first exhibition in the dark was supported by and housed at this organization. Soon after, when he decided to expand Dialogue in the Dark as a separate organization and to open additional exhibitions, he started to collaborate with other organizations and received financial support from various sources. They included government grants to train blind people, and corporate partners that supported the organization as part of their corporate social responsibility. Later on, to institutionalize the innovation, Heinecke looked for groups that were willing to do Dialogue in the Dark on their own and worked with them as social franchises. All along, the Dialogue in the Dark sought partners, supporters, and people to replicate the model.

Any person or group of people who contemplates innovation in nonprofit organizations ought to be prepared to work with many people and to be able to recruit support. The innovative idea needs allies, and the implementation needs people who will advocate for it and help carry it out. Not the least is the need to secure funds for the initial idea and for new developments. Funding often must come from such sources as foundations, government, corporations, and individuals. Networking with these sources and recruiting their commitment to establish the innovation's legitimacy is an essential part of the innovation process. A written report, as brilliant as it may be, is worthless without many partners and staff committed to implement it. At times, there is a need to raise funds and/or secure permits from various government units, and in all these cases the more supporters and collaborators, the better the chance for success.

7. Leadership

As mentioned above, hard work is a necessary but insufficient component of nonprofit innovation; one can work very hard but ineffectively and thus reach nowhere. Once social change agents make a commitment to investing hard work into their projects, leadership skills are required for success. Leadership is one of those concepts that have numerous definitions and variations. It is a topic that has been widely written about and widely researched. For the purpose of this chapter, we refer to a person's ability to cause others to support and follow his or her direction. A leader who is behind a nonprofit innovation is someone with a vision, willing to work, and capable of making others join and act in accordance with that vision.

For example, in the case of MTA in Washington, DC, we are told that:

> Tenner grew up in New Jersey, attended college in New York, and then moved west to begin his professional career in Seattle in 1992 as an outreach worker in a homeless youth organization. Because of his leadership skills, he was director of the program 5 years later.

Tenner came to the organization when it was in fiscal debt and introduced measures that were respected by board members, staff, and collaborating organizations. It was this leadership that enabled him to lead the change from a strictly service organization to a mix of advocacy and service. Following his leadership, the staff members internalized the innovation and identified with it.

The same is true regarding The Mind Trust in Indianapolis. The director, David Harris, was one of the mayor's policy advisors and a capable leader. Using his leadership skills, he managed to build a coalition around the educational mission, obtain large grants, and champion an impressive educational reform. Recruiting many influential people in Indianapolis and elsewhere to believe in and support his vision is emblematic of his effective leadership skills. People followed Harris' agenda and accepted him as a leader.

In the case of The Welfare Reform Liaison Project, founder Odell Cleveland had years of experience both running companies and being a religious leader. He immediately assumed the role of a leader. He made himself known to all the players in town and was able to negotiate with various public and private organizations. Cleveland's skills and reputation as a leader helped rally the community behind their organization, and this was crucial in making the innovation possible and successful.

In contrast to this project, in the case of Krembo Wings, 16-year-old founder Adi Altschuler's youth and inexperience did not prevent her from being an effective leader. In fact, in the early years of the organization, Adi was able to act as a young, bold entrepreneur who could get away with taking risks on behalf of her organization, such as confronting the mayor in a public place to get his support. While this approach would likely have been beneath an experienced entrepreneur, Adi took the risk and was seen as courageous and charming, and even became a symbol of the ideal Israeli youth. Krembo Wings and Adi herself gained public support, legitimacy, and funding, and she led the organization through two formative periods of evolution. Her case is a testament to the fact that unlikely leaders can become champions of their innovative ideas if they have the passion and tenacity to see it through, as Adi did.

In sum, to increase the probability of success, the leaders/social entrepreneurs must often double check and reassess their ideas, and if needed, redirect their ideas or the methods they used to implement them. The leaders are responsible to make sure they have a program that can succeed and will not cause harm to the clients or damage to the cause. MacMillan and Thompson (2014) call this leadership responsibility "the tough-love test," that is, the leader who is enamored with her plan of action must be strong enough to frequently reassess its actual feasibility, and, if so needed,, terminate it in order to significantly revise the plan to gain future success.

8. Ongoing Challenges

Those who spearhead an innovative project or an innovative nonprofit organization must be ready to face new challenges and crises as they arise. A successful step forward does not preclude the formation of a new crisis. The ability to overcome these challenges and crises is an essential factor in nonprofit innovation.

Charles Heying, in the chapter on Café au Play, wrote the following:

> No organization succeeds without encountering both minor and major crises. A resilient organization manages the crises and learns from them; a brittle organization will stumble and possibly fail. Café au Play has encountered two major crises: the first was an event that precipitated a change in board procedures; the second has been an ongoing financial struggle that became a full-blown crisis in the summer of 2012. From the second crisis we learned the limits of our revenue model and the need, even for a social enterprise, for effective fundraising strategies that build on organizational strengths.

Another example of a nonprofit facing ongoing challenges can be found in the case of Resto VanHarte. While the community restaurants host dining events to counter the rising social problem of loneliness in the Netherlands, it is important to the organization's mission that the events are attended by a broad audience of "lonely" people rather than a singular, small group of regular diners. Striking this balance is complex, because Resto VanHarte must not only be an occasional haven for the lonely;, it also must reach a broader community in order to be effective . Furthermore, because the meals served are quite affordable, healthy, and substantial, Resto VanHarte has to stay true to its mission of countering loneliness and avoid becoming simply a provider of cheap meals for the local poor. This is an ongoing challenge that the organization copes with any time a meal is planned and advertised.

Not only do new and emergent nonprofits face ongoing challenges. In Chapter 20, Björn Schmitz demonstrates that innovation is not only possible for formative or new organizations, but also within mature, well-established nonprofit organizations. However, this type of social intrapreneurship brings a set of ongoing challenges unique to mature organizations. Nonprofits and social welfare organizations that were founded prior to the modern era—such as Germany's Hephata, which was founded in 1859—have faced the necessity of altering their model to keep up with evolving social needs. However, the need to innovate and be flexible can be discouraged by long-existing bureaucratic procedures for decision making. Such rigid organizational structures and traditions can make it difficult to actualize necessary partnerships with far younger, more flexible organizations.

In sum, an idea alone is insufficient, and a long process of implementation is required for the idea to become a successful reality. However, even when the implementation process is in full force, new challenges and new crises are bound to appear. Nonprofit innovation requires the ability to face such negative developments with leadership and to solve these issues, while moving forward with the innovation.

9. Facing Resistance

Not all innovations are widely accepted. Often when an innovation is proposed or even introduced, other organizations stand to lose and accordingly amass opposition. The opposition can come from various sources and take many faces. Change is a frightening process, and people's usual intention is to avoid change. In many of the cases discussed in this volume, the resistance was not overt and was only mentioned in passing.

The case of the SZIA is a good example of facing resistance, with the resistance coming from many parts of society. While the new nonprofit organization was hailed for its development of service standards for the social welfare sector and the nonprofit sector, it also encountered major resistance from several sources. Nonprofit organizations publicly accepted the new standards but privately refused to implement them. The government was sympathetic to SZIA and appreciated their developed standards, but refused to make them official. Then, a subsequent new government wanted SZIA to go away, and it cut its support for the organization. Still, SZIA found ways to survive.

For mature organizations seeking to begin employing their new model or to start new projects, resistance to such innovation takes a different form,, as explained by Björn Schmitz in Chapter 20. Inside players in the organization, such as colleagues, other departments, and older employees, may perceive the innovation as wrong or perceive it as being done at their expense, and thus may mount an opposition (Oreg, 2006; Piderit, 2000). For example, the German organizations Hephata and Stiftung Liebenau were each founded in the mid-to-late 19th century, and as such have been members of a long-established social welfare climate. In their desire to innovate and to alter their approach to social welfare, mature organizations such as these change the climate in effect for all the other welfare organizations in the welfare system. As a result of being a new proactive force, they risked backlash and resistance from other mature organizations that may not be as willing to change.

In sum, whether new or mature, innovative nonprofits usually attract a large amount of resistance and find their survival at risk. Many of the studied organizations were or are at such risk, and they continually faced resistance and competition. Unfortunately, when discussing and planning an innovation, the resistance of the competing organizations and opposing forces are often forgotten. In many of the chapters in this volume, such challenges are obvious and make the understanding of nonprofit innovation more real and less idealized.

10. Demonstration of Measurable Outputs

Outputs are the direct products of the social innovation's process and may include types, levels, and targets of services delivered by it (cf. W. K. Kellogg Foundation, 2004, p. 2). In other words, one is seeing the accomplishments or "deliverables" of the intervention's activities.

The successful social innovation should have some kind of measurable outputs that demonstrate the accomplishments of its goals and objectives. This volume presents a wide array of the different types of outputs that nonprofits can produce. Some of the cases directly describe them and others allude to them. Ideally, some would objectively measure the services that are now provided, such as summarizing the hours provided by the different services that the YMCA has produced, and the numbers of people it has served over its long history, or count up the meals served and programs delivered by Resto Van Harte. Others would look at the financial resources that the nonprofit obtained, such as at HelpHOPELive, Living Cities, and GiveIndia, or the physical spaces built for nonprofits by Third Sector New England and the Center for Rural Development. Still others could describe the organizational innovations they produced, such as the advocacy activities developed by Metro Teen AIDS, or the collaborative meetings between government and nonprofits regarding the contracting system in New York City. Such outputs give credibility to the innovation, and they show that innovative actions have taken place.

OUTCOMES AND IMPACTS OF NONPROFIT SOCIAL INNOVATIONS

Outcomes represent the specific changes in the behavior, knowledge, skills, status, and level of functioning of individuals and organizations that have undergone social innovation. Usually, outcomes measure short-term, mid-term, and long-term changes in the well-being of individuals, (See Knowlton & Phillips, 2009, p. 45), and the degree of positive movement toward the accomplishment of the nonprofit's mission. Following such outcomes is impact, " the ultimate intended change in an organization, community, or other system" (Knowlton & Phillips, p. 38). For example, an educational public health program might seek the impact of improved health in a community. Its resources, activities and outputs might produce outcomes of greater health knowledge and awareness among citizens in the short term, enhance their skill and motivation in the midterm, and increase their strength, endurance, and healthier eating and exercise habits in the long-term. (See Knowlton & Phillips, p. 40). Thus, in the end, the desired impact of improved health has been ultimately achieved.

According to the W. K. Kellogg Foundation (2004),

> [s]hort-term outcomes should be attainable within 1 to 3 years, while longer-term outcomes should be achievable within a 4 to 6 year timeframe. The logical progression from short-term to long-term outcomes should be reflected in impact occurring within about 7 to 10 years. *Impact* is the fundamental intended or unintended change occurring in organizations, communities or systems as a result of program activities within 7 to 10 years. (p. 2)

11. Development of Measurable Outcomes and Impacts of Nonprofit Social Innovations

The cases in this volume have sought to achieve positive outcomes and notable impacts on their target populations and organizations, and ultimately on their communities and societies. They include: diminished loneliness through Café Au Play, Resto Van Harte, and Krembo Wings, thus increasing personal well-being and improving the quality of community life and social integration; improved quality of work life for nonprofit employees and ultimately their communities, as shown in the cases of the Center for Rural Development, Third Sector New England, the Jungbu Foundation, and the New York City contracting collaborative; and aspects of improved quality of life among individuals and communities served by the YMCA, Metro Teen AIDS, Living Cities, Dialogue in the Dark, GiveIndia, SZIA, Hephata and the Liebenau Foundation, Seacology, HelpHOPELive, The Mind Trust, and the Welfare Reform Liaison Project. Some of the social innovations studied herein are too new for their impacts to be established, but their trajectories are positive; the older cases have already displayed the impacts they have wrought. It is because of these often underpublicized accomplishments that we wrote this book.

SUMMARY AND CONCLUSIONS

As we noted above, the distance between a creative idea and the implementation of an actual innovation represents a long and arduous road. What we aimed to do in this chapter is to look critically at the many cases of nonprofit innovation that we have assembled and elicit commonalities. We have also tried to illustrate the positive difference that these organizations have actualized around the world.

We entered the process of writing this last chapter with an open mind and with no preplan. We allowed the cases and the stories behind them to dictate the themes herein and the logic model conceptual framework. After reading the chapters a few times and knowing them quite well, the themes emerged by themselves. We did not turn to other sources to guide us and shape our findings. The themes were there and obvious to any interested reader. We hope that we managed to unravel the most significant ones and that we did not miss any other important ones.

Readers can use this systems model and the themes to analyze these cases or other cases of nonprofit innovations not included in this volume. As noted above, the recurring themes in these cases of nonprofit innovations were as follows:

A. Inputs:

(1) There exists a social change agent(s) with an alternative vision of how things can be

(2) The expressed change may be large-scale and comprehensive, but it should also be single-focused and easily expressed

(3) Necessary attention is given to an adequately conducive ecology/environment surrounding the social innovation

B. Process:

(4) Resilience is relied upon to correct mistakes in the early stages of implementation

(5) Hard Work and Perseverance prevail

(6) The need to recruit others to support politically, emotionally, and fiscally is recognized and implemented

(7) Leadership is taken

(8) Ongoing challenges are met

(9) Resistance is faced and overcome

C. Outputs:

(10) Measurable outputs are demonstrated

D. Outcomes:

(11) Measurable outcomes and impacts of nonprofit social innovations are explained.

It is obviously easier to analyze these recurring themes in nonprofit innovation than to carry them out. Even a cursory look at the above list of themes indicates that initiating nonprofit innovation requires vision, and it is a long process that demands perseverance and the willingness to be adaptable and collaborative without losing sight of the end goal. This list, however, should not discourage people from coming up with creative ideas and making the effort to implement them; it is through such actions that the nonprofit world can better serve the public good.

Indeed, regardless of the enormity of the innovation process, we hope that this book as a whole, and this chapter in particular, will help readers think critically about nonprofit innovations and see them as desirable. For those who read the book from the vantage point of working in foundations or organizational headquarters, this volume and this chapter seek to help them see the merit of nonprofit innovation and encourage them to support new innovation quests. All in all, let the spirit of nonprofit innovation be celebrated and bring our world new, effective responses to our pressing needs.

REFERENCES

Amabile, T. M., Conti, R., Coon, H., Lazenby, J., & Herron, M. (1996). Assessing the work environment for creativity. *Academy of Management Journal, 39*(5), 1154–1184.

Damanpour, F. (1991). Organization innovation: A meta-analysis of effects of determinants and moderators. *Academy of Management Journal, 34*(3), 555–590.

Drori, G. S., Meyer, J. W., & Hwang, H. (Eds.). (2006). *Globalization and organization: World society and organizational change*. Oxford, United Kingdom: Oxford University Press.

Garrow, E., & Hasenfeld Y. (2010). "Contingency theory" in theoretical approaches to human service organizations. In Y. Hasenfeld (Ed.), *Human services as complex organizations* (pp. 37–38). Thousand Oaks, CA: Sage.

Hartley, J., Sørensen, E., & Torfing, J. (2013). Collaborative innovation: A viable alternative to market-competition and organizational entrepreneurship. *Public Administration Review, 73*(6), 821–830.

Harvard Business Review. (2011). *Inspiring and executing innovation*. Boston, MA: Harvard Business School Publishing Corporation.

Hickman, G. R. (2010). *Leading change in multiple contexts: Concepts and practices in organizational, community, political, social, and global change settings*. Thousand Oaks, CA: Sage.

Jones, J. M. (2006). Understanding environmental influence on human service organizations: A study of the influence of managed care on child caring institutions. *Administration in Social Work, 30*(4), 63–90.

Knowlton, L. W. & Phillips, C. C. (2009). *The logic model guidebook: Better strategies for great results.* Thousand Oaks, CA: SAGE.

MacMillan, I. C., & Thompson, J. D. (2014). *The social entrepreneur's playbook, expanded edition: Pressure test, plan, launch and scale your social enterprise* [E-reader version]. Philadelphia, PA: Wharton Digital Press.

Mulroy, E. A. (2004). Theoretical perspectives on the social environment to guide management and community practice: An organization-in-environment approach. *Administration in Social Work, 28*(1), 77–96.

Oreg, S. (2006). Personality, context and resistance to organizational change. *European Journal of Work and Organizational Psychology, 15*, 73–101.

Piderit, S. K. (2000). Rethinking resistance and recognizing ambivalence: A multidimensional view of attitudes toward an organizational change. *Academy of Management Review, 25*(4), 783–794.

Van de Ven, A. H. (1986). Central problems in the management of innovation. *Management Science, 32*(5), 590–607.

W. K. Kellogg Foundation. (2004). *Logic model development guide*. Battle Creek, MI: W. K. Kellogg Foundation.

About the Authors

Alan J. Abramson is a professor in the Department of Public and International Affairs at George Mason University and the founding director of Mason's Center on Nonprofit Management, Philanthropy, and Policy. Alan is also a Senior Fellow at the Aspen Institute and an Affiliated Scholar at the Urban Institute. He is the author and coauthor of numerous books and papers, and his work has twice won awards from the American Political Science Association. Alan received his PhD in political science from Yale University and his BA from Wesleyan University.

Michal Almog-Bar, PhD, is a lecturer (assistant professor) at the Paul Baerwald School of Social Work and Social Welfare, The Hebrew University of Jerusalem. Her research focuses on nonprofit organizations and their relations with government, philanthropic foundations, advocacy activities of human service organizations, and cross-sector partnerships.

Lehn M. Benjamin is an associate professor of Philanthropic Studies at the Lilly Family School of Philanthropy, Indiana University. Her research focuses on nonprofit performance, and she has published a number of articles on this topic. Her most recent project focuses on the work of frontline staff.

Wolfgang Bielefeld is Professor Emeritus at the School of Public and Environmental Affairs and the Lilly Family School of Philanthropy at Indiana University-Purdue University Indianapolis. He has also taught at the University of Texas at Dallas, the University of Minnesota, and Stanford University. In addition to social entrepreneurship, his research interests include the relations between nonprofit organizations and their environments and the dynamics of the nonprofit sector. He has authored numerous articles and coauthored a number of books, including *Managing Nonprofit Organizations; Nonprofit Organizations in an Age of Uncertainty;* and *Social Entrepreneurship: An Evidence-Based Approach to Creating Social Value*.

Odell Cleveland was the founder, President, and CEO of the Welfare Reform Liaison Project, Greensboro North Carolina, a project birthed out of the spiritual womb of Mt. Zion Baptist Church, in Greensboro, NC. Welfare Reform Liaison Project was Reverend Cleveland's outreach ministry of the church and the crown jewel of Mt. Zion's reach into the community. In February 2013, with the retirement of Bishop George W. Brooks of Mt. Zion, Reverend Cleveland was called back to the church to be its Chief Administrative Officer and face of the church in the broader community. He left Welfare Reform Liaison Project in the black financially and on solid footing in the community.

Ram A. Cnaan is a professor and director of the Program for Religion and Social Policy Research, as well as the faculty director of the Goldring Reentry Initiative at the School of Social Policy & Practice of the University of Pennsylvania. He is also a Global Eminent Scholar: Kyung Hee University, Graduate Institute for Peace Studies. Dr. Cnaan served as the president of ARNOVA (Association for Research on Nonprofit Organizations and Voluntary Action), and he studies volunteerism, religious social services, international social development, prisoner reentry, and social welfare policies.

Femida Handy is a professor at the University of Pennsylvania's School of Social Policy & Practice. She has published on various aspects of the economics of the nonprofit sector. Her current research includes global philanthropy, environmental philanthropy, social economy, and substitution between paid and volunteer labor. She is currently the editor-in-chief of *Nonprofit and Voluntary Sector Quarterly*.

Gábor Hegyesi is Professor Emeritus of Social Work at Eötvös Loránd University, Budapest, Hungary, where he served as the Head of the Department of Social Work for 20 years. He was one of the founders of the first nonstatutory social services in Hungary as early as 1982. Also, he served as the founding president of the Hungarian Association of Nonprofit Human Services for four terms (1992–2004). He is still serving in various roles in many nonprofit organizations. He has more than 100 publications. He received an award from the President of Hungary for his professional and nonprofit activities in 2005.

Charles Heying is Associate Professor of Urban Studies and Planning at Portland State University. He has coauthored a book and numerous articles on the politics and development of Olympic cities. Professor Heying's current research combines his interest in the arts with his passion for community-based economic development. His book, *Brew to Bikes: Portland's Artisan Economy*, describes how the transformation from an industrial to a postindustrial economy is being articulated in the trendsetting edges of Portland's artisan production. He has served on the board of Southeast Uplift Neighborhood Coalition and is a founding board member of Café au Play, a nonprofit community center coffee shop now operating in southeast Portland.

Henry Jones is the Communications Assistant at Seacology and a resident of Oakland, California. He holds master's degrees from UC Berkeley in Journalism and International and Area Studies.

Chulhee Kang, PhD, is a professor of Social Welfare and serves as the director of the Center for Social Welfare Research at Yonsei University in Seoul, Korea. He received his BA in theology from Yonsei University and his PhD in social welfare from the University of Pennsylvania. Chulhee Kang's research focuses on philanthropy and nonprofit organizations. He teaches courses in charity and philanthropy, management in NPOs, foundation, resource development in NPOs, social entrepreneurship and social enterprise, and research methodology in social science. He is currently the editor of *Korean Journal of Social Welfare Research* and previously served as the editor of both the Korean Journal of *Social Welfare* and the Journal of Korean Social Welfare Administration. In addition to his services as an editor, he has worked as a board member of several nonprofit organizations, including Korean Community Chest, the Jungbu Foundation, and ARNOVA.

Sangchul Lee, PhD, is an assistant professor of social welfare at Dong Seoul College. He received his BA in sociology and MA in psychology from Sungkyunkwan University and his PhD in social welfare from Yonsei University. Sangchul Lee's research focuses on human resource management in nonprofit organizations. He is a member of the Korean Academy of Social Welfare, Academy of Korean Social Welfare Administration, the Korean Association of Community Welfare, and the Korean Gerontological Society.

Lucas Meijs, PhD, is full professor of Strategic Philanthropy at the Erasmus Centre for Strategic Philanthropy and the Rotterdam School of Management, Erasmus University. His research focuses on philanthropy, volunteer and nonprofit management, business-community involvement, and civil society. He is coeditor of *Nonprofit and Voluntary Sector Quarterly*. He is an appointed member of the Dutch Council on Societal Development. He is also a member of the supervisory board of Resto VanHarte, the case presented in his chapter.

Lauren A. Miltenberger, PhD, is an Assistant Professor of Public Administration at Villanova University. Dr. Miltenberger teaches courses in Public and Nonprofit Human Resources, Decision Making, Public Policy and Public Administration. Her current research interests are human services system partnerships between nonprofits and the government and human capital management strategies within the nonprofit sector. Dr. Miltenberger has a PhD in Urban Affairs and Public Policy from the University of Delaware. Prior to joining the faculty at Villanova University, Dr. Miltenberger held executive leadership positions in the nonprofit sector.

Martti Muukkonen, ThD, MSS, is a Finnish theologian and social scientist who has focused his studies on nonprofit theory, the YMCA, and the history of welfare. He has worked as a local YMCA secretary as well as a university lecturer. Currently he serves as a chaplain of the Lutheran parish of Nurmijarvi in Southern Finland.

Lynne Coughlin Samson, Esq., was executive director for HelpHOPELive for 11 years. She previously practiced law in the area of medical malpractice defense for White and Williams in Philadelphia for 14 years. Lynne is also involved in other charitable endeavors including serving as a Deacon at Wayne Presbyterian Church and on the Board of the Radnor a Better Chance. She also serves as a grant reviewer for the Inglis Foundation and the Reeve F. Foundation. Her other interests include end of life care and military service as well as skiing, running, and gardening.

Björn Schmitz is the founder of Philiomondo, a nonprofit consulting firm in the field of innovation, innovation management, and organizational development in Heidelberg, Germany. Furthermore, he is responsible for cooperation and communications at the Schmid Foundation in Heidelberg, Germany. Formerly he worked as a project manager for the Centre for Social Investment (CSI) at the University of Heidelberg. He studied business administration in Mannheim, and sociology, philosophy, and psychology in Heidelberg. His main areas of interest are social innovation, social entrepreneurship, hybrid organizations, pro bono consulting, social impact measurement, and scaling of social innovation and social change.

Micheal L. Shier, PhD, is an assistant professor at the Factor-Inwentash Faculty of Social Work, University of Toronto. He has published on topics such as donating, labor market attachment, occupational health and subjective well-being among social workers, and the intraorganizational context of nonprofit human service organizations. His present research focuses on issues affecting young adult labor market attachment and the internal and external organization-level factors that contribute to nonprofit human service organizations being socially innovative.

Andreas Schröer, PhD, (Erlangen-Nuremberg) is a professor of Nonprofit Management at the University of Applied Sciences Darmstadt and the director of the Institute for Future Studies in Health and Social Management (IZGS). He is a senior fellow at the Centre for Social Investment at Heidelberg University and associate professor (by courtesy) of Public Administration at Portland State University. His work focuses on leadership in hybrid organizations, organizational learning, and social innovation.

Bruce Sievers is a visiting scholar and lecturer in Political Science at Stanford University and adjunct professor at the Institute for Nonprofit Organization Management at the University of San Francisco. He was the founding executive director of the California Council for the Humanities and CEO of the Walter and Elise Haas Fund, and he is currently a member of the National Council on the Humanities. His most recent book, *Civil Society, Philanthropy and the Fate of the Commons,* was published in 2010.

Margaret F. Sloan joined the School of Strategic Leadership Studies at James Madison University Harrisonburg, Virginia, as Assistant Professor of Strategic Leadership in 2012. Prior to her doctoral work at the University of Kentucky, she worked in the nonprofit sector for 10 years in a variety of management roles with a focus on community development, youth programs, the arts, and resource development.

Jonathan Spack has been Executive Director since 1988 at Third Sector New England, a Boston-based capacity-builder providing management and leadership resources to help nonprofits support healthy, just communities. He holds a law degree from New York University and a master's degree in Human Services Management from the Heller School at Brandeis University. Earlier in his career, Mr. Spack worked with community-based organizations in Massachusetts and New Jersey and with Native American groups in North Dakota and Zuni, New Mexico, as a VISTA volunteer and legal services attorney. He is coauthor of the *Executive Director's Guide*, published by TSNE in 2002, and is a cofounder and current board member of the Nonprofit Centers Network, the National Network of Fiscal Sponsors, and the Massachusetts Nonprofit Network.

Katalin Talyigás holds a doctorate in sociology, and she taught at Eotvos Lorand University between 1981 and 1992. She was the General Secretary of Hungarian Jewish Foundation founded by JDC NY, between 1992 and 2002. She also served as director of different projects of the Soros Foundation. In 2003, she was an expert of the Ministry of Equal Opportunity, and between 2004 and 2007 she served as an expert at the European Parliament in Brussels. Since 2007, she has served as the director of SZIA, the Social Innovation Foundation. She has numerous publications on social work and nonprofit organizations. In 2002, she received an award from the President of Hungary for her activities.

Stefan Toepler is associate professor in the Department of Public and International Affairs at George Mason University, where he teaches nonprofit management in the Master's of

Public Administration program. Prior to joining George Mason in 2002, he was on the research faculty of the Johns Hopkins Institute for Policy Studies, where he coordinated work on Central and Eastern Europe, the Middle East, and on NGO law in the Johns Hopkins Comparative Nonprofit Sector Project.

Jon Van Til is Professor Emeritus of Urban Studies and Community Planning at Rutgers University, New Jersey, USA. His 12 authored or coedited books include *Resolving Community Conflicts and Problems* (2011), *Breaching Derry's Walls* (2008), *Growing Civil Society* (2008, 2000), and *Mapping the Third Sector* (1988). He served as a Fulbright Specialist in Northern Ireland in 2006 and Hungary in 2010–2011. He is the past president of ARNOVA and the recipient of its career award for distinguished research and service.

Avis C. Vidal is a professor of Urban Planning at Wayne State University. Professor Vidal analyzes alternative approaches to strengthening poor neighborhoods. She is best known for her seminal research on the potential of community development corporations (CDCs) to strengthen poor neighborhoods. Prior to joining Wayne State, she served as Principal Research Associate at the Urban Institute, Director of the Community Development Research Center at the New School for Social Research, and Associate Professor at the Kennedy School of Government at Harvard.

Diane Kaplan Vinokur (publishing as Diane Vinokur-Kaplan) is an associate professor at the University of Michigan School of Social Work, Ann Arbor where she teaches courses in management of human services and nonprofit management. She is cofounder and past faculty director of the university's Nonprofit and Public Management Center, a collaboration of the Schools of Business, Public Policy, and Social Work. Her recent publications focus on interdisciplinary teams, work motivation, job satisfaction, and the benefits and challenges of nonprofit colocation.

Robert J. Wineburg is the Jefferson Pilot Excellence Professor at the University of North Carolina Greensboro and Visiting Professor of Religion and Community Service at Greensboro College. He is the author of three books and numerous scholarly works and articles written for nonacademic audiences. He has been an academic partner with his coauthor, Reverend Odell Cleveland, since 1996. In 2010, Cleveland and Wineburg authored *Pracademics and Community Change: How an Activist and a Scholar Created a 100 Million Dollar Nonprofit Organization.*

Index

Note: Page numbers in *italics* indicate figures and tables.